P9-DIW-494

Ready
When
You Are

Also by Elizabeth Schneider Colchie

BETTER THAN STORE-BOUGHT (*with Helen Witty*)

ELIZABETH SCHNEIDER COLCHIE

CROWN PUBLISHERS, INC.
NEW YORK

We acknowledge with thanks the material taken from:

Verses from 1929 On by Ogden Nash.
Copyright 1935 by Ogden Nash. First appeared in *Life* magazine.
By permission of Little, Brown and Company.

Farmer Boy by Laura Ingalls Wilder.
Copyright 1933 by Harper & Row, Publishers, Inc. Renewed © 1961 by Roder L. MacBride.
Reprinted by permission of Harper & Row, Publishers, Inc.

The Crack Up by F. Scott Fitzgerald.
Copyright 1945 by New Directions Publishing Corporation.
Reprinted by permission of New Directions.

Published by Crown Publishers, Inc.,
One Park Avenue, New York, New York 10016,
and simultaneously in Canada by General Publishing Company Limited

Manufactured in the United States of America

The majority of these recipes have appeared, in slightly different
form, in the *International Review of Food & Wine* magazine.
Several others have been published, also in a somewhat different form,
in *Bon Appétit*, *Cuisine*, *Family Circle*, and *Travel & Leisure*.

Library of Congress Cataloging in Publication Data

Colchie, Elizabeth Schneider.
Ready when you are.

Includes index.
1. Entertaining. 2. Cookery. I. Title.
TX731.C635 641.5'68 81-15211
ISBN: 0-517-543672 AACR2

Design by Deborah Bailey Kerner

10 9 8 7 6 5 4 3 2 1
First Edition

Contents

WINTER

SPRING

Recipes by Type

APPETIZERS AND HORS D'OEUVRES

SOUPS, *First Course*

SOUPS, *Main Course*

SEAFOOD, *Main Course*

SALADS, *Main Course*

SALADS, *Side Dish*

BREAKFAST AND BRUNCH DISHES

BREADS

DESSERTS

CAKES, COOKIES, AND PIE

DRINKS

Introduction

Entertaining, whether it means having two dozen guests for holiday brunch or celebrating a sunny day with close family, usually keeps the cook in the kitchen. *Fêtes accomplies*, or made-ahead parties, solve a good part of the kitchen-confinement problem. It does take time to assemble and fashion worthwhile dishes, particularly ones that reheat successfully, but the time can be spent before company comes, so you and your friends can relax together.

My definition of ready-when-you-are is broad. It means, first of all, food that needs no last-minute fussing: Turning on the oven and setting a timer, heating a soup, tossing a salad are tolerable tasks; but standing over a hot skillet to whip up a sauce, gild a garnish, or sauté a fish filet are not. Ready-when-you-are means dishes that offer no surprises near serving time. They are predictable, requiring no final adjustments when guests are on hand. Nor are the foods so fragile that they demand immediate service, as would a soufflé or delicate sauce. Recipes that entail constant hovering (will the roast be ready when guests arrive?) are not included in this repertoire. And the cooking schedule must be flexible, allowing for preparation over several days, if needed.

This volume of information and recipes was developed for hosts and hostesses who enjoy serving fine meals but can't bear missing lively conversation. It is also a book for those who care about the meaning of food, who linger over the assembly of beautiful ingredients, who are nourished by a balance of good food and talk; it is for people who savor.

Ready When You Are is arranged by season so that you can take advantage of the best of nature, when the best is least expensive.

Most of the chapters explain how to put together a complete meal, or several meals; recipes, important shopping information, and background material are included. Interspersed within each season are several chapters of another style. These focus on food subjects that are useful for a particular time of the year, rather than on complete meals. In this category you will find, for example, such chapters as "Salads That Make the Meal," which features main-course salads for summer, and "As Noble to Give As to Receive," a selection of winter holiday food to have on hand for guests or for gift-giving. When this subject format is followed, menus are provided, as they are in all chapters, but the recipe accompaniments suggested are to be found in other parts of the book, rather than being contained within the chapter.

An asterisk precedes menu suggestions for which recipes or explanations are provided. Occasionally a meal is best completed by a simple, familiar preparation that needs no recipe—such as a green salad, or sliced tomatoes with herbs. These foods are simply listed in the menu plans without an asterisk or page reference.

Generally speaking, the number of courses suggested for each menu is generous to allow for ample appetites. If you prefer trimmer meals, you might wish to tailor the repast by snipping out a soup or salad or vegetable when all are offered.

"Seasonal" is a broad concept. The fruits of late summer and early fall overlap, as do the vegetables of late fall and early winter. Sadly, there is no way to predict the date on which juicy grapefruits arrive in your market, or on which the sweetest melons will put in an appearance. Nor is it possible to take into consideration regional crop and market variations. But to every thing there *is* a season. It is up to you to sniff it out and bag it. Then choose menus that coordinate with whatever is loveliest in your neighborhood market, rather than allowing the seasonal rubric to dictate your ingredients.

Summer

1
An Elegant, All-Vegetable Lunch

Summer seems the suitable season for a lengthy luncheon, for a conversation filled with detours and stopovers, for a meal that encourages meandering. This sunny menu is built around the glorious vegetables that deserve center stage at this time of year.

AN ELEGANT, ALL-VEGETABLE LUNCH FOR SIX

Chilled Dry Sherry *or* Dry Vermouth
*Marinated Mushrooms
*Radishes with Anchovy Butter/Toasted Rounds of French Bread
*Iced Beet Soup
*Corn Timbales with Basil Cream
Wine: Gamay Rosé *or* a Rosé of Cabernet
*Zucchini Salad with Tomato-Herb Dressing
*Rich Carrot-Walnut Cake/Espresso

MARINATED MUSHROOMS

Not surprisingly, the first extensive cultivation of mushrooms took place in France. In 1707 the state of the art had developed to such an extent that a complete description of mushroom farming was recorded by the French botanist Joseph de Tournefort. Caves from which building stone had been quarried were sites for the lucrative business that flourished outside Paris. By the late eighteenth century mushroom production had gone mad: Documents show that among the many caves that were farmed at the time, one had twenty-one miles of mushroom beds, producing 3,000 pounds daily.

Mushroom cultivation in the United States was started by English gardeners, who had learned the procedures from the French. The fledgling industry centered around New York, then expanded to Pennsylvania, which now has the largest production of any state. American mushrooms are presently cultivated at the rate of more than 470 million pounds annually. If only some of this commercial attention was devoted to a fungus (or two, or more) that had a bit more character than the bland, pleasant *Agaricus bisporus*.

Prepare this recipe about a week before serving. It will provide you with enough to keep on hand for the next guests you might have, as well.

Makes about 1½ quarts

2 quarts water
2½ tablespoons coarse (kosher) salt
2 pounds medium-size mushrooms, trimmed and rinsed
1 cup white wine vinegar
1 tablespoon coriander seeds
2 bay leaves
1½ teaspoons sugar
½ teaspoon black peppercorns
½ teaspoon whole allspice
1 tiny dried hot chile pepper (or use about ⅛ teaspoon red pepper flakes)
¾ teaspoon dried thyme
1 shallot, sliced
1 garlic clove, halved
About 1 cup olive oil

1. In a large pot combine the water and 1½ tablespoons of the salt and bring to a boil. Add the mushrooms and boil 2 minutes. Drain, reserving 1 cup liquid.
2. In a saucepan combine the reserved mushroom liquid, vinegar, coriander seeds, bay leaves, sugar, peppercorns, allspice, hot pepper, thyme, and remaining 1 tablespoon salt. Boil 5 minutes.
3. Pack the mushrooms into a heat-resistant clean container (preferably a jar of 6- to 8-cup capacity with a tight-fitting cap). Pour the hot liquid over them, then add the shallot and garlic. Add enough olive oil to cover the mushrooms by about an inch.
4. Cool, cap, and refrigerate for about a week before using, stirring or shaking whenever you remember.

RADISHES WITH ANCHOVY BUTTER

Alexis Soyer, in his ambitious, witty, and pedantic history of food in ancient times, *The Pantropheon* (1853), had this to say about radishes:

> Writers of antiquity . . . fancied that at the end of three years, the seed of this plant produced very good cabbages, which must have been rather vexatious, at times, to honest gardeners who might have preferred radishes.
>
> In times of popular tumult this root was often transformed into an ignominious projectile, with which the mob pursued persons whose political opinions rendered them obnoxious to *the majority*, as we might say in the present day. As soon as calm was re-established, the insulting vegetable was placed in the pot to boil, and afterwards eaten with oil and a little vinegar.

TO PREPARE RADISHES WITH ANCHOVY BUTTER: Rinse and trim a selection of red and white radishes, keeping intact as many leaves as possible. Dry the radishes, arrange them on a serving dish, and refrigerate until needed. Rinse and very finely chop enough anchovies to measure about 2 tablespoons. Mash them, then beat together with 1 stick softened unsalted butter. Taste and season with pepper and lemon juice, then smooth into a small crock and chill. Serve, slightly softened, with the radishes, supplying your guests with small knives with which to spread the seasoned butter on the radishes.

ICED BEET SOUP

Beets are among those love-it-or-loathe-it vegetables, which divide the best of families and create warring factions among the chroniclers of food. Martial, the epigrammatist (first century A.D.), called them insipid, while his contemporary, the Roman cook Apicius, upheld their goodness. John Gerard in his *Herball* (1597) considered the brilliant beet enticing enough to leave to the cook's imagination:

> But what might be made of the red and beautiful root (which is to be preferred before the leaves, as well in beautie as in goodnesse) I refer unto the curious and cunning cooke, who no doubt when hee had the view there, and is assured that it is both good and wholesome, will make thereof many and divers dishes, both faire and good.

If beets cause rifts at your dining table, a cold cucumber soup will do as well.

Makes 6 servings

2 bunches medium-size beets, preferably with perky leaves (or buy about 2 pounds beets without tops)
2 celery stalks with leaves, coarsely chunked
1 large garlic clove, sliced
1 onion, sliced
1 quart light beef stock or broth, entirely skimmed of fat
1 quart water
2 tiny dried hot chile peppers, seeded and crumbled (or use about 1/4 teaspoon red pepper flakes)
1 teaspoon salt
2 tablespoons sugar
1/3 cup lime juice
GARNISH: Lime slices

1. Scrub and coarsely grate or shred half the beets. Wash and chop the tops, if available. Combine both chopped beets and tops in a saucepan with the celery, garlic, onion, stock, water, and hot pepper. Simmer, partly covered, for about 45 minutes.
2. Strain the soup into a clean saucepan through a sieve, pressing down firmly to extract all the stock. Discard the solids.
3. Remove and discard the tops (if any) from the second bunch of beets; scrub the beets thoroughly, but leave them whole. Add the beets to the stock and simmer, covered, until tender—which may vary from 1/2 to 1 1/2 hours, so test.
4. Remove the beets. Peel and trim them. Strain the stock into a bowl through a piece of fine-mesh cotton cheesecloth (or doubled wide-mesh cloth), then return to the rinsed-out pan. Add the salt and sugar. Cut the beets into very fine julienne strips using a knife, the shredding or julienne blade of a food processor, or a vegetable cutter. Return to the stock and taste for seasoning, then cool and chill thoroughly.
5. *To serve:* Add the lime juice, season, then ladle the soup into 6 chilled bowls, preferably glass ones. Cut a slit in a slice of lime and fit it onto the rim of each bowl.

CORN TIMBALES WITH BASIL CREAM

Well! If ever there was a "nothing new under the sun" affirmation, corn timbales is it. Having worked on the corn timbale recipe, I began nosing around old cookbooks for additional luncheon notions. What should I find in one book (*The Good Housekeeping Hostess*, 1904) but a complete "corn luncheon" featuring corn timbales, which I had fancied to be so terribly original.

As for using a corn motif throughout, as the author Eleanor M. Lucas advises, it might be a bit much, even for the most devoted lover of these sweet kernels. Her menu is made up of eleven dishes, six of which include corn in one form or another. She also suggests table appointments which, although undeniably corny, sound charming:

> The table was covered with white damask, and for a center piece ears of corn formed an elongated enclosure. Perfect ears had been selected and the pale green husks had been drawn back and made to lie flat like the sepals of a flower, and from them rose the pearly ears of corn, standing upright, partly veiled in filmy corn silk. Arranged within and overrunning this enclosure were bright blue cornflowers and asparagus ferns. Both are so enduring that no water was required . . . and flowers were arranged in a loose mass . . . trailing down the table and, wherever they encountered a candlestick, wreathing themselves about it.

As for blessed basil, the splendid leaf that perfumes the cream sauce, it has played many contradictory roles in the Mediterranean myths in which it figures. It is the symbol of lovers in some regions of Italy, but often of hate in Greece. In other parts of Italy, legend has it that basil generates scorpions in the brain, while in still other areas it is eaten to cure their sting. I have read that if it is consumed regularly, basil will have an aggrandizing effect upon the male member; or, for those seeking a more spiritual benefit, that it will promote good cheer.

A magical invention, these re-puffing petite soufflés. Rich, elegant, bathed in an herbal cream—and foolproof. The point of departure for this dish was Simone Beck's recipe "Petits Soufflés d'Alençon" (from *Simca's Cuisine,* Alfred A. Knopf, 1972). The addition of corn, among other changes, makes for pouf-y little hassocks that are even hardier than the originals. And difficult as it may be to believe, you really can refrigerate the timbales overnight before the final baking. They will be as light and inflated as if freshly assembled.

Makes 6 servings, as a main course

TIMBALES:

3 medium ears of tiny-kerneled corn (or 1½ cups canned tiny corn kernels)
1 cup milk
¼ cup all-purpose flour
¼ teaspoon salt
⅛ teaspoon white pepper
Big pinch of grated nutmeg
3 egg yolks
4 egg whites
½ cup finely grated Swiss cheese (about 2 ounces)

SAUCE:

1¼ cups heavy cream
½ teaspoon salt
⅛ teaspoon black pepper
2 tablespoons or more finely slivered fresh basil leaves, packed (or, if you have none, use 1 teaspoon finely crumbled dried basil leaves and ¼ teaspoon tarragon leaves—both steeped in the cream while you prepare the timbales)

1. Drop the corn ears into a kettle of boiling water and return to a boil. Remove the ears and cut the kernels into a measuring cup. There should be about 1½ cups. (If you are using canned corn, simply drain and measure it.)
2. Combine half the kernels and the milk in a processor or blender; purée until smooth, then strain through a sieve.
3. Butter twelve ½-cup dariole (timbale) molds, or a cupcake pan with twelve "cups" of that capacity, and set aside. Preheat oven to 375°.
4. In a small saucepan stir the milk-corn purée gradually into the flour, using a whisk. Add the ¼ teaspoon salt, the white pepper, and nutmeg. Stir with a whisk over low heat until thick and pasty. Off heat, stir to cool a bit. Beat in the yolks, one at a time, using the whisk.
5. In a small, deep bowl beat the whites with a pinch of salt until soft peaks form. Stir a quarter of the whites into the yolk mixture,

blending thoroughly. Gently fold the remaining whites into the mixture with a rubber spatula. Fold in the cheese, then the remaining corn kernels.

6. Divide the mixture among the molds and place them in a large roasting pan. Set in the oven and pour in boiling water to come halfway up the side of the molds. Bake 15–20 minutes, or until the little soufflés are puffed and golden. Remove the molds from the water.

7. You can let the timbales stand at room temperature for up to 4 hours, or you can store them in the refrigerator up to 24 hours, after they have cooled.

8. *To heat and serve the timbales:* Replace the molds in a pan half filled with boiling water. Heat in a preheated 350° oven for 5 minutes (if they've been held at room temperature) or 10 minutes (if refrigerated).

9. Run a knife carefully around the edge of each little cup and unmold the timbale onto a buttered baking/serving dish to hold them all with an inch between. They look pretty browned side up, but if you unmold them this way, be careful not to break them.

10. Bring the sauce ingredients to a simmer in a small pan and pour over the timbales. Bake in the center of the oven for 10–15 minutes, or until the timbales have re-puffed, browned, and absorbed much of the sauce.

ZUCCHINI SALAD WITH TOMATO-HERB DRESSING

Tomatoes and zucchini have been romantically intertwined for as long as vegetable gossipers can remember—perhaps as a result of the original neglect, and in the case of tomatoes, the outright rejection they have suffered—as well as their natural affinity. Tomatoes have endured some pretty poisonous press over the ages, probably because of their unfortunate membership in the same large family as the deadly nightshade (the potato, eggplant, and pepper are other family members). Well after Europeans had come to enjoy the tomato in sauces, in salads, and "eaten as a boiled vegetable," it was still avoided in the United States. When an Italian painter attempted to introduce the lovely love apple to Salem, Massachusetts, in 1802, he couldn't even persuade people to take a taste. The town, of course, is not famous for its open-mindedness. It seems a pity that the tomato, a South American native, should have taken so long to come round to the northern part of its continent of origin. As late as 1838, William Alcott, certainly the most dour cookbook author of the nineteenth century, wrote that the tomato

> is chiefly employed as a sauce or condiment. None, it is believed, regards it as very nutritious; it belongs . . . to a family of plants, some of the individuals of which are extremely poisonous. Some persons are even injured . . . by the acid of the tomato. Dr. Dunglison says it is very wholesome and valuable; but a very slight acquaintance leads me to a very different position (*The Young Housekeeper, or Thoughts on Food*).

Makes 6 servings

2 pounds medium-small zucchini, well scrubbed
2 pounds ripe tomatoes
1/4 cup pine nuts (pignolias)
3/4 teaspoon salt
1 1/2 teaspoons sugar
1/4 teaspoon black pepper
3 tablespoons red wine vinegar
1/3 cup olive oil
2 tablespoons finely minced fresh chives
3 tablespoons finely minced fresh parsley

1. Preheat the oven to 300°. Drop the zucchini into a large pot of boiling salted water. Boil for about 4–5 minutes, or until the squash can just barely be dented with the fingers when pressed. Remove the squash with tongs, leaving the water in the kettle, and set in a bowl of ice water until cooled through.
2. Remove the zucchini from the ice water, leaving the ice water in the bowl. Trim off the ends of the squash. Cut into strips about 2 × 1/4 × 1/4 inches. Arrange in a wide serving dish, cover, and chill.
3. Drop the tomatoes into the same kettle of hot water, return to a boil, then drain. Cool in the ice water. Remove the cores and peels. Halve each tomato and squeeze out the seeds. Cut half the tomatoes into 1/2-inch dice. Coarsely slice the remainder.
4. Spread the pine nuts in a pan and toast for about 15 minutes in the oven, or until they are just golden. Do not overbrown. Reserve.

5. Meanwhile, combine the coarsely sliced tomatoes in the container of a processor or blender with the salt, sugar, pepper, and vinegar and whirl until smooth. Add the oil and mix.
6. Set aside half the tomato dice in a small dish; cover and refrigerate. Combine the remaining dice in a bowl with the tomato dressing. Stir in the chives and parsley. Season, adding herbs to taste. Cover until serving time, refrigerating if you'll be waiting more than a few hours.
7. *To serve:* Drain off any liquid that has accumulated in the platter of zucchini or bowl of tomato dice. Pour the dressing over the zucchini. Top with the reserved tomato dice and pine nuts.

RICH CARROT-WALNUT CAKE

Poets and historians have not waxed lyrical when faced with carrots, perhaps because the sturdy, simple root has been overshadowed by some of the many other fragrant offshoots of the *Umbelliferae* clan, which includes parsley, caraway, dill, anise, coriander, and fennel among its 2,500-odd members. Even the usually appreciative Mrs. Beeton sounds unenthusiastic: "The carrot is said by naturalists not to contain much nourishing matter and, generally speaking, is somewhat difficult of digestion" (*The Book of Household Management*, 1861).

But cake eaters (which, like lounge lizards and tea drinkers, is an old American term for those who are habituated to a life of ease) may be pleased with the pretty orange flecks, firm texture, and moistness that carrots contribute to this compact, Cognac-scented cake. Incidentally, the cake freezes well, if you care to double the recipe.

Makes 1 small tube cake

1 cup all-purpose flour
3/4 teaspoon baking powder
1/4 teaspoon salt
1/2 teaspoon ground cinnamon
2/3 cup walnuts
1 slice white bread
1 stick (8 tablespoons) butter, softened
1/3 cup Cognac or brandy
1 teaspoon vanilla
3 eggs, at room temperature
3/4 cup sugar
1 cup peeled, finely shredded (not chopped) carrots
About 1 pint small strawberries, rinsed and hulled
Whipped cream flavored with Cognac (optional)

1. Sift together into a bowl the flour, baking powder, salt, and cinnamon. Combine 2 tablespoons of the mixture in a processor with the nuts and grind to a fairly fine texture. Or grate the nuts in a rotary handmill, then toss with the 2 tablespoons flour. Do not use a blender to chop the nuts.
2. Toast the bread in a low oven (250°) until it is dry throughout, not brown. Whirl in a blender or processor to make very fine crumbs. (Or use 3–4 tablespoons commercial crumbs.) Butter generously a tube pan of 5- to 6- cup capacity, preferably one with a decorative form (a bundt or kugelhopf). Coat thoroughly with the crumbs, tapping out any excess.
3. In a medium-size bowl cream the butter with an electric mixer until very soft. Add the Cognac gradually and beat until incorporated. Add the vanilla. On lowest speed add the remaining flour mixture, about one third at a time. Raise the oven temperature to 350°.
4. With clean beaters whip the eggs in a deep, narrow bowl until they are pale and thick. Gradually add the sugar and beat on high speed for about 15 minutes, until the mixture is firm and shiny.
5. Mix half the egg mixture with the butter-flour mixture, blending well with a rubber spatula. Stir in the carrots. Fold in half the remaining egg mixture delicately with a spatula. Sprinkle in a handful of nuts, then fold in gently. Alternate nuts and remaining egg mixture, folding to blend throughly, but taking care not to deflate the mixture.
6. Gently pour the batter into the prepared pan. Bake in the center of the oven for 45 minutes, or until a tester inserted in the center comes out clean.
7. Let cool on a rack for 10 minutes, then invert on a cake rack, remove the pan, and cool completely. Wrap and store for a day at room temperature before serving.
8. *To serve:* Heap the strawberries in the center and top with the cream or not, as you wish.

2
Two Buffets for the Hot Times

One Brunch, One Dinner

There are parts of the country where July and August would be best spent lying in the picnic cooler with the beer. At this time of year small buffets seem the most sensible party form. They take some of the burden off both hosts and guests, permitting a generally slouchier atmosphere. But while self-service entertaining can be a boon, balancing plates and glasses in midair is tiresome. Consequently, do not allow the number of diners to exceed the seating available at your table(s). Eight people is usually a manageable number for the sultry season, but if your preference is for crowds, all the recipes can easily be doubled.

BUFFET BRUNCH (OR LIGHT SUPPER) FOR EIGHT

*Rum-Orange Punch
Sliced Ham or Cold Roast Chicken
*Delicate Corn Custard
Wine: California Fumé Blanc *or* Alsatian Pinot Blanc
Green Salad
*Processor "French" Bread (page 139) *or* Bakery Italian or French Bread
*Nectarines in Blueberry Sauce
*Petite Macaroons (page 43) *or* store-bought cookies
Iced Coffee

RUM-ORANGE PUNCH

Makes about 2 quarts

1 quart boiling water
5 heaping teaspoons strong, black tea leaves
About 1/2 cup sugar
2 or 3 oranges, as needed
2 or 3 lemons, as needed
2 medium-size cinnamon sticks, broken up
6–8 whole allspice
About 2 cups dark rum
Thinly sliced oranges and lemons, as desired

1. Pour the boiling water over the tea leaves and let steep for 5 minutes. Strain the tea into a pitcher and stir in the sugar to taste.
2. Remove the thin layer of colored peel from 1 orange and 1 lemon with a swivel peeler, setting fruit aside. Add the peel to the tea, along with the cinnamon and allspice. Cover and refrigerate for several hours.
3. Squeeze the juice from the peeled orange and lemon. Squeeze the juice from more oranges and lemons as needed, until you've measured about 1 1/2 cups orange and 1/2 cup lemon juice. Strain into a serving pitcher. Strain in the tea and discard the peels and spices. Add the rum gradually, tasting until you have the balance that suits your taste. Chill until serving time.
4. *To serve:* Garnish the punch with fruit slices. Serve "straight up" or in tall glasses over ice.

DELICATE CORN CUSTARD

Although this may seem like a lot of custard for eight, it appears to slip down remarkably easily.

Makes 8–10 servings

4 1/2 cups milk (or 3 1/2 cups milk plus 1 cup juice drained from canned corn)
1 cup heavy cream
1/2 stick (4 tablespoons) unsalted butter
1/4 cup all-purpose flour
1 1/4 teaspoons salt
1/2 teaspoon white pepper
1/4 teaspoon ground mace
6 large eggs
3 cups small corn kernels, freshly cut from the cob (or use canned kernels: Drain and reserve the juice; replace 1 cup of the milk with 1 cup of the juice)

1. Preheat the oven to 325°. Butter 2 baking dishes, each of about 6-cup capacity. Scald together in a saucepan the milk (and corn juice, if you are using it) and cream.
2. Meanwhile, in another heavy pan melt the butter. Stir in the flour and cook for a few minutes over moderate heat, stirring. Add the scalded milk-cream mixture and stir with a whisk over moderate heat until the mixture boils up and thickens. Add the salt, white pepper, and mace. Remove the pan from the heat.
3. In a large bowl beat the eggs to just blend. Gradually add the milk mixture, beating constantly with the whisk. Turn the mixture into the buttered baking dishes. Distribute the corn evenly among the dishes and mix, then place the dishes in a large roasting pan.
4. Pour hot water into the pan to reach at least halfway up the dishes. Bake the custard for about 1 hour, or until it is barely set in the center. Let stand in the water bath until cooled.
5. *To serve:* You can serve the custard hot from the oven, or lukewarm (to show off its texture and flavor), at room temperature, or cold.

NECTARINES IN BLUEBERRY SAUCE

Makes 8 servings

8 very large, ripe nectarines (or 12 medium-large ones)
2 1/2 cups water
1 1/2 cups sugar
1/2 lemon, thickly sliced
1 pint blueberries, picked over and rinsed
About 1 tablespoon kirsch (or mirabelle)

1. Because many nectarines are not freestones, it is advisable to prepare them as follows: Halve each one lengthwise (through the stem end), then grasp both halves firmly and twist in opposite directions until one side pulls free of the pit. If you cannot easily pry the pit from the other half, use a grapefruit knife to cut it out neatly. Repeat until all the nectarines have been pitted.
2. In a large (12-inch) skillet or saucepan combine the water and sugar and bring to a boil, stirring. Add the lemon slices. Set the nectarines skin side down in the syrup. Cover the pan and barely simmer for 3–5 minutes, or until the halves are slightly tender. Gently turn over each half and barely simmer, covered, about 2 minutes longer, or until the fruit is slightly softened.

(Continued)

3. With a slotted spoon remove the fruit from the syrup. Discard the lemon pieces; reserve the syrup. When cool enough to handle, carefully pull the skin from each nectarine half. Set all the halves, cut side down, in a dish large enough to hold them in one layer. Spoon a little syrup over each half, cover, and refrigerate until serving time.
4. Add the berries to the remaining syrup. Simmer until soft, about 4 minutes. With a slotted spoon, transfer the berries to the container of a processor or blender. Whirl to a fine purée. Press through a fine sieve into a bowl. Add enough of the cooking syrup to produce a fairly thick, but liquid sauce. Add the kirsch to taste. Refrigerate until serving time.
5. *To serve:* Pour the sauce into a very wide, deep serving platter. Set the nectarines very gently into the sauce (so as not to splash them with purple), their cut sides down.

BUFFET DINNER FOR EIGHT

*Feta-Walnut Pastries
*Yogurt-Marinated Spiced Chicken
*Cracked-Wheat Salad with Avocados and Radishes
*Eggplant Purée with Tomatoes and Olives
Wine: Frascati *or* Rioja Clarete
Sesame Pita Bread
*Fruit-Filled Honeydew (page 335)
Mint Tea

FETA-WALNUT PASTRIES

These crackling-crisp appetizer pastries are the only hot spot in a cool feast. To allow for a minimum of last-minute attention when they are served, four alternative methods of storing and heating are provided at the end of the recipe, so you can choose whichever best suits your schedule.

Makes 24 appetizers

$^1/_2$ cup very finely crumbled feta cheese
$^1/_3$ cup medium-fine chopped walnuts
$^1/_3$ cup large-curd cottage cheese
$^1/_2$ teaspoon black pepper
About 6 sheets phyllo or strudel dough (see note below), at room temperature
$^1/_2$ stick (4 tablespoons) unsalted butter, melted and cooled

1. Combine the feta cheese, walnuts, cottage cheese, and pepper in a bowl and blend with a fork.

2. Remove one sheet of dough from the package and wrap the remaining sheets in a damp towel. Cut the exposed sheet into strips about $2^1/_2$ inches wide and 16–19 inches long (depending upon the length of the brand you've purchased). Leave 4 of these narrow strips on the working surface and wrap the remainder in the damp-toweled package of dough.

3. Dip a soft pastry brush in the butter, press out some excess, and sparingly brush 2 strips of the dough all over. Cover each of these strips with a second strip and brush again with butter. Place a scant teaspoon of the filling on one of the two top strips and fold over a corner of the dough to make a small triangle (see diagram). Continue folding the dough down to form a little triangle with each turn. Brush the top of the triangle lightly with butter and place the pastry on an ungreased baking sheet.

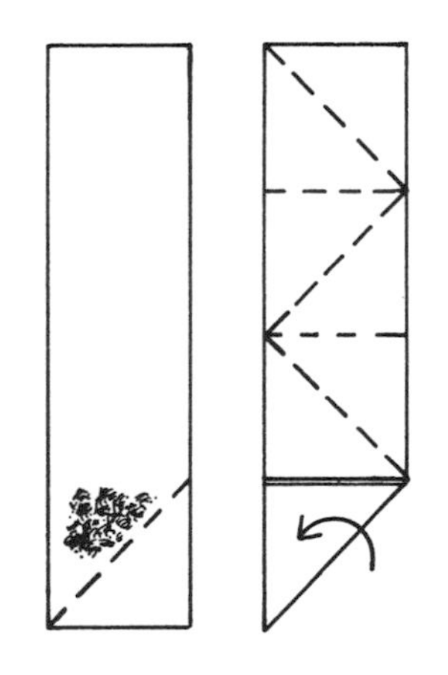

(Continued)

4. Continue until all the filling is used up; makes about 24 pastries.
5. *To store and serve:* Proceed to one of the following, depending upon your needs:

- Bake the pastries in a preheated 350° oven for 25–30 minutes, or until they are golden. Serve immediately.
- Refrigerate the raw pastries, on their baking sheet, covered with plastic, for up to 24 hours. Bake in a preheated 350° oven for about 30 minutes, or until browned. Serve immediately.
- Bake the pastries in a preheated 350° oven until they are golden, then cool completely on a rack. Wrap the pastries, on their baking sheet, in foil and refrigerate or freeze for several days. Unwrap and reheat in a preheated 350° oven until the pastries are hot and sizzling, about 10 minutes for refrigerated pastries, about 15 minutes for frozen ones.
- Freeze the raw pastries up to a month, tightly wrapped. Unwrap the pastries and let them stand for about 30 minutes at room temperature before baking in a preheated 350° oven until browned, about 30 minutes.

NOTE: As sheets of phyllo and strudel dough vary in size from one brand to another, no specific measurement can be given for the cheese triangles. Packages marked strudel or phyllo will both serve the purpose here. You will find that most sheets measure 19 × 19, or 23 × 17, or 16 × 12 inches.

YOGURT-MARINATED SPICED CHICKEN

This is another useful dish, which, like the Delicate Corn Custard on page 14, can be served hot, warm, or cold.

Makes about 8 servings

4 tiny dried hot chile peppers, seeds removed
2 tablespoons coriander seeds
1 teaspoon cumin seeds
1/4 teaspoon saffron threads
1 tablespoon boiling water
2 1/2 teaspoons coarse (kosher) salt
3 tablespoons lime juice
1 tablespoon sugar
2 chickens (each about 2 1/2–3 pounds), cut into serving pieces
1 bunch scallions, bulbs and light green only (reserve the greens for another use)
2 tablespoons peanut or corn oil
1 1/2 cups yogurt

1. In a small pan combine the chiles, coriander seeds, and cumin seeds and toast them over low heat, stirring, for about 2 minutes, or until the seeds barely begin to darken and start to make a crackling sound. Do not brown or burn the spices. Reserve and cool.
2. Combine the saffron and boiling water in a dish and let steep about 5 minutes. Add the salt, lime juice, and sugar and stir to mix.
3. Grind the spices to a powder in a spice mill or a mortar. Add to the lime juice mixture and stir well. Scrape half of the mixture into a small dish.
4. Prick the chicken pieces thoroughly all over with a skewer or the tip of a sharp knife. Rub each piece with some of the spice mixture, using up one small bowl to coat the pieces. Place them in a large bowl as you finish.
5. Combine the remaining spice mixture in the container of a blender or processor with the scallions, peanut oil, and yogurt and whirl to a fine purée. Pour the mixture over the chicken and stir to cover all the pieces. Cover the bowl with plastic and refrigerate for about 24 hours, stirring occasionally.
6. When you are ready to cook the chicken, remove the pieces from the marinade (do not wipe them) and set them on a broiler pan, skin side down. Broil about 4 inches away from the heat source, turning once, until the chicken is nicely browned, but not blackened or charred. This usually takes about 30 minutes. (If you have an outdoor grill, it is perfect for this. Be careful, however, to keep the heat low so that the poultry does not burn.)
7. *To serve:* Either serve the chicken at once, or let it rest at room temperature up to 1½ hours (at most, in hot weather) before serving. Or you can refrigerate the chicken and let it return to room temperature to serve.

CRACKED-WHEAT SALAD WITH AVOCADOS AND RADISHES

Cracked wheat is also sold as bulgur and wheat pilaf. If you are buying the wheat in the package, not loose from a bulk supplier, be sure to buy the kind that does not contain a seasoning mix. If your supermarket does not carry this, try a health-food store (or see list of mail-order sources, page 353).

Makes about 8 servings

$1\frac{1}{2}$ cups cracked wheat
5–6 cups hot tap water
2 teaspoons salt
$\frac{1}{2}$ cup plus 2 tablespoons lemon juice
8 tablespoons olive oil
$\frac{1}{2}$–1 cup chopped red onion (about 1 small onion), to taste
1 cup finely minced fresh parsley
2 medium-small avocados, peeled and cut into $\frac{1}{2}$-inch cubes
1 cup sliced red radishes
2 cucumbers, peeled and sliced (seeded, if large ones)
GARNISH: Small whole radishes

1. Combine the wheat and hot water in a bowl and let stand for 30 minutes to an hour, or until the grains are no longer hard at the core. Time will vary, depending upon granulation. The grains should be firm-tender, not crunchy. Pour into a sieve lined with fine-mesh cotton cheesecloth and let the water drain out. Squeeze the wheat in the cloth to extract all the liquid. Spread the wheat on a towel and toss it to dry and separate the grains somewhat.
2. In a small bowl combine the salt and the $\frac{1}{2}$ cup lemon juice. Stir to dissolve the salt. Add 6 tablespoons of the olive oil.
3. In a large bowl combine the wheat, lemon and oil mixture, onion, and parsley and toss throughly. Cover and refrigerate for several hours or more.
4. No more than 2 hours before serving, cut up the avocado and toss with the 2 tablespoons lemon juice and remaining oil to coat the pieces thoroughly, mixing very gently to avoid mushing the avocado. Let stand, covered, until ready to serve.
5. *To serve:* Add the sliced radishes to the wheat mixture and mix well. Add the avocado and mix gingerly. Mound in the center of a platter and surround with the cucumbers and radish garnish.

EGGPLANT PURÉE WITH TOMATOES AND OLIVES

Prepare the purée 12–48 hours before serving, to allow the flavors to develop. The garlic, incidentally, is very mild when treated this way. Decorate with the olives and tomatoes when you set up the buffet table.

Makes 8 servings

6–10 medium-size garlic cloves, cut into long slivers
1$^1/_2$ teaspoons ground allspice
1$^1/_2$ teaspoons ground cinnamon
$^1/_2$ cup plus $^1/_2$ teaspoon olive oil
4–6 equal-size eggplants (do not use large ones), to make a total of 5 pounds
1 teaspoon sugar
1$^1/_2$ tablespoons coarse (kosher) salt
2 tablespoons red wine vinegar
Sliced plum tomatoes
Black olives, preferably the tiny Niçoise or pointed, purplish Calamata variety (see list of mail-order sources, page 353, for both)

1. In a small dish combine the garlic slivers with the allspice, cinnamon, and the $^1/_2$ teaspoon olive oil; mix well.
2. To insert the garlic slivers into the eggplants, cut a deep slit into an eggplant; hold it open with the knife tip and insert a garlic sliver. Press the garlic into the flesh with the knife tip until it disappears. Continue distributing the slivers equally, until all the garlic and spices are used up. If any spice mixture remains, rub it on the eggplants.
3. Set the whole, untrimmed eggplants on a pan and set them as far from the heating element on a broiler as possible. Broil, turning once, until the skin is very wrinkled and blackened and the eggplants have collapsed. This usually takes 20 minutes, or longer. Remove the eggplants from the broiler, cover with foil and let stand for about 10 minutes.
4. Holding the stem of a still-hot eggplant, gently peel off the skin with a small knife. Discard the skin and stems and place the flesh in a strainer (preferably enameled or stainless steel) to drain. Continue until all the eggplants have been placed in the strainer.
5. Combine half the eggplant flesh with half the sugar, half the salt, and half the vinegar in the container of a food processor or blender. Whirl to just barely mix. Add $^1/_4$ cup of the oil in a thin trickle with the machine running. Incorporate the oil, but do not overprocess the purée to a homogenized mass. It should have some texture. Scrape into a bowl.
6. Repeat step 5 with the remaining eggplant, sugar, salt, vinegar, and oil. Combine the purées in the bowl, blend together, and season to taste with additional salt, allspice, oil, cinnamon, and vinegar.
7. Chill the purée, covered, for 12–48 hours.
8. *To serve:* Mound the purée in the center of a platter and surround with the sliced tomatoes and the olives. Scoop up the purée with small wedges of pita bread.

3
Salads That Make the Meal

Seven Main-Course Salads

Even the most torrid times can be tempered by a well-conceived repast, but creating such a meal for heat-wan diners can be difficult. Although light food is in order, rabbit nibbles do not seem to revive flagging spirits, nor does a shapeless meal that leaves guests feeling they've been eating hors d'oeuvres alone. The most successful dinner to serve is one made up of several courses composed of particularly lively textured, colored, and flavored foods. This provides form and focus for hazy taste buds. Nothing, I think, could better fill the bill than a main-dish salad, with appropriate accompaniments.

Although specific ingredients and quantities are supplied in the recipes, salads are particularly well disposed to variation and experimentation. If you can save yourself a trip to the market by substituting lemon juice for wine vinegar, or carrots for red peppers, do. If you have a garden, use whatever begs to be picked. But avoid the everything-but-the-kitchen-sink approach. The freshness of greens, the toasty flavor of nuts, the succulence of poached fish, the tartness of an unexpected fruit—all are lost if diverting flavors and texture vie for dominance. Beware of overkill in the salad bowl, lest you wind up with a creation of the kind that motivated Ogden Nash to write "My Dear, How Ever Did You Think Up This Delicious Salad?"

> This is a very sad ballad,
> Because it's about the way too many people make a salad
> Generally they start with bananas,
> And they might just as well use Gila monsters or iguanas.
> Pineapples are another popular ingredient,
> Although there is one school that holds preserved pears or peaches
> more expedient. . . .

Because if you think the foundation sounds unenticing,
Just wait until we get to the dressing, or rather, the icing.
There are various methods of covering up the body, and to some, marshmallows are the pall supreme.
And others prefer whipped cream,
And then they deck the grave with ground-up peanuts and maraschinos
And you get the effect of a funeral like Valentino's. . . .

(*Verses from 1929 On,* Little, Brown & Co., 1935.)

SUMMER SALAD MENU 1 (FOR FOUR)

Guacamole/Tortillas *or* Tostadas
*Shrimp, Corn, and Tomato Salad
Rosé Wine *or* Mexican Beer
*Peach Sherbet (page 68) *or* Fresh Berries
Iced Cinnamon-Flavored Coffee

SHRIMP, CORN, AND TOMATO SALAD

Makes about 4 servings

5 medium-size ears of corn, husked
1 teaspoon ground cumin
3 tablespoons red wine vinegar
2 teaspoons salt
1/3 cup finely minced cilantro (also called fresh coriander or Chinese parsley)
1 small, fresh hot pepper, seeds and ribs removed, finely minced (about 2 teaspoons)
3/4 cup plus 1 tablespoon olive oil
1 small red onion
6 cups water
1 teaspoon black peppercorns
1 1/2 pounds small shrimp in the shell
1 very small tomato, peeled, seeded, and diced
1 egg yolk
3 medium-size tomatoes
1 jar (2 ounces) small stuffed green olives, drained and sliced

1. Drop the corn into a large pot of boiling salted water. Return to the boil over highest heat. When the water returns to the boil, remove the pot from heat and drain the corn.
2. Slice off the kernels, which should measure about 3 cups. Combine in a bowl with the cumin, 2 tablespoons of the vinegar, 1/2 teaspoon of the salt, 2 tablespoons of the cilantro, 1 teaspoon of the hot

(Continued)

peppers, and 1 tablespoon of the olive oil. Peel and very finely mince half the onion (reserve the remainder for later). Add to the bowl and toss. Cover the bowl and chill.

3. Combine the water, 1 teaspoon of the salt, and the peppercorns and bring to a boil. Add the shrimp and remove from the heat. Let stand about 20 minutes. Drain and peel the shrimp; devein if necessary. Cover and chill.

4. In the container of a blender or processor, combine the remaining 1 tablespoon vinegar, 1/2 teaspoon salt, 1 teaspoon hot pepper, the very small tomato, and egg yolk. Whirl to a light, fluffy texture. Gradually add the remaining oil, keeping the motor running. Add 2 tablespoons of the cilantro and mix to just blend. Chill the dressing until about 1/2 hour before serving time. It should be softly spoonable.

5. *To serve:* Slice the remaining half onion thin and separate into slivers. Slice the medium-size tomatoes and arrange with the onions around the edge of a serving platter. Mound the corn in the center, leaving a central depression for the shrimp. Toss the shrimp with about one fourth of the dressing and arrange it in the center of the platter. Garnish the salad with the olives and sprinkle with the remaining cilantro. (The salad can be arranged an hour or so before serving.) Pass the dressing separately.

SUMMER SALAD MENU 2 (FOR FOUR)

Selection of Olives, Radishes
Breadsticks
*Tuna, Pasta, and Broccoli Salad
Wine: Chianti Classico
Bowl of Ripe Peaches or Nectarines/Almond or Anise Toast
Iced Espresso

TUNA, PASTA, AND BROCCOLI SALAD

Makes about 4 servings

1/2 cup olive oil
1 small garlic clove, finely minced
3/4 teaspoon salt
1/4 teaspoon black pepper
1 teaspoon oregano
2 tablespoons red wine vinegar
2 tablespoons drained capers, preferably nonpareil (the small ones)
8 ounces farfalle (also called bowties) or shell macaroni
1 large bunch broccoli
3 medium-size red bell peppers, cut into 1-inch pieces
2 cans (7 1/2 ounces each) solid white tuna, drained and coarsely chunked

1. Combine the olive oil, garlic, salt, pepper, oregano, red wine vinegar, and capers in a jar. Cap tightly and shake to blend.
2. Drop the farfalle into a large pot of boiling salted water and continue boiling until just tender, not soft. Drain, toss with a tablespoon of the dressing, and reserve.
3. Peel the broccoli stems. Cut them on the bias into slices 1/2 inch wide. Divide the blossoms into approximately 1-inch florets. Steam the stem and floret pieces in separate batches over boiling water, covered, until the vegetable just barely loses its hard, raw texture—but retains some crunchiness. Check often; broccoli cooks in minutes. Cool each batch under cold running water; drain and pat dry. Toss the florets in a bowl with about half the dressing.
4. Combine the pasta, peppers, and broccoli stems in a serving bowl; toss gently with the remaining dressing. Add the tuna and toss gingerly. Arrange the broccoli florets around the edge of the bowl.
5. Chill the salad for several hours or more before serving.

SUMMER SALAD MENU 3 (FOR FOUR)

*Tiny Tomatoes Stuffed with Taramosalata (page 49)
Warm Pita Bread, cut into wedges
*Zucchini, Carrot, and Lima Salad with Cheese, Yogurt, and Nuts
Wine: Iced Sicilian White such as Corvo or Bianco Alcamo
Fresh Plums and Figs/Iced Mint Tea

ZUCCHINI, CARROT, AND LIMA SALAD WITH CHEESE, YOGURT, AND NUTS

Makes about 4 servings

3/4 pound small firm zucchini, scrubbed and trimmed
3/4 pound small-medium carrots, peeled and trimmed
1 package (10 ounces) frozen baby lima beans
1 teaspoon salt
1/2 cup water
2 tablespoons lemon juice
1/4 teaspoon oregano, crumbled to a powder
1/4 teaspoon summer savory, crumbled to a powder
1/4 teaspoon black pepper
1 tiny garlic clove, very finely minced or pushed through a press
1 1/4 cups yogurt
4–6 ounces feta cheese, cut into very small cubes
3/4 cup coarsely chopped walnuts

1. Drop the zucchini into a large pot of boiling water. Boil vigorously for 2–4 minutes, or until the squash is softened just enough to indent slightly when pressed. Remove with tongs; keep the water boiling in the pot. Cool the squash thoroughly under cold running water or in ice water. Chill.

2. Drop the carrots into the boiling water. Boil until they are just slightly tender, about 4–5 minutes. Remove from the water with tongs. Cool under running water or in ice water. Chill.

3. In a saucepan, combine the lima beans with 1/2 teaspoon of the salt and the water. Boil gently, covered, until just tender, about 10 minutes. Drain and chill.

4. Combine the remaining 1/2 teaspoon salt, the lemon juice, oregano, summer savory, pepper, and garlic in a small bowl. Stir in the yogurt and chill for at least 1 hour.

5. Halve the zucchini crosswise, then cut each half in two lengthwise. Place each of these quarters flat side down and cut into 4 strips.

6. Cut carrots in half crosswise, then halve each piece lengthwise. Place flat side down and cut the quarters into uniform strips.

7. Mix together the limas and feta. Arrange the vegetables all together on a serving platter. Either store in the refrigerator up to several hours, or serve.

8. *To serve:* Spoon the yogurt dressing over the vegetables and sprinkle with the nuts.

SUMMER SALAD MENU 4 (FOR FOUR)

Cold Cucumber Soup *or* Tomato Soup
*Salad of Shellfish and Buckwheat Noodles (Soba)
Japanese or Thai Beer
Fresh Pineapple/Almond Cookies
Iced Tea

SALAD OF SHELLFISH AND BUCKWHEAT NOODLES (SOBA)

Makes about 4 servings

7 cups water
1 1/2 teaspoons salt
3/4 pound large sea scallops
1/2 pound small shrimp in the shell
1 1/2–2 pounds small mussels
Salt and flour for cleaning mussels
1 tiny onion, halved
3 scallions
10 tablespoons rice vinegar
1/4 cup peanut oil
1/2 pound fine Japanese buckwheat noodles (soba) or another kind of thin, dark, whole-grain pasta (see note below)
1 tablespoon plus 1/2 teaspoon sugar
1 tablespoon soy sauce
2 tablespoons Oriental (dark) sesame oil (see list of mail-order sources, page 353)
1 1/2 tablespoons peeled, chopped fresh ginger
About 3/4 pound small tender spinach leaves, trimmed, washed, dried, and thinly slivered
1/4 pound small, very fresh mushrooms, thinly sliced

1. In a large pot (it will hold the noodles later) bring the water and 1 1/4 teaspoons of the salt to a boil. Turn off the heat. Add the scallops and shrimp, then cover and let stand 15 minutes. With a slotted spoon remove the shellfish from the pot; reserve the cooking liquid.
2. Meanwhile, scrub the mussels thoroughly and pull off their "beards." Soak in several changes of water mixed with a handful each of salt and flour for about 15 minutes total. Discard any open mussels that will not close when you tap their shells and any ones that open easily when you slide the shells apart in opposite directions.

(Continued)

3. Place the mussels in a pot with the onion. Cover tightly and cook over high heat, shaking often, until the mussels open. Lift out the mussels and reserve the broth. Remove the mussels from the shells to a sieve set over a bowl (if you like, save a few shells for decoration). Strain the mussel broth through several layers of fine-mesh cotton cheesecloth to remove any sand. Pour the broth over the mussels to clean them. Strain broth again, if necessary, then add to the reserved cooking liquid.
4. Peel shrimp, devein if necessary, and halve lengthwise if they are not tiny ones. Cut scallops across into 1/4-inch-thick slices. Mix shrimp and scallops with mussels in a bowl. Mince one of the scallions fine. Sprinkle over the seafood, along with 1/8 teaspoon of the salt, 2 tablespoons of the vinegar, and 2 tablespoons of the peanut oil. Mix gently, cover, and refrigerate.
5. Boil noodles until just tender in the reserved cooking liquid. Meanwhile, prepare the dressing. In the container of a processor or blender combine the remaining scallions (sliced), 6 tablespoons of the vinegar, remaining 2 tablespoons peanut oil, 1 tablespoon of the sugar, the soy sauce, sesame oil, and ginger. Whirl to a fine purée. Drain the noodles and toss with the dressing. Let cool, then refrigerate.
6. *To serve:* Toss the spinach with the remaining 2 tablespoons vinegar, the 1/2 teaspoon sugar, and remaining 1/8 teaspoon salt. Arrange on a platter. Mound the noodles on the spinach, arrange the shellfish over the noodles, then decorate with the thinly sliced mushrooms.

NOTE: Oriental and health-food stores usually offer several varieties of whole-grain noodles. Or see the list of mail-order sources on page 353.

SUMMER SALAD MENU 5 (FOR FOUR)

Sliced Ripe Tomatoes
*Rustic Wheat Loaves (page 137) *or* Italian Bread
*Potato, Ham, and Cheese Salad with Shallot Dressing
Alsatian Sylvaner Wine *or* Light Beer
*Peaches in Vanilla Syrup (page 64) *or* Fresh Fruit
Ginger Cookies/Coffee

POTATO, HAM, AND CHEESE SALAD WITH SHALLOT DRESSING

Makes 4 servings

1 1/2 pounds small new potatoes, well scrubbed
1/2 cup walnut halves
3/4 pound firm, smoky ham
1/2 pound Emmenthaler, Gruyère, or Swiss cheese
3/4 teaspoon salt
1/4 teaspoon black pepper
3 tablespoons white wine or dry vermouth
2 tablespoons white wine vinegar
2 tablespoons very finely minced shallots
1 1/2 tablespoons sharp mustard
1/4 cup finely minced fresh parsley
1/2 cup olive oil
Very finely shredded red cabbage or coarsely shredded chicory (about 3–4 cups)

1. Preheat the oven to 325°. Drop the potatoes into lightly salted boiling water and cook until just barely tender; drain. When just cool enough to handle, cut into pieces about 1 inch square and 1/2 inch thick, peeling off the skin only if it is thick.
2. While the potatoes are cooking, toast the walnuts in a pan in the oven for 15 minutes. Let cool. Cut the ham and cheese into extremely thin strips.
3. Combine the salt, pepper, white wine, vinegar, shallots, and mustard in a jar; cap and shake to combine. Add the parsley and oil and shake to blend thoroughly. Gently mix about two thirds of the dressing with the warm potatoes. Let cool completely.
4. Gently toss the ham and cheese with half the remaining dressing and add to the potatoes. Toss the remaining dressing with the cabbage or chicory and arrange on a platter. Mound the mixed salad in the center. Sprinkle with the walnuts. Chill until about 1/2 hour before serving time.

SUMMER SALAD MENU 6 (FOR FOUR)

*Chickpea Dip with Vegetable Strips (page 343)
*Minted Fish and Rice Salad
Wine: California Rkatsiteli *or* California Fumé Blanc
*Watermelon Ice (page 37), with Sliced, Sugared Strawberries
Iced Tea

MINTED FISH AND RICE SALAD

Makes about 4 servings

2 1/2 cups water
Few parsley sprigs
Few onion slices
1 carrot, sliced
1/4 teaspoon dried thyme
About 1 3/4 pounds fish steak in one piece (such as swordfish, salmon, king mackerel [kingfish], tile fish, striped bass; or whatever steak-cut fish seems freshest in your market)
1 3/4 teaspoons salt
1 1/2 cups long-grain white rice
1/3 cup lemon juice
1/4 teaspoon black pepper
1/3 cup olive oil
2 scallions, thinly sliced
3–4 tablespoons minced fresh mint, to taste
2 large cucumbers, peeled
About 3 cups shredded lettuce
GARNISH: Whole mint leaves and lemon slices

1. In a heavy saucepan (about 2-quart size) bring to a boil the water, parsley, onion, carrot, and thyme. Boil for a few minutes. Add the fish, cover, and cook over lowest heat until the fish is not quite cooked through, about 10 minutes. Transfer the fish steak to a dish, reserving the cooking liquid.
2. Strain the broth and return it to the rinsed-out pot. Add 1 teaspoon of the salt and the rice. Bring to a rolling boil, stirring occasionally. Turn heat to lowest point, cover, and cook 20 minutes. Remove pot from the heat and let rest, covered, for at least 15 minutes.
3. Meanwhile, combine 1/2 teaspoon of the salt, the lemon juice, pepper, oil, and scallions in a jar. Shake to blend. Coarsely chunk the fish, discard the bones, and mix in about 1/4 cup of the dressing. Cover and refrigerate. Gently mix the remaining dressing and the minced mint with the rice. Refrigerate until serving time.

4. Halve the cucumbers lengthwise. Remove the seeds with a melon ball cutter or teaspoon. Cut the cucumbers across into thin slices. Sprinkle with the remaining 1/4 teaspoon salt and refrigerate, covered.
5. *To serve:* Arrange a layer of greens on a platter. Gently toss together the fish and rice and transfer to the platter. Drain the cucumbers and arrange them around the mixture. Decorate with mint leaves and lemon slices.

NOTE: If you happen to have about 2 1/2 cups cooked leftover fish, you can use this instead of the fresh. Simply ignore step 1, then substitute half water–half clam juice (broth) for the fish stock.

SUMMER SALAD MENU 7 (FOR FOUR)

*Salad of Squid, Grilled Peppers, Red Onion, and Olives
Italian Bread *or* Genoa Toast *or*
*Processor "French" Bread (page 139)
Wine: Verdicchio *or* Pinot Grigio
Sliced Strawberries and Peaches with Rum and Sugar

SALAD OF SQUID, GRILLED PEPPERS, RED ONION, AND OLIVES

Makes about 4 servings

1 1/2 pounds small, cleaned squid or 2 pounds uncleaned
1 bay leaf
1 teaspoon coriander seeds
1/4 teaspoon fennel seeds
1/2 teaspoon dried thyme
1 small onion, halved
1 celery stalk with leaves, sliced
1/2 teaspoon black peppercorns
2 garlic cloves, peeled
1/2 teaspoon plus 1/8 teaspoon salt
About 1/2 cup lemon juice
1 1/2 cups water
1/4 cup plus 2 tablespoons olive oil
2 medium-large, straight-sided red bell peppers
2 medium-large, straight-sided green bell peppers
1 teaspoon vinegar
1 very small head chicory, washed, dried, and slivered
1 small red onion, thinly sliced and separated into rings
1/3 cup pitted, sliced, oil-cured black olives

1. *To clean squid:* If you have never cleaned squid, don't be reluctant to do so. It is a simple, neat job. You may follow these instructions or not, but the whole procedure will be pretty obvious once you have the squid in front of you. First grasp the tentacles with one hand, the hood (or mantle) with the other. Gently but firmly pull the tentacles to separate them (and their attached parts) from the mantle. Cut off and discard the sacs and eyes and keep the tentacles. Pop out the little beak in the center of the tentacles. Slip out the remarkable leaf-shaped, plastic-clear "pen" that serves as the inner structure for the squid; discard. Rinse the whole works, inside and out. Holding the mantle under running water, strip off the speckled membrane.

2. In a 2- to 3-quart saucepan combine the bay leaf, coriander seeds, fennel seeds, thyme, onion, celery, peppercorns, garlic, the 1/2 teaspoon salt, 1/3 cup of the lemon juice, the water, and the 1/4 cup oil and bring to a boil. Cover and boil gently for 15–20 minutes.

3. Meanwhile, cut the cleaned squid mantles across into rings 1/8–1/4 inch thick. Divide the tentacles into manageable mouthfuls, or cut them in pieces if they are large.

4. Strain the stock and return it to the saucepan. Add the squid and simmer for about 1 minute, stirring, until the squid is curled at the edges. Remove the squid to a bowl with a slotted spoon.

5. Boil the liquid to reduce it to 1/2 cup. Add to the squid. Cool, cover, and refrigerate.

6. Place the peppers directly in the flame of the gas burners of your stove (or as close to the broiling element as possible, if you don't have a gas stove). Keep turning them in the flames until they are blackened all over. Set aside for a few minutes, then place them in a plastic bag and let stand for 15–20 minutes.

7. Remove the peppers from the bag and halve them lengthwise. Scrape off the stems, seeds, ribs, and skins. Rinse. Cut each half into eighths, lengthwise. Rinse the peppers and pat them dry.

8. Combine 1 tablespoon of the oil, the 1/8 teaspoon salt, and 1 teaspoon vinegar in a bowl. Add the pepper strips and refrigerate until serving time—which can be up to 24 hours later.

9. *To serve:* Arrange the chicory on a large serving platter. Toss the squid with about 2 tablespoons lemon juice, 1 tablespoon oil, and pepper to taste (this dish can stand plenty of it). Arrange over the chicory with the pepper strips, onion rings, and olives.

4
An Ice Cream Party for All Ages

*Watermelon Ice
*Banana Milk Sherbet with Strawberry Swirls
*Lemon Custard Ice Cream
*Blackberry Frozen Mousse
*Apricot-Ginger Ice Cream
Lemonade from *Lemon Syrup for Lemonade
Iced Tea
*Cinnamon-Sugar Strips
*Petite Macaroons
Wine: Asti Spumante

Ice cream gatherings are a uniquely American tradition. At the most common variety, neighbors assembled to raise money for a benevolent purpose, such as a school building, the purchase of a new church bell, or, later, for the benefit of an organization like the Girl Scouts. These events, planned for a "cause," have been dubbed "ice cream suppers," "ice cream socials," and, most endearingly, "ice cream sociables." Affairs such as our Ice Cream Party for All Ages were designated "ice cream festivals" and "ice cream parties" and were simply get-togethers at which the chief diversion was the eating of ice cream.

Ice cream was probably first manufactured in Italy, where, as early as the end of the sixteenth century, huge storage pits of snow, kept throughout the year, were used for cooling. There was even an academy devoted to the art of ice and ice cream making. Through contact with their Italian neighbors, the French courtiers soon developed their own frozen delicacies, molded in exquisite forms. During the 1660s, snow storage wells were constructed in England, as well, to cool desserts for royal tables.

It is not difficult to judge how popular ice and ice cream making had become in Britain by the time Mrs. A. B. Marshall made known her thoughts on the subject in *The Book of Ices* (1885). In addition to more than a hundred recipes, Mrs. Marshall's book included advertisements for freezers and a thousand-odd molds that she carried in her London cookware shop. When Charles Dickens was fêted at a dinner at the Delmonico restaurant in New York, he was served sorbet à l'américaine, a popular dish of the time, which Mrs. Marshall described in her book:

> Sorbet à l'américaine is peculiarly interesting, as it was first served in the cups or glasses formed of raw ice prepared in moulds in imitation of wine-glasses or cups. Its flavouring, when prepared in New York, is the sparkling . . . Catawba. . . . The moulds for making these ice cups or glasses consist of two parts, an inner and outer cup, so that when fixed together they have the appearance of one cup; but between the two parts is a space which is filled with pure or coloured water. These are set in the ice-cave till the water is frozen; the ice-cups are then turned out of the moulds and used. The pretty effects which can be produced by real ice-glasses prepared in this way are so numerous that these moulds are now being used for sorbets of any kind.

As was then customary, Mrs. Marshall divided her ice creams into categories according to the amount of eggs and cream used: "Very Rich," "Ordinary," "Common," and "Cheap." With similar brevity, Pierre Blot expressed his ideas on ice cream in the *Hand-Book of Practical Cookery* (1869): "Made with cream it is richer than with milk. With eggs it is better and richer than without, and those that advocate it without eggs either have no palate, or do not know how to use them in making it. The addition of starch, . . . arrowroot, flour, meal, etc. spoils it." The same advice still goes.

In America the fancy dinner novelty called "iced cream" appeared at the homes of the wealthy around the time the Declaration of Independence was being conceived. Not long thereafter, limited quantities were produced commercially to be served up in parlors, saloons, and cafés in New York and Philadelphia. Until 1846, when one Nancy Johnson invented—but neglected to patent—a hand-cranked portable freezer for home use, most ice cream was made as described below by Laura Ingalls Wilder, whose husband-to-be, Almanzo, was left alone one day in 1868 to do the chores with his siblings:

> "Let's make ice-cream!" Royal shouted.
>
> Eliza Jane loved ice-cream. She hesitated, and said, "Well—" Almanzo ran after Royal to the ice-house. They dug a block of ice out of the sawdust and put it in a grain sack. They laid the sack on the back porch and pounded it with hatchets till the ice was crushed. Alice came out to watch them while she whipped egg-whites on a platter. She beat them with a fork, till they were too stiff to slip when she tilted the platter.
>
> Eliza Jane measured milk and cream, and dipped sugar from the barrel in the pantry. It was not common maple sugar, but white sugar bought from the store. Mother used it only when company came . . .
>
> She made a big milk-pail full of yellow custard. They set the pail in a tub and packed the snowy crushed ice around it, with salt, and they covered it with a blanket. Every few minutes they took off the blanket and uncovered the pail, and stirred the freezing ice-cream.
>
> When it was frozen, Alice brought saucers and spoons, and Almanzo brought out a cake and the butcher knife. He cut enormous pieces of cake, while Eliza Jane heaped the saucers. They could eat all the ice-cream and cake they wanted to; no one would stop them (*Farmer Boy*, Harper & Row, 1933, 1961).

It is interesting to remember that until the mid–late nineteenth century ice was not made artificially. Ice harvesting was a flourishing industry in which huge fortunes were amassed. Practical New Englanders devised ways to transport blocks of the precious ice to sweltering lands as far flung as South America, the Middle East, China, the East Indies, the Philippines, and Australia. When commercial ice-making methods were devised the industry grew even larger, and survived until the 1940s, when practical home refrigeration became common.

Although lemonade and iced tea are the principal survivors in the realm of summer party liquid refreshment (other delicacies having died out with the advent of such hardy brews as canned and bottled sodas), a broad spectrum of cool, colorful quaffs was once an important part of languorous afternoon gatherings all over the United States. My old cookbooks reveal a rainbow of recipes for syrups of apricots, blackberries, cherries, currants, limes, oranges, peaches, plums, strawberries, raspberries, and almonds, as well as violets, roses, and maidenhair. In the South, flavored syrups known as *eaux sucrées* were particularly popular. Lemonade and *eau sucrée* parties were famous in New Orleans

> in those happy, innocent days when friend met friend in social gatherings for the pleasure of social intercourse, and not for the sake of the "grand spread" of fancy viands and wines that have become a source of terror in our day to the housewife of limited means. . . . With that beautiful old-time courtesy so peculiar to the Creoles, the poor young woman who entertained was placed on an equal with her richer sister, for it became a kind of unwritten law that beyond a glass of lemonade and cake . . . nothing more was expected. . . . [People] laughed and sang and danced . . . on iced Lemonade . . . and Iced Creams, with as much zest as when grand suppers were spread and champagne flowed; there were no heartaches, no pangs, no sad thoughts, because Madame So-and-So, who lived in the Rue Esplanade or Rue Rampart had given a grander ball (*The Picayune's Creole Cook Book*, 1901).

As real ice cream has become a relative luxury, the financial burden of an ice cream/lemonade/cookie party is a bit weightier than a century ago, but such a gathering is still a relative bargain when compared with the cost of assembling a large group of kids of all ages for a meal. Although ice cream and cookies are often thought to be children's fare, my experience suggests that it is "grown-ups" who finish every crumb and melted bit of cream on their plates. So why not involve everyone in an old-fashioned, informal gathering where sweets are (just once a summer) the only refreshments? Although the hand-cranked machines that necessitated a strong group spirit to produce an icy confection are a thing of the past, the idea of assembling young and old for an ice cream party can be a merry present reality.

A Note on Ice Cream Makers and Recipe Yields

To test many of these recipes, I used a 2-quart Waring Ice Cream Parlor machine. The directions provided by each manufacturer should be followed for the freezing. In general, keep in mind that the smoothest ice cream results from a moderate rate of freezing. Too high a proportion of salt results in too-fast freezing and makes for coarse crystals. Therefore, use the minimum amount of salt your freezer instructions advise. The Waring machine, so simple to use, as it employs ordinary ice cubes and table salt, works best with 4–5 trays of ice cubes and 1¼ cups table salt.

It is impossible to predict how much ice cream your machine will yield. There is a considerable range in the volume produced by various freezers, so don't be surprised if you wind up with more or less than I did.

I have not indicated the number of people to be served, as sweet tolerance is a personal affair. Figure on a total yield of at least 6½ quarts of dessert (which will be much richer than store-bought), then count heads, or sweet tooths, or whatever you count.

WATERMELON ICE

Most people find that this ice has more taste and verve than real watermelon. The fruit-sweet flavor is icy clean, and the look is of crystalline, sparkling pink snow. The ice is made by "still-freezing," which requires only an occasional mixing by hand, rather than the constant agitation of a mechanical freezer.

Makes about 1 quart

1 cup sugar
¾ cup water
4 cups chopped, seeded watermelon pulp
⅓ cup lemon juice, or to taste

1. Combine the sugar and water in a pot over high heat. Holding the handle of the pot, swirl the syrup until it boils. Turn down the heat and boil gently, covered, for 4 minutes. Cool.
2. Purée the fruit in a blender or processor. There should be about 2½ cups. Pour into a bowl or, if you are in a hurry, into a wide pan (both preferably stainless steel). Stir in the sugar syrup and lemon juice to taste. The flavor should be tart.
3. Freeze the mixture until a fairly solid rim of ice forms around the edge and the center is mushy-frozen, no longer liquid. This may take as few as 4 hours, as many as 8, depending upon the efficiency of your freezer.

(Continued)

4. Beat the ice briefly with a whisk or electric mixer until it resembles a uniform slush. Return to the freezer and chill, covered, until icy-mushy throughout, about an hour or more.
5. Beat the ice briefly again until it is light but not liquefied.
6. Cover closely and freeze, preferably no longer than 4–5 days.

BANANA MILK SHERBET WITH STRAWBERRY SWIRLS

The addition of egg whites (and/or milk) transforms an ice into a sherbet. This one, "still-frozen" like the watermelon ice, is particularly rich flavored and pretty. For a presentation that makes the most of the rosy strawberry whorls, scoop out balls of sherbet, arrange them in a glass bowl, and refreeze, covered, until serving time. This method also makes serving simpler. Use it for the ice creams, as well.

Makes 1–1 1/2 quarts

3 medium-size ripe bananas
1/4 cup lemon juice
1/2 cup plus 2 tablespoons sugar
1/4 cup light corn syrup
1 1/2 cups milk
1/4 teaspoon vanilla
2 egg whites
1 pint strawberries, rinsed and hulled

1. Purée the bananas, lemon juice, 1/2 cup sugar, corn syrup, milk, and vanilla in a blender or processor. Strain through a sieve.
2. Beat the egg whites to form soft peaks. Beat in the banana mixture gradually, on lowest speed. Pour into a bowl, preferably stainless steel. Cover and set in the freezer.
3. When the sherbet has frozen around the edge and is no longer liquid in the center, beat it vigorously until it is smooth and creamy. Return to the freezer and chill, covered, until the sherbet freezes again.
4. While the sherbet is refreezing, purée the strawberries with the 2 tablespoons sugar. Strain them, if you like.
5. When the sherbet is almost firm, beat it briefly again until it is almost smooth; do not let it liquefy. Quickly fold in the purée to make vivid streaks; do not blend.
6. Cover and return to the freezer. Let "ripen" overnight before serving.

LEMON CUSTARD ICE CREAM

This velvety, classic ice cream is the kind that evokes passionate praise, such as this:

> What a wave of grateful coolness the ice and its yet more seductive sister, ice-cream, contribute when the dog-star reigns and cicadas have begun to shrill. Who among the calumniators of sweets would wish them banished in support of a fallacious theory that sweetmeats render woman more capricious, and are injurious to the roses and lilies of her skin? (George Ellwanger, *The Pleasures of the Table*, 1902).

Makes 1–1½ quarts

3 large lemons, washed
¾ cup sugar
4 egg yolks
⅛ teaspoon salt
2 cups milk
2 cups heavy cream, preferably not ultrapasteurized

1. Remove the outer yellow rind from the lemons with a swivel peeler and combine it in a processor container with ½ cup of the sugar. (Or simply grate the lemon rind, if you don't have a processor, and use the ½ cup sugar in step 3.) Whirl to a fine texture.
2. In a small bowl beat together with a whisk, rotary beater, or electric mixer the remaining ¼ cup sugar, egg yolks, and salt until the mixture is very pale and thick.
3. Heat the milk, cream, lemon sugar (or grated rind and sugar) in a heavy 2½- to 3-quart saucepan until it almost simmers. Beat half of it gradually into the yolk mixture, scraping down the sides of the bowl.
4. Pour the egg mixture into the remaining milk-cream in the pot and stir over moderately low heat until the custard almost simmers, stirring constantly. Set immediately into a sink containing cold water and let cool entirely, stirring occasionally. Refrigerate, covered, for several hours or overnight.
5. Squeeze enough of the peeled lemons to make ¼ cup juice and stir into the custard. Strain into the container of an ice cream machine and freeze according to the manufacturer's directions.
6. Pack the ice cream into a freezer container and let "ripen" for a day in the freezer before serving. The ice cream will be at its best if served within a week.

BLACKBERRY FROZEN MOUSSE

The perfume of rose water lends a mysterious, lovely undertone to this rich, deep-colored frozen cream.

Makes about 1 1/2 quarts

3–4 cups blackberries, rinsed
1 tablespoon rose water (optional; see list of mail-order sources, page 353)
1/4 teaspoon almond extract
1/3 cup water
1 cup sugar
1/8 teaspoon salt
4 egg whites
1 cup heavy cream, preferably not ultrapasteurized

1. Combine the berries, optional rose water, and almond extract in the container of a blender or processor and whirl to a purée. Press through a fine sieve and chill.
2. In a small heavy pan heat the water, sugar, and salt, swirling the pan until the syrup boils. Cover and boil for 1 minute, then insert a candy thermometer into the syrup and boil to 240°, uncovered.
3. Meanwhile, using a stand mixer, beat the egg whites to form soft peaks. When the syrup reaches 240°, pour it gradually into the whites, beating the meringue and scraping down the sides of the bowl. Continue beating on high speed for about 15 minutes, or until the meringue is cooled, thick, and shiny.
4. In a small bowl whip the cream until it forms soft peaks. Do not beat to stiff peaks or the mousse will taste greasy.
5. Gradually and thoroughly fold the chilled berry purée into the meringue, using a rubber spatula. Fold in the whipped cream. Turn the mixture into a serving dish that will withstand freezing, cover, and freeze for at least 6 hours, or up to 3 days.
6. *To serve:* Allow the mousse to soften in the refrigerator for an hour.

APRICOT-GINGER ICE CREAM

Ice cream made without eggs, in the so-called Philadelphia style, is considered to be the all-American way. The pale, sunny coloring and full-fruit flavor of dried apricots might be a welcome finale to many meals, year round. I prefer to serve this exceptionally creamy dessert with a vivid, tart gingery Apricot Sauce (page 126) to cut the soft richness and underscore the fruit flavor.

Makes about 1 1/2 quarts

1 cup dried California apricots (about 4–5 ounces)
3/4 cup water
1/4 cup drained, chopped preserved stem ginger in syrup (see list of mail-order sources, page 353)
1 tablespoon lemon juice
1/2 teaspoon almond extract
3/4 cup sugar
2 cups heavy cream, preferably not ultrapasteurized
2 cups milk
1/8 teaspoon salt

1. Combine the apricots and water in a small heavy saucepan and cook over low heat, covered, until the fruit is very soft—about 25 minutes. Pour into the container of a processor or blender; add the ginger and whirl to a very fine purée. Add the lemon juice and mix. Scrape into a bowl; cool somewhat. Add the almond extract; cover and refrigerate.
2. Heat together in a heavy saucepan the sugar, cream, milk, and salt, stirring occasionally until the mixture comes just to a simmer. Cool, cover, then refrigerate.
3. When both apricots and cream are thoroughly chilled, gradually stir the cream mixture into the apricots. Turn into the container of an ice cream machine and freeze according to the manufacturer's directions.
4. Pack the ice cream into a freezer container and let "ripen" for a day or two in the freezer before serving.
5. *To serve:* Let soften for about an hour in the refrigerator.

LEMON SYRUP FOR LEMONADE

This style of lemonade—pungent and full-flavored—deserves a revival.

Makes about 1 quart syrup, or about 4 quarts lemonade

6 large lemons, washed
2 cups sugar
2 cups water
GARNISH: Lemon slices

1. Roll the lemons against a countertop to soften them so they'll yield more juice. Remove the outer yellow rind with a swivel peeler.
2. In a heavy saucepan heat the sugar and water over moderate heat, swirling the pan until the syrup boils. Add the peel and boil gently, covered, for 3–4 minutes. Strain out the peel and reserve it for drinks or baking. Cool the syrup.
3. Squeeze the lemons, strain the juice, and add to the syrup. Refrigerate and use as needed. Will keep for weeks.
4. *To serve:* Combine the syrup with water, using about 3 parts water to 1 part syrup. Add ice and sliced fresh lemon.

CINNAMON-SUGAR STRIPS

Around 1700, when Gulielma Penn, spouse of William, had her family recipes transcribed, preheating an oven was not a simple matter. She advised, in a recipe for "bisketts," that "you must not goe to breke your eggs till youre oven is hott." The same advice holds true for these quickly assembled, thin, melting crisp cookies.

Makes about 2½ dozen

1¼ cups sifted all-purpose flour
⅛ teaspoon salt
¼ teaspoon baking powder
1 stick (8 tablespoons) unsalted butter, softened
½ cup sugar
1 egg, separated
2 tablespoons brandy or Calvados
1 tablespoon water
⅓ cup large-crystal (decorating) sugar or ½ cup sugar cubes
1 teaspoon ground cinnamon

1. Preheat the oven to 375°. Butter a large, heavy baking sheet, or use a nonstick baking sheet. Sift the flour, salt, and baking powder into a bowl.
2. In the small bowl of an electric mixer beat the butter until light. Add the sugar and beat until pale; add the egg yolk and brandy or Calvados and beat until smooth and fluffy. Add the flour mixture all at once and stir to blend.
3. Using a wet metal spatula, spread the batter thin and as evenly as possible on the baking sheet, leaving a 1-inch margin all around. Smooth the batter with a wet knife or spatula.
4. Beat the egg white in a small bowl with the water until frothy. Gently and thoroughly spread a coating over the batter. Mix the decorating sugar and cinnamon and sprinkle evenly over the sheet of batter. (If you're using the sugar cubes, first wrap them in a towel and crush them into quite small pieces, using a heavy object such as a meat pounder or rolling pin.)
5. Bake in the center of the oven for about 12 minutes, or until the sheet of pastry is nicely browned. Remove from the oven and, using a pastry cutter or sharp knife, immediately trim the edges to form a neat rectangle. Cut the pastry into strips about 4 × 1½ inches.
6. Transfer the cookies to a rack and cool thoroughly. Store in an airtight tin.

PETITE MACAROONS

Macaroons have been prepared in Europe and America in pretty much the same way for centuries. At present, however, the bitter almonds (rich in poisonous prussic acid) that were used to flavor them are virtually unavailable, except in their processed form, as almond extract. Orange flower or rose water was sprinkled over the almonds while they were being pounded (or "brayed"), a lovely addition for those who appreciate the delicate perfumes. The pastry bag used to form the neat rounds was originally called a "squirt," a delightfully apt appellation.

Makes about 40–50

1 cup (about 5 ounces) whole, unblanched almonds
3/4 cup confectioners' sugar
2 egg whites ("large")
Pinch of salt
2 tablespoons plus 4 teaspoons sugar
1/2 teaspoon almond extract
1/4 teaspoon vanilla extract

1. Combine the almonds and confectioners' sugar in the container of a processor and whirl to an extremely fine texture. Scrape the resulting nut-sugar powder into a medium bowl.
2. Preheat the oven to 325°. Cover a large baking sheet with parchment or grease and flour it, knocking off any excess flour; or use a nonstick sheet.
3. In a small mixing bowl beat the egg whites with the salt until soft peaks form. Add the 2 tablespoons sugar, one at a time, beating for 1 minute on high speed after each addition. Beat in the almond extract and vanilla.
4. Fold the almond powder thoroughly into the egg whites, using a rubber spatula.
5. Fit a pastry bag with a plain tip opening about 1/2 inch in diameter and fill the bag with the almond mixture. Press out 40–50 rounds, each about 1 1/4 inches in diameter, onto the sheet. With a wet spoon or fingertip smooth the top of each round. Sprinkle the cookies with the remaining 4 teaspoons sugar, which will give them a shiny, crackled top.
6. Bake in the center of the oven for about 15 minutes, or until the cookies are firm and colored a very pale beige but are not browned. Remove from the oven and let stand 10–15 minutes to firm up. Transfer to a rack and let cool completely.
7. Store the completely cooled cookies in an airtight tin, where they'll keep for weeks.

5
A No-Cook Buffet—When the Heat Is On

A heat-heavy day does not ordinarily stimulate a desire to rattle the pots and pans. As a matter of fact, there are days when the mere thought of being in the same room with a toaster in action, no less an oven, dampens the brow. But social life, after all, does go on despite the intemperate temperature, and postponing entertaining until the first breath of cool weather arrives could be pretty lonely.

Here is a meal that does not require even one teeny bit of oven, toaster, or range energy—only your own. It does take a fair amount of time to assemble in attractive fashion an interesting, full-size buffet, even one without any cooking whatsoever, but the pleasure of entertaining a goodly number of guests coolly, beautifully, is a splendid reward.

NO-COOK BUFFET FOR NINE OR TEN

*Icy Minted Gazpacho
*Tiny Tomatoes Stuffed with Taramosalata
*Smoked Oysters and Horseradish Cream in Cucumber Cups
*Tapenade-Filled Celery
*Salad of Cracked Wheat, Olives, Cilantro, and Peppers
*Salad of Layered Cheeses, Salami, Basil, and Tomatoes
*Beans, Peppers, and Ham in Mustard Dressing
*Salad of Kiwis and Avocados

(Continued)

Crusty French or Italian Bread
Wine: Italian White Wine such as Verdicchio, Pinot Grigio, Colli Albani, or Frascati
Clusters of Several Grape Varieties
Bowl of Ripe Peaches
Bitter Chocolates
Optional (if you feel like boiling water): Spiced Iced Espresso
*Raspberry Cordial

Preparations were made in the following order, more or less:

At least 10 days ahead:
Prepare raspberry cordial

The day before entertaining:
Shop for everything but bread
Prepare taramosalata filling
Make tapenade mixture
Make mustard dressing for the bean and ham salad
Freeze tomato juice cubes
Assemble serving dishes, glasses, napkins, etc. (This kind of Mediterranean spread looks lovely in rustic ceramic dishes, if you have them)

The day of entertaining:
Buy bread
Prepare gazpacho
Soak cracked wheat for salad
Prepare bean and ham salad
Prepare cracked-wheat salad
Make horseradish cream
Trim and soak celery
Prepare cucumber cases
Prepare tomato cases
Prepare cheese and salami salad
Fill and refrigerate cucumbers
Fill and refrigerate tomatoes
Fill and refrigerate celery
Prepare avocado and kiwi salad

ICY MINTED GAZPACHO

This soup is an uncommonly clean, direct, and refreshing one. Gazpacho has become enormously popular in the United States in recent years. Often it is served with pretty little dishes of chopped vegetables for garnish, but in this case a smooth-textured soup is in order, since the meal contains a wide array of fresh, crunchy vegetable bits.

On the Iberian peninsula, to which gazpacho was carried by the Moors, gazpacho is still served in dozens of different styles. Some that I have tasted in Portugal are remarkably close to the original form of the soup, which contained only boiling water, garlic, dried bread slices and sometimes lemon and herbs. It must have been one of the less delicate versions that prompted the French Romantic poet-critic (and snob), Theophile Gautier, to record his memories of a meal of the soup. Gazpacho, he wrote,

> is worthy of a special description, and we shall here give the recipe, which would have made the hair of the late Brillat-Savarin stand on end. You pour some water into a soup tureen, and to this water you add a dash of vinegar, some cloves of garlic, some onions cut into quarters, some slices of cucumber, a few pieces of pimento, a pinch of salt; then one cuts some bread and sets it to soak in the pleasing mixture, serving it cold. At home, a dog of any breeding would refuse to sully its nose with such a compromising mixture. It is the favorite dish of the Andalusians, and the prettiest women do not shrink from swallowing bowlfuls of this hell-broth of an evening (*Un Voyage en Espagne*, tr. by Catherine Alison Phillips, published by Alfred A. Knopf, 1926, as *A Romantic in Spain*).

Prepare the following version of gazpacho, which I trust will sound more appealing, at least a few hours ahead of serving time, preferably the morning of the day you entertain.

Makes 9–10 servings

1½ cups soft, white bread crumbs (about 4 slices bread, crusts removed)
1 or 2 large garlic cloves, pushed through a press
1½ teaspoons ground cumin
¼ cup red wine vinegar
¼ cup olive oil
About 1¼ teaspoons mild pure chile powder, also called ground mild chiles (see list of mail-order sources, page 353; or substitute a big pinch of cayenne)
1 tablespoon coarse (kosher) salt
5 large, ripe tomatoes (about 1¾–2 pounds)
1 cup lightly packed, coarsely chopped fresh mint leaves (about 1 good-size bunch)
1 medium-large red onion, coarsely chopped
2 medium-size red bell peppers, chopped
2 medium-size cucumbers, peeled, seeded, and chunked
1 tablespoon tomato paste
About 3 cups cold water
Tomato juice frozen in ice-cube trays

1. In a large bowl mix the bread crumbs, garlic, cumin, vinegar, oil, chile powder, and salt.

2. Core the tomatoes and halve them crosswise. Squeeze out and discard the seeds. Chop the flesh coarsely and add to the bowl. Add the mint, onion, peppers, cucumbers, tomato paste, and 2 cups water. Mix together well.

3. In batches, purée the mixture to a fine texture in a blender or food processor. Press each batch through the medium disc of a food mill into a bowl after you purée it. Add water to create the desired consistency.

4. Chill the soup for several hours or more, covered. Season.

5. *To serve:* Ladle into cups with a cube or two of the frozen tomato juice in each to keep the chill.

TINY TOMATOES STUFFED WITH TARAMOSALATA

If you have never tasted the creamy, pale, peach-colored concoction, taramosalata, don't be fooled by its delicate appearance; an intense fish flavor lurks in the fluffy mélange. Tarama, the fish eggs used to make the salata, can be from mullet, carp, mackerel, or cod and are commonly salt-preserved. Be sure that you ask for the plain tarama (check for the jar in the refrigerator section of specialty shops or Greek groceries), not the already-mixed taramosalata.

You'll probably have a bit left over, but since this rich assertive mixture will keep for at least two weeks in the refrigerator, it seems worthwhile to make extra.

Makes 2 1/2 dozen, plus extra filling

1/2 cup tarama (about 5 ounces)
1 cup soft, white bread crumbs (about 2–3 slices bread, crusts removed)
2 teaspoons very finely minced onion
About 2 tablespoons lemon juice
Pinch of sugar
1/4 cup light vegetable oil (such as safflower or corn)
About 1/3 cup olive oil
Tabasco
About 2 1/2 dozen tiny plum tomatoes or large cherry tomatoes
Small bunch fresh dill

1. Line a sieve with 2 layers of fine-mesh cotton cheesecloth, scoop in the tarama, and rinse very gently. Press lightly to extract liquid.
2. Soak the bread crumbs in water to cover, then squeeze dry. Combine in a processor or blender with the onion, 2 tablespoons lemon juice, and sugar. Add the tarama and whirl to blend.
3. With the motor running, slowly add the vegetable oil in a thin trickle; next, pour in 1/3 cup olive oil, scraping down the sides to blend evenly. Add more olive oil as necessary to obtain the texture of a lightly fluffy mayonnaise. Season with Tabasco and more lemon juice, if needed. Chill for at least 12 hours, covered.
4. No more than a few hours before serving, prepare the tomatoes for filling. Remove the stems, if any, to make a flat base. Cut a thin slice off the rounded, nonstem ends. With a small melon ball cutter, remove and discard the seeds and pulp. Sprinkle the cases lightly

(Continued)

with salt and sugar and invert them on a cake rack set over a plate for an hour or so to allow the juices to drain out.

5. Finely chop enough dill to equal a few tablespoons. Sprinkle a little into each tomato case, then arrange the cases close together on a serving dish. Fill a pastry tube fitted with a star tip with the taramosalata mixture. Pipe in the cream to almost overflowing. Poke a sprig of dill into each filling. Refrigerate, covered, until serving time.

SMOKED OYSTERS AND HORSERADISH CREAM IN CUCUMBER CUPS

Speaking of horseradish, we are told in a book published in 1852, the title page of which reads as follows:

LADIES'
INDISPENSABLE ASSISTANT.
Being A Companion For The
SISTER, MOTHER, AND WIFE.
Containing More Information For The Price Than Any Other Work Upon the Subject.
HERE ARE THE VERY BEST DIRECTIONS FOR THE
BEHAVIOR AND ETIQUETTE OF
LADIES AND GENTLEMEN,
LADIES' TOILETTE TABLE,
Directions For Managing Canary Birds,
ALSO
SAFE DIRECTIONS FOR THE MANAGEMENT OF CHILDREN;
INSTRUCTIONS FOR
LADIES UNDER VARIOUS CIRCUMSTANCES;
A GREAT VARIETY OF VALUABLE RECIPES, FORMING A COMPLETE SYSTEM OF
FAMILY MEDICINE.
Thus Enabling Each Person To Become His Or Her Own Physician:
To Which Is Added One Of The Best Systems of
COOKERY
Ever Published;
Many Of These Recipes Are Entirely New And Should Be In the Possesion of Every Person In The Land.

that horseradish "is useful in hoarseness, when made into a syrup."

Makes about 2½ dozen small cucumber cups

2 tablespoons prepared horseradish
1 package (3 ounces) cream cheese, softened
1 tablespoon lemon juice
½ teaspoon sugar
½ teaspoon coarse (kosher) salt
¼ cup heavy cream, whipped
About 4 firm, straight cucumbers, each about 7–8 inches long and 1½–2 inches in diameter
1 bunch fresh parsley, very finely chopped
1 tin (3¾ ounces) smoked oysters (or smoked clams)

1. Place the horseradish in a small sieve and press to drain off the liquid. Combine the drained horseradish, cream cheese, lemon juice, sugar, and salt in a small bowl and beat to blend thoroughly. Fold in the whipped cream with a rubber spatula. Cover the bowl with plastic and refrigerate.
2. Peel the cucumbers, leaving a thin layer of the green beneath the skin, if it's not bitter. Trim off the ends. Using a citrus stripper or the tines of a fork, cut grooves about ½–¼ inch apart along the length of each cucumber. Cut each cucumber into 1-inch lengths. With a melon ball cutter, remove the interior spongy central flesh and seeds from each piece, leaving the other cut side intact to form a tiny, flat-bottomed cup. You should have about 2½ dozen. Lightly salt and sugar the interior of the cups and invert them on a cake rack set over a plate to drain for about ½ hour.
3. Turn the cucumbers upright and sprinkle the interiors lavishly with parsley. Place an oyster half (or whole one, if they're tiny) in each cup. When all the cups have been filled, set them in a serving dish. Fill a pastry bag fitted with a tip with a fairly wide opening with the horseradish cream. Pipe the cream in an overflowing mound over each oyster.
4. Refrigerate, covered, several hours before serving.

TAPENADE-FILLED CELERY

Tapenade is a traditional Provençal specialty. The word derives from the regional word for capers, which is difficult to understand, considering how few capers are actually in the dish. I had always assumed that the spread—an intense, dark mixture (downright primeval looking)—was an ancient concoction. Then I read the ever-instructive Elizabeth David on the subject and discovered that "it was invented less than a hundred years ago by the chef at the Maison Dorée in Marseille, although it must certainly have been based on some existing sauce" (*French Provincial Cooking*, 1969).

The embellished version that follows is considerably lighter than the original, which consisted only of olives, capers, anchovies, and sometimes brandy, olive oil, garlic, and lemon juice. Prepare the mixture a day before serving, to allow flavors to mellow.

Makes about 30 small lengths of filled celery

1/2 cup walnut halves
1/2 cup pitted oil-cured black olives
1 tablespoon capers
1 tablespoon lemon juice
1 tin (3 3/4 ounces) sardines in oil, drained
1/2 teaspoon sharp mustard
1 tablespoon brandy or gin
2 tablespoons olive oil
1 bunch celery
A few tablespoons minced fresh parsley

1. In a processor (or with a heavy knife) chop the nuts to a medium-coarse texture. Reserve.
2. Combine the olives, capers, and lemon juice in the container of a processor or blender and chop to a coarse purée. Add the sardines, mustard, brandy, olive oil, and pepper and whirl briefly to form a medium-coarse purée. Add the walnuts and whirl to just blend. Cover, and chill overnight.
3. With a small, sharp knife pull out any coarse "strings" from the firmest, least pithy celery stalks, then zip them down and off (like banana skins). Cut the stalks into 2-inch lengths and drop into a bowl of cold water. Refrigerate for a few hours, until assembly time.
4. Neatly spread a healthy amount of the tapenade in each piece of celery. Arrange the filled celery in a serving dish. Sprinkle each piece with minced parsley in narrow stripes. Refrigerate, covered, until serving time.

SALAD OF CRACKED WHEAT, OLIVES, CILANTRO, AND PEPPERS

Cilantro and hot peppers, like kidneys and oysters, seem to divide the food lovers of the world into two distinct camps. If you don't care for them, you might substitute the traditional mint and parsley mixture that one finds in tabbouli, the Middle Eastern cracked-wheat salad. You might use sweet peppers alone, if you don't relish "heat."

To avoid skin irritation, clean hot peppers under cold running water, or lightly cover your hands with shortening, or wear thin rubber gloves.

Makes 9–10 servings

1½ cups cracked wheat (see note below)
5 cups hot tap water
½ cup diced red onion (1 tiny onion)
¾ cup finely minced, lightly packed cilantro (also called fresh coriander or Chinese parsley)
½ cup pitted, sliced green olives (the Sicilian ones are good)
About 1 cup very finely minced peppers, a judicious selection of colors, sweetness, and hotness
1½ teaspoons salt
⅓ cup lemon juice
¼ cup olive oil
Romaine leaves

1. Combine the cracked wheat and water in a bowl and let stand about ½–1 hour, or until the grains are no longer hard-hearted; they should be firm-tender, not crunchy. The timing will depend upon the fineness of granulation. Pour into a fine sieve and drain. Squeeze out all water, then spread on a towel. Toss and turn until somewhat dried.
2. In a large bowl combine the onion, cilantro, olives, peppers, and wheat. In a small jar combine the salt, lemon juice, and oil; cover and shake to blend. Pour the dressing over the cracked-wheat mixture and toss, then cover with plastic and chill until serving time.
3. *To serve:* Spread the romaine on a deep platter and mound the wheat salad in the center. Decorate, if you like, with a tiny hot pepper, cut into petals, which will warn diners of the warmth within.

NOTE: Cracked wheat is also called bulgur and wheat pilaf. It is usually available in health-food stores and many markets. Don't buy the brand with seasoning. If you can't find it, see the list of mail-order sources on page 353.

SALAD OF LAYERED CHEESES, SALAMI, BASIL, AND TOMATOES

This is one of the many antipasto-style variations on a familiar combination of Italian ingredients. You might consider serving the salad as a main course, with bread and fruit for a simple dinner on another occasion, as well as in the array of dishes for the buffet.

Makes 9–10 servings

4 ounces provolone, cut into 1/4-inch dice
1/2 pound Emmenthaler or Swiss cheese, cut into 1/4-inch dice
3/4 cup lightly packed small, fresh basil leaves
2 tablespoons white wine vinegar
1/2 teaspoon coarse (kosher) salt
1/4 cup olive oil
2 tablespoons finely minced shallots
4–6 ounces thinly sliced Genoa salami, or a combination of varieties
3–4 medium-size ripe tomatoes
Watercress sprigs, trimmed

1. Spread the cheeses in a serving dish and sprinkle with about three fourths of the basil.
2. In a jar combine the vinegar, salt, oil, and shallots; cap and shake to blend thoroughly, then pour half the dressing over the cheese.
3. Cut the salami slices in half and spread over the cheeses. Slice the tomatoes and spread on top. Pour the remaining dressing over all. Sprinkle the remaining basil leaves over all.
4. Cover with plastic and refrigerate several hours before serving.
5. *To serve:* Tuck the watercress around the edge of the salad.

BEANS, PEPPERS, AND HAM IN MUSTARD DRESSING

Fresh, firm-cooked beans will taste better than canned ones, but there are some fine *al dente* brands that are worth the compromise during the dog days. Incidentally, although there will be too much dressing, it's nice to have on hand for the next day or two—and halving an egg seems silly.

Makes 9–10 servings

1 egg, at room temperature
1 tablespoon cider vinegar
2 tablespoons sharp mustard
1 teaspoon coarse (kosher) salt
1/3 cup light vegetable oil, such as corn or safflower
1/3 cup olive oil
1 can (about 1 pound) dark red beans, rinsed and drained
1 can (about 1 pound) white beans, rinsed and drained
3/4 pound firm, smoky ham, cut into 1/4-inch cubes (about 1 1/2 cups)
1 large green bell pepper, cut into 1/4-inch dice
1 large red bell pepper, cut into 1/4-inch dice
1–2 scallions, thinly sliced
Chicory leaves, washed, dried, and shredded

1. Blend the egg, vinegar, mustard, and salt in the container of a processor or blender. With the motor running, gradually pour in the vegetable oil, then the olive oil. Scrape the mixture into a dish and refrigerate, covered, for at least several hours or overnight.
2. In a bowl combine the beans, ham, peppers, and scallions. Scoop in half the dressing and mix very gently with a rubber spatula, being careful not to mash the beans. Taste and add dressing as needed. Add pepper to taste. Chill until serving time, covered.
3. *To serve:* Spread the chicory on a deep platter and mound the salad in the center.

SALAD OF KIWIS AND AVOCADOS

Tart-sweet, fuzzy-skinned kiwi fruits are natives of China (they are sometimes called Chinese gooseberries), although their commercial home is New Zealand. They are presently being raised in California as well. The production from both sources assures a supply virtually year round. Soft, sliceable, parrot-green, the fruit is dotted with black seeds that form a symmetrical pattern, making kiwis ideal for decoration—and the darling of the Nouvelle Cuisine.

In the recipe that follows, the acid fruit, whose taste mingles characteristics of melon, strawberry, rhubarb, and plum, is arranged with bland avocado and tangy orange slices in a slightly nutty sauce. This is not a salad, strictly speaking, but a fresh fruit plate, enhanced with a light touch of dressing to prevent the avocado from darkening and to point up the natural flavors.

Makes 9–10 servings

2 large, ripe avocados
1 large navel orange
1/4 cup lime juice
1/4 teaspoon salt
2 tablespoons walnut oil (see note below)
1 teaspoon honey
2 tablespoons light vegetable oil (such as safflower or almond)
4 large kiwi fruits

1. Run a knife around the avocados lengthwise. Grasp both halves and twist in opposite directions to separate them. Jab a knife deeply into the pit and pull it out. Slice each half in half once again lengthwise, and gently pull off the skin.
2. Set one quarter, with a cut side down, on a board. Cut across on the bias into fairly thin slices. Slide a spatula or pancake turner under the whole quarter and pick it up, keeping the slices together. Slip the whole onto a serving platter and fan out the slices slightly into a graceful design. Continue until all the avocado is sliced and arranged.
3. Peel the orange, removing all the white pith with a sharp knife. Holding the orange over a dish to catch the juice, cut in between the membranes to remove the sections. Arrange with the avocado.
4. Into the dish containing the orange juice pour the lime juice, salt, walnut oil, honey, and vegetable oil. Spoon over the oranges and avocados, being careful to coat each piece of avocado.
5. Using a swivel peeler or a small, sharp knife, remove the skin from the kiwi fruit. Cut the fruit in thin slices, crosswise. Arrange over the avocados.
6. Cover the dish with plastic wrap and refrigerate until serving time, preferably no more than an hour.
7. *To serve:* Tip the platter and spoon a little dressing over all.

NOTE: Nut oils, particularly walnut and hazelnut, should be stored in the refrigerator, or they will quickly turn rancid or musty flavored. If you cannot find walnut oil where you live, see the list of mail-order sources on page 353.

RASPBERRY CORDIAL

Flamboyantly colored, easy to put together, sweet-smelling, this liqueur makes a lovely iced after-dinner quaff on a summer's eve. Or spike iced vodka or dry vermouth with a splash for a vivid apéritif. Notice that you'll need to put together the drink at least 10 days before serving, to allow it to mellow.

Makes about 3 cups

1 pint fresh raspberries
2 1/2 cups good-quality vodka
1 vanilla bean, cut into 1-inch pieces
1/2 teaspoon peppercorns, bruised (lightly pounded in a mortar, but not broken)
1/4 teaspoon whole allspice, bruised
About 1/3 cup light corn syrup

1. Crush the berries roughly in a bowl, using a potato masher or wooden spoon. Scrape into a 1-quart wide-mouthed canning jar or any wide-mouthed container that closes tightly. Add the vodka, vanilla, peppercorns, and allspice. Cover tightly and shake well.
2. Let stand for a week to 10 days, shaking the bottle heartily whenever you pass by.
3. Strain the liqueur, a small batch at a time, through a layer of damp fine-mesh cheesecloth, or several layers of wide-meshed cheesecloth, lining a sieve, which has been set over a 1-quart measuring cup or a bowl with a spout. Press down lightly on the berries to extract the juice, discard the solids, and pour in another small batch of berries and liquid.
4. Rinse the cloth and fold to form 2–3 layers, if fine, or 5–6 if wide-meshed. Strain the cordial through this. Add corn syrup to taste. Pour into a bottle that does not allow much airspace and store for months.

6
Two Meals from One—with Scents of Summer

When summer is finished, so are tomatoes and peaches. Although among the more common pleasures of the garden and orchard, the prickly scent of tomatoes and flowery aroma of peaches surprise and enchant anew every year. To me, their smells are as seasonally significant as perfumed McIntosh apples, or a resinous Scotch pine. It seems fitting to usher out the summer with meals that include both of these fruits.

The two meals that follow are really one, with variations that make for a second night's dining. The dinners are for four or five, but if you're in the mood for a grander scale, simply cook the first night's meal to feed eight to ten.

INFORMAL LATE-SUMMER DINNER 1 (FOR FOUR)

*Spinach and Sorrel Soup
*Pork and Veal Loaf with Fresh Tomato Sauce
*Baked Summer Squash
Crusty Wheat Bread
Wine: Light Red Wine such as Periquita (Portugal)
or a Beaujolais
*Peaches in Vanilla Syrup
Iced Tea
*Orange Sugar Wafers

SPINACH AND SORREL SOUP

The success of dishes that have few components generally depends upon the quality of the ingredients. So it is with this utterly simple soup. Here is one place, for example, where frozen spinach—one of the vegetables that freezes admirably—is less satisfactory, and where canned broths would dull the delicacy of the flavors. You should try to find genuine Parmesan as well, because it adds a pungent edge to the lightly seasoned vegetables and stock. If you are unable to buy sorrel, add another pound of spinach and a generous amount of lemon juice for tartness.

Makes 4 servings (when half is reserved for Dinner 2)

1½ pounds tender, fresh spinach
¾ pound fresh sorrel
4 scallions, trimmed and sliced
7 cups chicken or veal stock, entirely fat-free
Pinch of grated nutmeg
1½ cups freshly shredded or grated Parmesan cheese (about 5 ounces)

1. Remove and discard the stems and any yellowed leaves from the spinach and sorrel. Wash the greens well in several changes of water. Take handfuls of the leaves and cut them into shreds. There should be about 10 packed cups.
2. Cook the spinach, sorrel, and scallions in a large enameled or stainless-steel pot over high heat, stirring until the vegetables have wilted, about 3 minutes. (You can complete this step up until a few hours before your guests arrive.) Set aside until serving time.
3. *To serve:* Add the stock and nutmeg to the greens and bring to a boil. Remove and chill 3 cups of the soup for the next night's Chilled Cream of Spinach and Sorrel Soup. Divide the remainder among 4 bowls and sprinkle each with 2–3 tablespoons of the cheese. Serve the remaining cheese at the table.

PORK AND VEAL LOAF/PÂTÉ

This double-duty recipe makes two loaves—one to be served hot, the other cool. Although the meat mixture is the same in both, the cooking methods are not, which creates two different textures. If your first reaction is that the recipe looks a bit lengthy for what is, after all, only a simple meat loaf, it may be tempered by the realization that not only do you get two meals from one day's cooking, but that as pâté procedures go, this one is most uncomplicated. Note that the mellowing process requires two to five days.

Makes 2 loaves

1 tablespoon coarse (kosher) salt
1 teaspoon sugar
1/2 teaspoon dried savory
1/2 teaspoon dried thyme
1/4 teaspoon grated nutmeg
1 1/2 pounds trimmed pork (shoulder, butt, or loin), cut in 1- to 1 1/2-inch cubes
1 pound trimmed veal (shoulder or breast), cut in 1- to 1 1/2-inch cubes
1/2 pound pork or calf's liver, membrane removed
3/4 pound fresh pork fat (fatback), cut in 1/2- to 3/4-inch cubes
4 medium-size shallots, finely minced
1 medium-size garlic clove, finely minced
4 tablespoons freshly melted pork fat, suet, or lard
2 eggs
3–4 ounces firm, smoked ham (such as Westphalian), cut into 2 thick slices, then into 1/8- to 1/4-inch dice
1 tablespoon pink or green peppercorns, drained, if packed in liquid (see list of mail-order sources, page 353)

1. Combine the salt, sugar, savory, thyme, and nutmeg in a small bowl. Crush slightly with a pestle. Combine the pork, veal, liver, and fat in a bowl. Sprinkle evenly with the spice mixture, tossing to coat the pieces, then cover the bowl with plastic and refrigerate for 1-1 1/2 days.
2. Chill a 4- to 5-cup loaf pan. Preheat the oven to 325°.
3. Cook the shallots and garlic for 1 minute in a small skillet in 1 tablespoon of the melted fat. Set aside.
4. Remove the bowl of meats from the refrigerator and set aside

the liver. Chop about 2 cups of the meat at a time to a coarse texture in the processor, using a "pulse," or turning the machine on and off quickly. As you finish a batch, scrape it into a bowl. (See note below if you prefer to use a meat grinder.)

5. Combine the liver, shallot-garlic mixture, and eggs in the container of the processor and whirl to a fine texture. Pour into the bowl of meats. Add the ham and peppercorns and mix well with your hands.

6. Heat the remaining 3 tablespoons fat and paint the entire interior of the chilled loaf pan generously with it. Very firmly pack half the meat mixture into this; smooth the top. Paint the top generously with more fat. Cover tightly with foil and set the pan in a baking dish half-filled with hot water. This is the pâté.

7. Pack the remaining half of the meat mixture into a 5- to 6-cup loaf pan and paint the top with any remaining fat. This is the meat loaf.

8. Set both pans in the oven (the uncovered pan should be directly on the oven rack, not in the dish of water). Bake 1 hour 15 minutes. With an instant-reading thermometer, check the temperature of the open loaf. When it has reached 165°, remove it from the oven. It should take an additional 20 minutes or so for the covered loaf to reach this temperature; test it.

9. Let both loaves cool 1/2 hour, uncovered. Pour the fat and broth from the pâté into a cup. Skim off the fat and reheat the broth. Pour it back into the pan with the pâté and let cool. Pour out and discard the fat and broth from the meat loaf. Let cool.

10. Refrigerate both loaves, covered. You should allow the pâté to mellow for 1–2 days before serving; the meat loaf can be reheated any time.

11. *To serve the meat loaf:* Remove the loaf from the pan and cut it into slices. Arrange the slices, overlapping, in a baking-serving dish. Bake for about 20 minutes in a preheated 375° oven until the meat is hot through. Heat the sauce (see the following recipe) and pour half over the meat. Serve the remainder separately.

NOTE: If you prefer to use a meat grinder to chop the meat, cut the pork, veal, and fat into strips about 2–3 inches long and 1/2–1 inch wide, instead of into cubes.

FRESH TOMATO SAUCE

This is a clean, light tomato sauce. Make it when you have time (it will keep for days) and reheat for dinner. If you have a splendid stock of tomatoes, prepare more sauce and freeze it in small containers. If you plan to follow the convertible dinner scheme, remember to set aside 1/2 cup for Dinner 2.

Makes about 2 1/2 cups

2 1/2 pounds ripe tomatoes, preferably plum tomatoes
2 tablespoons olive oil
1/4 cup chopped onion
1/4 cup chopped carrot
1/4 cup chopped celery
Large pinch dried thyme
Large pinch dried rosemary
About 1/2 teaspoon sugar
1 long strip orange peel

1. Drop the tomatoes into a large pot of boiling water. Let the water return to a boil; boil 30 seconds. Pour the tomatoes into a colander. Peel and core the tomatoes; halve crosswise and squeeze out most of the seeds. Chop coarsely; there should be about 5 cups.
2. In a medium-size skillet or saucepan heat the oil. Add the onion, carrot, and celery and cook over low heat, covered, until the vegetables are very soft, about 15 minutes. Add the tomatoes, thyme, rosemary, and 1/2 teaspoon sugar and simmer, covered, for about 15 minutes.
3. Press the sauce through the medium disc of a food mill. Return to the pan. Add the orange peel and simmer, uncovered, until the sauce is somewhat thickened. Season with sugar. Remove the orange peel.
4. Set aside 1/2 cup of the sauce for Dinner 2. Pour the rest into a heatproof jar. Cool, cover, and chill.
5. *To serve:* Reheat briefly, stirring.

NOTE: The sauce is deliberately left unsalted to accompany the highly seasoned meat loaf.

BAKED SUMMER SQUASH

Prepare the squash whenever you have the time. If you plan to serve it the same day, you can leave it out until serving time. If prepared a day ahead, be sure to let it return to room temperature before serving. If you make the stuffed peppers for Dinner 2, save at least a cup of the mixture for the stuffing.

Makes 4 servings (with 1 cup reserved for Dinner 2)

2½ pounds firm, medium-size yellow summer squash or zucchini
2 medium-size onions, sliced and separated into rings
2 garlic cloves, sliced
1 teaspoon dried oregano
1 bay leaf, crumbled
¼ teaspoon black pepper
1 teaspoon salt
⅓ cup olive oil
1 tablespoon vinegar

1. Preheat the oven to 375°. Scrub the squash and trim off the stem and blossom ends. Slice the squash across into rounds ½ inch thick.
2. Oil a shallow baking dish large enough to hold the squash in one overlapping layer; spread half the onion rings and half the garlic in it. Sprinkle with half the oregano, bay leaf, pepper, and salt. Spread the squash over this and cover it with the remaining onions, garlic, oregano, bay leaf, pepper, and salt. Drizzle the oil over the top and sprinkle with the vinegar. Cover the dish tightly with foil.
3. Bake for 20 minutes. Uncover the dish and toss the vegetables. Bake for 10 minutes longer, uncovered, until the squash is just *barely* tender. Do not let it cook through and get soft, as it will continue to cook in the dish when removed from the oven. It should have a firm consistency.
4. *To serve:* The squash may be served warm or at room temperature, where it can remain all day. Reserve and chill 1 cup for Dinner 2.

PEACHES IN VANILLA SYRUP

Not only do peaches smell and taste heavenly, but they miraculously turn sunset colors when poached.

Makes 4 servings (if half is reserved to make the sherbet for Dinner 2)

3 cups water
2 1/4 cups sugar
1/2 vanilla bean, halved across
16 medium-small freestone peaches (about 3 pounds), ripe but not soft
A few tablespoons of framboise (raspberry brandy), if desired

1. In a very large skillet combine the water, sugar, and vanilla. Boil gently for 5 minutes, covered.
2. Add the peaches and simmer very gently, uncovered, until they are not quite tender, turning once. The fruit is usually cooked sufficiently in 8–10 minutes, but timing varies—so test by pressing.
3. Remove the peaches from the syrup with a slotted spoon and transfer them to a rack. When cool enough to handle, peel, halve, and stone them. Divide them equally between two bowls, placing all the prettiest halves in one bowl to be served with the syrup. The other peaches will go into the sherbet for Dinner 2.
4. Pour a little syrup and, if desired, framboise to taste over the peaches to be served that night. Cover the bowls with plastic wrap. Chill the peaches. Chill the remaining syrup separately.

ORANGE SUGAR WAFERS

Thin, crisp, sparkly topped cookies are quick to make and last well.

Makes 2 dozen

1/2 cup sugar, plus sugar for tops of cookies
1 stick (8 tablespoons) unsalted butter, softened
1/4 teaspoon salt
2 egg whites ("large" or "extra-large")
2 teaspoons grated orange rind
2 teaspoons orange flower water (see list of mail-order sources, page 353), or use orange juice
3/4 cup all-purpose flour
2 tablespoons cornstarch

1. Preheat the oven to 375°. Get out 2 nonstick baking sheets (preferably) or cover 2 baking sheets with parchment.
2. Beat the sugar, butter, and salt together in a mixing bowl to blend. Add the egg whites, orange rind, and orange flower water and mix until well blended. Sift in the flour and cornstarch and blend thoroughly, but do not overbeat.
3. Fit a pastry bag with a 1/2-inch plain tip and fill with the batter. Pipe 12 flattened rounds about 1 1/2 inches in diameter, evenly spaced, on each baking sheet. With a wet fingertip, flatten their topknots. Sprinkle the top of each cookie with sugar, using about 1 1/2 tablespoons for the entire amount.
4. Set the sheets on two shelves in the center of the oven. Bake for 7–8 minutes. Turn the pans around and switch racks. Continue baking for about 5–6 minutes longer, or until the cookies have a pale brown rim about 1/4 inch wide.
5. Let the sheets rest for a minute on a rack, then carefully transfer the cookies to the rack to cool completely. Stored airtight, the cookies will last up to a week.

INFORMAL LATE-SUMMER DINNER 2 (FOR FOUR)

*Chilled Cream of Spinach and Sorrel Soup
*Pork and Veal Pâté
*Peppers Stuffed with Rice and Squash
Wine: Valpolicella *or* Bardolino
*Processor "French" Bread (page 139) *or* Bakery White Bread
*Peach Sherbet
*Orange Sugar Wafers

CHILLED CREAM OF SPINACH AND SORREL SOUP

Prepare this with the reserved Spinach and Sorrel Soup from Dinner 1, either the night that you serve the hot soup or the next day.

Makes 4 servings

3 cups Spinach and Sorrel Soup (page 59)
Salt, as desired
4 teaspoons cornstarch
About 1/2 cup heavy cream, chilled
Very finely shredded sorrel or spinach for garnish
Thinly sliced scallion greens

1. Purée the soup through the fine disc of a food mill. Add salt to taste.
2. Combine 3 tablespoons of the puréed soup with the cornstarch and stir until the mixture is smooth. Add it to the soup.
3. Bring the soup to a boil over moderate heat, stirring constantly. Simmer for 2 minutes, stirring constantly.
4. Pour the soup into a bowl and cool it, stirring now and then. Chill the soup, covered, for several hours or overnight.
5. *To serve:* Stir in 1/2 cup cream, or to taste. Ladle the soup into chilled serving bowls and sprinkle with the sorrel and scallions.

PORK AND VEAL PÂTÉ

See Pork and Veal Loaf/Pâté, page 67. *To serve the pâté:* Remove it from the loaf pan and scrape off all the fat and jellied broth. Cut it into fairly thin slices and arrange on a platter with sliced plum tomatoes. Serve at room temperature.

PEPPERS STUFFED WITH RICE AND SQUASH

Makes 4 servings

8 very small, straight-sided red and/or green bell peppers
About 2 1/2 cups cooked rice
1/2 cup Fresh Tomato Sauce, reserved from Dinner 1 (page 62)
1 cup Baked Summer Squash, reserved from Dinner 1 (page 63), drained and coarsely chopped
1/2 teaspoon dried thyme
1/4 cup minced fresh parsley
1 tablespoon capers, preferably nonpareil (the tiny kind) if possible
2–3 tablespoons pitted, thinly sliced oil-cured black olives
1/4 cup olive oil

1. Drop the peppers into a pot of boiling water. Let them return to a boil, then boil gently for 4–5 minutes, until slightly softened. Turn several times. Preheat the oven to 425°.
2. Drain the peppers and place in a bowl of ice water to cool. Cut around the center stems and remove them, as well as the seeds and ribs.
3. Combine the rice, sauce, squash, thyme, parsley, capers, salt, pepper, and olives in a bowl. Toss gently. Season assertively.
4. Fill the peppers with the stuffing, mounding the centers. Spread 1 tablespoon of the olive oil in a baking dish that will hold all the peppers upright, pressed close together. When the peppers are filled and fitted into the baking dish, drizzle the remaining oil over them. Bake for 20 minutes. Let cool to room temperature.
5. Serve peppers when convenient. They can remain at room temperature all day.

PEACH SHERBET

To make a simple sherbet, you purée the poached peaches in their cooking syrup and freeze the mixture, stirring it up several times to break up the large ice crystals that form.

Makes 1 quart

8 Peaches in Vanilla Syrup (or half the recipe total), reserved from Dinner 1 (page 64)
1 1/4 cups vanilla syrup (reserved from Peaches in Vanilla Syrup)
1/2 cup cold water
About 1/4 cup fresh lemon juice
GARNISH: Fresh mint leaves

1. Purée the fruit through the medium disc of a food mill. It should make about 2 cups.
2. Add the reserved vanilla syrup and the cold water and mix. Add 1/4 cup lemon juice, or to taste, making the mixture slightly tarter than you like it. It will mellow in freezing.
3. Pour the purée into a metal pan, cover, and freeze until solid around the edge and no longer liquid in the center. Timing varies; begin checking at about 1 hour. Beat vigorously with a whisk to make an even-textured, not liquefied slush. Freeze again, which will take somewhat less time. Beat the mixture again.
4. Pack into a quart container and freeze 4 hours or more before serving, preferably overnight.
5. *To serve:* Let the sherbet soften for 1/2 hour in the refrigerator, then garnish, if you like, with mint leaves.

7
Main-Dish Vegetable Variations

Meatless Main Courses for Casual Meals

For various reasons involving taste, budget, and health, we have never consumed a great deal of meat in our home—and for all the same reasons, we are buying even less now. Although it is almost impossible to feel confident about a choice of diet when bombarded daily with information that alternately damns and praises nearly every food that might pass our lips, there does appear to be substantial evidence that a diet rich in vegetable starches and proteins and low in animal fats is beneficial.

While this is by no means the only chapter featuring meatless entrées, the grouping of a wide range of such dishes presents the opportunity to stress the pleasures and virtues of several valuable and occasionally overlooked sources of high-quality, low-cost forms of nourishment.

SUGGESTED MENU FOR FOUR OR FIVE

*Brown Rice, Zucchini, and Walnut Loaf with Cheddar Sauce
Baked Tomatoes
Wine: Valpolicella *or* Chianti
Arugula and Mushroom Salad
*Fresh Grapefruit Gelatin with Cream (page 312)

BROWN RICE, ZUCCHINI, AND WALNUT LOAF WITH CHEDDAR SAUCE

This moist, firm, herbed loaf has distinctive texture and a full-flavored, slightly acid sauce. It is one of those rare dishes that seems to please everyone.

Makes 4–5 servings

1 cup long-grain brown rice
1 1/2 cups water
1 teaspoon salt
Scant 1 pound small zucchini, scrubbed and trimmed
3 scallions, thinly sliced
3/4 cup walnuts, coarsely chopped (except a few halves for the top of the loaf)
1/4 teaspoon black pepper
1/2 teaspoon dried sage
1/4 teaspoon dried rosemary
1/2 teaspoon dried marjoram
3 eggs

SAUCE:
1 1/4 cups milk
2 tablespoons butter
5 teapoons potato starch (preferably) or 3 tablespoons all-purpose flour
2 teaspoons sharp mustard
4 ounces sharp Cheddar cheese, finely shredded
About 1/2 cup buttermilk

1. Combine the rice, water, and 1/2 teaspoon of the salt in a hesaucepan. Bring to a full boil, stirring occasionally. Turn the heat to its lowest level, cover the pot, and cook for 35 minutes. Remove from the heat and let stand, covered, for at least 20 minutes.
2. Meanwhile, coarsely grate the zucchini and scrape into a sieve set over a bowl. Toss with the remaining 1/2 teaspoon salt and let drain for at least 30 minutes.
3. Combine the scallions, walnuts, pepper, sage, rosemary, and marjoram in a bowl with the rice. Let cool for a few minutes, tossing often.
4. Press down firmly on the zucchini to extract as much liquid as possible; discard the liquid. Blend the eggs in a bowl and stir in the zucchini, mixing well to separate the strands. Add to the rice mixture and blend thoroughly.

5. Scoop the mixture into a well-buttered, loaf-shaped baking dish with about a 6-cup capacity. Let the mixture cool, then cover tightly with foil. Store in the refrigerator up to 12 hours.
6. *To make the sauce:* In a small pot bring the milk to a bare simmer; reserve. Melt the butter in a small heavy saucepan. Stir in the potato starch or flour and stir over moderate heat for a few minutes until lightly colored. Add the milk, all at once, and bring to a simmer, stirring constantly with a whisk. Add the mustard and cheese and stir until the cheese melts. The sauce will be much too thick, but will be thinned later on. Let cool completely, then cover and refrigerate until serving time.
7. *To bake and serve:* Preheat oven to 350°. Bake the foil-covered loaf for 50 minutes. Remove the foil and bake 10–15 minutes longer, or until the surface of the loaf is dry and firm. Let rest at room temperature for 5–10 minutes.
8. Meanwhile, heat the sauce over low heat, stirring often. Gradually stir in the buttermilk, until it reaches the desired consistency. Add salt to taste.
9. Run a knife around the edge of the loaf, set a platter over it, and invert. Pour about one third of the sauce over the loaf; pour the remainder into a hot gravy boat or small pitcher. Arrange the walnut halves on the loaf and serve.

SUGGESTED MENU FOR FIVE

Melon and Prosciutto
*Lasagne with Eggplant, Peppers, and Onions in Garlic Cream Sauce
Wine: Frascati *or* Colli Albani
*Processor "French" Bread (page 139) *or* Italian Bread
Salad of Watercress with Walnuts and Lemon-Oil Dressing
*Peach Sherbet (page 68)

LASAGNE WITH EGGPLANT, PEPPERS, AND ONIONS IN GARLIC CREAM SAUCE

Lasagne receives an unusual treatment in this made-ahead meal that can be refrigerated or frozen. The fennel- and garlic-enlivened sauce is a pale pinky coral color.

Makes 2 casseroles (5 servings each)

3 medium eggplants (3 1/2 pounds total weight)
2 1/2 teaspoons coarse (kosher) salt
7 tablespoons butter
4 medium onions, cut into 1/2-inch dice
2 red bell peppers, cut into 1/2-inch dice
2 green bell peppers, cut into 1/2-inch dice
2 large garlic cloves, finely minced or pushed through a press
1/3 cup all-purpose flour
3 cups milk
3–4 ounces freshly shredded or grated Parmesan cheese (1–1 1/3 cups)
2 1/2 cups tomato juice
1/2 teaspoon fennel seeds, slightly crushed in a mortar
1 package (1 pound) lasagne (24 noodles)
2 dozen olives, pitted and sliced (optional)

1. Rinse the eggplants and cut into 3/4-inch dice (do not peel). Combine in a stainless-steel or enameled colander with 2 teaspoons of the salt; toss well. Set a plate and a heavy weight on top of the eggplant and allow to drain for at least 1/2 hour.
2. In a large skillet melt 2 tablespoons of the butter. Stir in the onions and peppers and cook over moderate heat until softened, about 10 minutes, stirring often. Transfer to a dish.
3. Melt the remaining 5 tablespoons butter in the same skillet. Stir in the garlic, then the flour, and continue stirring over moderate heat for 2 minutes. Add the milk, all at once, and stir over high heat with a whisk until the sauce simmers. Lower the heat and continue cooking for about 10 minutes, stirring often. The sauce should not quite simmer. Stir in the cheese and remaining 1/2 teaspoon salt and remove from the heat.
4. Press down on the eggplant to express as much liquid as possible.

Spread the cubes on paper towels and pat dry a bit. Combine in a very large skillet or casserole with 1½ cups of the tomato juice and the fennel seeds. Cook over high heat for about 10 minutes, stirring often, until the eggplant is tender and the liquid has evaporated.

5. Meanwhile, bring to a boil a very large pot of salted water. Drop in the noodles, one at a time, keeping the water at a boil. Stir gently to keep the water from boiling over and the noodles from sticking together. Boil until the strips are just pliable, not tender, about 5 minutes. Drain, then cover with cold water.

6. Set out two rectangular baking dishes, about 11 × 8 × 2½ inches. Line one with foil. Stir the remaining 1 cup tomato juice into the cream sauce, using a whisk. Spread about ½ cup each of the pepper-onion mixture and the eggplant in each dish. Dot each with a scant ½ cup sauce. Over this spread 4 noodles lengthwise, to cover, on each. Spread 1 cup of the onion-pepper on each noodle layer, then cover with another layer of noodles, placed crosswise and trimmed to fit. Divide the remaining eggplant between the two dishes and dot with ½ cup of the sauce. Cover each dish with the remaining noodles, placed in the same direction as the first layer—that is, lengthwise. Divide the remaining sauce over the tops and smooth evenly with a spatula. Cover with foil.

7. *To store:* The foil-lined dish should be set in the freezer. When frozen solid, remove the foil package and seal and label, then return to the freezer for storage up to 3 months. Store the other dish in the refrigerator up to 24 hours.

8. *To reheat the lasagne from the freezer:* Unwrap and entirely defrost the frozen lasagne in the appropriate dish (see Reminders about Freezing, page 352). Set on the upper shelf of the oven and turn to 350°. Heat, covered, for 30 minutes, until hot in the center. Remove the foil, turn the heat to 425°, sprinkle with half the optional olives, and bake for 15 minutes, until lightly browned and bubbling.

To reheat the lasagne from the refrigerator: Set it on the upper shelf of a turned-off oven. Turn the heat to 375° and bake, covered, for 20 minutes. Remove the foil, scatter half the optional olives over the top, and bake about 25 minutes longer, until the top is lightly browned and bubbling.

SUGGESTED MENU FOR NINE

*Icy Minted Gazpacho (page 47)
*Strudel of Kasha, Cabbage, and Walnuts with Dill Sauce
Wine: A Sparkling White Wine
Large Bowl of Fruits
*Cinnamon-Sugar Strips (page 42)

STRUDEL OF KASHA, CABBAGE, AND WALNUTS WITH DILL SAUCE

Why buckwheat (in its roasted form called kasha) is not universally adored is incomprehensible to me. In the United States it seems to be appreciated almost exclusively by the descendants of Central Europeans and by "health-food" fanatics. Yet whenever I serve the earthy, nutty grains, guests are delighted. And if the appealing texture and flavor are not sufficient grounds for more attention, consider these bonuses: Kasha is easy to prepare, cheap, and nutritious.

Strudel or phyllo (or filo) dough is available in the refrigerator sections of many supermarkets and specialty stores. Although the sizes vary from brand to brand, any would do here. If you have never used this tissue-thin miracle dough, don't hesitate. It is not difficult to handle and produces a perfect crust every time.

Makes 3 strudel rolls (about 3 generous main-course servings each)

1 head (3 pounds) red cabbage
2 tablespoons coarse (kosher) salt
1 medium or large egg, beaten
1 cup medium kasha (see list of mail-order sources, page 353)
1 3/4 cups boiling water
1/2 teaspoon salt
1 1/4 sticks (10 tablespoons) unsalted butter
1/2 cup walnut oil (see list of mail-order sources, page 353)
4 medium onions, coarsely chopped
1/2 teaspoon dill seed
1/2 teaspoon caraway seeds
2 cups walnuts
1 pound strudel (phyllo) dough
3/4 cup dry bread crumbs
1 1/2 teaspoons poppy seeds

SAUCE (FOR ALL 3 ROLLS):

1 cup sour cream
2 cups yogurt
3 tablespoons finely snipped fresh dill

1. Remove and discard the tough outer leaves of the cabbage. Quarter and core the cabbage, then rinse well. Shred very fine, being sure there are no large chunks. Combine in a stainless steel or enameled colander with the coarse salt. Toss to mix. Set a plate to almost cover on the cabbage and place a heavy weight on this. Let the cabbage drain at least 1/2 hour, or longer.
2. Combine the egg and kasha in a bowl and mix until all the grains are coated. Scrape into a heavy saucepan. Over moderate heat stir until all the grains are dry and separated. Add the boiling water and salt. Turn the heat to its lowest point. Cover and cook the kasha 15 minutes. Remove from the heat and let stand, covered, 10 minutes. Fluff the kasha into a bowl to cool.
3. Melt the butter in a small pan over low heat. Carefully remove and discard the foam. Pour off and reserve the clear yellow liquid and discard the milky residue that remains. Add the walnut oil to the clarified butter.
4. In a very large skillet sauté the cabbage and onions in 1/4 cup of the butter-oil mixture. Stir over moderate heat until the vegetables are very tender and no liquid remains, about 15 minutes. Add the dill seed and caraway seeds and scrape into a large dish to cool.
5. When both cabbage and kasha are cooled, combine them in a bowl and add plenty of pepper. Coarsely chop the nuts and reserve.
6. Wet 2 dish towels and wring them out thoroughly. Spread horizontally in front of you and cover each with a sheet of waxed paper. Unwrap and open out the strudel dough and place on one sheet of the waxed paper. Turn in the towel edges to cover the dough. Remove one sheet of the dough and place on the other towel.
7. Brush all over with a thin coating of the butter-oil mixture. Lay another strudel leaf on top of this and brush sparingly all over with the butter-oil. Sprinkle with a rounded tablespoon of bread crumbs. Continue thus, making 7–8 layers, using up 1/4 cup crumbs on alternate layers. When you've buttered the last layer, sprinkle evenly with one third of the walnuts. Lay on another sheet of dough and butter it.
8. Spread one third of the filling a few inches in from the closest edge and from the two short ends. Turn the short ends inward about 1 1/2 inches to enclose the filling. With the aid of the towel, roll the strudel, jelly-roll fashion, to make an even cylinder. Do not roll tightly.

(Continued)

9. Set the roll, seam side down, on a nonstick or lightly oiled baking sheet. Brush lavishly with the butter-oil. Sprinkle the top with the poppy seeds.
10. Repeat the filling, rolling, and finishing steps to make two more rolls.
11. *To refrigerate, then bake:* Refrigerate the strudel rolls until the butter coat is firm, then cover loosely with plastic wrap and store in the refrigerator up to 24 hours. To bake, preheat the oven to 425°. Set the baking sheet in the center of the oven for 10 minutes. Lower the heat to 350° and bake the rolls about 25–30 minutes longer, or until they are crisp and evenly browned. You can serve the strudels hot or warm. Bake an hour or two before you plan to serve.
12. *To freeze, then bake:* Refrigerate the strudel rolls until the butter coat is firm. Then carefully wrap, label, and seal the rolls, which can be stored up to 1 month. Before baking, defrost overnight in the refrigerator. Then unwrap, set on a baking sheet, and let reach room temperature before baking as above. The crust will be less crisp when strudel is frozen before baking.
13. *To make the sauce:* Combine the sour cream, yogurt, dill, and pepper to taste. Cover and store in the fridge until serving time, then serve with the strudel rolls.

SUGGESTED MENU FOR FOUR

*Tapenade-Filled Celery (page 52; halve the recipe)
*Gratin of Zucchini, Bread, and Ricotta
Wine: Vernaccia di San Gimignano *or* Chianti
Salad of Mushrooms and Endive
*Petite Macaroons (page 43)/Fresh Fruit

GRATIN OF ZUCCHINI, BREAD, AND RICOTTA

There are few one-dish meals as easy to assemble as this fresh, simple mélange.

Makes 4 servings

2 pounds small or medium-size zucchini, well scrubbed
1 1/2 teaspoons coarse (kosher) salt
1 can (1 pound) peeled tomatoes
1 container (15 ounces) part-skim ricotta cheese (or use fresh, bulk ricotta if you can get it in your neighborhood)
1/2 cup buttermilk
2 eggs
1/4 teaspoon grated nutmeg
1/4 teaspoon black pepper
2 medium shallots, minced
1/2 teaspoon dried tarragon
About 8 firm slices whole-wheat bread, or as needed

1. Coarsely grate or shred the zucchini. Combine with 1 teaspoon of the salt in a colander, preferably enameled or stainless. Set the colander over a dish. Place a plate on top of the squash to almost cover it, put a heavy weight on top of this and let the squash drain for at least 30 minutes.
2. Meanwhile, purée the tomatoes and their liquid in a processor or blender. Press through a sieve so that all the pulp is strained. Discard the seeds. Boil gently in a small saucepan, stirring often, until the purée is reduced to 3/4–1 cup. Cool, cover, and refrigerate.
3. Combine the ricotta, buttermilk, eggs, remaining 1/2 teaspoon salt, the nutmeg, and pepper in a processor or blender and mix well.
4. Press as much moisture as possible from the zucchini. Toss well with the minced shallots and tarragon. Spread evenly in a well-buttered shallow baking/serving dish of about 2-quart capacity.
5. Overlap the bread slices slightly to cover the squash; about 8 sandwich-size slices should suffice. Pour the ricotta mixture over this. With a knife tip pierce through the bread here and there to absorb the mixture. Cover and store in the refrigerator up to 12 hours. Or you can let stand for 30 minutes and then bake.
6. *To bake and serve:* Remove the gratin from the refrigerator (if you refrigerated it) while you preheat the oven to 400°. Drizzle the reserved tomato purée in a design over the top of the gratin. Bake in the center of the oven, uncovered, for about 45 minutes, or until the top is puffed and browned.

SUGGESTED MENU FOR SIX

*Crisp Savory Almonds (page 289; halve the recipe)
*Creamed Root Vegetables
*Brown Rice (page 176)
White Wine from Bordeaux *or* Light Beer
Sliced Oranges and Strawberries

CREAMED ROOT VEGETABLES

This is a casual dish, to be served to vegetable-loving friends. Although it may look finicky to supply the size of the vegetable pieces, it is important that the dice be uniform, or they will finish cooking at different times, making for an undistinguished stew of over- and undercooked vegetables. When cooked *al dente*, the pretty root vegetables are a treat. This is a late summer dish.

Makes about 6 servings

3/4 stick (6 tablespoons) butter

1 medium-size leek, split lengthwise, meticulously washed, then sliced thin, roots and dark green leaf tops removed

About 1 1/4 pounds carrots, peeled and cut into 1/2- to 3/4-inch pieces (about 3 cups)

About 3/4 pound small, fresh white turnips, cut into 1/2- to 3/4-inch cubes (peel only if large and tough-skinned)

About 3/4 pound rutabaga, peeled and cut into 1/2- to 3/4-inch cubes (about 2 cups)

About 3/4 pound parsnips, peeled and cut into 1/2- to 3/4-inch pieces (about 2 cups)

About 3/4 pound all-purpose potatoes, peeled and cut into 1/2- to 3/4-inch cubes (about 2 cups)

3 cups chicken or veal broth

1 cup milk

3 tablespoons all-purpose flour

3/4 teaspoon dried dillweed

1 teaspoon dried basil

1/2 cup heavy cream

1. Melt 3 tablespoons of the butter in a large, heavy casserole or Dutch oven. Add the leek and stir over moderate heat until softened, about 5 minutes. Add the carrots, turnips, rutabaga, parsnips, and potatoes and cook over moderately high heat for 4–5 minutes, tossing.
2. Add the broth and milk and boil gently, partly covered, for 5–8 minutes, stirring often, until the vegetables are not quite tender. Drain and reserve the vegetables and liquid separately.
3. Melt 2 tablespoons butter in the same pot in which the vegetables cooked. Add the flour and cook about 2 minutes, stirring. Add the reserved cooking liquid, dill, and basil and stir over moderate heat for a few minutes. Add the cream and vegetables and bring to a simmer, stirring. Taste for salt.
4. Remove from the heat and set the pot in a sink containing cold water. Stir often until the mixture is cooled. Cover and store in the refrigerator up to 36 hours.
5. *To serve:* Set the pot of creamed vegetables over moderate heat and stir often, until just heated through, 5–10 minutes. Do not cook or the vegetables will become too soft. Serve over Brown Rice.

SUGGESTED MENU FOR SIX

*Deviled Eggs (page 186; halve the recipe)
or *Icy Minted Gazpacho (page 47)
*Warm Soybean Salad with Cheese, Peppers, and Olives
*Processor "French" Bread (page 139) *or* Bakery French Bread
Wine: Petite Sirah from California
Melon

WARM SOYBEAN SALAD WITH CHEESE, PEPPERS, AND OLIVES

Although you could use any dried bean in this recipe, soybeans are to be preferred for their extremely firm texture. They retain both their shape and smoothness of skin, and thus reheat without stickiness.

Makes about 6 servings

1 pound dried soybeans
1 teaspoon salt
1/2 cup strong-flavored olive oil, such as the Spanish brands
3/4 cup diced red bell pepper
3/4 cup diced green bell pepper
2 medium garlic cloves, minced
1 tablespoon ground cumin
1–2 tablespoons diced, peeled hot green chiles (fresh, frozen, or canned)
2 cups sliced scallions
1/2 pound feta or Bryndza cheese, cut into 1/2-inch dice
1/4 cup pitted, sliced, oil-cured black olives
Lemon juice
Finely minced fresh parsley

1. Soak the soybeans overnight in water to cover by 3–4 inches.
2. Drain and rinse the beans briefly. Combine in a heavy saucepan with water to cover by about 4 inches. Simmer, partly covered, until tender, which can take from 2 1/2 to 4 hours, depending upon the state of dehydration. Soybeans never become as soft as other beans—and it is virtually impossible to overcook them. Toward the end of their cooking period, add the salt. Drain. If you wish, you can store the beans for a day or two in the refrigerator, covered.
3. Heat the oil in a large skillet. Add the red and green peppers and sauté for a few minutes to soften very slightly. Add the garlic and stir for a minute. Add the cumin, chiles to taste, and scallions and stir over high heat for less than a minute.
4. Combine the beans and the contents of the skillet and toss. Cool, if necessary. Add the cheese and olives and cover. Store in the refrigerator if you'll be serving the dish the next day. Otherwise, keep at room temperature.
5. *To serve:* In a large skillet stir the salad over moderate heat for a few minutes to *just* warm. The cheese should just begin to soften, not melt. Add lemon juice, parsley, and pepper and salt to taste.

A TOFU DETOUR, OR CURDS AND WAYS

Of the myriad magical products created from the humble soybean, bean curd is the one that is most popular in this country. It is not hard to understand why. The soft, bland, ivory-colored cakes take well to just about any treatment the cook can offer: Bean curd can be eaten fresh, steamed, broiled, baked, simmered, deep fried, or vividly sauced. And along with pleasant flavor and texture, bean curd is uncommonly nutritious. The soybean is the only vegetable considered to be a complete protein (that is, one with all the essential amino acids), and in its curd form it provides a food that is both high in protein and extremely easy to digest. Bean curd is unique among high-protein foods in that it is low in calories and saturated fats, and contains no cholesterol. When you add to this the fact that bean curd is also packed with vitamins and minerals, it is no wonder that people all over this country have begun to pay attention to this simple source of nourishment, one that has been revered for centuries by the Chinese and Japanese.

Perhaps it is the association with traditional Oriental cuisine that has made some people reluctant to cook bean curd, believing that a knowledge of Oriental cooking techniques or special equipment and ingredients is necessary for the preparation of these bean cakes. While it is true that the Japanese and Chinese have made of soybean cookery an art unto itself, it is neither necessary to have exotic supplies, nor to "think Oriental" in order to enjoy the many virtues of this versatile substance.

Although bean curd can appear in the market in no less than twenty guises, the forms most often encountered are the simple, off-white, square cakes called tofu (Japanese) and dow foo (Chinese). To make these, soybeans are soaked and puréed, then curdled by the addition of a coagulant. The curds are pressed into squares of varying tenderness that may range from delicately custardy ("silken" tofu) to firm and bouncy (the small, Chinese-style pressed dow foo). Most often you will find the spongy, straight-sided cubes of a medium-tender texture (tofu) and the somewhat firmer version of the same (dow foo) in ordinary markets. Both kinds are immersed in large containers of water from which they are scooped and sold by the piece; or you can buy them in small, sealed plastic tubs, also water-filled. When you buy bean curd loose (that is, not sealed) look for a super-clean shop, or purchase from someone with whom you've dealt before, as bean curd should be very fresh and immaculate.

SUGGESTED MENU FOR FOUR OR FIVE

*Bean Curd in Chile Tomato Sauce
Cornbread
Beer
Avocado and Grapefruit Salad
Fresh Fruit *or* *Watermelon Ice (page 37)

BEAN CURD IN CHILE TOMATO SAUCE

A curious and delicious hybrid, this is a combination of southwestern chile and Peking-style bean curd. It is spicy, quick to make, and lighter than either of its ancestors. You can make the sauce hours or days ahead, then heat it up and add the bean curd at serving time.

Makes 4–5 servings

3/4 pound fatty pork (about 2/3 lean, 1/3 fat), chilled
1 large onion, coarsely chopped (1 cup)
1 medium green bell pepper, coarsely chopped (1/2 cup)
3–4 medium garlic cloves, minced (1 1/2–2 teaspoons)
1 tablespoon all-purpose flour
2 teaspoons dried oregano
1 teaspoon ground cumin
1 tablespoon ground coriander
2 tablespoons mild pure chile powder or a smaller amount of ground hot chiles (see list of mail-order sources, page 353)
1 can (1 pound 12 ounces) Italian plum tomatoes (see note below)
1 cup water
6 bean curd cakes (firm or tender), rinsed
Cilantro (fresh coriander or Chinese parsley)

1. If you are using a food processor to chop the meat, cut it into 1-inch cubes and process to a medium-coarse grind. With a meat grinder, cut into strips about 3 × 1/2 inches and press through the coarse disc of the grinder.
2. Heat a large, heavy saucepan over high heat; drop in the pork and stir, breaking up the pork, until it is no longer pink. Add the onion and green pepper and stir until softened, about 3–4 minutes. Add the garlic, flour, oregano, cumin, coriander, and chile powder and lower the heat to moderate. Stir for about 3 minutes.
3. With kitchen scissors, snip the tomatoes in the can into small bits. Pour into the saucepan. Add the water and simmer for 30 minutes. Taste and add salt as needed. Cool, cover, and refrigerate until serving time.
4. *To serve:* Halve the bean curd horizontally, then cut into 1/2-inch cubes. Heat the reserved sauce, stirring. Add the cubes to the sauce and barely simmer, stirring often, until the curd is puffy and softened, about 15 minutes.

NOTE: Canned tomatoes have been used so that this dish can be prepared year round, as it fits other seasons equally well. If you use fresh tomatoes, buy about 1 3/4 pounds plum tomatoes. Drop them into a pot of boiling water. Let the water return to a full boil over highest heat. Drain the tomatoes. Peel and core them and chop coarsely, then add.

SUGGESTED MENU FOR FOUR

*Bean Curd in Paprika Cream Sauce
*Brown Rice (for 4–5, page 176) *or* *Millet (page 178)
Crisp-Cooked Green Beans
Wine: Pinot Grigio *or* Soave
Salad of Cucumbers and Endive with Dill-Lemon Dressing
*Fruit-Filled Honeydew (page 335)

BEAN CURD IN PAPRIKA CREAM SAUCE

This is a rich, filling dish that will probably please even the most stalwart carnivores.

Makes 4 servings

3 tablespoons butter
About 6 small yellow onions, sliced into 1/4-inch-thick rings (to make 2 cups)
3 tablespoons all-purpose flour
2 teaspoons sweet Hungarian paprika
1/4 teaspoon sugar
1 large tomato, puréed and strained (3/4 cup), or use an 8-ounce can tomatoes, pressed through a food mill
1 cup beef broth
1/4 teaspoon dried marjoram
1/2 cup heavy cream
6 bean curd cakes (firm or tender), rinsed

1. Heat the butter in a large skillet. Stir in the onion rings and cook over moderately low heat until they are somewhat soft but not browned, about 10 minutes.
2. Sprinkle over them the flour and paprika and stir for 2 minutes. Add the sugar, tomato, broth, and marjoram and simmer, stirring constantly, for 4–5 minutes, until the mixture is thick and smooth. Stir in the cream, a little at a time. Season with salt and remove from the heat.
3. Pour half the sauce and onions into a shallow baking/serving dish about 10 × 6 inches. Cut the bean curd crosswise into slices 1/2 inch thick. Spread the slices, closely overlapping, on the sauce. Sprinkle lightly with salt and pepper. Pour the remaining sauce and onions on top. Cool, cover, and store in the refrigerator up to 24 hours.
4. *To heat and serve:* Remove the dish from the fridge and uncover it while you preheat the oven to 350°. Set the dish in the upper level of the oven and bake about 35 minutes, or until heated through.

8
The Last Outdoor Supper

The last outdoor supper of the season is, for apartment dwellers like me, simply a state of mind. For others, who live in parts of the country where the seasons almost always (or almost never) allow for alfresco dining, the last supper of summer will have a different meaning. Whatever the images evoked, most of us sense a transition from a relatively relaxed pace of life to the brisker, more demanding mode that distinguishes the fall season.

It is that change of tone that is being acknowledged here. Wearing sandals and loose robes, linger over the last of summer's beauties—ripe tomatoes and pungent basil, most estival of herbs. Savor the bittersweet blackberries. Then, when you've momentarily mourned the passing of the leisurely season, look forward to the busy bounty of fall.

LAST OUTDOOR SUPPER FOR SIX

Radishes with Leaves/Breadsticks/Black Olives
Wine: Verdicchio *or* Orvieto Secco
*Puréed Fennel and Leek Soup
*Spinach-Stuffed Boned Rock Cornish Hens
*Tomatoes Stuffed with Rice and Basil
*Summer Squash, Red Pepper, and Zucchini Salad
Wine: Beaujolais Villages *or* Côtes du Rhône-Villages
Iced or Hot Tea (a flowery variety would be nice)
*Summer Pudding *or* *Blackberry Pie

PURÉED FENNEL AND LEEK SOUP

The lack of popularity of fennel, licorice, and anise in America is puzzling. In many European countries (France, Germany, Portugal, and Spain, to name a few) one encounters the complex, penetrating savor of these herbs in beverages, cookies, cakes, and candies as frequently as one might vanilla or lemon in the United States. For some mysterious reason, Americans consider this family of flavors to be strange, often distasteful.

The soup made from the bulb of this delicately flavored fresh vegetable is not forcefully fennel-y, so perhaps even nonadmirers will give it a chance. Fennel shows up under the name of "finocchio" or "anise" in the market, where it is irregularly available all year round on the East Coast, from late September to April in a good many states, and from November to January just about everywhere. If it is difficult to come by, celery makes a very appealing alternative.

As the moisture content of celery and fennel can vary considerably, be sure to add the milk and cream when the soup has finished cooking, so that you can adjust the thickness to taste. If the evening is coolish, serve the soup hot; if it's Indian summer, you might want it iced.

Makes 6 servings

Wing tips, necks, bones, and gizzards from the 3 Rock Cornish hens (see step 1 of Spinach-Stuffed Boned Rock Cornish Hens, page 88; see also note below)
2 quarts water
1 bay leaf
2 carrots
1/4 teaspoon dried thyme
2 onions, rinsed (no need to peel)
3 tablespoons butter
1 medium leek, dark leaf tips removed, meticulously washed, then thinly sliced (2 cups)
1 very large head of fennel, feathery tops trimmed off and reserved, very finely minced; bulb and stalks thinly sliced crosswise (about 5 cups)
1 medium-large potato, peeled and thinly sliced (about 1 1/2 cups)
1 1/2 teaspoons salt
1/4–1 cup milk, or as needed
1 tablespoon cornstarch
About 1/2 cup cream
1 1/2 tablespoons anise-flavored liquor, such as Ricard or Pernod
Lime or lemon juice to taste

1. Combine all the leftover scraps from the hens in a large pot with the water. Bring to a boil, skimming off the froth. Reduce the heat and add the bay leaf, carrots, thyme, and onions and simmer gently, partly covered, for about 2 hours, adding water if needed to keep the bones covered. Strain the broth (discard the solids); skim and cool. Refrigerate if you're not planning to make the soup within a few hours. There should be 5½–6 cups broth. Add water, if necessary, to make that amount.
2. Melt the butter in a large, heavy pot. Stir in the leek and sliced fennel and cook over moderate heat until softened, about 10 minutes, stirring often. Stir in the potato and the salt. Add the broth and simmer, covered, for 25–35 minutes, or until the vegetables are very soft.
3. In batches, process the soup in a blender or processor to a very fine purée. Press through a sieve to remove the fibers, straining into the washed-out pot.
4. Mix together ¼ cup milk and the cornstarch. Add to the soup. Bring the mixture to a simmer over moderately low heat, stirring often. Simmer 1 minute, stirring. Add ½ cup cream and the anise liquor and remove from the heat. Adjust the thickness by adding milk, a little at a time. Let cool to room temperature, then cover and chill up to 1½ days, if desired.
5. *To serve:* Season the soup with lime or lemon juice, anise liquor, and salt and pepper. Thin to the desired consistency with milk or cream. If you are serving the soup hot, first warm it over low heat, stirring often, then put in additional liquids (not before heating). Sprinkle the top with the very finely minced fennel leaves.

NOTE: If you have chicken stock available, or for some reason do not want to make the broth, omit step 1 of the recipe and substitute 6 cups of prepared broth. Do not add the salt to the recipe if your stock is salted.

TO MAKE CELERY AND LEEK SOUP: Substitute 6 cups sliced celery with leaves for the fennel. Add ⅛ teaspoon celery seed when you add the broth. Use 1½ tablespoons cornstarch and 3 tablespoons anise liquor.

SPINACH-STUFFED BONED ROCK CORNISH HENS

Although Rock Cornish hens, commercially speaking, are a relatively new product, the breed itself is ancient. What confuses is the use of the term "Cornish hen" to denote size, rather than a breed. While it is usual for birds called Cornish hens to be the result of a cross between a Cornish male and a White Plymouth Rock female, what is most important is the size of the bird at slaughter—generally 1½–2 pounds, aged 5 weeks. Theoretically, other crosses could be termed Cornish hens if they were slaughtered at that size, although the chances of the Cornish chicken being part of the act are great, since the Cornish appears to be the father of virtually every breed extant today. (Incidentally, if allowed to mature, the birds would be mighty hefty—up to 18 pounds, according to one geneticist.

Whatever the true story of the origin of the succulent hen, there are predictable characteristics to the bird that we find in the butcher's case. Fifty years of genetic work have produced a juicy, small, flavorful, all-white-meat bird with a high proportion of flesh to bone. The average dressed weight per bird is about 1¼ pounds. Although available both fresh and frozen, the fresh are far superior, especially if you can find them free of vacuum-sealed containers.

In my opinion, Cornish hens are considerably too large to feed one person, and often too small for two. Stuffing produces a moist, savory bird that amply feeds two. Boned and sliced Cornish hen is an elegant entrée, easier to prepare than a galantine, which it closely resembles. If you've never boned poultry before, you may find this the simplest bird with which to begin, as the flesh is so tender and the bones so flexible you can accomplish the job almost entirely without a knife, thereby avoiding the most common boning hazard—holes pierced in the skin.

Makes 6 servings

3 fresh Rock Cornish hens (about 1½ pounds each)
¼ cup minced shallots
3 tablespoons olive oil
2 packages (10 ounces) frozen chopped spinach, defrosted
Grated rind of 1 large lemon
1–1¼ cups whole-milk ricotta
1 cup soft, fresh white bread crumbs, lightly packed
1½ teaspoons dried tarragon
2 eggs, beaten
2 teaspoons coarse (kosher) salt
¼ teaspoon black pepper

1. Remove and discard any loose interior fat from the birds. Cut off and reserve the wingtips along with the gizzard and all bones to come, for the soup stock for Puréed Fennel and Leek Soup (page 86). Reserve the hearts and livers for the stuffing.
2. *To bone the birds:* If you keep in mind that you are going to gradually peel the flesh and skin downward from the neck opening, the job is simpler. If you're using a knife, never turn the blade toward the flesh; it should always be headed boneward. Set the bird on end, neck up, and cut a firm line down the center back from neck to tail. With your fingers press the flesh off the wishbone and snap the bone loose. Peel flesh and skin off the bone in a downward motion. Use a knife to cut the ball joints that hold the wings to the breast. Working slowly downward, gently pull the flesh and skin from the breast, pushing both toward the tail. When you get down to the ball joints that attach the thighs, sever them. At this point you should be able to work out and remove the whole carcass, leaving only the wing, leg, and thigh bones in the bird. Spread the bird flat, skin side down. Sever the connection between thigh and drumstick. Scrape out and remove the thigh bones, using a knife or your fingers. With a knife scrape away the flesh to free the leg bones, holding the knife blade against the bone. With a firm yank, pull the entire drumstick inward; cut the flesh and skin at the tip to release the bone. Keep the drumstick meat turned inside out (like the sleeve of a sweater); flatten it with your hands or a meat pounder so it will cover the exposed skin more or less evenly. Repeat the thigh-leg boning operation on the other side. The bird should now be flat, except for wings, which remain intact. Try to distribute the flesh more or less uniformly over the skin so that an even layer of meat will surround the stuffing. Repeat with the remaining birds. (You can refrigerate the hens at this point, if you'd rather stuff them later.)
3. *To make the stuffing:* Soften the shallots in 1 tablespoon of the oil, cooking until lightly browned. Chop the reserved hearts and livers. Add them to the pan and brown lightly. Pour all into a bowl. Press all liquid from the spinach, squeezing firmly; discard the liquid. Add the spinach to the shallot mixture; add the lemon rind, ricotta, crumbs, tarragon, eggs, salt, and pepper. Mix vigorously to blend.
4. *To stuff the birds:* Spread one third of the stuffing in an even mound running from neck to tail of one bird. There will be a slightly V-shaped opening at the tail. Using doubled white cotton thread and

(Continued)

a large needle, sew this closed to make a more or less rectangular form. Fold both sides of the bird over the stuffing and continue sewing around the tail, over all the stuffing, up to the neck. Leave a margin of at least 1/4 inch from the edge of the skin, or the birds may open up. If there are any holes, sew them closed. Tie the bird with 3 pieces of white cotton string, not too tightly, to make a neat cylinder. Pour the remaining 2 tablespoons olive oil into a large baking dish and spread evenly. Set the tied-up bird in this. Repeat the process with the other two.

5. *To cook:* Preheat the oven to 350°. Gently roll each bird in the oil to coat it. Using the strings, pull each onto one side and press it gently so it remains in this position. Sprinkle lightly with salt and pepper and set in the oven. Roast 30 minutes. Pull the strings on each bird to turn gently onto its other side. Sprinkle with salt and pepper. Roast 20 minutes longer. Pull each bird (again with the string) onto its back. Roast breast upward for about 20 minutes, or until lightly browned. Again using the strings, gently lift each bird to a board to cool. When completely cooled, wrap and refrigerate until serving time (up to 1 day in the fridge).

6. *To serve:* Cut off the strings. Delicately pull out the threads, then slice the birds across into neat ovals. Overlap on a serving platter and let stand at room temperature while you serve nibbles and the soup course.

TOMATOES STUFFED WITH RICE AND BASIL

Makes 6 or more servings

1 1/4 cups long-grain white rice
2 cups cold water
1/4 cup lemon juice
1 teaspoon salt
1 teaspoon sharp mustard
1/8 teaspoon black pepper
1/3 cup olive oil
About 1/4 cup finely minced fresh basil
1/4 cup finely minced fresh parsley
1/4 cup finely minced scallions
8 medium-size firm-ripe tomatoes
Sugar
About 16 large basil leaves, to line the tomatoes
Tiny basil sprigs for garnish

1. Combine the rice and water in a heavy saucepan. Bring to a rolling boil, then reduce the heat to its lowest point. Cover and cook 20 minutes. Remove from the heat and let stand, covered, for 20 minutes.
2. In a small jar combine the lemon juice, salt, mustard, and pepper and stir to mix. Add the olive oil, cover, and shake to blend.
3. Using a large fork, fluff the cooked rice into a mixing bowl. Add the dressing, 1/4 cup minced basil (or to taste), parsley, and scallions and mix well. Check the seasoning. Refrigerate for several hours or more (overnight will do).
4. Cut about 1/2 inch off the stem ends of the tomatoes. Gently squeeze out the seeds. With a melon ball cutter, scoop out the central tomato flesh, leaving the case intact (discard any seeds and woody parts you find along the way). Chop this pulp, then combine it in a strainer set over a bowl with a sprinkle of salt, pepper, and sugar. Sprinkle the interior of the shells with salt, pepper, and sugar, then invert them on a rack to drain. Let both pulp and shells drain for at least 30 minutes.
5. Line the bottom of each tomato shell with basil leaves—which will both flavor the rice and prevent absorption of tomato juices. Toss the drained pulp with the rice mixture. Divide the mixture among the shells, pressing it in firmly and mounding smoothly on top (a rubber spatula makes a neat shape). Top each with a tiny basil sprig.
6. Arrange the tomatoes in a serving dish and refrigerate until about an hour before serving time.

SUMMER SQUASH, RED PEPPER, AND ZUCCHINI SALAD

These ribbons of color are particularly ravishing in glazed earthenware, if you have it. Remember that although pepper-peeling is a bother, the before and after are worlds apart.

Makes 6 servings

About 1 1/2 pounds red bell peppers (6 medium-size)
3/4 pound small, firm, straight-sided zucchini
3/4 pound small, firm, straight-sided summer squash (yellow squash)
1 teaspoon salt
1 teaspoon finely minced garlic
1 teaspoon vinegar
1/3 cup olive oil

1. Place the peppers directly in the high flame of the gas burners of your stove, or as close as possible to the broiler if you don't have a gas range. Keep turning the peppers until they are blackened all over. Cool for a few minutes; place in a plastic bag to steam off the peel.
2. Meanwhile, drop the squash (both varieties) into a large pot of boiling water. Boil vigorously for 2–4 minutes, or until the squash is softened just enough to indent slightly when pressed. Keep testing; don't overcook. Drain, then cool completely in a bowl of ice water.
3. Remove the peppers from the bag. Halve lengthwise; scrape out the seeds, ribs, and stems. Scrape off all the black skin, then rinse each piece. Cut each piece into even strips about 1/4 inch wide. Spread on towels to dry.
4. Cut the squash into strips about 2 inches long and 1/4 inch wide. Combine in a bowl with the peppers.
5. Mix salt and garlic in a small bowl. Add the vinegar and stir. Mix in the oil. Pour over the vegetables and toss gently with a spatula.
6. Chill for at least 2 hours before serving. Season to taste.

A CHOICE OF DESSERTS

Since both blackberries and currants are difficult to find in some parts of the country, here are two desserts to choose from, so that you can enjoy whichever fruit is more readily available in your area, without passing up a quintessentially summer sweet.

SUMMER PUDDING

This time-honored English creation is synonymous with summer, as are its main ingredients—raspberries and red currants. There are more than 400 defined species of raspberries and numerous intermediate forms that grow in North and South America, China, and Europe. Some berries reach maturity colored purple, amber, or white, although by far the most common form is the lovely ruby red. Oddly, this finest of fruits was not cultivated in America until the eighteenth century, nor has a great deal been written about its existence prior to that. Before the sixteenth century, wild raspberries were known as "hindberries" in Britain. From then on, an impenetrable etymological briar patch appears to have grown up over the poor berry. And if you look to other languages for help (French, *framboise;* Italian, *lampone;* German, *Himbeere*), you can really get scratched in the brambles!

Glassy currants, both red and black, are considerably more popular in Europe than in the United States. For centuries they have been allotted the respect due a cookable fruit with such a pleasing astringency by being part of sauces, desserts, cordials, and wines. Happily, crème de cassis, a liqueur composed of perfumey black currants from France, has recently found plenty of fans in America by way of the simple apéritif Kir, made of chilled white wine (or Champagne, for Kir Royale) and cassis. Currants are not produced commercially in America, but they do grow wild. They are sent to market in many regions, generally through August. Raspberries have become more readily available in recent years, but the season is erratic, generally peaking in July.

Astonishingly, if you care to hold onto the fleeting moment when raspberries and currants coexist, summer pudding freezes fabulously well. Just let it defrost in the fridge overnight before serving.

Makes about 8 servings

1 quart red currants, rinsed
2 tablespoons water
1 quart raspberries, rinsed
About 2/3 cup sugar
1 loaf firm homemade or bakery white bread (or better, if you can get it, is a slightly sweet egg bread, such as challah)
Crème fraîche (or use a mixture of sour cream and heavy cream)
Candied violets or rose petals (optional; see list of mail-order sources, page 353)

1. Remove the stems from the currants and discard them along with any mushy berries. There should be 3–3 1/2 cups. Combine them in a heavy enameled or stainless-steel saucepan with the water. Bring to a boil, covered. Lower the heat and simmer for 2 minutes. Uncover and continue cooking briefly, until soft.

2. Press the currants and their juices through the fine disc of a food mill. Discard the seeds. Return the puréed currants to the saucepan. Add the raspberries and sugar and bring to a boil. Boil, stirring, for about 2 minutes, or until the sugar has dissolved and the raspberries have softened and lost some juice. Reserve.

(Continued)

3. Slice the bread 1/4 inch thick and trim off the crusts. Line a 6-cup soufflé dish, or a bowl or mold this size, with the bread slices. Cut the pieces to fit together tightly and cover both bottom and sides.

4. Pour the berries into the mold, cover with more bread cut to fit, then cover loosely with plastic wrap. Locate a bowl, pot top, pan, or dish with a diameter about an inch less than the mold's. Set this on top of the plastic and place a 3–4 pound weight on it. Refrigerate for about 24 hours.

5. *To serve:* Run a knife around the edge of the dish. Set a serving dish with a rim on top of the bowl, then quickly invert both. Cut the gaudily red dessert into slices and top with the cream and a few candied flowers.

BLACKBERRY PIE

Blackberries, dewberries, and raspberries are all members of the rose family. So prolific is this dark-brilliant berry that the first records we have of it in agricultural journals provided methods of killing off the fierce bramble, rather than cultivating it. Only as wild areas were razed was commercial culture undertaken.

At present, blackberries are cultivated mainly on the West Coast in the United States, but they do still grow wild on the East Coast, as well. Blackberries without thorns are now grown commercially, but production of blackberries in any form is extremely minimal when compared to strawberries, blueberries, or raspberries. If you can get your hands (preferably gloved) on wild berries, they are usually sweeter and more pungently scented than the cultivated varieties.

Three variations on the blackberry—the boysenberry, youngberry, and loganberry—flourish on the Pacific coast. They are among those unusual twentieth-century productions that have been created virtually full blown, rather than having evolved over centuries. It will probably surprise no one to hear that the berries were cultivated by three gentlemen named, respectively, Boysen, Young, and Logan.

NOTE: As the wine-y, sugar-glazed pie that follows freezes very well, you might make more than one to hoard for the winter. A baked pie will keep well for about 3–4 months. To reheat it, remove from the freezer, unwrap, and bake the frozen pie on the lowest oven rack. Bake at 350° for about 40 minutes, or until it is just warm throughout.

Makes one 9-inch double-crust pie

CRUST:

1¾ cups unbleached all-purpose flour
½ teaspoon salt
1 stick (8 tablespoons) unsalted butter, chilled
2 tablespoons solid vegetable shortening, chilled
About 4 tablespoons ice water

FILLING:

4 cups cleaned, rinsed blackberries (see note below)
½ cup sugar, or more to taste if berries are very tart
1–2 tablespoons cornstarch
⅛ teaspoon almond extract
Pinch salt
2 teaspoons orange flower water (see list of mail-order sources, page 353; or use orange juice)
1 tablespoon water
Scant teaspoon grated orange rind

GLAZE:

1 egg white
2 teaspoons orange flower water (or use orange juice)
2 teaspoons sugar

1. *To make the crust:* Sift the flour and salt into a mixing bowl. Cut the butter and shortening into tiny bits and add to the flour. Using a pastry blender, 2 knives, or your fingertips, work the mixture into small even particles of fat and flour. The butter and shortening should no longer be visible. Drizzle in 1 tablespoon ice water at a time, tossing the flour mixture with a fork to incorporate the liquid evenly. When you have added all the water, you will probably be able to mass the pieces into a ball by simply pressing them together. If the pieces separate, sprinkle in a little more water. Form the dough into 2 circles, each about ½ inch thick. Wrap each in plastic and refrigerate for at least an hour—up to 2 days.

2. *To make the filling:* Toss the berries and the ½ cup sugar together in a bowl. To determine how much cornstarch you'll require, taste

(Continued)

a few berries. If they're soft and juicy, use 2 tablespoons; if they're firm and small, use 1 tablespoon. In a cup mix together the cornstarch, the almond extract, a pinch of salt, 2 teaspoons orange flower water, 1 tablespoon water, and the orange rind. Add to the berries. Let stand for about 1/2 hour, tossing occasionally.

3. Preheat the oven to 450°, having first set an old roasting pan, baking sheet, or jelly-roll pan in the lower third of the oven. (The heated pan will help set the lower pastry quickly and prevent juice spillover into the oven. Do not use a "good" baking pan, as it may warp or get sticky with syrup.)

4. Roll one portion of the dough on a lightly floured surface to form an even circle about 11 inches in diameter. Trim, if needed, to form this. Fold the dough in quarters. Place the center point in the middle of a 9-inch pie pan and unfold the dough carefully, easing it into the pan. Trim the edge to form a neat 1/2–1 inch overhang.

5. *To make the glaze:* Beat together the egg white and 2 teaspoons orange flower water. Brush the pastry sparingly with this. Roll out the remaining dough to form a circle that will fit the top of the pie exactly, trimming to even it out. Pour the berry mixture into the pastry and spread flat. Moisten the exposed pastry rim with the glaze. Set the top crust on this and press down lightly. Bend the overhanging edge of the lower crust over and press down. Seal firmly by pressing with the tines of a fork or the dull side of a knife blade. Cut 4 or 5 slits in the top, each about an inch long.

6. Brush the pie with the remaining glaze. If you like decorations, cut the dough scraps into pretty shapes, set them on the glaze, then brush each decoration with more glaze. Sprinkle evenly with the 2 teaspoons sugar.

7. Set the pie in the preheated pan and bake for 15 minutes. Lower the oven heat to 350° and bake 35–40 minutes longer, or until the pie is well browned. Set on a rack and cool completely.

NOTE: If you cannot find fresh blackberries, there are several high-quality frozen brands, sold loose pack (that is, without syrup) either in pint-sized plastic containers or in plastic bags. Be sure, in either case, that the berries are loose, not clumped together, which would indicate that they had been refrozen after defrosting. Measure the berries in a frozen state, then let them thaw completely before proceeding with the recipe. Or you can substitute fresh blueberries (3 1/2 cups) and use the maximum amount of cornstarch.

Fall

9
Cook Once—Dine Twice

Two Small Dinners from One, for Early Fall

Two small, informal dinners for four result from one day's culinary effort to permit you to entertain twice. The early fall menus incorporate the last of the hot season's most fragrant gifts—tomatoes, basil, mint, thyme, and peaches—while the pork sausage and hearty whole-wheat bread herald the cooler times. If it is convenient to do so, you can prepare all the dishes for both dinners at one time, with the exception of the Brandied Peach Whip in Dinner 2, which is assembled the day it is served.

EARLY FALL DINNER 1 (FOR FOUR)

*Diced Eggplant and Peppers
*Crusty Whole-Wheat Loaves
*Poached Pork and Fennel Sausage
*Fresh Shell Beans with Herbs
Wine: Côtes du Rhône, Bardolino, *or* Valpolicella
Espresso
*Peaches with Cream and Almonds

DICED EGGPLANT AND PEPPERS

If it is more convenient to prepare the dinner piecemeal, this appetizer can be finished as much as two days ahead.

Makes 4 generous servings (with 2 cups reserved for Dinner 2)

6 large, smooth red and/or green bell peppers
3 or 4 small eggplants (about 2 pounds)
1 tablespoon plus 1/2 teaspoon coarse (kosher) salt
1/3 cup peanut oil
1–2 large garlic cloves, minced or pushed through a press
1/4 cup red wine vinegar
1 tablespoon brown sugar

1. Place the peppers directly on the gas burners of your stove on a high flame, or as close to the broiling element as possible if you don't have a gas stove. Keep turning them until the skin is quite blackened. Remove from the burners (or broiler), let stand 5 minutes, then enclose in a plastic bag.
2. Cut the eggplants into 1/2-inch dice (do not peel). There should be roughly 3 quarts. Combine in a stainless-steel or enameled colander with the 1 tablespoon salt; toss well. Set a plate and a heavy weight on top of the eggplant and let drain for about an hour.
3. Meanwhile, remove the peppers from the bag. Halve them lengthwise and remove the seeds, stems, and ribs. Scrape off all the black skin with a knife. Rinse briefly, then cut into 1/2-inch squares. Pat dry with a towel. Set aside and refrigerate 3/4 cup for Dinner 2.
4. Spread the eggplant pieces on paper towels and dry lightly. Heat 2 tablespoons of the oil in a large skillet, preferably a nonstick one, and brown half the eggplant dice over moderate heat on all sides, which will take about 5 minutes. Transfer to a dish. Repeat with 2 tablespoons of the remaining oil and the remaining eggplant. Transfer to the dish, reserving 1 cup for the Stuffed Zucchini and Peppers for Dinner 2. Add the diced pepper to the dish.
5. Heat the remaining oil in the skillet over moderate heat and stir in the garlic. Add the vinegar, sugar, and the 1/2 teaspoon salt and simmer for a minute. Pour over the eggplant-pepper mixture and toss gently with a spatula. Cool, cover, and refrigerate overnight, or longer.
6. *To serve:* Season to taste with additional salt, pepper, sugar, and vinegar, as needed.

CRUSTY WHOLE-WHEAT LOAVES

This fairly large recipe makes two hefty, round loaves—wheaty, moist, fairly light in texture—sometimes called "hearth" or "farmer style." Although there might be a bit too much bread for four to finish off at each meal, it is no hardship to crunch the bread as morning toast, as well. If you prefer, you can wrap and freeze one loaf for several months, after it has cooled completely.

Makes 2 large, round loaves

2¼ cups warm (not hot) water
2 packages dry yeast
2 tablespoons honey
1 tablespoon salt
2½ cups whole-wheat flour
1 cup coarse, unprocessed bran
About 4 cups bread flour (available in specialty stores and many supermarkets)
3 tablespoons melted butter
Cornmeal for the pans
Glaze: 1 teaspoon cornstarch mixed with ¾ cup water

1. Combine ½ cup of the warm water in a small bowl with the yeast and ½ teaspoon of the honey. Stir and let stand about 5 minutes, or until the mixture is fluffy. If the mixture does not foam up, start again with fresh ingredients.
2. Combine the yeast mixture in the large bowl of an electric mixer with the remaining water, honey, salt, whole-wheat flour, bran, 1 cup of the bread flour, and the melted butter. Beat on moderate speed for about 3–4 minutes. Remove the bowl from the beater stand and stir in 2 cups bread flour.
3. Spread the remaining bread flour on a kneading surface. Turn the dough out onto it and knead vigorously until the dough is elastic and no longer very sticky, adding flour as necessary to keep the dough from sticking to the board. (Doughs made from whole wheat will never be as smooth as the ones made from white flour; they remain a bit tacky.) Ten minutes of kneading should do.
4. Form the dough into a ball, place it in a large buttered bowl, and turn to coat all sides with butter. Cover the bowl with plastic. Let the dough rise at room temperature until doubled in bulk, about an hour or more.
5. Punch down the dough and divide it into 2 equal pieces on a lightly floured work surface. Form each piece into a round ball by gently pulling and pinching the base until no seams or wrinkles show on top. Flatten each ball very slightly.
6. Sprinkle 2 round cake pans 9 inches in diameter with cornmeal. Set a loaf in each pan, pinched side down. Cover each with a towel and let rise until doubled in size, about 45 minutes.
7. Preheat the oven to 400°. Stir together the cornstarch and water in a tiny saucepan. Bring to a boil, stirring, then set aside.

(Continued)

8. When the loaves have risen, paint each one with the cornstarch glaze, being careful not to let it drip onto the pan. Holding a sharp knife or razor almost parallel to the bread's surface, cut 6 curves at least 1/4 inch deep in the top of each loaf, radiating from the center like petals.
9. Bake the loaves for 30 minutes in the center of the oven. Brush again with the glaze and reduce the heat to 350°. Switch the pan positions in the oven and bake for about 25–30 minutes longer, until the loaves are well browned all over. Let the loaves cool entirely on a rack before serving.
10. *To serve:* If baked a day before serving, warm the bread for 10 minutes in a 300° oven shortly before dinner.

POACHED PORK AND FENNEL SAUSAGE

To make these large sausages, you need no special equipment or casings, but a food processor will simplify the job. The sausages can be assembled as much as three days before serving.

Makes 2 large sausages (with part reserved for Dinner 2)

4 teaspoons coarse (kosher) salt
1 tablespoon fennel seeds
1/2 teaspoon black peppercorns
1/4 teaspoon whole allspice
1/4 teaspoon dried thyme
2 pounds lean, well-trimmed pork (shoulder, loin, butt, or leg), cut into 1- to 1 1/2-inch dice and chilled (see note below if you're using a meat grinder)
3/4 pound fresh pork fat (preferably hard fatback, but loin or belly fat will do), cut into 1/2-inch dice and chilled (see note below if you're using a meat grinder)
1/4 cup coarsely chopped celery leaves
2 medium shallots, sliced
1/3 cup coarse, fresh white bread crumbs
1/4 cup chilled red wine
Melted lard or vegetable oil for the cheesecloth

1. Combine the salt, fennel seeds, peppercorns, allspice, and thyme in an electric spice mill or mortar; grind to a fairly coarse, but even blend. Toss with the meat and fat in a large bowl to coat the pieces well.

2. With the motor running, drop the celery leaves, shallots, and bread crumbs into the feed tube of a food processor and chop fine. Add about one quarter of the meat mixture and the wine and process to an extremely fine texture. Transfer to a bowl. (See note below if you're using a meat grinder.)

3. Chop the remaining meat mixture (in 2 batches) to a coarse grind—about 1/8-inch pieces. Add to the puréed meat in the bowl. Blend very well, then cover and refrigerate for 1–2 days to develop the flavors.

4. Divide the sausage mixture in half and form two 8- to 9-inch cylinders. Place each cylinder on a large sheet of fine-mesh cotton cheesecloth (or a doubled sheet of wide-mesh cloth) that has been brushed generously with melted lard or vegetable oil. Roll the cloth to encase each sausage neatly and firmly. Tie the ends with string.

5. Place the sausages in a large pot or pan or deep skillet filled with simmering water to cover generously. Cook at just under a simmer until an instant-reading thermometer registers 170°, about an hour.

6. Skim and reserve the floating fat on the water to use with the Fresh Shell Beans with Herbs (see following recipe). Remove the sausages and let them cool for up to 2 hours, or proceed to the next step immediately.

7. Cut off and refrigerate half to three quarters of one sausage to use for Dinner 2. *To serve the remaining sausages:* Cut into slices 1/2 inch thick. Brown them on both sides in a large skillet and arrange them, overlapping, around the warm beans.

NOTE: If you use a meat grinder instead of a processor, cut the meat into strips about 3 inches long and 1/2–1 inch wide instead of dicing it. Toss with the spice mixture (step 1) and grind with the medium-coarse disc in place. Remove one quarter of the mixture, combine it with the celery leaves and shallots (both very finely chopped) and the bread crumbs, and grind twice, using the fine disc. Beat in the wine, then combine this mixture with the coarsely ground meat and fat. Refrigerate 1–2 days to develop flavor, then proceed with step 4.

FRESH SHELL BEANS WITH HERBS

Fresh shell beans are a treat, but erratically available. I used the beautiful beige, burgundy-speckled cranberry beans, which are plump, smooth, and meaty. Beans in pods, ready to be popped out for cooking, are to be had all over the country—but with such an array of regional names and seasons that it is hopeless to try to categorize them definitively. Some fairly common ones are broad (or fava) beans, which should be used when small; limas; butter beans; speckled limas; and black-eyed peas. Whichever you use, you'll need 5–6 cups shelled beans for the amount required for both these meals.

Makes 4 servings (with 2 cups reserved for Dinner 2)

4–5 pounds cranberry beans (about 2 pounds, shelled, or 5–6 cups)
1–2 tablespoons of the fat reserved from simmering the Poached Pork and Fennel Sausage (see preceding recipe)
5 tablespoons olive oil
2 tablespoons lemon juice
About 3/4 teaspoon salt
About 1/4 teaspoon black pepper
2 tablespoons minced fresh chives (or thinly sliced scallions)
3–4 tablespoons minced fresh parsley
1 tablespoon minced fresh thyme or summer savory (or substitute 1/4 teaspoon dried rosemary or 1/2 teaspoon dried thyme if you haven't access to fresh herbs)
GARNISH: Lemon slices

1. Drop the beans into a large pot of boiling water, add the reserved sausage fat, then lower the heat and simmer, partly covered, until they are just tender, which will take about 30 minutes; but timing can vary enormously, so taste often. (*Note:* If you're using the *dried* herbs, add them during the last few minutes of cooking.) Drain the beans in a colander. Set aside 2 cups for Dinner 2 and toss with 1 tablespoon of the olive oil.
2. Toss the remaining hot beans (about 4–5 cups) with the remaining olive oil, the lemon juice, salt, and pepper. Let them stand at room temperature for several hours, until you wish to heat them.
3. *To serve:* Reheat the beans briefly, covered. Toss with the chives, parsley, and fresh thyme or savory and mound on a hot platter large enough to hold the sausage as well. Surround with the sliced sausage and decorate with lemon slices. The platter can be kept warm briefly, if necessary.

PEACHES WITH CREAM AND ALMONDS

Simple and sweet: peaches in an amber-rose syrup with a lightly spicy aroma.

Makes 4 servings (with half reserved for Dinner 2)

24 very small freestone peaches, or 16 medium ones (about 2 1/2 pounds)
1 cup brown sugar (dark or light), lightly packed
1/2 cup white sugar
8 cloves
1 cup water
1/4 cup whole, blanched almonds
1/2 cup heavy cream
1/3 cup sour cream

1. Drop the peaches into a large pot of boiling water set over high heat. When the water returns to a boil, count to 30, then cool the peaches briefly in ice water. Drain in a colander. Peel off and discard the skins.
2. Combine the brown and white sugars, cloves, and water in a wide skillet that will hold the peaches in a single layer (or poach them in 2 batches). Bring the syrup to a boil, then simmer for 3–4 minutes. Add the peaches and cover the pan. Turn down the heat and barely simmer for about 5 minutes, or until the undersides are not quite tender. Turn over gently and simmer until barely tender when pierced through with a cake tester. Do not overcook.
3. Transfer the peaches and syrup to a dish. Cool, cover, and refrigerate until serving time.
4. Spread the almonds in a pan and toast in a 325° oven for about 15–20 minutes, stirring occasionally, until lightly beige. Cool, then sliver or chop and reserve.
5. Whip the cream to form soft peaks, then fold together gently with the sour cream, using a spatula. Cover and refrigerate for up to several hours (or overnight, if you prefer).
6. *To serve:* Neatly halve and pit half the peaches (reserve the rest for Dinner 2). Pour a little syrup into each serving dish, arrange 4 or 6 halves in each (depending on the number of peaches you've poached), and drop a tidy dollop of cream into each cavity. Sprinkle with the toasted almonds and serve. (Reserve 3/4 cup of the remaining syrup for Dinner 2.)

EARLY FALL DINNER 2 (FOR FOUR)

*Iced Yogurt Soup with Tomato Garnish
Mixed Olives
*Stuffed Zucchini and Peppers
*Crusty Whole-Wheat Loaves
Wine: Chianti Classico *or* Zinfandel Rosé
Iced Espresso
*Brandied Peach Whip

ICED YOGURT SOUP WITH TOMATO GARNISH

This quickly prepared, no-cook soup can be made a day before serving, or the morning of the day that you serve Dinner 2. It is a tart, bracing starter for a meal.

Makes 4 servings

1 teaspoon salt
1/4 teaspoon white pepper
1/2 teaspoon sugar
1/2 cup cold water
2 cups yogurt
1/3 cup sour cream
2 medium cucumbers, peeled, seeded, and coarsely shredded (1 cup)
2–3 tablespoons very finely slivered scallion greens
3–4 tablespoons chopped fresh basil (or 2 tablespoons fresh mint)
Ice water, as needed
1 cup finely diced, seeded, and skinned tomatoes (3 medium tomatoes)

1. Combine the salt, pepper, sugar, and 1/2 cup cold water in a bowl. Whisk in the yogurt and sour cream. Stir in the cucumbers, scallion greens, and basil. Chill several hours, or overnight.
2. *To serve:* Stir the soup and add ice water as needed to make a smooth, easily pourable consistency (I used 1/2 cup). Season to taste. Ladle into 4 chilled bowls and sprinkle a share of the diced tomato evenly over each.

NOTE: To peel tomatoes, drop them into boiling water and let the water return to a full boil. Remove and peel tomatoes, then halve crosswise and squeeze out the seeds. Dice.

STUFFED ZUCCHINI AND PEPPERS

Just about everything that you made for Dinner 1 goes into the stuffed vegetables for Dinner 2. If you like to get all the work done at once, prepare the stuffed vegetables completely the night before and simply slip them into the oven when you're almost ready to dine.

Makes 4 servings

4 medium-large zucchini (each about 9 inches long, 2 inches in diameter)
1/2–3/4 Poached Pork and Fennel Sausage (page 102), cut into 1/4-inch chunks
3 tablespoons olive oil
1 small onion, chopped
1 medium-size garlic clove, minced
1 cup reserved eggplant from Diced Eggplant and Peppers (page 99)
3/4 cup reserved peppers from Diced Eggplant and Peppers (page 99)
2 cups reserved, cooked shell beans from Fresh Shell Beans with Herbs (page 104)
1/3 cup finely minced fresh parsley
3 large, smooth, straight-sided green bell peppers, halved lengthwise

1. Drop the zucchini into a large pot of boiling water. Boil for about 5 minutes, or until your fingers barely make an impression in the skin when you press it. Cool under running water. Halve lengthwise, then scoop out the flesh with a melon ball cutter, leaving a shell of 1/2 inch on the bottom and 1/4 inch on the sides. Chop and reserve the flesh. Sprinkle the shells with salt and invert on a rack to drain.
2. Brown the sausage pieces in a large skillet in 1 tablespoon of the oil. Transfer to a dish. Add the onion, garlic, and the zucchini flesh to the skillet and sauté until lightly colored. Add the reserved eggplant, peppers, beans, and parsley and stir to blend. Season with salt and pepper.

(Continued)

3. Mound the stuffing compactly into the halved zucchini and peppers. Fit into oiled baking dishes, packing snugly. Drizzle the remaining oil evenly over the vegetables. Either cover and refrigerate overnight, leave at room temperature up to several hours, or go immediately to the next step.
4. *To serve:* Preheat the oven to 400°. Bake the stuffed vegetables in the oven center for 30–35 minutes, until sizzling. (If you're taking the vegetables from the refrigerator, add about 10 minutes to the baking time.) Serve hot, or warm.

BRANDIED PEACH WHIP

Makes 4 servings

Peaches reserved from Peaches with Cream and Almonds (page 105)
1 tablespoon Cognac, brandy, or Calvados
3/4 cup reserved peach syrup
2 egg whites
1/2 cup heavy cream
2–3 tablespoons finely chopped pistachios or pecans

1. Purée the peaches and Cognac in a blender or processor until smooth. Cover and reserve in the refrigerator.
2. Gently boil the reserved syrup in a small heavy pot until it is very thick and syrupy, being very careful not to let it caramelize or burn.
3. While the syrup is cooking down, beat the egg whites in the small bowl of an electric mixer until they are very fluffy. Beating on high speed, gradually pour in the thick syrup. Beat for about 5 minutes, until the meringue is thick, cooled, and slightly shiny.
4. Whip the cream to form soft peaks. Gently fold into the cooled meringue, using a rubber spatula. Delicately fold the puréed peaches into the meringue-cream. Cover with plastic and refrigerate for several hours.
5. *To serve:* Spoon into chilled glass dishes or stem glasses and serve, sprinkled with the nuts.

10
One Leg of Lamb = Three Main Dishes

Recipes That Make Lamb Economical

Leg of lamb is full-flavored, versatile, and much appreciated in Europe. It is also loved by people of Mediterranean and Jewish backgrounds in the New York metropolitan area, where 39 percent of the country's lamb is shipped. Ironically, consumers in the block of central states, where 81 percent of our lamb is produced, barely touch the stuff. Not that there is much difference between "barely touch" and the average per capita consumption: In 1980 Americans ate 1.5 pounds of lamb annually, compared to 107 pounds of beef.

This national neglect makes lamb an expensive item, especially if you're thinking of sharing it with friends. But, however expensive it may be, leg of lamb lends itself extremely well to dishes in which it is "expanded" by other ingredients—such as vegetables, grains, and pasta—as its distinct flavor does not get lost in combination with others. The bones, too, yield a broth that is sufficiently full bodied to produce a soup of great character, with few other ingredients needed.

Dividing one leg into components for three nights' dining is an economical and delicious proposition. The first meal, of rare, marinated lamb, treated almost like steak, is one that demands attention fairly close to mealtime. It makes use of the lamb "straight," with no frills. The second meal incorporates cooked leftover lamb into a macaroni custard of Greek origin, which can be prepared a day in advance. The third variation on the leg is a thick, spicy soup, made from the bones and scraps. It can be made at least a day or two before serving, or it can be frozen for months.

LAMB DINNER 1 (FOR FOUR)

*Tiny Tomatoes Stuffed with Taramosalata (page 49; halve the recipe)
or *Leek and Potato Soup with Cucumbers (page 344)
*Butterflied, Pepper-Marinated Lamb Leg
*Diced Eggplant and Peppers (page 99), at room temperature
*Walnut-Wheat Bread (page 160) *or*
*Crusty Whole-Wheat Loaves (page 100)
Wine: Zinfandel *or* Medium-Bodied Dão, from Portugal
Ripe Pears/*Sugared Almonds (page 208)

BUTTERFLIED, PEPPER-MARINATED LAMB LEG

Although this dish is assembled in advance (it requires two days of marinating), it should be broiled fairly close to serving time. A flavorful, piquant marinade tenderizes and moistens the meat. It also adds a zestiness that meat served at room temperature seems to require.

Since very rare meat is not to everyone's taste, be warned that this dish is designed to be really rare. It will not suffer dreadfully if you prefer to cook it longer, but rare meat is softer, which is particularly desirable when lukewarm. If you don't fancy lamb at this temperature, simply ignore the final made-ahead aspect and serve the meat hot off the broiler.

Makes about 4 servings (with 1 pound cooked meat reserved for use in Lamb Dinner 2 and 1/4 pound in Lamb Dinner 3)

1 fresh, not frozen, lamb leg (7 pounds)

MARINADE:

4 bay leaves, crumbled
2 1/2 teaspoons coarse (kosher) salt
1 teaspoon black peppercorns
1 tablespoon Szechuan peppercorns (see list of mail-order sources, page 353)
1/2 teaspoon sugar
1/2 cup strong red wine
1/4 cup red wine vinegar
1/3 cup peanut oil
2 garlic cloves, quartered

SAUCE:

2 teaspoons Szechuan peppercorns
1 teaspoon coarse (kosher) salt
3 tablespoons red wine vinegar
1 tablespoon Oriental sesame oil (see list of mail-order sources, page 353)
2 scallion greens, very finely minced
1/2 teaspoon sugar

GARNISH: **1/2 bunch watercress**

1. Have the butcher bone and butterfly the leg, saving all the meat scraps and bones. Remind him to trim off all the membrane (the fell) and fat. If you do the job yourself, proceed as follows: Remove the fell and all exterior fat. Turn the side that was once covered with membrane (the rounded side) down onto the cutting surface.

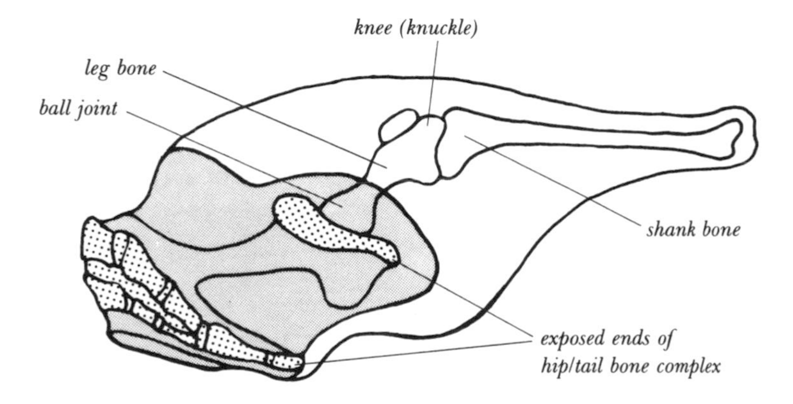

Holding a boning knife against the tail bone part of the tail-hip assembly, begin scraping against the bone, cutting around it until you can free the entire hip-tail complex. Remove and discard any fat as you work. Reserve all meat scraps. When you get to the ball joint at the leg bone, cut free the hip-tail assembly and reserve it.

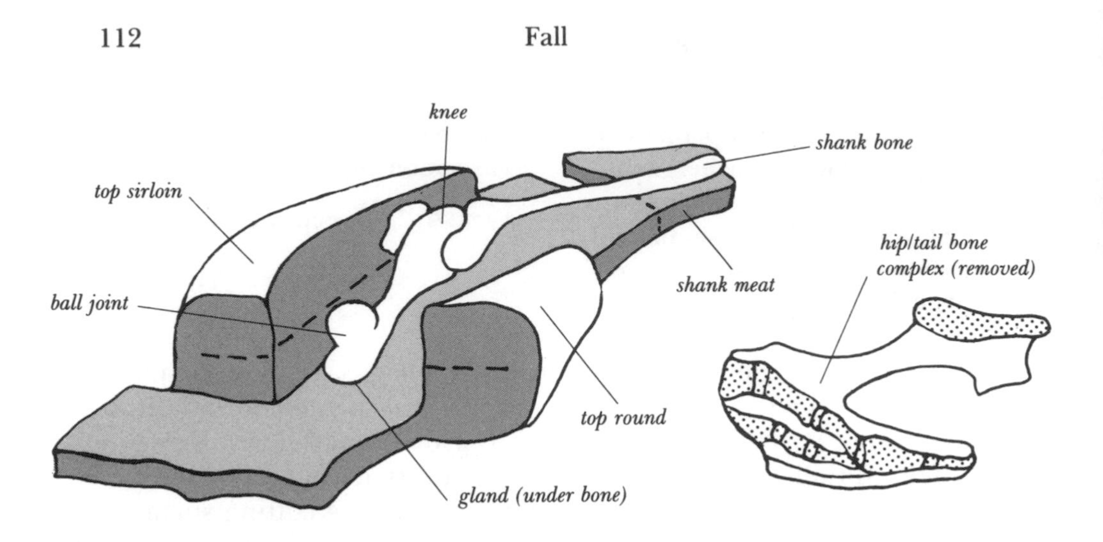

Holding the knife against the leg bone, scrape around the ball joint until you've freed it from the surrounding flesh. Then, following the conformation of the bone, cut a line from ball joint to the knee to the end of the shank bone to uncover them all. Cut out the leg and shank bones and reserve them. Gradually cut into the large piece of top round, about halfway through, to open it out flat. Trim off the tough shank end of the meat and reserve it.

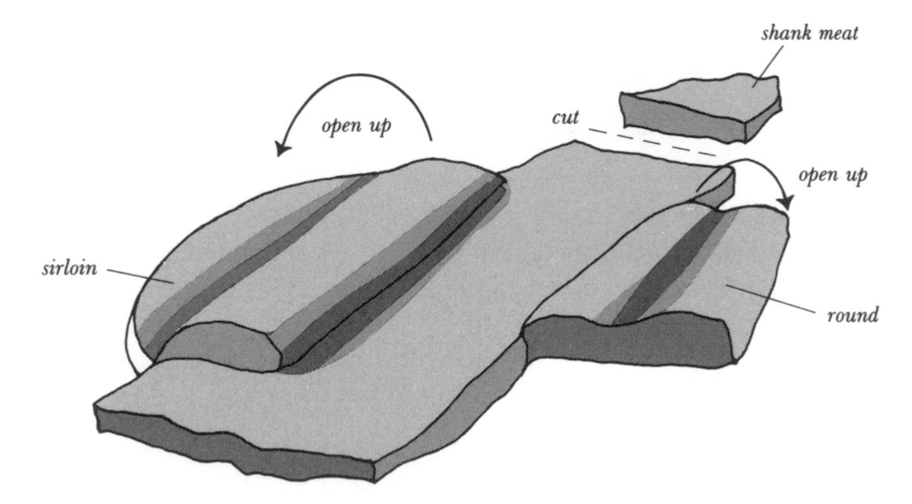

Cut out any pockets of fat and the glands hidden in that fat that lie directly under the ball joint. Cut into the top sirloin slightly to open it out. It is not important to have a neat piece of meat, as the lamb will be presented in thin slices, not as an ungainly chunk. Wrap and reserve all the scraps and bones for the Curried Lima and Lamb Soup (page 116).

NOTE: The diagrams show the left leg of a lamb. If you have a right leg, directions should follow a mirror image of this.

2. *To make the marinade:* Combine the bay leaves, 2 teaspoons of the salt, the black peppercorns, and Szechuan peppercorns in a spice mill and grind fine. Place the spice mixture in a nonmetal dish large enough to hold the meat. Add the sugar, wine, vinegar, oil, and garlic. Turn the meat in the marinade. Cover with plastic wrap and refrigerate for 1½–2 days, or thereabouts.

3. About 1–1½ hours before serving the meat, preheat the broiler. At the same time remove the meat from the refrigerator. When the broiler is hot, scrape off most of the spice mixture. With the bone side up, place the meat on the broiler pan as close to the heat as possible. Sprinkle ¼ teaspoon salt over this. Broil 10 minutes, until slightly crisp and brown. Carefully turn the meat. Sprinkle with ¼ teaspoon salt. Broil 10–15 minutes longer, for tender, rare meat. If you're using an instant-reading thermometer, which is highly recommended, the thickest part of the meat should measure 120°. Because of the range of thickness, there will be parts of the meat that are well done, too.

4. Transfer the meat to a board and let it stand until shortly before serving time, not longer than 1 hour. *Assemble the sauce.* In a tiny pan roast the peppercorns a minute or two, until they smell fragrant and sound sizzly. Let cool, then crush fine in a spice mill or mortar. Sift through a coarse sieve to remove the hulls. Mix the pepper in a small bowl with the salt, vinegar, the sesame oil, scallion greens, and ½ teaspoon sugar (or to taste). Let stand at room temperature.

5. Cut off, wrap, and refrigerate about 1¼ pounds of the lamb, choosing the least attractive bits, as this meat will be chopped. This will be used for Lamb Dinners 2 and 3.

6. *To serve:* Carve the lamb into very thin, even strips cut on the bias. Because of the uneven thickness, there will be slices ranging from rare to well done. It is easiest to arrange them on a platter in that order, so that guests can choose. Spoon a little bit of the sauce over the meat and serve the rest separately. Surround the meat with the watercress and serve.

LAMB DINNER 2 (FOR EIGHT)
(Based on leftover Butterflied, Pepper-Marinated Lamb Leg, page 110)

*Chickpea Dip with Vegetable Strips (page 343)
*Pastitsio (Lamb and Macaroni Layers with Cheese Custard)
Green Salad
Wine: Greek White Wine *or* Sicilian White such as Bianco Alcamo
Coffee
*Orange Sugar Wafers (page 65)/Seckel Pears/Clementines

PASTITSIO
(Lamb and Macaroni Layers with Cheese Custard)

This homey, substantial main dish, made from the leftover Butterflied, Pepper-Marinated Lamb, is lovely for an informal sit-down dinner or a buffet.

Makes about 8 servings

LAMB AND MACARONI:

1 pound cooked lamb (reserved from Butterflied, Pepper-Marinated Lamb Leg, page 110), well trimmed
1 medium-large onion, chopped
7 tablespoons olive oil
1 can (1 pound) peeled tomatoes
2 tablespoons tomato paste
1/4 teaspoon ground cinnamon
1 1/2 teaspoons dried oregano
1/2 cup strong red wine
1/4 teaspoon salt
1/2 teaspoon black pepper
1 pound hollow macaroni (such as ziti, ditalini, penne)
1 egg, beaten

CUSTARD:

1/4 cup water
2 tablespoons cornstarch
3 cups milk
1 tablespoon butter
1/2 teaspoon salt
4 eggs
1/4 teaspoon cinnamon
6–8 ounces Parmesan, Romano, or Kefalotiri cheese, grated

1. Cut the meat into 1½-inch cubes and chop it coarsely in a food processor. (Or you can cut it into strips about 2 × 1 × ½ inches and push it through the coarse disc of a meat grinder.) Reserve.
2. In a large skillet stir the onion over moderate heat in ¼ cup of the oil until just softened. Using kitchen scissors, snip the tomatoes in the can into small bits. Pour into the pan. Add the tomato paste, cinnamon, the oregano, wine, salt, and the pepper. Cover and cook over low heat for 5 minutes. Add the meat, uncover, and cook 10 minutes longer over moderately low heat, stirring occasionally. Season and reserve.
3. Boil the macaroni in a large pot of salted water until it is not quite tender; do not overcook. Drain, then toss with 1 tablespoon of the remaining oil. Stir the beaten egg into the cooled meat sauce.
4. *Make the custard:* Combine the water and cornstarch in a cup and mix well. In a heavy saucepan heat the milk and butter and salt until bubbles form around the edge. Stir the cornstarch mixture into the milk mixture with a whisk. Continue stirring over moderate heat until the mixture bubbles up and thickens. Beat the eggs together in a bowl to just blend. Beating constantly with a whisk, pour the milk mixture gradually into the eggs. Add the cinnamon.
5. Spread the remaining 2 tablespoons oil in a baking/serving dish about 9 × 15 × 3 inches (or two 8-inch square pans, or two 9-inch round ones). Spread half the macaroni evenly in the dish; top with the meat mixture. Sprinkle half the cheese over this. Cover evenly with the remaining macaroni. Pour the custard mixture over all, then sprinkle with the remaining cheese. (You can now go to the next step, or else refrigerate the pastitsio for several hours.)
6. Preheat the oven to 325°. Bake the pastitsio in the center of the oven for about 50 minutes, or until the custard just barely sets and the top is light golden.
7. *Serve* the pastitsio warm, or cooled to room temperature, cut into hefty squares. If you prefer, you can cool and refrigerate the baked pastitsio and reheat it, covered, the next day. It will taste fine, although the texture will be better if served freshly baked.

LAMB DINNER 3 (FOR SIX)
(Based on leftover bones and scraps from Butterflied, Pepper-Marinated Lamb Leg, page 110)

*Mushroom-Egg Pirozhki (page 231)
*Curried Lima and Lamb Soup
Beer or Ale
Cucumber Salad
Fresh Pineapple

CURRIED LIMA AND LAMB SOUP

This thick, delicious, sweet-smelling soup is made with the bones and meat scraps left from the leg of lamb (page 110). Chances are you'll want to freeze it, since the Butterflied, Pepper-Marinated Lamb Leg and the Pastitsio will provide two company dinners for one week—probably plenty. Or, if you prefer, you can keep the soup for three days in the refrigerator before serving.

Makes about 6 servings

BROTH:

Bones and trimmings reserved from Butterflied, Pepper-Marinated Lamb Leg (page 110)
1 large onion, rinsed (no need to peel)
2 carrots, scrubbed and coarsely sliced
2 bay leaves
2 large celery stalks with leaves
2 1/2 quarts water

SOUP ASSEMBLY:

1 pound large dried lima beans
2 large garlic cloves, thinly sliced
2 tablespoons butter
2 large onions, coarsely diced
2 teaspoons mild curry powder
1 tablespoon coarse (kosher) salt
3 medium-size carrots, peeled and very thinly sliced
About 1/4 pound leftover lamb (reserved from Butterflied, Pepper-Marinated Lamb Leg, page 110), well trimmed and diced small
Yogurt to taste

1. Combine the broth ingredients in a large pot and bring to a boil, skimming. Skim thoroughly. Keep at a bare simmer, partly covered, for about 3 hours or more, adding water as needed to keep the bones almost covered. Strain, discarding the solids. Then cool, cover, and chill. Remove all fat.
2. In a large pot combine the beans with water to cover by about 3 inches. Bring to a boil and simmer for 2 minutes. Cover and let stand 1 hour. Drain and leave uncovered.
3. Measure the broth. There should be 2 quarts. Add water to make this amount, if necessary. In a large pot stir the diced onions in the butter until softened. Add the garlic and stir a few minutes. Add the curry powder and stir. Add the beans, broth, and 1 tablespoon salt and simmer gently, partly covered, until the beans are just tender. Timing varies considerably. Begin testing at about 25 minutes.
4. Remove the pot from the heat. Scoop out 1 1/2 cups beans with a slotted spoon. Purée in a processor or blender until smooth. Return to the soup along with the thinly sliced carrots and the diced lamb. Simmer until the carrots are just barely tender, about 5 minutes.
5. Set the pot in a sink containing cold water and stir now and then until cooled. Refrigerate up to 3 days. Or pack for freezing and store up to 3 months in the freezer.
6. *To serve:* Either heat the soup, stirring gently, over low heat or, if frozen, defrost entirely, then heat just until hot through; do not cook. Season to taste. Ladle into large bowls and place a dollop of yogurt on each.

11
A Low-Cost, Mexican-Style Dinner Party

Turkey in a hot-spicy, cornbread-crusted guise is perfect party fare. It is reasonably priced, reheats beautifully, and is enjoyed by many. (Incidentally, it is also high in protein, low in fat.) Simmered in a rich, nutty, highly seasoned sauce, the meat remains moist and well flavored. There will be no leftover problem with this turkey treatment, as there often is with a plain-roasted bird, which dries out so easily. When faced with the question of what to do with such a post-holiday roast, F. Scott Fitzgerald fashioned this unusual recipe:

> Obtain a gross of small white boxes such as are used for a bride's cake. Cut the turkey into small squares, roast stuff, kill, boil, bake, and allow to skewer. Now we are ready to begin. Fill each box with a quantity of soup stock and pile in a handy place. As the liquid elapses, the prepared turkey is added until the guests arrive. The boxes delicately tied with white ribbons are then placed in the handbags of the ladies, or in the men's side pockets (*The Crack-Up*, A New Directions Paperback, 1945).

A LOW-COST, MEXICAN-STYLE DINNER PARTY FOR EIGHT

Bloody Marias (the same as Marys, but substitute tequila for vodka)
*Seviche with Avocado and Cherry Tomatoes
*Turkey in Chile-Nut Sauce with Cornbread Crust
*Orange, Onion, and Chicory Salad
Wine: Spanish Wine from the Rioja Region *or* a Cabernet Sauvignon from Chile
*Coconut Cream with Apricot Sauce
Coffee, brewed with a bit of cinnamon

SEVICHE WITH AVOCADO AND CHERRY TOMATOES

The popular Latin American appetizer seviche (also ceviche, cebiche, and more) takes many forms. Although in the United States it is customary to use only the most delicate (and expensive) fish and shellfish, the dish works well with any fresh, nonoily fish that will hold its shape when cubed. Sea bass, tuna, halibut, king mackerel, and scallops have all been well received in my home.

Makes 8 servings

1¼ pounds boneless, skinned fish—whichever is leanest, freshest, and cheapest—cut ½ inch thick
1 cup lime juice (or lemon and lime mixed)
3 scallion greens, thinly sliced
1 pint cherry tomatoes, hulled
3–4 chiles jalapeños (or serranos) en escabeche (see note below)
3 tablespoons olive oil, preferably a strong-flavored variety
1 teaspoon salt
¼ cup finely minced fresh parsley
2 tablespoons finely minced cilantro (also called fresh coriander or Chinese parsley)
1 large, ripe avocado
Finely shredded lettuce

1. Cut the fish with a sharp knife into ½-inch cubes. Combine with the lime juice and scallion greens; cover and refrigerate for at least 1 hour, stirring once or twice, if you think of it.
2. Thinly slice about three quarters of the tomatoes; chop 3 of the hot peppers fine. Add both to the fish along with the olive oil, salt, parsley, and cilantro. Cover and refrigerate for about an hour longer.
3. *To serve:* Peel the avocado and cut it into ½-inch cubes. Gently toss with the fish, using a rubber spatula. Taste for seasoning, adding more hot peppers to taste. Arrange on the shredded lettuce and garnish with the remaining tomatoes, halved.

NOTE: These small, hot green peppers are packed in jars or small cans in a flavored pickling brine. They are commonly available in large supermarkets and in stores that sell Mexican products. If you cannot find them, you can use hot Italian peppers packed in vinegar, but use a larger amount, as the Italian peppers are milder.

TURKEY IN CHILE-NUT SAUCE WITH CORNBREAD CRUST

No doubt about it. This recipe is ridiculously long to read. It is just one of those recipes that, if it is to be useful to many people, requires extra explanation about alternative methods of preparation and ingredient substitution.

For those who prefer to cook in stages, the recipe is divided to allow for preparation over several days. Those who prefer to tackle the job in one fell swoop can just bomb along. Whichever method you choose, leave time for the dish to rest at least 24 hours before serving, to blend the spices.

Makes 2 large casseroles, each to make 8–10 servings

TO COOK THE TURKEY AND MAKE THE BROTH:

1 turkey (about 14 pounds) with giblets, cut into pieces for the pot
About 4 quarts water
2 teaspoons salt
1 garlic clove, peeled
1 onion, rinsed and halved (no need to peel)

1. Slice the turkey gizzard and combine it with the neck and cut-up turkey parts in your largest stockpot. Add the water to just cover, adjusting the amount as needed. Add the salt, garlic, and onion. Cover, and keep at just under a simmer for 35 minutes. Let cool, uncovered.
2. Remove the turkey pieces from the broth and set aside. Strain the stock and discard the solids. Skim off and discard the fat from the broth. Chill 10 cups of the stock to use for the sauce. Freeze whatever stock remains for another use.
3. Remove and discard the skin and bones from the turkey. Cut the flesh into large, neat chunks. Store the meat, well wrapped, in the refrigerator until it is convenient to make the sauce, or go directly to the next operation.

TO MAKE THE SAUCE:

10 large, mild dried hot chile peppers (or use 1/3–1/2 cup pure mild chile powder or chile powder mix; see note below)
About 10 cups reserved turkey broth
1 cup blanched almonds
4 medium-size garlic cloves, unpeeled
1 cup sunflower seeds, preferably unroasted
1/4 cup fine dry bread crumbs
2 large onions, coarsely chopped
1 tablespoon sugar
2 cans (1 pound each) tomatoes, undrained
2 teaspoons ground coriander
1 teaspoon ground cinnamon
1 1/2 teaspoons ground cumin
1 tablespoon salt
1/2 cup lard

1. *If you're not using whole dried chiles, go on to the next step.* Working under cold running water, or wearing thin rubber gloves, remove the stems, seeds, and ribs from the chiles and tear them into bits. Use enough to make about 2 cups. Heat 3 cups of the turkey broth and pour it over the chiles, using enough to cover by at least an inch. Let stand for at least 20 minutes.
2. Stir the almonds, garlic cloves, and sunflower seeds over medium-low heat in a skillet until lightly golden, not browned, about 5 minutes. Cool. Remove and reserve the garlic.
3. Grind the almonds, sunflower seeds, and bread crumbs to a fine texture in a processor or blender. Set aside.
4. *If you're not using whole dried chiles, go on to the next step.* Purée the chiles and broth in a blender or processor until smooth. Pour into a container and reserve.
5. In several batches purée the onions, sugar, tomatoes and their juice, coriander, cinnamon, cumin, salt (and chile powder if you're using it) in the container of a blender or processor with the reserved garlic cloves, which have been pushed through a press. Combine the batches as they're puréed and mix with the chile purée (if you're using it).
6. Melt the lard in a very large, heavy pot. Chop the reserved turkey liver and heart and sauté for a minute in the fat. Pour in the purée and simmer, partly covered, for 10 minutes, stirring often. Be careful of splatters. Add the ground nut mixture and stir to blend.

(Continued)

7. Add 6–7 cups turkey broth, or enough to make a very generous amount of thick but easily poured sauce. Simmer for 5 minutes. Add the reserved turkey chunks and simmer for 5 minutes. Add broth, if needed, to make a very generous amount of thick sauce.
8. Distribute the turkey and sauce equally between two large, broad baking/serving dishes, each about 3 1/2-quart capacity, one lined with foil. Cool, uncovered. Then wrap and store the unlined dish in the fridge. Cover the foil-lined dish with foil, then label and freeze up to 6 months (see Reminders about Freezing, page 352). When you wish to serve the dish, remove the foil, then thaw the mixture in the dish in which it was frozen before going on to the recipe for the crust.

NOTE: If you can't find whole dried chiles or pure mild chile powder (see list of mail-order sources, page 353, for both), buy the combination of spices called "chili powder." Buy the powder mixture with the shortest ingredient list, preferably without garlic powder. If you use the mixed spices, halve the quantities of coriander, cinnamon, cumin, and salt called for in the sauce recipe. *Note also* that the thickening power of different chiles and of the powder varies, so add the broth gradually to obtain a sauce of the proper consistency.

TO MAKE THE CORNBREAD CRUST (PREPARE THE DAY YOU SERVE THE DISH):

1 1/4 cups all-purpose flour
1 teaspoon baking powder
1/2 teaspoon salt
2 teaspoons sugar
1/2 teaspoon baking soda
1 cup yellow cornmeal, preferably stone-ground
2 eggs
1 cup buttermilk
1/4 cup melted lard
3/4 cup finely minced red bell peppers, or a combination of red and green

1. Preheat the oven to 425°. Grease and flour a jelly-roll pan or baking sheet (see note below). Invert it over the dish that contains the turkey and trace the outline of the baking dish on the floured pan.
2. Sift together into a bowl the flour, baking powder, salt, sugar, and baking soda. Whisk in the cornmeal.
3. In a small bowl beat together the eggs and buttermilk. Pour into the dry ingredients. Immediately add the melted lard and mix to just blend the ingredients well; do not overbeat. Fold in the peppers quickly.
4. Scoop the mixture into a large pastry bag fitted with a 1/2-inch star tip. Indenting 1/2 inch from the edge of the line traced on the baking sheet, begin to pipe the cornbread batter to fill in the form entirely. If there is any extra left in the bag, you can make designs on top of the complete layer—squiggles around the edge, blobs in the center, whatever suits your fancy.
5. Bake the crust in the center of the oven for 15–20 minutes, until the top is lightly browned. Let cool on the pan for a few minutes, then lift *carefully* onto a large rack (using large spatulas). Cool until needed—sometime that day.

NOTE: Although the batter looks more festive when piped from a pastry bag, you can also make the crust in a baking pan. Select a pan the same size or slightly smaller than the dish in which you have the turkey (I used a standard 9 × 13-inch roasting pan for both crust and turkey). Grease the pan and spread the batter evenly in it. Bake at 425° for 15–20 minutes, until the top is lightly browned. Cool for 10 minutes, then gently unmold onto a rack.

TO ASSEMBLE THE CASSEROLE AND CRUST FOR SERVING:
1. Heat the turkey casserole in a 400° oven until it is bubbling throughout. This will take about 25 minutes, heated from room temperature, about 35 minutes from the refrigerator. Stir well. Set the crust on top and heat for about 10 minutes longer, until the cornbread is hot.
2. *To serve:* Cut through the topping with a sharp knife. Place a wedge of the cornbread on each plate, then spoon a portion of the turkey and sauce alongside.

ORANGE, ONION, AND CHICORY SALAD

This salad is designed to be served on the plate with the turkey, as the tastes and textures are complementary. The clean, sharp-sweet citrus flavor cuts the density of the hot-thick sauce; the crisp, bitter chicory offers a freshening background for the soft turkey chunks.

Makes 8 servings

1 large head curly chicory
5 large navel oranges, chilled
1 teaspoon coriander seeds (or use ground coriander)
1 teaspoon coarse (kosher) salt
3–4 tablespoons lemon juice
1/4 cup olive oil
1/4 cup peanut oil, almond oil, or corn oil
Big pinch of sugar
2 large red onions, chilled

1. Wash and dry the chicory. Cut into fine slivers and spread in a deep serving platter. Chill until serving time.
2. Peel the oranges, removing all the white pith, then halve lengthwise. Cut each half across into thin half-circles, saving any juice. Set both slices and juice aside in a bowl.
3. Pour any juice from the bowl into a small jar. Using a spice mill or mortar and pestle, crack the coriander seeds to a fine texture and add to the juice (or add the ground coriander). Add the salt, lemon juice to taste, olive oil, peanut oil, and sugar. Cap the jar and shake to blend.
4. Peel the onions. Cut them in half lengthwise, then across into paper-thin half-circles.
5. *To serve:* Arrange the onions and oranges over the chicory and pour the dressing over all. You can refrigerate the salad for up to 2 hours. Tip the serving dish to spoon the dressing over the salad before serving.

COCONUT CREAM WITH APRICOT SAUCE

This is a creamy white, melting, smooth molded cream, surrounded by a bright apricot sauce. It is surprisingly delicate for a coconut dessert. Blancmange (from the French, meaning "white food") and manjar-blanco, the Latin American version of the dessert, are sweet, thickened, milk-based confections, quite different from the medieval dish from which they descended. The Victorian journalist E. S. Dallas discussed the original form in *Kettner's Book of the Table* (1877): "It is needless to give the old receipt . . . because nobody would eat it. In the days of the English king Richard II it was a fowl first roasted, then cut to pieces and served in syrup which was whitened with milk, rice, and almond paste." By the eighteenth century the English term "blancmanger" referred only to a dessert of almonds, sugar, milk, and starch or isinglass (a form of gelatin made from fish).

Having tried both fresh and canned coconut for this dessert, it must be admitted that there is no reason to go through the bother of shelling, peeling, and grating the real thing. But do select the sweetened canned coconut that contains only added sugar, or sugar and water—not the brand with a labful of preservatives. The tart, gingery apricot sauce can be made days ahead.

Makes 8 servings

2 cans (7 ounces each) sweetened coconut flakes
1 3/4 cups cold water
2 envelopes unflavored gelatin
1 1/2 cups milk
Pinch of salt
1/3 cup sugar
2 tablespoons amaretto, coconut amaretto, or coconut liqueur
1 cup heavy cream, chilled
Apricot Sauce (recipe follows)
GARNISH: Peeled, sliced kiwi fruit or halved strawberries

1. Preheat the oven to 350°. Spread the coconut on a jelly-roll pan and bake, tossing frequently, until the flakes are pale beige, not brown, about 15 minutes. Watch closely to prevent burning.
2. Meanwhile, pour 3/4 cup of the water into a small pot and sprinkle with the gelatin.
3. Combine the remaining 1 cup water, the coconut, milk, salt, and sugar in a saucepan and bring to a boil, stirring. In a processor or blender whirl the mixture to chop the coconut as fine as possible.
4. Pour the coconut mixture through a sieve lined with fine-mesh cotton cheesecloth into a bowl. Press down hard on the coconut. Let cool until you can pick up the corners of the cheesecloth and squeeze and twist to extract all the milk; discard the solids. Add the amaretto to the coconut milk.

(Continued)

5. Over low heat, stir the gelatin until it dissolves, leaving no visible granules. Stir the gelatin into the coconut milk with a whisk. Set the bowl in a larger bowl of ice and water and stir often until the mixture is very thick, almost set.
6. As the coconut mixture begins to solidify rapidly, remove it from the ice. Beat the heavy cream in a small bowl until it just begins to form very soft peaks. Do not overbeat.
7. With a whisk, stir the coconut cream to make a smooth consistency. Immediately fold the cream in, gently. Pour the mixture into a lightly oiled, simply decorated 5-cup mold. Cover with plastic wrap and chill for at least 3 hours.
8. *To serve:* Run a knife carefully around the very edge of the mold—do not try to reach deep inside. Set a wet serving plate over this, so you'll be able to slide the cream into place, and invert the two. Wait for a minute. If the cream does not drop from the mold, dip a towel in very hot water, wring it out thoroughly, and wrap around the mold. Repeat until the cream is released. Surround with the apricot sauce and decorate with the kiwis or strawberries.

APRICOT SAUCE

1/2–2/3 cup dried California apricots (3 ounces)
1 1/4 cups water
2 tablespoons chopped preserved ginger in syrup (see list of mail-order sources, page 353)
2 tablespoons rum
Ginger syrup from the preserved ginger in syrup
About 2 tablespoons amaretto, coconut amaretto, or coconut liqueur

1. Combine the apricots and water in a small, heavy pot. Cook over very low heat, covered, until the fruit is very tender, about 1/2 hour.
2. Combine the apricots and liquid with the chopped ginger in a processor or blender and whirl to a very fine purée. If any shreds of ginger remain, strain through a fine sieve. Add the rum, ginger syrup, and amaretto to taste. Thin with water, if needed, to achieve a pourable consistency.
3. Cover and store in the refrigerator.

12
Sup on Soup

Four Main-Course Soups, with Breads to Match

What cool-weather meal could feel cozier and more comforting than one made up of steaming soup and homemade bread? Yet how often do we serve such a homey meal to company, or partake of such simple pleasures when we are guests? And soup is such a sensible solution to the problem of what to prepare on those days when entertaining and working appear to be mutually exclusive. It will wait serenely on a back burner until you're ready for it, demands no final fussing, and offers no last-minute surprises. And, perhaps best of all, a soup meal puts guests at ease; informality reigns.

What lifts a soup meal out of the ordinary is homemade bread. Crusty, real breads deserve a place of honor at any meal—as main dishes, not as accoutrements. Filling, delicious loaves are the natural companion to soups, not only because their tastes and textures are complementary, but because the combination of proteins and complex carbohydrates provides the basis for a nutritionally superior meal.

A General Note on Soup and Stockpiling

While it is always the right time to have a freezerful of reduced stocks made from all kinds of meat and poultry (mine are often mutts), soups are bulky, and not much of an advantage unless you have loads of space. While it may not be sensible to freeze composite soups, they do benefit from resting and blending for at least a day or two in the refrigerator before serving, so you can be quite flexible about your spontaneous entertaining.

If broth-brewing has been ignored in your home of late, let me remind you how very simple it is to keep this necessity on hand. Most important is to wrap, label (include date), and freeze every scrap of meat and bone that comes your way: poultry giblets (use hearts and livers elsewhere) and wing tips; bones from pork, veal, or beef roasts; little ribs left over from boning a duck or chicken breast; ham bones, etc. Also, freeze any leftover sauces, meat juices, and gravies to enliven future soups. When time permits, such as a day when you'll be paying bills or doing housework, haul out a batch of compatibly flavored bones and meat scraps and combine them with water to cover in a large pot. Simmer and skim for a few minutes, then add an onion or leek, a few branches of celery, a carrot or two, bay leaf, and thyme. Partly cover the pot and let the liquid barely bubble for as long as you can—preferably at least a few hours. Strain, cool, and skim. Or you can mix up the stock fixings in a large slow-cooker and leave them while you're gone for the day, or overnight.

It makes sense to boil down stocks so that they won't take up so much storage space. If you have the time to cook them down to a syrupy texture (called glace de viande), you will fit the strength of about 8 quarts of stock into a 2-cup container, from which you can then withdraw potent spoonfuls whenever you wish to enrich a sauce, stew, or soup, or when you want to reconstitute the broth.

SOUP AND BREAD MEALS FOR SIX

Apéritif of Ricard or Pernod
Green and Black Olives (brine- and oil-cured)
Cubed Feta Cheese, Marinated with Herbs and Olive Oil
*Fish Chowder Provençal
*Rustic Wheat Loaves *or* *Processor "French" Bread
Wine: White Bordeaux *or* California Sauvignon Blanc
Baked Pears in Syrup

*Deviled Eggs (page 186; halve the recipe)
*Soup of Winter Vegetables,
Ham, Chestnuts, and Dried Mushrooms
*Processor "French" Bread *or* *Cracked-Oat Bread (page 347)
Wine: Alsatian Sylvaner *or* Italian Tocai
Fresh Pineapple/*Petite Macaroons (page 43)
Tea

*Soup of Chickpeas, Kale, Brown Rice, and Salt Pork
*Rustic Wheat Loaves *or* *Processor "French" Bread
Wine: Merlot del Trentino *or* a Rioja Clarete—either one cooled
Bosc, Seckel, and Anjou Pears
Several Soft Cheeses
Espresso/Candied Fruit Peels

*Cock-a-Leekie Soup
*Rustic Wheat Loaves *or* *Cracked-Oat Bread (page 347)
Dark Beer *or* Beer and Stout
Waldorf Salad (celery, apples, and walnuts with mayonnaise)
Coffee/Gingerbread

FISH CHOWDER PROVENÇAL

The English word "chowder" comes from the French *chaudière*, a huge pot. Into such a pot the fishermen of Brittany would toss a selection of fish from their day's catch. It is reasonable to assume that they carried this custom with them to Newfoundland, then Nova Scotia, and on to New England. Amelia Simmons, who in 1796 wrote what some consider to be the first American cookbook, included a recipe for "chouder." Her version incorporates bass, salt pork, and crackers soaked in water. She suggested an accompaniment of potatoes, pickles, applesauce, and "mangoes" (a term that described stuffed, pickled fruit). It is surprising how very close this mix of flavors is to what might be served today in New England.

What surprises even more is that Hannah Glasse (*The Art of Cookery Made Plain and Easy*, London, 1796) offered a recipe "To make Chouder, a Sea Dish" that begins in just the same way as does a traditional New England one—with salt pork, onions, dried herbs, cod, and crackers. Her recipe, however, then strikes off in its own direction: "When you take it up and lay it in the dish, pour in a glass of hot Maderia [*sic*] wine, and a very little India pepper: if you have oysters, or truffles, or morels, it is still better; thicken it with butter." To top it all off, the soup becomes a pie, covered with a thick crust.

What follows is neither of these, nor is it a real New England chowder. It is, rather, a chowder in the style of New England, thick with fish and potatoes, the New World addition to the soup, enhanced with the powerful aromas of Provence—garlic, saffron, fennel.

Makes 6 servings

1 tablespoon coarse (kosher) salt
2 medium-size garlic cloves
1 teaspoon fennel seeds
1/4 teaspoon dried thyme
2 pounds lean fish filets (cod, hake, haddock), cut into 2-inch pieces
1–2 large fish skeletons (heads and bones; about 2 pounds), of lean white fish
6 cups water
1 cup dry white wine
3–4 medium-size onions, thinly sliced (to make 4 cups)
1/4 cup olive oil
1/4 cup all-purpose flour
2 teaspoons dried basil
1/2 teaspoon dried summer savory
1 bay leaf, crumbled or snipped small
1/2 teaspoon saffron threads, steeped in 1/4 cup hot water
1 3/4 pounds large new potatoes, peeled and sliced into pieces about 1 inch square and 1/4 inch thick (about 5 cups)
About 1/2 cup light or heavy cream
Minced fresh basil or thyme (optional)

1. Crush together 1 teaspoon of the salt, 1 garlic clove, the fennel seeds, and dried thyme in a mortar, or chop fine with a heavy knife. Rub the mixture evenly over the fish pieces, then cover with plastic and refrigerate overnight or leave several hours at room temperature.
2. Remove the gills from the fish heads. Chop the skeletons into manageable pieces and combine with the water in a large pot. Simmer, partly covered, for 5 minutes. Scrape off any large pieces of meat from the bones and refrigerate them. Return the bones to the pot; add the wine and simmer gently for 20 minutes. Strain through a sieve, then through fine-mesh cotton cheesecloth. Set aside.

3. In a large soup pot cook the onions in the olive oil until very soft. Slice the remaining garlic, add to the pot, and stir for a minute. Add the flour and stir and scrape for about 2 minutes. Pour in the fish stock; add the dried basil, savory, bay leaf, saffron, and the remaining 2 teaspoons salt. Bring to a boil, stirring.
4. Add the potatoes and simmer gently for about 15 minutes, or until the potatoes are not quite cooked through. Stir in the reserved raw and cooked fish. Gently stir for about 1 minute, or until the outside of the raw fish turns white, but the fish is not cooked through.
5. Set the pot in a sink containing cold water. Stir the soup now and then until cool. Refrigerate, covered, overnight.
6. *To serve:* Warm the soup over low heat, stirring gently so as not to break up the fish. Add the cream to taste and stir; sprinkle with the fresh herbs, if available, and serve.

SOUP OF WINTER VEGETABLES, HAM, CHESTNUTS, AND DRIED MUSHROOMS

If you were to cross a French vegetable soup with Chinese hot-and-sour soup, then added a soupçon of sweet-and-sour sauce, you'd have something along these lines—substantial, but at the same time fresh tasting, and rather exotic.

Makes 6 servings

1 cup dried chestnuts (see note below)
2–2½ pounds ham hocks (smoked pork knuckles)
2½ quarts water
About 10 large dried Japanese or Chinese mushrooms (see list of mail-order sources, page 353)
2 leeks, roots and dark green leaf tops removed, split, well washed, and thinly sliced (about 2½ cups)
2 medium-size parsnips, peeled and cut into ½-inch cubes (1¼ cups)
3–4 small white turnips, peeled and cut into ½-inch cubes (2 cups)
3 medium-size parsley roots (also called root parsley), peeled and cut into ½-inch cubes—about 1¼ cups (or use celeriac or celery root if you can't get the parsley)
1 butternut squash (about 1¾ pounds), peeled, seeded, and cut into 1-inch cubes (about 4 cups)
¼ teaspoon crushed red pepper flakes (or use 1 tiny dried hot chile pepper, crumbled)
1 tablespoon coarse (kosher) salt
3 tablespoons cornstarch
3 tablespoons rice vinegar or white wine vinegar

1. Soak the chestnuts overnight in water to cover by several inches. Drain, then pick off any loose bits of husk. Simmer in a covered saucepan, with several inches of water over the nuts, until the nuts are tender but not falling apart. Timing for this can vary from 1 to 3 hours. Drain and measure the liquid, adding water to make 2 cups, if needed. Halve the chestnuts, unless they are tiny.
2. While the chestnuts are simmering, place the ham hocks in a large soup pot with 2 quarts of the water; bring to a boil and skim the surface for 1 minute. Simmer, covered, for about 1 hour, or until the meat is tender but not falling from the bones. Remove the hocks, reserving the broth, and let cool a bit, then discard the skin and bones. Cut the meat into 1/4- to 1/2-inch dice.
3. While the ham hocks are cooking, soak the mushrooms in 2 cups hot water. When they are softened sufficiently, cut off and discard the stems. Cut the caps into halves or quarters, depending upon their size. Strain the soaking liquid through a paper towel or several layers of fine-mesh cotton cheesecloth and reserve it.
4. Add the chestnuts and liquid, mushrooms and their liquid, and diced ham to the broth in the soup pot, then add the leeks, parsnips, parsley root, butternut squash, turnips, red pepper flakes, and salt. Bring to a boil, then lower the heat and simmer for 15–20 minutes, until the vegetables are not quite fully cooked. Do not let them become soft.
5. Set the pot in a sink containing cold water. Stir the soup gently, now and then, until cool; refrigerate, covered, until serving time—up to 2 days.
6. *To serve:* Warm the soup over low heat, stirring occasionally. Mix together the cornstarch and vinegar and stir in. Bring to a bare simmer, stirring often, and gently. Simmer about 2 minutes, until the broth is clear and thickened.

NOTE: It is simplest to use the dried chestnuts that can be found year round, usually in specialty shops or Hungarian, Oriental, and Italian groceries (or see list of mail-order sources, page 353). If you prefer the fresh chestnuts, you'll need to buy about 1 pound. To peel the bothersome creatures in a not-too-trying manner, rinse the nuts, lay them flat side down on a cutting board, and chop them in half with a cleaver or heavy knife. Drop into a pot of boiling water and boil for about 4–10 minutes, until the meats can be pried easily from the shells. Timing can vary considerably, so test frequently. Pour off most of the water, leaving enough to keep the nuts barely covered with the liquid. Pick out the nuts, one at a time, and discard the shells. When all the nuts have been cleaned, simmer them gently in fresh water to cover until almost tender.

SOUP OF CHICKPEAS, KALE, BROWN RICE, AND SALT PORK

This is a most satisfying main-course soup: It has a variety of flavors, textures, and aromas as interesting as those of many a whole meal. Not only that, but the soup is nutritious, and it smells heavenly while simmering. But—there is so often a little drawback—the chickpeas are a nuisance to skin. It is not absolutely necessary to do this, but if you have the patience, you'll be rewarded with chickpeas that are tastier, prettier, firmer, and considerably easier to digest. It simplifies matters to take care of the pea-peeling job a day or two before the meal, with a good conversationalist of any age (my daughter is ideal). Incidentally, we wound up with 4 cups of chickpeas to 2 cups of skins—which is a lot of husk to swallow.

If you've not tasted kale, a vegetable that thrives on wintery winds, it is definitely worth trying. Curly blue-green leaves with a dusky bloom have a firm texture and full, earthy flavor. Kale's vitamin and mineral content are unbelievably high, its calorie count—nil. Generally speaking, kale has a peak season of November through early April. If you aren't able to get it when you want to make this soup, you can substitute fresh or frozen collard greens, chard, or spinach. For chard, add the cut stems first and shorten the cooking time for the leaves; for spinach, simply stir in the leaves at the end of the cooking time.

Makes about 6 servings

$^3/_4$ pound (about 2 cups) dried chickpeas (also called cecis or garbanzos)
3 garlic cloves, peeled
2 teaspoons coarse (kosher) salt
$^1/_2$ pound salt pork or slab bacon (as lean as possible), cut into $^1/_4$-inch dice
2 medium-size onions, coarsely chopped
$^3/_4$ cup brown rice
2 teaspoons ground cumin
1 teaspoon ground cardamom
$^1/_4$ teaspoon grated nutmeg
Light meat stock and/or water
1 pound fresh, tender kale
Cherry tomatoes, thinly sliced

1. Soak the chickpeas overnight in water to cover by at least 3 inches. Drain. Turn into a pot with water to cover by at least 3 inches. Add garlic and simmer, partly covered, until just tender not soft, adding water as needed to cover the peas by at least 1 inch. Add the salt toward the end of the cooking time. Time required varies considerably—it can be as long as 3 hours, as little as 1 hour—so keep tasting. Dip the peas out into a bowl and reserve the cooking liquid and garlic.
2. When peas are cool enough to handle, squeeze each one gently between thumb and forefinger to slip off the skin; discard the skins. Mash the garlic cloves and add to the reserved cooking liquid. Cover and refrigerate the peas and stock separately, until convenient to proceed. Or go directly to step 3.
3. In a large soup pot brown the pork on all sides. Add the onions and stir until soft and lightly browned. Add the rice and stir a few moments, until lightly browned. Add the cumin, cardamom, and nutmeg, and stir. Add enough stock and/or water to the cooking liquid to equal 12 cups. Pour into the pot with the pork and onions and bring to a boil. Lower the heat and simmer, partly covered, until the rice just barely begins to become tender, about $^1/_2$ hour.
4. Meanwhile, strip off the stems from the kale and discard them. Wash the leaves well, then shred very fine. Add to the soup along with the chickpeas, and simmer for about 5 minutes, uncovered, or until the kale is softened but not quite tender and the rice is almost the proper consistency. Don't overcook, as both kale and rice will continue to soften while the soup cools and when it is reheated.

5. Set the pot in a sink containing cold water; stir the soup now and then until cool, then refrigerate, covered.
6. *To serve:* Warm over low heat, stirring gently. Season with pepper. Slice enough cherry tomatoes to almost cover the top of the soup, and heat through.

COCK-A-LEEKIE SOUP

If you open up a book of Scottish cookery, you're more than likely to find yourself in a kettle of soup, thick with names that are as down-to-earth as the burly brews: hotchpotch, feather fowlie, pow-sowdie, cullen skink, red pottage, neep brose. In this company you'll encounter a grizzled veteran that has traveled widely, suffered the tampering of chefs and kings, and endured a goofy name—cock-a-leekie. In its "purest" form, the soup contained a cock (some sources maintain that in the days of cockfighting the loser was the starting point for cock-a-leekie), masses of leeks, prunes, and salt. Along its 400-year history, first in an English form and then in a Scottish one, it has picked up a few embellishments: barley, oatmeal, or rice, and, commonly, a pleasant dose of sweet spice. The amount of leeks has been cut down (an early formula suggested eighteen leeks to each quart of broth) and a fowl (boiling hen), capon, or chicken has replaced the cock.

Oddly, one of the more weighty indignities the soup has had to bear is the admiration of *two* celebrated Frenchmen—the bishop-statesman-gastronome Talleyrand and Alexis Soyer, chef and culinary historian *extraordinaire.* The praise of the French, whose ideas about food were thought to be fussy and fancy, was not considered a high honor by some Scots. Talleyrand, it is written, preferred his cock-a-leekie pruneless. I recommend their inclusion, even if you're not a prune fancier. They lend a mellow wininess to the broth, and as they puff up their flavor becomes delicately tea-like, not cloying. All, however, do not concur on this monumental subject, as is immediately evident from this statement from Christopher North's *Noctes Ambrosianae* (1822–35): "Speakin' o' cocky-leekie, the man was an atheist that first polluted it with prunes." See for yourself.

Makes 6 servings

1 chicken (2½ pounds)
3 quarts light meat or poultry stock
2 pounds veal bones, sawed into manageable pieces
1 large carrot, scrubbed and chunked
2 whole cloves
2 celery stalks with leaves
2 bay leaves
Handful of fresh parsley with stems
6 large leeks
½ cup barley
1 teaspoon ground allspice
1 teaspoon curry powder
2 teaspoons coarse (kosher) salt
12 prunes, pitted
Worcestershire sauce to taste

1. Combine the chicken, stock, and veal bones in a large soup pot and bring to a simmer. Simmer gently for a few minutes, skimming. Add the carrot, cloves, celery, bay leaves, parsley, and 1 leek, split and well washed. Cover and keep at a gentle simmer for 1 hour.
2. Remove the chicken from the pot and set it aside on a cutting board. Discard all the vegetables and veal bones. Skim the fat from the stock.
3. Cut off and discard the tough dark green tops and the roots from the 5 remaining leeks, then halve them lengthwise. Wash very well to remove all traces of sand and soil and cut into 1-inch lengths. Either add the leeks to the broth, if you like a strong leek flavor, or, for a very pale leek flavor, drop the leeks into a pot of boiling water, return the water to a boil, drain the leeks and then add them to the broth.
4. Add the barley, allspice, curry powder, and 2 teaspoons of the salt. Simmer for 45 minutes, partly covered, until the barley is tender.
5. While the soup simmers, remove and discard the skin and bones from the chicken. Cut the meat into small slivers.
6. Add the chicken meat and prunes to the soup and stir for 2 minutes. Remove from the heat and set the pot in a sink containing cold water. Stir the soup now and then until cool, then refrigerate, covered.
7. *To serve:* Warm the soup over low heat. Add Worcestershire sauce to taste (this is based on an Indian sauce adopted by the British, but chances are good that the venerable seasoning had Roman ancestors, as well). Simmer for a few minutes longer, season, and serve.

RUSTIC WHEAT LOAVES

Leafing through a British baking manual entitled simply *Manna* (by Walter T. Banfield, 1937[?]), I met up with a group of crunchy-crusted, coarse breads that are called variously "cottage," "farmhouse," "country," and "crusty" loaves—all highly appetizing appellations. The idea of "rolling a doughpiece whilst . . . 'green' [unbaked] in cracked wheat" seemed most appealing, especially as the text goes on to promise that the "loaf eats and keeps exceptionally moist." I enjoy the crackly exterior that the grains produce, but if your preference is not for the hard and crunchy, omit the final 1/4 cup cracked wheat for coating.

A word on baking pans: It is useful to make the three loaves that the recipe yields in different shapes for different uses. Certainly the most adorable is the fat, round, puffed-top loaf, for which you need a charlotte mold or soufflé dish of 1-quart capacity. However, you can use any metal or oven-glass pan that has a 1-quart capacity. Lower the oven temperature by 25° when you bake in glass.

Makes 3 loaves (each 1–1 1/4 pounds)

1 cup cracked wheat (also called bulgur or wheat pilaf; see list of mail-order sources, page 353)
4 teaspoons salt
1 1/2 cups boiling water
2 1/4 cups lukewarm water
Big pinch of sugar
2 packets dry yeast
2 tablespoons olive oil
3 cups whole-wheat flour
About 4–5 cups bread flour (available in specialty stores and many supermarkets)

1. Sprinkle 3/4 cup of the cracked wheat and 1/2 teaspoon of the salt into the 1 1/2 cups boiling water; simmer, covered, for 5 minutes. Scrape into a large bowl and let cool.

2. In a small bowl whisk together 1/2 cup of the warm water, the sugar, and yeast. Let stand about 5 minutes, until fluffy. If mixture does not foam, start again with fresh ingredients. Add the remaining 1 3/4 cups water, the oil, and 3 1/2 teaspoons salt to the cracked wheat. Stir in the yeast mixture.

(Continued)

3. Stir the whole-wheat flour into the cracked-wheat mixture. Gradually stir in 2 cups bread flour. Spread 2 cups more on a kneading surface and turn out the dough onto this. Gradually knead in the flour, adding enough to make dough of a medium consistency. Cover with a bowl and let stand 15 minutes. If the dough is sticky, knead in more flour. Continue to knead the dough until it no longer sticks to your hands. It should be a very full, bouncy dough, but do not expect it to be satiny, as whole-wheat doughs are always a bit sticky.
4. Set the dough in a large oiled bowl and cover. Let rise until doubled in bulk, about an hour. (Don't set in a warm place; 75° is best.)
5. Punch down the dough and divide into thirds on a very lightly floured board. Flatten each piece, then shape it to fit the pan you have chosen. Roll the bottom and sides of each loaf in about 1 tablespoon of the cracked wheat. Oil the pans well, then fit the loaves into each pan. Cover with towels and let rise above the edges of the pan to at least double in volume, about an hour. Preheat the oven to 375°.
6. Sprinkle a teaspoon or so of flour evenly over each loaf. Cut a large cross on top of any round loaves; leave rectangular loaves in pans unslashed. Bake 45 minutes in the center of the oven. Remove the loaves from the pans and set them directly on the oven shelf. Bake about 10–15 minutes longer, or until the loaves are well browned. Cool on racks.
7. *To store and serve within a day or two:* Leave the bread unwrapped, at room temperature. Re-crisp in a 275° oven for 10 minutes shortly before serving. *To freeze and reheat:* Wrap tightly in freezer paper, seal, label, and freeze (up to 2 months). To serve, unwrap the loaf and enclose in a clean towel to thaw entirely. Freshen in a 275° oven for 15 minutes shortly before serving.

PROCESSOR "FRENCH" BREAD

Obviously, any bread made in a processor is not the "original" version. But this simply assembled loaf is virtually all crackly crisp crust, long and narrow, and properly yeasty and wheaty. To achieve the crustiness, you'll need a plant mister or sprayer. To lend a bit more flavor and substance, a small amount of whole-wheat flour is included. If you're not serving these with a meal, nothing makes a better ham or cheese sandwich.

Makes 4 very thin loaves (about 5 ounces each)

1 cup lukewarm water
1 packet dry yeast
Big pinch of sugar
1/2 cup whole-wheat flour
About 2 1/2 cups all-purpose unbleached flour
1 1/2 teaspoons salt
1/4 cup very warm water
Cornmeal to sprinkle on the baking sheets

1. Combine 1/2 cup of the lukewarm water with the yeast and sugar in the processor container. Switch the machine on and off a few times to blend. Let the mixture stand until it is frothy, about 5–10 minutes. If it doesn't fluff up, begin again with fresh ingredients.
2. Add the remaining 1/2 cup lukewarm water, the whole-wheat flour, and 2 cups of the all-purpose flour. Process 15 seconds.
3. Stir together the salt and very warm water until the salt dissolves. Pour into the container of the processor with the remaining 1/2 cup all-purpose flour and process for 20 seconds.
4. Turn the dough out onto a very lightly floured board and knead for a few minutes to make a springy, fairly soft dough. Do not add flour unless the dough is very sticky.
5. Sprinkle a bowl lightly with flour. Place the dough in it, sprinkle a little flour on top, and cover the bowl with plastic. Let the dough rise until at least double in bulk—almost tripled, if you have the time—from 1 to 2 hours.
6. Scrape the dough out of the bowl and knead it for a moment to make a smooth ball. Return to the bowl, cover with plastic, and let double in volume, about 1 hour.

(Continued)

7. Turn the dough out onto a lightly floured board and cut into 4 equal pieces. Fold each piece over on itself to make a sandwich and cover with plastic.
8. Take one piece of dough and pat it to form a rough rectangle about 8 × 6 inches. Roll toward you from one long side to the other to form a cylinder. Pinch the seam closed. Flatten the dough again to form a rectangle about 12 inches long and about 2 inches wide. With the side of your hand press a trench down the center of the rectangle, lengthwise. Follow this mark to fold the dough in half lengthwise. Pinch the seam closed. Turn seam side down and with your fingertips gently roll the rope to make an even loaf about 15 inches long.
9. Sprinkle 2 baking sheets thinly and evenly with cornmeal. Set the formed loaf on one (it will be soft and wobbly) and even it out gently.
10. Repeat steps 8 and 9 to make 4 loaves. Set 2 on each sheet. Cover the loaves with towels and let them double in size—about an hour or less. Preheat the oven to 400°. Remove the light bulb from your oven or turn it off, so that it won't shatter when the oven is sprayed with water.
11. You can leave the loaves smooth and cylindrical. Or you can make 3 long diagonal slashes in each, using a very sharp knife or razor and cutting 1/4 inch deep. Set the pans on the middle and upper shelves of your oven and spray them and the surrounding oven furiously with the plant mister for 30 seconds.
12. Bake 10 minutes, then spray for 15 seconds. Bake for 5 minutes. Reverse the pans and switch shelves. Bake about 10 minutes longer, until the loaves are well browned all over and have no pale lines along the sides. Cool entirely on racks.
13. *To serve that day:* Leave, uncovered, at room temperature until serving time, then heat for 5 minutes in a 300° oven shortly before serving. *To freeze and reheat:* Wrap the loaves in freezer paper, seal, and label them. Return to the freezer for up to 1 month. When ready to use, let the loaves defrost at room temperature, wrapped. Unwrap and heat in a 300° oven for 5–10 minutes shortly before serving.

13
A Traditional Thanksgiving–Updated

Without the media pressures surrounding Christmas or the frantic gaiety that always seems to go with New Year's Eve, Thanksgiving does what a holiday is supposed to do: It encourages people to sit down together and spend the day talking, reviewing—and eating—in a relatively informal atmosphere.

American eating styles have altered drastically since the Pilgrims gave thanks for their survival in 1620, inaugurating our first national celebration. The change during the last century has been particularly marked, with a lightened approach becoming more apparent every year. To a contemporary diner, working through the gargantuan meals that were popular in this country early in the century would hardly be cause for thankfulness. One such Thanksgiving meal, overwhelming—if delightful—in its variety, appeared in the *Picayune Creole Cook Book* (1901), reproduced here as it was originally printed.

Oysters on Half Shell.
Cream of Asparagus Soup
Spanish Olives. Celery. Mixed Pickles.
Radishes. Salted Almonds.
Baked Red Snapper à la Créole
Mashed Potatoes
Lamb Chops au Petits Pois
Chicken Sauté aux Champignons.
Cauliflower, Sauce Blanche.
Pineapple Fritters au Rhum.
Pâtes de Foies Gras.
Stuffed Tomatoes
Turkey Stuffed with Chestnuts, Cranberry Sauce.
Endive Salad, French Dressing.

Pababotte à la Creole. [a game bird from Louisiana]
Plum Pudding, Hard or Brandy Sauce.
Pumpkin Pie.
Lemon Sherbet. Assorted Cakes.
Assorted Fruits. Assorted Nuts. Raisins.
Neufchatel.
Quince Marmalade. Crackers.
Café Noir.

Although the tone of the meal is distinctively Creole, the size of the menu and arrangement of courses is typically American, approximating a well-to-do Thanksgiving dinner anywhere in the country.

As the dinner was considered substantial, even for that epoch, the recommended breakfast Thanksgiving morning was unusually light:

Grapes.
Oatflakes and Milk.
Oysters on Toast.
Broiled Tenderloin Steaks. Potato Chips.
Milk Biscuits. Butter
Rice Griddle Cakes. Louisiana Syrup.
Cafe Noir.

The evening supper that followed Thanksgiving dinner was so light as to be virtually nonexistent:

Cold Turkey.
Tomato Salad.
Crackers.
Cake. Fruit. Tea.

For our American ancestors of the time, there were as many rules and regulations with regard to etiquette and aesthetics as there were courses in the meal. For a correct bachelor's Thanksgiving, cautions *The Good Housekeeping Hostess* (1904), "much will depend upon the quality and the proper laying of the cloth. An ideal bachelor's dinner is elegant, but rather severe in appointments. . . . Yellow color effects are always satisfactory." Acceptable diversions were specified, too— as bachelors might tend to become rowdy without some planned entertainment. The author recommends that "after the soup is removed, the butler should pass a tray on which are numbered tickets. Each guest takes one. Immediately the turkey is brought in 'decorated' with corresponding tickets, each cut being numbered." The author assures the reader that this "unusual 'turkey raffle' is sure to occasion a great deal of interest and amusement." As would another Thanksgiving surprise—serving a dessert of turkey cake for which great pains were taken to create a bird of startling verisimilitude. Directions advise that "while icing is still soft, take a coarse-meshed strainer and press all over it to imitate the grain of the turkey's skin." The author added gravely that parsley might be used for garnish "if intense realism is desired."

While neither raffles for a choice cut nor turkey cakes are recommended in the dinner that follows, the ingredients are quite traditional, although their treatment may not be orthodox. The meal is a patchwork affair, not focused on any particular part of the United States, taking, rather, bits and pieces from several regions. Although there must be some last-minute reheating and assembling for a lengthy celebration meal of this kind, all dishes are completed ahead of the guests' arrival. The recipes were developed for a rather small group (eight or nine), as most people seem to prefer full-scale meals such as this sitting at the table, conversing. And, as with meals, families today are smaller than they used to be.

THANKSGIVING DINNER FOR EIGHT OR NINE

Champagne *or* Sparkling Dry White Wine
*Oysters with Piquant Sauce
*Chestnut Soup
*Smoked Turkey
Wine: Gewürztraminer from Alsace or California *or*
Dry California Johannisberg Riesling
*Braised Celery
*Rutabaga Purée
*Coarse Cranberry Relish
*Smooth Cranberry-Apple Sauce
*Romaine, Orange, and Watercress Salad with
Mustard Cream Dressing
*Butternut-Maple Fanchonettes with Glacéed Pecans
Coffee/Port

OYSTERS WITH PIQUANT SAUCE

North, South, East, West—oysters have long been traditional openers for the Thanksgiving feast, although the once cheap shellfish has become a coquillage de luxe. Sharp, peppery-vinegary sauces were the usual accompaniment to raw oysters on the half shell, but I think that most of these overwhelm. One exception is the sauce devised by the Delmonico chef Alessandro Filippini, a recipe for which was published in his book, *The Table* (1889). Although sharp, it is not too fierce, pointing up rather than annihilating the ephemeral oyster flavor and delicate texture. The recipe, entitled "Oysters à l'Alexandre Dumas," has been altered, but the ingredients are generally the same as those of the original.

The sauce, which should be made 8–24 hours ahead of time, will be sufficient for about 4 dozen oysters—enough for a first course for eight. Serve with a *teeny* spoon, as a sprinkle on each oyster is ample.

Makes 8 or 9 servings

1 teaspoon salt
1 teaspoon white pepper
2 tablespoons very finely minced shallots
1 1/2 tablespoons very finely minced fresh parsley
1 1/2 teaspoons olive oil
About 8 drops Tabasco
3/4 teaspoon Worcestershire sauce
1/4 cup white wine tarragon vinegar
About 4 dozen oysters on the half shell

Mix all the ingredients (except the oysters!) in a bowl and cover with plastic. Refrigerate from 8 to 24 hours before serving.

CHESTNUT SOUP

Soup made by this recipe is sweet, smoky, rich, and predominantly chestnutty—unlike a late eighteenth-century Virginian recipe that I once came upon, which contained (in addition to the chestnuts and vegetables) ham, beef, veal, pigeons, several kinds of stuffed birds, and veal broth, as well as bread snippets for garnish. A Creole cookbook recommends adding small dumplings to chestnut soup and using "oyster water" on fast days instead of the usual beef broth.

If they are available to you, dried chestnuts—sold in specialty shops and Italian, Hungarian, and Oriental groceries—are to be preferred. Not only will you be freed from the bothersome task of peeling the chestnuts, but the flavor of this soup is improved by using the dried nuts. The intensified smokiness is very appealing here, as is the fact that the dried chestnuts, which are available all year, make this a much more useful dish than one that depends upon fresh chestnuts, which have a short season. (Do be cautious, however: If dried nuts smell stale, or have wormholes, don't buy them.)

Makes 8 or 9 servings

2 cups dried chestnuts (see list of mail-order sources, page 353; or use 2 pounds fresh chestnuts—see note below)
6 tablespoons butter
1 medium leek, split lengthwise, meticulously washed, and thinly sliced, roots and dark green leaf tops removed
About 3/4 pound carrots, sliced or chopped (2 cups)
About 1 celery stalk, chopped (3/4 cup)
About 6 cups light veal, chicken, duck, or turkey stock (or enough to make 7 cups when combined with the reserved chestnut cooking liquid)
About 2 teaspoons salt
1/2 teaspoon dried savory
1/4 teaspoon grated nutmeg
1/4 teaspoon black pepper
1 cup milk
1 1/2 tablespoons cornstarch
3 tablespoons water
A few tablespoons of the dinner wine

1. Soak the chestnuts overnight in a cool place in water to cover by several inches. Pick out the loose husks. Simmer until soft in fresh water to cover in a covered saucepan. Timing will vary considerably, depending upon the state of dehydration of the nuts. It can take as long as several hours. Drain, reserving the liquid. Remove any husks that still cling to the nuts. There should be about 4 cups of chestnuts.
2. Melt the butter in a large pot. Add the leek, carrots, and celery and cook over moderate heat, stirring, for 10 minutes, or until the vegetables are lightly colored. Add the chestnuts and stir. Add the reserved chestnut cooking liquid and stock, salt, savory, nutmeg, and pepper. Bring to a simmer.
3. Cover and simmer for about 1 hour, or until the chestnuts and vegetables are very soft.

(Continued)

4. Purée the soup in batches in a food processor or blender with the milk. The purée should be very smooth. Press through a fine sieve into the rinsed-out pot. Stir together the cornstarch and water and add to the soup. Bring to a simmer, stirring.
5. Cool the soup by setting the pot in a sink containing cold water. Refrigerate, covered, for 1–2 days before serving.
6. *To serve:* Bring to a simmer and add broth if soup is too thick. Add a few splashes of the dinner wine to point up the flavor. Season and serve.

NOTE: If you can't get the dried chestnuts, prepare fresh ones in this relatively simple way: Rinse and halve about 2 pounds large, weighty chestnuts with a heavy knife or cleaver, laying them flat side down to do this. Combine the nuts with water to cover by a few inches in a large saucepan. Boil for about 5–10 minutes, or until the shells can be easily removed. Pick out the nuts from the water, a few at a time, and discard both shells and husks. Simmer gently until almost tender in fresh water to cover.

SMOKED TURKEY

Roasted turkey is one of those foods that can be delicious—or utterly tasteless, depending upon your skill and luck. So why not chance a skill-less, precooked smoked turkey this year? Curing and smoking techniques vary: Some birds are given a quick bath in brine, while others are slowly dry-salted, like ham; some turkeys are smoked lightly, others very heavily. Smoked turkeys (virtually all are frozen) are available in many supermarkets and butcher shops, or by mail (see list of mail-order sources, page 353). In the latter category you will have a large choice that includes turkeys long and short cured, long and short smoked, and ranging in size from 5 to 25 pounds. The smallest supermarket size available is usually about 10 pounds.

Whichever turkey you choose, it will probably need to be defrosted—which is best accomplished slowly, in the refrigerator. Allow at least two days for this.

TO SERVE SMOKED TURKEY: Carve the meat into thin slices (do this with the legs and second joints as well, which are too rich to eat in larger pieces, as you might a roasted turkey). Arrange the slices on a platter, cover with plastic, and refrigerate until serving time.

BRAISED CELERY

The strong herbal flavor of braised celery complements smoked meat superbly. Choose tender, compact stalks, without holes or heavy fibers, for this classic vegetable dish.

Makes 8–9 servings

6 celery hearts (or 6 small bunches tender celery)
1/2 stick (4 tablespoons) butter
2 tablespoons olive oil
1 small onion, finely chopped
1 medium-size carrot, finely chopped
1 medium-size garlic clove, thinly sliced
1/2 teaspoon dried marjoram
1 bay leaf, crushed
1 teaspoon dried basil
1 cup water
1 1/2 teaspoons salt
1/4 teaspoon black pepper
1 cup white wine

1. Trim the celery hearts and separate the ribs. (If using the bunches, remove the outer stalks, any other tough ones, and the leaves.) Wash the celery well and cut across into 3- to 4-inch sections. Place them in a very large kettle with cold water to cover, bring to a boil over high heat, then drain and rinse with cold water. Preheat the oven to 350°.

2. In a medium-size skillet heat the butter and oil; add the onions, carrot, and garlic and stir over moderate heat for 5 minutes, or until the vegetables have softened. Stir in the marjoram, bay leaf, and basil. Spread half the mixture in a large, shallow baking-serving dish, then spread the celery over this. The dish should be very full, as the vegetable will cook down.

3. Add the 1 cup water, salt, pepper, and wine to the vegetables remaining in the skillet and bring to a boil. Pour over the celery. Cover with buttered wax paper, then with foil or a lid. Bake for 1 to 1 1/2 hours, or until the celery is tender, basting once. Uncover the dish and let it stand at room temperature until you are ready for dinner. Or refrigerate the celery if you're preparing it a day ahead of time.

4. *To serve:* Drain off the juices from the celery into a small saucepan and boil them until they are reduced to about 1/2–3/4 cup. At the same time reheat the celery in a preheated 400° oven for about 25 minutes, until hot. Pour the reduced juices over the stalks and serve.

RUTABAGA PURÉE

With their strong, earthy, autumnal flavor, rutabagas are among the finest of Thanksgiving traditions. They are considerably mellowed by simmering in a simple stock, but if you don't have any bones on hand, or you just don't feel like making stock, you can substitute canned broth enriched with a few strips of smoked bacon.

Makes 8–9 servings

Trimmings from a smoked turkey (see page 146; cut off the tail, wing tips, and any other readily available bony parts; use the neck and giblets if they come with your turkey)
Bones and meat scraps from your freezer, including any stray bits of pork, goose, turkey, duck, chicken, or game birds
1 onion stuck with 2 cloves
1 carrot, sliced
1/2 teaspoon dried thyme
1 bay leaf, crumbled or snipped fine
A few celery leaves
A few black peppercorns
About 6 cups water
4 pounds rutabagas
1 1/2 teaspoons salt
1–1 1/2 teaspoons dried sage
1/4 teaspoon black pepper
1/2 stick (4 tablespoons) butter
1/4 cup all-purpose flour

1. Chop the smoked turkey trimmings and bones into manageable pieces that can be placed in a 3-quart saucepan. Combine with the onion, carrot, thyme, bay leaf, celery leaves, peppercorns, and enough water to just cover. Bring to a simmer and skim. Simmer, partly covered, for about 1 1/2 hours.
2. Cool, uncovered, then strain into a bowl. There should be about 1 quart of liquid. Add water to make this amount, if needed. Chill until you are ready to cook the turnips, at which point you should skim off and reserve 1 1/2 tablespoons of the fat and discard the rest.
3. Peel the rutabagas and cut them into 1- to 2-inch cubes. Combine in a large pot with the skimmed stock, salt, sage, and pepper and simmer, partly covered, for 40–50 minutes, until tender.
4. Drain, reserving the stock. Press the turnips through the medium disc of a food mill into a bowl and reserve.
5. Heat 3 tablespoons of the butter and reserved 1 1/2 tablespoons of fat in the rinsed-out pot in which the rutabagas cooked. Add the flour and stir over moderate heat for a few minutes, until lightly

browned. Add 1 1/2 cups of the reserved stock and stir over moderate heat for about 5 minutes. Add the puréed turnips and stir to blend thoroughly. Taste and season.

6. Scrape the turnips into a buttered heatproof serving casserole and let them rest at room temperature, uncovered, until needed. Or, if preparing the day before serving, cover and refrigerate.

7. *To serve:* Dot the turnips with the remaining tablespoon butter, cover, and bake in a preheated 400° oven for about 25 minutes (a bit longer if they were refrigerated) or until they are hot through.

COARSE CRANBERRY RELISH

Remember to freeze cranberries when they are in season. No fruit or vegetable remains as undaunted by the freezing process—and nothing else but pumpkin is so absurdly seasonal in the market. Cranberries are a wonderful, perky asset to use all year—so stock up. Simply pop the unopened bags of fresh berries in the freezer and keep them as long as you like—at least until the next cranberry season. Don't even defrost them before you use them; a rinse is enough.

Makes about 3 cups

1 pound cranberries (fresh or frozen), rinsed and picked over
1 cup sugar
1/4 cup gin

1. Coarsely chop the berries in a food processor or with a heavy stainless-steel knife, or press through a meat grinder, using the coarse disc. Scrape into a bowl.

2. Stir in the sugar and gin gradually, adding more or less to taste. Cover and refrigerate for at least 1 day before serving.

SMOOTH CRANBERRY-APPLE SAUCE

Don't wait for "turkey time" to serve this. It is a smoothly soft, spoonable sauce (not a relish) that has just the right amount of tartness to complement rich meats, such as duck and pork—whether cured, smoked, or fresh. Scoop any leftover sauce over yogurt and sliced bananas for breakfast. You can prepare this days ahead.

Makes about 3 cups

1 cup sugar
2 cups water
1 pound cranberries (fresh or frozen), rinsed and picked over
1 large tart apple, coarsely chopped (not cored or peeled)
1 teaspoon grated lemon rind

1. In a heavy saucepan combine the sugar and water and bring to a boil, stirring. Cover and boil gently for 4–5 minutes.
2. Add the berries and apple and cook, uncovered, stirring often, until the berries are all popped, about 10 minutes. Add the lemon rind.
3. In 2 batches purée the mixture in a blender or processor until it is very smooth. Rub through a fine sieve to remove all the bits of skin and seeds. Cool, then chill.

ROMAINE, ORANGE, AND WATERCRESS SALAD WITH MUSTARD CREAM DRESSING

We should be grateful that the composed salad vogue of the twenties and thirties is no longer with us. At that time, all manner of fruits, meats, and vegetables were cemented together in aspics and creams, then decorated within an inch of their lives with cheese swirls, pimiento cutouts, and ribbons. For the most part, salads are accorded more respectful treatment at present, in that the components are allowed to maintain recognizable and separate identities.

It is fun, however, to dig back into the past and try to re-create tastes that pleased diners in other eras. Although we might safely dispense with a "Salad Dressing without Oil," in which the author suggests that the oil in an ordinary mayonnaise be replaced with chicken fat, there are some pleasant combinations that deserve revival. Oranges, romaine or endive, and onions appeared often at Thanksgiving dinners with dressings that were richly eggy and/or creamy, rather than tart and light. Although less cloying, thinner, and sharper than the recipe on which it is based (from *The Boston Cooking School Cook Book* by Fanny Merritt Farmer, 1896), the following dressing is creamy and sweet, in the style of dressings popular at that time.

Makes 8–9 servings

DRESSING:

3/4 teaspoon salt
1 1/2 teaspoons sharp mustard
1 1/4 teaspoons sugar
1 tablespoon melted butter, cooled
1 egg, beaten
1/3 cup heavy cream
2 1/2 tablespoons cider vinegar
1/8–1/4 teaspoon black pepper (or use 1/2 teaspoon crushed green peppercorns)

SALAD:

3 or 4 navel oranges
2 small heads romaine lettuce, washed and dried
1 bunch watercress, trimmed, washed, and dried
Green part of 4 scallions, thinly sliced
2 tablespoons orange juice

1. Combine all the dressing ingredients in the order listed above in the top part of a double boiler. Mix well with a whisk. Set over simmering water and stir constantly until the sauce thickens, about 5 minutes.
2. Scrape into a dish and cool. Cover and store in the refrigerator up to a day.
3. Slice the peel and pith from the oranges. Cut them in half lengthwise, then into crosswise slices. Place in a bowl, cover with plastic wrap, and refrigerate until serving time.
4. Cut or tear the romaine into serving pieces. Toss in a serving bowl with the watercress, cover with plastic, and refrigerate until serving time.
5. *To serve:* Arrange the orange slices on the greens and sprinkle the scallions over them. Stir the orange juice into the dressing and taste for seasoning. Pour the dressing over the salad at the table and toss.

BUTTERNUT-MAPLE FANCHONETTES WITH GLACÉED PECANS

The Good Housekeeping Hostess (1904) recommends serving "Pumpkin Fanchonettes" as a "convenient way in which to present an old friend under a new name." To me, "fanchonette" sounded more like a frou-frou turn-of-the-century affectation than a dessert, but I was wrong. Sitting between Nougat and Plum-Cake in a charming French cookbook of the same era (*La Cuisine Pratique* by Albert Maillard) was a recipe for custard-filled bouchées ("mouthfuls," in French) called Fanchonettes. Four more variations came to light in mid-nineteenth-century cookbooks from Britain, the most detailed of which was included in *The Modern Cook* by Queen Victoria's chef, Francatelli. In his version, pastry-lined tartlet molds are filled with different flavors of pastry cream, topped with a decorative piping of meringue, and browned lightly.

There was a time, believe it or not, when maple sugar was the inexpensive, everyday sweetener, and refined white sugar was saved only for company. If you can't find pure maple syrup, or don't care to spend the extra money, this filling is one preparation in which maple-flavored corn syrup blends can be used with surprisingly good results.

The recipe calls for cupcake or muffin tins, rather than individual tartlet pans, because they allow for a softer and more generous helping of custard than the shallower, albeit more elegant, French-type molds. The pastry, incidentally, is not a crisp-flaky one, but a slightly soft cookie-type crust that gives a more uniform texture to the dessert and makes it easier to consume hand-to-mouth style, if you so desire. Bake the fanchonettes as close to dinnertime as convenient, so the crust stays firm. Don't bother to form perfectly tidy edges on the pastry, as the circumference will be piped over with cream. The glacéed pecans are optional but highly recommended, as they are a lovely touch, for texture, flavor, and decoration.

If you prefer to make a dessert that can be finished the day before, you might want to double the recipe for Pumpkin or Squash Flan (page 267)—although there will be some left over. If you're serving eight people who aren't dessert crazy, you can make only one mold. You might make the maple-glacéed pecans and serve them on the side, like candy.

Makes 18 tartlets (about 2½ inches in diameter)

TO MAKE THE MAPLE-GLACÉED PECANS:

36 pecan halves
½ cup pure maple syrup (no blends should be used here)
1 tablespoon dark or light corn syrup

1. Preheat the oven to 325°.
2. Spread the nuts in a pan and bake them for 15 minutes, tossing a few times. Cool. Meanwhile, oil a baking sheet or large piece of aluminum foil, or take out a nonstick baking sheet.
3. In a small, heavy pan combine the maple and corn syrups and bring to a boil over high heat, swirling the pan by the handle. Lower the heat and continue cooking for a few minutes and gently swirling until the syrup is a caramel brown, not a deep, burned color.
4. Working very quickly (and carefully—the syrup is *hot*), stick a small skewer or knife tip into a pecan; rapidly twirl it in the syrup, then drop it onto the prepared sheet. If someone can help you dip, all the better, as the syrup hardens quickly. If it sets too soon, reheat by setting the pan into a larger pan of simmering water. The syrup will soften. Let the nuts cool completely. (There is another, easier method, but the nuts will not be as neatly coated. When the syrup is caramelized, dump in all the nuts, swirl in the syrup to coat them, then pour onto the prepared sheet. With buttered knives or forks, immediately separate the pecans and let them cool. When they are cold, crack apart those nuts that have remained stuck together.)
5. *To store:* Arrange the nuts between layers of waxed paper in an airtight tin, not touching. They will stay fresh and crisp for at least 3 days, if you care to make them ahead of time.

TO MAKE THE CRUST:

1 stick (8 tablespoons) unsalted butter, softened
1 cup confectioners' sugar
2 eggs (large or extra-large)
½ teaspoon vanilla
Scant 2 cups all-purpose flour
½ teaspoon baking powder
¼ teaspoon salt
Softened butter or shortening for the baking tins

1. In the small bowl of an electric mixer, cream the butter until light; gradually beat in the confectioners' sugar. Add the eggs, incorporating them one at a time. Add the vanilla.

(Continued)

2. Sift together into a bowl the flour, baking powder, and salt. Gradually add the creamed ingredients. Turn out onto a sheet of plastic or waxed paper, wrap tightly, and refrigerate for at least 2 hours.
3. Brush 18 muffin or cupcake cups, each about 2½ inches in diameter, with softened butter or shortening. Halve the dough and replace one part in the refrigerator.
4. Roll the dough on a floured surface into a very thin sheet. With a biscuit cutter, pot top, or empty can, cut out circles about 4–4½ inches in diameter. Place them gently in the cups. When all have been cut and placed, press the dough evenly into the molds, shaping it to reach the tops. Repeat with the remaining half of the dough.
5. Chill for at least 30 minutes. Meanwhile, preheat the oven to 375° with a baking sheet (an old one that can afford to be warped) placed on a shelf in the lower third.

TO MAKE THE FILLING:

2 eggs plus 2 egg yolks
1 tablespoon all-purpose flour
2 cups squash or pumpkin purée, fresh-cooked, frozen, or canned (see note below)
1 teaspoon ground coriander (optional)
¼ teaspoon salt
¼ teaspoon grated nutmeg
¾ cup pure maple syrup or maple-flavored syrup
1¾ cups heavy cream, chilled
½ cup milk
¼ cup pecans
4 gingersnaps (or use other dry cookies)

1. Beat the eggs, egg yolks, and flour with a whisk to blend. Beat in the squash purée, optional coriander, salt, and nutmeg. Stir in the maple syrup, ¾ cup of the cream, and the milk.
2. Pulverize the pecans and cookies together in a food processor or blender and divide the crumbs among the pastry cases. Ladle the filling into them to come up to the top, using about ¼ cup for each.

TO BAKE AND SERVE THE FANCHONETTES:

1. Place the tins on the preheated sheet and bake for 20 minutes. Lower the heat to 300° and bake about 15 minutes longer, or until the filling is puffed and slightly bubbling, but not entirely set in the center.

2. Cool 15 minutes on a rack. Carefully unmold the fanchonettes and place them on the rack to cool completely. Do not refrigerate.
3. *To serve:* At serving time, whip the remaining 1 cup cream until it forms fairly firm peaks. Scoop into a pastry bag fitted with a smallish star tip and pipe a generous rim around each tart, then place a large puff of cream in each center. Garnish with two of the maple-glacéed pecans and serve.

NOTE: If you have the time or inclination, freshly cooked butternut squash (or frozen butternut—also called winter squash on some packages) is really the best filling to use for any preparation that calls for squash or pumpkin. It is sweet, smooth, flavorful, and a ravishing vivid orange. To prepare squash for purée, bake it on a sheet or in a baking dish in a 350° oven until it is completely tender (about 1½ hours for a 2-pound squash, which is what would be needed here). Halve the vegetable and cool it a bit, scoop out the seeds, remove the peel and press the squash through the medium disc of a food mill. Cool the purée in a fine sieve so that some of the liquid drips off.

14
Brunch from Alsace—Especially for Bakers

Steep vineyard slopes surround tiny towns, which hold fast to the banks of cascading rivers. Brilliant flowers shine from clay pots set in niches, a fountain bubbles in a tiny square, and a ruined citadel looms in the background like the magician's castle in Swan Lake. You could be in one of many French regions—were it not for the culinary clues. Although the soft-hued, half-timbered houses reveal that the town is probably Alsatian, the drink and food leave no doubt. Eau-de-vie, a potent, crystal-clear brandy, abounds. The dry fresh wines named for their grapes are in evidence everywhere: Riesling, Gewürztraminer, Sylvaner, Pinot Blanc, Muscat, and Pinot Gris (Tokay d'Alsace). Tidy charcuteries beckon from each lane, their display windows overflowing with symmetrically arranged smoked meats, sausages, and rich pâtés—this is foie gras country. And judging from the number of shops, the region of Alsace must have as many bakeries and pastry shops as it does families.

This brunch menu, culled from a glorious visit to Alsace, is not authentic, since brunch does not even exist in France, but the flavors are true to the region. Each dish has been adapted from one tasted there, although the sequence might be considered curious by some of the cooks whose ideas were borrowed. The meal would also probably be considered pathetically insufficient by those chefs, as meals in Alsace are generally enormous.

Although these recipes have been developed for six, with no extra trouble they can be doubled for a large group. If you are feeding twice the number, though, you needn't increase the amount of Walnut-Wheat Bread or Alsatian Fruit Bread.

ALSATIAN BRUNCH FOR SIX (OR TWELVE)

*Mirabelle with White Grape Juice/
*Framboise with Pineapple Juice
*Smoked Meats with Cranberry Cream Sauce
and Horseradish Sauce
*Walnut-Wheat Bread
*Apple Slices in Anise Syrup
Wine: Pinot Gris (Tokay d'Alsace) *or* Pinot Blanc from Alsace
Coffee and Tea
*Alsatian Fruit Bread
Honeys/Butter

MIRABELLE WITH WHITE GRAPE JUICE/ FRAMBOISE WITH PINEAPPLE JUICE

For those unfamiliar with eaux-de-vie ("waters of life"), these brandies are worth a detour. Stunningly aromatic and bone dry (and not to be confused with various sweet, fruit-flavored brandies), they are produced in Alsace, Germany, and Switzerland. There are twenty-odd fruit bases used to create eaux-de-vie in Europe, but only a few are available in the United States. The most common one is kirsch (cherry), followed by framboise (raspberry), mirabelle (plum), and poire (pear). In Alsace the gamut includes such delicacies as holly, gentian, wild sloe, and bilberry brandies.

Eaux-de-vie are also termed "alcool blancs," because they are always colorless, or "white." In fact, all distilled spirits start out clear. Their coloring is imparted from wooden barrels, oxidation, and sometimes the addition of caramel. Fruit brandies are not subjected to aging in wood, as it would alter their fresh bouquet. Instead they usually undergo an aging, mellowing process in glass. As with any good brandies, eaux-de-vie are expensive. There are good reasons for this, not the least of which is the staggering amount of fruit required for their production. When you realize that thirty pounds of raspberries can go into one bottle of framboise, the manufacture deserves comparison with the distillation of rose petals or gardenia blossoms into perfume.

There is no need to provide measured recipes for these drinks. Simply combine ice cubes and framboise or mirabelle to taste in a tall glass, add the juice, and mix. If you would like a somewhat less sweet, less potent concoction, add a little sparkling water, too. Once you've had the pleasure of these brandies, you'll probably be delighted to finish off rich dinners with their clean perfume—chilled, as they drink them in Alsace, or as you would Cognac. In the summertime, nothing makes a more vivid dessert ice.

SMOKED MEATS WITH CRANBERRY CREAM SAUCE AND HORSERADISH SAUCE

At the Restaurant L'Ecurie, a refurbished seventeenth-century stable in Riquewihr, Chef Michel Roelly prepared a splendid, gargantuan meal. The appetizer might have served for the whole, and it is on that that this brunch is based. Marcassin (wild boar less than six months old), cured and smoked, was served with sauces of red currants, tart berries and cream, and horseradish, and was accompanied by a firm, unsweetened walnut bread. Along with this we drank Sporen, the charming wine produced by a blending of several grape varieties from a local vineyard. All other Alsatian wines are pure varietals.

The strict game laws in Alsace make for an area of extraordinary abundance, where deer, boar, hare, grouse, quail, and partridge roam in abundance. During a short period in the fall the deer, which eat the valuable grapes, ready for harvest, are declared "vermin" and are up for grabs. When Chef Roelly takes his daily jeep trip to the forest, he calls forth his pet boars with *"Papa est là! Venez!"* and they trot out to be fed and patted. These, he explained, are his pals. Deeper in the forest, a different territory supplies the subjects for his meals. It could only be in crazily gastronomic France that such elaborate distinctions for wild boar could exist: A wild boar up to the age of six months is called marcassin;

> from six months to a year, a *bête rousse;* between one year and two, a *bête de compagnie;* after two years, a *ragot;* at three years, a wild boar *à son tiers an;* at four years he is a *quartenier;* older, a *porc entier;* and finally, when he is advanced in age, he is given the name of *solitaire* or *ermite* (*Larousse Gastronomique*).

Only the very youngest animals are eaten, as the flesh becomes tough later on. Although the head of older boars is eaten, it is after a complete renovation, involving marinating, stuffing, and considerable garnishing—a transformation not unlike the one that produces head cheese.

Although not a great deal of boar is available commercially in the United States, hunters have said there is plenty to be had all over the country, especially around Cape Canaveral in Florida. Most of us will have to make do with a substitute, which should be easy to find, as marcassin tastes much like slow-cured, heavily smoked domestic pig. But just about any selection of smoked meats will do for this meal.

Makes 6 servings

CRANBERRY SAUCE:

2 cups fresh (or frozen) cranberries, rinsed
1/4 cup water
Big pinch of salt
2–5 tablespoons sugar, depending upon the tartness of the berries
2 tablespoons sour cream
1/3 cup heavy cream

HORSERADISH SAUCE:

1 1/2 tablespoons prepared horseradish
1 1/2 teaspoons Dijon mustard
1/4 teaspoon salt
White pepper
2/3 cup heavy cream
Drops of lemon juice
1 1/2 pounds smoked meats (see note below)

1. *To make the cranberry sauce:* Combine the berries and water in a small, heavy pot. Simmer, covered, stirring often, until the berries are very soft and most are broken up—about 5 minutes. Add sugar to taste, keeping the sauce quite tart, to provide a keen accompaniment to the meat. Cool, cover, and refrigerate for at least 2 hours (or up to several days, if you prefer), then blend together the sour cream and heavy cream and stir into the berry sauce. Either cover and chill up to a day, or serve.
2. *To make the horseradish sauce:* Combine the horseradish, mustard, salt, and pepper to taste in a bowl and mix to blend. In a small bowl beat the cream to form soft peaks (a hand rotary beater works best). Fold the cream into the horseradish mixture, using a rubber spatula to blend. Add drops of lemon and salt to flavor. Cover the bowl with plastic and refrigerate up to 12 hours, or serve at once.
3. *To serve:* Arrange the meats decoratively, overlapping on large plates. Either serve at once, or cover and refrigerate until serving time. Pass the sauces alongside the meat, in separate bowls, so that guests can spoon a dollop of each onto their plates. Serve the Walnut-Wheat Bread (see following recipe), sliced and halved, to make open-faced sandwiches with the meat and sauces.

NOTE: When you choose the smoked meats, you might consider turkey or chicken (see list of mail-order sources, page 353), duck, goose, beef (bundnerfleisch or bresaola), or any of a dozen kinds of smoked ham, particularly Westphalian. If you buy poultry with bones, you'll want to get more than the suggested 1½ pounds. Leftover meat on the bone will keep for about 1 week, wrapped, in the refrigerator. If you have a good selection available, you might want to choose a dark meat (such as duck), a light meat (such as chicken), and some type of ham.

WALNUT-WHEAT BREAD

This is a firm, even-textured, medium-dark whole-wheat bread studded with flavorful walnuts. If you like the taste of juniper, the nuts are subtly enhanced by the addition of this traditional seasoning for wild boar.

Makes 2 loaves (each about 1 1/2 pounds)

1 3/4 cups milk
3 tablespoons butter
1 packet dry yeast
1/3 cup warm (not hot) water
Pinch of sugar
2 teaspoons juniper berries (optional)
1/4 teaspoon black peppercorns
2 tablespoons walnut oil (see list of mail-order sources, page 353)
1 tablespoon salt
1/4 cup coarse, unprocessed bran
2 tablespoons honey
3 cups whole-wheat flour
About 2 1/2–3 cups bread flour (available in specialty stores and many supermarkets)
1 1/2 cups walnuts, coarsely chopped

1. Heat the milk and butter until almost simmering. Pour into a large mixing bowl to cool.
2. Combine the yeast, water, and a pinch of sugar in a cup and mix until the yeast dissolves. Let stand about 10 minutes, until the mixture is very fluffy. If it doesn't puff up, begin again with fresh ingredients.
3. Grind the juniper berries and peppercorns in a spice mill or mortar to a fine texture. Add to the bowl of milk along with the oil, salt, bran, and honey. Gradually stir in the whole-wheat flour.
4. Add the bread flour gradually, stirring it in until the dough becomes too stiff to handle. Spread some of the remaining flour on a work surface and turn out the dough; continue kneading in flour as necessary until you have a firm, bouncy dough that is no longer sticky, which takes about 15 minutes. Whole-grain doughs never become as smooth as white ones; they always remain a bit tacky.
5. Place the dough in an oiled bowl and turn over to coat all sides. Cover the bowl with plastic and let the dough rise until it has more than doubled in bulk, about 1 1/2–2 hours.
6. Divide the dough in half. Cover one piece with plastic. On a very lightly floured surface roll or pat the other piece to form a rectangle 12 × 9 inches. Brush the surface with water and spread half the nuts evenly over it. Using a rolling pin, press the nuts lightly into the dough. Starting from one short end, firmly roll up the dough without stretching it. Pinch closed the seam. Turn the ends under slightly and set the loaf, seam side down, into a greased loaf pan approximately 9 × 5 × 3 inches.

(Continued)

7. Repeat the filling and forming process with the second piece of dough and remaining walnuts. Cover both loaves with a clean towel and let them rise until not quite doubled, about 1–1½ hours.
8. Brush each loaf top very lightly with water, then sprinkle each evenly with about 2 teaspoons flour. With a razor blade or sharp knife cut a gash about ¼ inch deep almost the length of each loaf. Set the pans in a cold oven and turn the heat to 400° (or 375° if you're using oven glass).
9. Bake 35 minutes, or until the loaves are browned and sound hollow when you remove them from the pans and thump the undersides. Set the loaves directly on the oven racks (no pans) and bake for 5–10 minutes longer, until well browned on all sides. Cool completely on a rack.
10. *To serve within a day or two:* Store uncovered, at room temperature. Refresh for about 10 minutes in a 275° oven shortly before serving. *To freeze and reheat:* Wrap the bread airtight, label, and freeze up to 2 months. When ready to use, unwrap the bread, enclose in a clean towel, and let thaw entirely. Warm for about 15 minutes in a 275° oven shortly before serving.

APPLE SLICES IN ANISE SYRUP

Anise is not a traditional Alsatian flavoring for apples. But neither was the Calvados (from Normandy) in which they were glazed when we ate them with the boar in Riquewihr. The apple brandy (Calvados) has been left out, as there already seemed to be plenty of liquor in this early-afternoon meal.

Makes 6 servings

1½ cups water
⅓ cup sugar
¼ teaspoon anise seeds
6 very large Delicious apples (or use Rome Beauties)

1. Combine the water, sugar, and anise seeds in a large deep skillet or wide pot. Bring to a boil, stirring. Simmer gently for 5 minutes.
2. Meanwhile quarter, core, and peel the apples, then halve each quarter lengthwise to make eighths. Drop into the hot syrup.

3. Cover the pan and simmer the apples very gently, stirring often and carefully, to avoid breaking up the slices. Simmer only until the apples are not quite tender. Timing can vary from about 5 to 10 minutes, depending upon the apple variety. Test often to prevent overcooking. The apples should be firm.
4. Turn the apples and syrup into a dish. Cool, then cover and refrigerate, up to several days, if you like.
5. *To serve:* Either spoon the cold apples onto the plates like a relish, or heat them as follows: Drain most of the syrup from the slices and cook the apples in a large skillet with 2 tablespoons butter, tossing gently for a few minutes until the fruit is just heated through. Turn into a warm dish and serve at once.

ALSATIAN FRUIT BREAD

On a misty morning walk through the tiny town of Kayserburg, I picked up a spicy, heavy loaf of a fruit- and nut-laden bread known locally as Bierewecke (pear bread), which has appeared over the years under many aliases. In the oldest versions, a simple cinnamon-scented bread dough barely encloses a bursting quantity of softened, kirsch-soaked dried fruits and a variety of nuts. Madeleine Kamman, the French cooking teacher and author, relates that in the mid-sixteenth century the city of Strasbourg ordered the complete separation of breadmaking and cake baking—just in case you imagined that unions might be a modern invention. The ordinance stated that among many preparations Bierewecke, also known as Hurzelknopf and Schnitzbrod, was to be made exclusively by bread bakers. In many small villages, however, there remained only one shop, in which both cakes and breads were prepared. As a result, some versions of the bread became sweet, rich, and cake-like.

The authentic Bierewecke should be a mass of dried fruits held together with a modicum of bread. Such is the bread that follows. Because the loaf is sweetened only with fruits, and has neither the dessert-y richness of baked-in butter, nor eggs, it is particularly delicious for brunch, coated with sweet butter and topped with a goodly portion of pungent honey.

Makes 3 medium or 2 large loaves

8 ounces dried pears, cut into ½-inch pieces (about 1½ cups)
3 ounces dried figs (preferably Kadota or Calimyrna, not Mission), cut into ½-inch pieces (about ½ cup)
2 ounces pitted prunes, halved (about ⅓ cup)
4 ounces raisins (about 1 cup)
⅓ cup kirsch (or use rum or brandy)
3–4 tablespoons honey
⅔ cup hot water
1 teaspoon grated lemon rind
1 package dry yeast
½ teaspoon sugar
1 cup warm (not hot) water
1 egg
2 teaspoons ground cinnamon
1 teaspoon ground anise seeds
¾ teaspoon salt
About 4 cups all-purpose flour
½ cup walnuts
½ cup unblanched almonds
½ cup hazelnuts (filberts)
1 egg yolk

1. Combine pears, figs, prunes, and raisins (see note below) in a bowl. Stir together the kirsch, honey, hot water, and lemon rind and pour over the fruits. Stir, cover, and let stand overnight, or until most of the liquid is absorbed. Stir occasionally.
2. Mix together the yeast, sugar, and ¼ cup of the warm water in a small bowl. Allow to stand until fluffy, about 10 minutes. If the mixture doesn't puff up, begin again with fresh ingredients.
3. Combine the yeast mixture in a large bowl with the remaining ¾ cup warm water, the egg, cinnamon, anise seeds, and salt. Beat to blend. Gradually add flour until the mixture is too stiff to stir (about 2½–3 cups). Turn out the dough on a floured surface and knead, adding flour as needed, until the dough is smooth and elastic, 5–10 minutes of kneading.
4. Set the dough in a buttered bowl. Turn to coat on all sides, then cover the bowl and let the dough double in bulk, which takes about 1 hour. Meanwhile, set the fruit in a sieve over a bowl to drain. Reserve the syrup. Preheat the oven to 325°.
5. Toast the almonds and hazelnuts in two separate pans in the oven for 15–20 minutes. Rub the hazelnuts around in a coarse wire sieve, protecting your hand with a pot holder, until most of the husks are removed. Discard these. Chop both nuts coarsely.

6. Now comes the messy part: Gradually knead the fruits and nuts into the dough, working on a heavily floured surface. Add flour as needed to keep the dough from sticking. Roll dough to form an even cylinder about 4 inches thick. The cylinder will not be too neat, but lumpy with fruit and nuts.
7. Cut the dough across into 2 or 3 pieces, as you wish. Pinch together the cut ends to seal them. Roll each cylinder with palms of hands to form a loaf about 15 inches long (for 2 large loaves) or 10 inches long (for 3 small ones). Place the loaves well apart on a nonstick baking sheet or one covered with parchment or foil. Cover with a towel and let rise until doubled, about 1½ hours.
8. Preheat the oven to 350°. Whisk together the yolk, reserved fruit syrup, and enough water (about 1 tablespoon) to make an easily brushable wash. Brush the tops and sides of the risen loaves with the wash.
9. Bake 15 minutes, then carefully and thoroughly brush the loaves again with the wash. Turn the baking sheet around in the oven. Bake until the loaves are well browned, about 20–25 minutes for the smaller loaves, 30–35 minutes for the larger ones.
10. Transfer the loaves to a rack to cool completely. Wrap tightly and let ripen at room temperature for 1–6 days before serving. Or you can freeze the loaves, tightly wrapped, up to 3 months.
11. *To serve:* Slice the bread and arrange on a plate. Accompany with butter and honey. The bread is lovely toasted, as well.

NOTE: This recipe has been tested with the soft, moist style of dried fruits that are most commonly available. If you are using hard-dried fruits, simmer them very briefly in water until tenderized, then drain. Then go on to the first step.

15 A Sensuous Birthday Dinner, on the Lavish Side

In our home the birthday celebrant gets to choose the party dinner. This usually results in one of two things: a request for an enormous amount of one or two favorite foods; or a petition for a meal that is particular enough to virtually define the philosophic and sensual aesthetic of the person being fêted. This following dinner of earth flavors and soft textures—raw fish, sweetbreads, Oriental mushrooms, arugula—obviously falls into the latter category. In the "enormous amount" department, I remember a dinner of my very early youth composed of a large bowl of spaghetti and butter and an equally large bowl of whipped cream and colored sprinkles.

A BIRTHDAY DINNER FOR SIX

*Peppered Raw Salmon Appetizer
Wine: Sancerre or California Chardonnay
*Sweetbreads with Chestnuts
*Wild Rice with Dried Mushrooms
Wine: Margaux
*Avocado and Arugula Salad
*Tart Lemon Mousse with Berry Sauce
Wine (for later in the evening, after dinner): Extra-Dry Champagne *or* a Moscato di Pantelleria Spumante

PEPPERED RAW SALMON APPETIZER

A taste for rosy, peppery, naked salmon flesh is not cultivated by all, which is just as well, considering its present cost.

Makes about 6 servings, as an appetizer

1 pound firm, very fresh salmon (preferably a narrow piece, near the tail)
1½ tablespoons drained pink peppercorns or use green peppercorns, if not available (see list of mail-order sources, page 353)
2 teaspoons sugar
1½ tablespoons coarse (kosher) salt
1 tablespoon gin
3 tablespoons unsalted butter
1 tablespoon sour cream
About ½ tablespoon grainy mustard
Finely snipped chives or scallions
6 slices firm homemade or bakery white bread (rectangular or square)

1. Using a sharp boning knife, halve the fish to remove the bone, or have the fish dealer do this. Separate the halves, and with tweezers pull out any small bones that remain.
2. Combine the peppercorns, sugar, and salt in a mortar and crush slightly. Add the gin and mix. Rub this all over the fish, on all sides. Re-sandwich the halves together and place them in a close-fitting, nonmetal dish.
3. Cover the dish with plastic wrap, pressing it tightly against the fish, then draping the excess very loosely over the sides of the dish. Set a plate or bowl on the fish. Into this set 2–3 pounds weight. Refrigerate the salmon for 1–2 days, turning and basting inside and out several times. If you like a stronger flavor and firmer fish, refrigerate for another day.
4. Shortly before serving, remove the weights and plastic. Gently scrape most of the spice mixture off the fish. Set the fish pieces, skin side down, on a carving board and slice them into very thin, even slices. Cut on the bias and free each slice at the skin with a firm cut. Arrange petal-fashion on a plate, cover with plastic, and refrigerate until serving time.
5. Make a mustard butter by creaming the butter until light, beating in the sour cream and mustard to blend, then adding chives to taste. Beat until smooth, pack into a small dish, and chill until serving time, covered.

(Continued)

6. Trim the crusts off the bread, then slice the bread into thirds. Spread on a baking sheet and toast in a 350° oven until golden, about 15 minutes. Arrange the toast fingers on a plate.
7. *To serve:* Set out the salmon, mustard butter, and toast. Supply the guests with small plates and butter knives and let them assemble their own canapés, to taste.

SWEETBREADS WITH CHESTNUTS

This is a lush dish, earth-toned and deep-scented as a Bordeaux. The toffee-colored sauce, full-bodied from the rich stock, is enriched and thickened with puréed chestnuts, which have equal billing with the sweetbreads in this dish, both in terms of quantity and importance.

Although this dish might be considered rich in our time, prior to the nineteenth century it would undoubtedly have been stark and bland to many English and American diners who, for the most part, preferred more complicated tastes and loads of butter, cream, and pastry. Sweetbreads (the pancreas and thymus of a calf), a longtime favorite, were almost always combined with a wide variety of other foods and rich sauces, or were baked in a closed crust, or "coffin."

Never have I encountered a recipe in which the delicate flavor and texture of this organ meat were more ruthlessly obliterated than the one that appears in the transcription of a seventeenth-century manuscript which belonged to Martha Washington (*Martha Washington's Booke of Cookery*, with introduction and commentary by Karen Hess): "To make a pie of seuerall [*sic*] things," you first make your coffin, then fill it with the palates of beef, calves or sheep; cocks' combs; sweetbreads, kidneys, and tongues of veal; sweetbreads and tongues of sheep; chicken, rabbit, or fowl to taste; "hartychoak" bottoms; skirrets (a species of water parsnip) and potatoes (sweet); oranges, citron, dates, suckets (candied fruits or vegetables); biscuit; salt, pepper, mace, and nutmeg; butter; broth made from meat and wine; sugar.

About 200 years later (1824), Mrs. Mary Randolph gave directions in her lovely book, *The Virginia Housewife*, to "make a pie of sweetbreads and oysters" that called for cream, butter, egg yolks, oysters, and sweetbreads in a puff paste. She claimed that it was "the most delicate pie" that might be made, adding that the "sweetbread of veal is the most delicious part, and may be broiled, fried, or dressed in any way, and is always good." Agreed.

Makes 6 servings

2 pairs sweetbreads (about 2 3/4 pounds), fresh or frozen, thawed
1 pound prepared chestnuts, either vacuum-packed, roasted (see list of mail-order sources, page 353) or the frozen Italian variety, or peeled fresh (to make 3 cups peeled nuts)
About 3 cups rich, homemade beef stock or a combination of beef and veal stocks
3/4 stick (6 tablespoons) butter
1 medium carrot, very finely minced (about 1/2 cup)
4–5 medium shallots, very finely minced (1/4 cup)
2–3 small tender celery stalks with leaves, finely minced (1/2 cup)
2 ounces ham, finely minced (about 1/3 cup)
1 tablespoon ground cardamom
1/4 teaspoon black pepper
1/4 teaspoon dried thyme
1/4 cup Port or Madeira
1/4 cup Cognac, Calvados, or brandy

1. Soak the sweetbreads for an hour or two in ice water, changing the water 3 or 4 times. Drain, then gently trim off as much fat and heavy membrane as possible without damaging the sweetbreads.
2. Combine the chestnuts and stock and simmer, covered, until the chestnuts are very tender but not falling apart. Test often for tenderness. Drain and reserve the stock. Cool the chestnuts, set aside 1 cup for the sauce, and cover the remainder with plastic wrap. Refrigerate.
3. Melt 3 tablespoons of the butter in a large casserole or Dutch oven. Add the carrot, shallots, celery, and ham and cook over moderately low heat until softened but not brown, about 10 minutes.
4. Preheat the oven to 300°. Boil the reserved stock to reduce it to 2 cups.
5. Add the cardamom, pepper, thyme, and reserved 1 cup of chestnuts to the vegetable mixture. Stir for a minute or two. Add the Port, Cognac, and reduced stock and bring to a simmer. Gently slip in the sweetbreads and return to a bare simmer. Cover, set in the oven, and bake for 45 minutes. Uncover, and let cool a bit. Then transfer the sweetbreads to a dish to cool completely.

(Continued)

6. Purée the stock-vegetable-chestnut mixture in a processor or blender (in batches) to as fine a texture as possible. Strain through a fine sieve into a heavy saucepan. Boil gently, stirring often, until the sauce is thickened and a rich caramel color. (Mine reached a desirable flavor and texture balance at about 3¼ cups, but timing will vary with the gelatin content of the stock.) Season to taste. Cool, then cover and store in the refrigerator up to 24 hours.
7. Cover the cooled sweetbreads with plastic wrap and set a plate on top. On the plate set 2–3 pounds weight. Store in the refrigerator up to 24 hours. Shortly before the final assembly, trim the sweetbreads and cut them into neat ½-inch slices. Wrap and chill until needed (or slice the sweetbreads just before heating to serve).
8. *To serve:* Preheat the oven to 400°. Heat the sauce to boiling, stirring constantly. Remove from the heat and stir in the remaining 3 tablespoons butter. Pour one third of the sauce into a baking/serving dish large enough to just hold the sweetbreads in a single, overlapping layer. Arrange the meat slices on the sauce, then top with the reserved whole chestnuts. Pour the remaining sauce over all and cover with foil. Bake 20 minutes in the upper third of the oven. Remove the foil and bake about 15 minutes longer, until bubbling hot, basting a few times to keep the sweetbreads covered with the sauce.

WILD RICE WITH DRIED MUSHROOMS

The sensation of eating this earthy, chewy combination may come as close as politely possible to pressing your face to a mound of wet autumn leaves on a rainy afternoon—which may not be a treat for everyone.

Makes 6 servings for lovers of wild rice

About 12 large Chinese or Japanese dried mushrooms (see list of mail-order sources, page 353)
1 tablespoon walnut or peanut oil
1½ cups wild rice (about ½ pound), well picked over and rinsed (see list of mail-order sources, page 353)
2 tablespoons butter

1. Combine the mushrooms in a bowl with the oil and warm water to cover. Soak for about 1/2 hour. Strain the soaking liquid through several layers of fine-mesh cotton cheesecloth to be sure no sand remains. Reserve the liquid.
2. Add enough water to the mushroom liquid to make 3 cups. Combine in a heavy pot with the rice and bring to a full boil, stirring. Cover the pot and cook over lowest heat until the rice is tender but still firm. Time can vary considerably, so begin tasting after about 35 minutes—although it may take longer than an hour. Add liquid, if needed. Drain off the liquid when rice is tender.
3. Cut stems from mushrooms (you can save them to flavor soups). Quarter the caps. Combine in a baking/serving dish with the cooked rice, butter, and salt and pepper to taste. Mix well and let cool. If you wish to make the rice the day before serving, cover the dish with foil and refrigerate.
4. *To serve:* Cover the dish with foil, if you have not already done so. Set in the upper third of a preheated 400° oven with the sweetbreads and bake for 20 minutes, covered. Remove the foil, stir the rice gently, and bake about 15 minutes longer, until hot.

AVOCADO AND ARUGULA SALAD

For most meals it is desirable to offer a contrast of textures and colors. Not so this birthday special, in which tender tendencies predominate. In keeping with the softness, a salad without crispness is suitable: smooth avocado, crunchless arugula, and a mellow dressing without bite. Assemble about one hour before serving.

Makes 6 servings

3 tablespoons balsamic vinegar (a deep brown, aged white wine vinegar available in many specialty shops, or see list of mail-order sources, page 353)
1 tablespoon hazelnut oil (available in specialty shops, or see list of mail-order sources, page 353)
1/4 cup olive oil
1/2 teaspoon coarse (kosher) salt
2 large, ripe avocados, cut into 1/2-inch dice
2 bunches arugula, stems trimmed, gently washed, thoroughly dried
1–2 tablespoons snipped fresh chives

1. Combine the vinegar, oils, and salt in a jar; cover and shake to mix. Pour over the diced avocados and mix gingerly with a rubber spatula to coat each piece. Cover with plastic and leave at room temperature until serving time, preferably no more than an hour.
2. *To serve:* Spread the arugula on a serving platter; pour the avocados and dressing over the arugula and sprinkle with chives.

NOTE: If ingredients for this salad are difficult to find, you might serve a simple salad of Boston lettuce and endive, dressed with lemon juice, olive oil, and a bit of chives or scallion.

TART LEMON MOUSSE WITH BERRY SAUCE

Although this mousse is extremely soft and billowy, pale and fragile to behold, its lemon flavor is defined, bracing.

Makes 6 servings

MOUSSE:
1 envelope unflavored gelatin
1/4 cup cold water
2 or 3 large lemons, as needed
3/4 cup sugar
4 egg whites
Pinch of salt
1 cup heavy cream (preferably not ultrapasteurized)

SAUCE/DECORATION:
1 package (10 ounces) quick-thaw raspberries in syrup, thawed
1 pint fresh strawberries, rinsed and hulled (reserve 4 for decoration)
About 2 tablespoons sugar
About 3 tablespoons framboise (or use kirsch)
Optional: transparent-thin slivers of candied angelica (an aromatic root) or candied mint leaves (see list of mail-order sources, page 353, for both)

1. Prepare a 4-cup straight-sided glass dish or soufflé dish by pinning a collar of folded wax paper around it to extend at least 2 inches above the rim.
2. In a small saucepan combine the gelatin and cold water and let stand for at least 5 minutes. Grate the rind off 2 lemons and squeeze and strain the juice; there should be about 1 1/2 tablespoons rind and

2/3 cup juice. If there is not enough, grate and squeeze another lemon to make that amount.

3. Stir the gelatin mixture over low heat until the gelatin dissolves. Add 1/2 cup sugar and stir until it dissolves. Remove the pan from the heat and stir in the rind and juice. Set the saucepan in a bowl of ice water and stir often until the gelatin is almost but not quite set. It will have the consistency of a soft jelly. Remove from the ice and stir vigorously.

4. Immediately beat the egg whites and salt to form very soft peaks. Beat in 1/4 cup sugar, 1 tablespoon at a time, until the whites are firm and glossy, not dry and stiff. Whip the cream until it mounds gently. Do not beat stiff or the mousse will be greasy, not soft and creamy.

5. Fold the gelatin mixture thoroughly into the egg whites, using a rubber spatula. Gently fold in the whipped cream. Turn the mousse into the prepared mold and chill for at least 4 hours.

6. Make a sauce by combining the berries and their syrup, 2 tablespoons sugar, and 2 tablespoons framboise and allow to macerate for at least 1/2 hour. Purée to a fine texture in a processor or blender, then press through a fine sieve. Taste and add sugar and framboise. Cover and chill until serving time.

7. *To serve:* Gently pull the waxed paper off the mousse. Halve the reserved strawberries lengthwise and press them gently, flat side down, onto the mousse. Decorate with the angelica "leaves" or the mint. Pour a few spoonfuls of the sauce onto each of your 6 prettiest dessert plates. Divide the mousse among the plates. Serve additional sauce in a small pitcher.

16
An Aside on the Subject of Grains

Grain Side Dishes for All Manner of Meals

Grains as a main subject deserve volumes. When considered simply as a lovely way of filling out a meal, complementing a sharp sauce, creating a textural background for a rich stew, a chapter will do. Treated kindly from the outset, most cereals are remarkably amenable to the double cooking process required for made-ahead dishes. And since few meals do not benefit fron the inclusion of one of these nourishing plants, a small selection of grain dishes follows, from which choices can be made, as needed.

NOTE: Although specific timing and temperature recommendations are given in each recipe, there will be times when they will not coordinate with other dishes you are heating for the same meal. If the temperature at which the main course is heating is 25° or 50° higher than the one specified for the grain, bake the grain 5 or 10 minutes less. If the temperature required for the entrée is 25° or 50° lower, add 5 or 10 minutes to the heating time for the grain.

PERFECT WHITE RICE

Among the great foods of the earth, elegant, subtle grains of polished white rice have sustained a large part of the world's population for longer than the recording of recipes. The following Oriental cooking method takes a bit longer than some others, but it ensures firm, separate grains when freshly cooked or when reheated.

4–5 servings	*6–8 servings*	
1 1/2 cups	**2 1/4 cups**	**long-grain white rice**
2 1/2 cups	**3 1/2 cups**	**water**
3/4 teaspoon	**1 teaspoon**	**salt**
1 tablespoon	**2 tablespoons**	**butter**

1. Combine the rice, water, and salt in a heavy saucepan and bring to a full, rolling boil over high heat, stirring occasionally. Turn heat to its lowest point, then cover the pan.
2. Cook 20 minutes. Remove the pan from the heat and let stand, covered, for 20 minutes longer. With a rubber spatula, gently mix in the butter.
3. Spread the rice in a well-buttered, shallow baking/serving dish and let cool. Cover with foil and store in the refrigerator for up to 1 1/2 days.
4. *To serve:* Set the foil-covered dish in a cold oven and turn the heat to 375°. Bake until hot throughout, about 35 minutes, fluffing the rice once halfway through heating to redistribute the grains.

SAFFRON RICE

When a slightly aromatic, more assertive flavor is desirable, season long-grain rice with saffron, underscored very delicately by garlic and thyme.

4–5 servings	*6–8 servings*	
1 1/2 cups	**2 1/4 cups**	**long-grain white rice**
2 1/2 cups	**3 1/2 cups**	**water**
3/4 teaspoon	**1 teaspoon**	**salt**
Large pinch	**2 large pinches**	**saffron threads, crumbled**
1/4 teaspoon	**1/2 teaspoon**	**dried thyme**
1 medium	**1 large**	**garlic clove, peeled and halved**
1 tablespoon	**2 tablespoons**	**butter or olive oil**

1. Combine the rice, water, and salt in a heavy saucepan. Bring to a full, rolling boil over high heat, stirring occasionally. Turn the heat to its lowest point. Stir in the saffron, thyme, and garlic.

(Continued)

2. Cover and cook 20 minutes. Remove from the heat and let stand, covered, for 20 minutes longer. With a rubber spatula, gently mix in the butter or olive oil, separating the grains.
3. Spread in a well-buttered shallow baking/serving dish and let cool. Cover with foil and store in the refrigerator up to 1 1/2 days.
4. *To serve:* Set the foil-covered dish in a cold oven and turn the oven to 375°. Bake for about 35 minutes, fluffing the rice once halfway through the heating time to redistribute the grains.

BROWN RICE

With some of the bran intact, brown rice is the most nutritious, firm textured, and flavorful form of the grain. The initial heating of the grains produces fluffy, cream-beige rice, with no stickiness.

4 servings	*6 servings*	
1 1/4 cups	**2 cups**	**long-grain brown rice**
2 cups	**3 cups**	**water**
1/2 teaspoon	**3/4 teaspoon**	**salt**
1 tablespoon	**2 tablespoons**	**butter**

1. In a heavy saucepan stir the rice over moderate heat until it is lightly browned, about 5 minutes. It will crack and pop around the pan as you stir for the last few minutes.
2. Stir in the water, salt, and butter and bring to a rolling boil. Turn the heat to its lowest point, cover the pot, and cook for 35 minutes. Remove the pot from the heat and let stand, covered, for 20 minutes.
3. Turn the rice into a well-buttered, shallow baking/serving dish and cool. Cover with foil and store in the refrigerator up to 1 1/2 days.
4. *To serve:* Set the foil-covered dish in a cold oven and turn the heat to 375°. Bake for about 35 minutes, fluffing the rice once halfway through the heating time to redistribute the grains.

WILD RICE

Wild rice is not a sauce sopper-upper, nor a retiring flavor that obediently blends in with its plate-mates. It has an assertive, earthy taste and firm texture that match its dark, wild color. Serve it "straight" to wild rice fans and mix half-and-half with white or brown rice for less ardent admirers.

Makes 6–8 servings

1½ cups wild rice (about ½ pound), well picked over and rinsed (see list of mail-order sources, page 353)
3 cups water or light meat broth
2 tablespoons butter (or use walnut, hazelnut, or olive oil)

1. Combine the rice and liquid in a heavy saucepan and bring to a rolling boil over high heat, stirring. Turn the heat to its lowest point and cover the pot.
2. Cook until the rice is firm-tender, which can vary from 30 minutes to upwards of an hour, so taste often. Do not let the grains get mushy. Add liquid, as necessary.
3. When the rice is cooked, drain off any liquid if it remains. Add the butter and mix gently with a rubber spatula. Season with salt and plenty of black pepper.
4. Spread in a well-buttered shallow baking/serving dish and let cool. Cover with foil and store in the refrigerator up to 1½ days.
5. *To serve:* Set the foil-covered dish in a cold oven. Turn the heat to 400° and bake for 25 minutes. Remove the foil, toss the grains, and bake about 10 minutes longer, or until hot through.

MILLET

It is difficult to understand why this pleasantly firm, fluffy, small-size grain is so widely ignored in this country. The tiny seeds, available in health-food stores, puff up slightly when toasted and have a delightful flavor reminiscent of both rice and popcorn. The simplicity of preparation and delicate taste make this a fine foil for all kinds of sauced and highly seasoned dishes.

4–5 servings	*7–8 servings*	
1¼ cups	**2 cups**	**hulled millet seeds**
2½ cups	**3¾ cups**	**boiling water**
½ teaspoon	**1 teaspoon**	**salt**
1 tablespoon	**2 tablespoons**	**butter**

1. In a heavy saucepan stir the millet over moderate heat until the seeds are golden brown. They'll crackle and pop lightly for the last few minutes. If it is necessary to remove them from the heat a few times to prevent burning, do so, but do allow for a complete browning. Otherwise the grains will be rigid and coarse instead of light and fluffy.
2. Turn the heat to its lowest point and stir in the boiling water all at once. Add the salt and butter, cover, and cook 20 minutes. Remove from the heat and let stand, covered, 20 minutes longer.
3. Fluff into a well-buttered baking/serving dish and let cool. Cover with foil and refrigerate up to 1½ days.
4. *To serve:* Set the dish in a cold oven, with the foil tightly covering it. Turn the heat to 375° and heat for 35–40 minutes, stirring once halfway through the baking time to redistribute the grains.

KASHA

In its whole-grain form buckwheat has long been a mainstay in the cuisines of Russia, Poland, Czechoslovakia, Hungary, Romania, Bulgaria, Yugoslavia, and parts of eastern Germany and northern France. The word *kasha,* translated as porridge from Slavic languages, has come to mean roasted buckwheat grains in our usage. When buckwheat kernels are harvested, the dark brown hulls are removed, leaving the creamy ivory groat. While the raw, pale form is marketed in some areas of the country, most groats are roasted and labeled kasha. It is available in many supermarkets and health-food stores, or you can order it from a mail-order source (see page 353). Although you could use the medium-granulation kasha, the whole form is preferable for reheating.

4 servings	*6–8 servings*	
1 1/4 cups	**2 cups**	**whole kasha**
1 medium or large	**1 extra-large or jumbo**	**egg, beaten**
2 cups	**3 1/4 cups**	**boiling water or broth**
1/2 teaspoon	**1 teaspoon**	**salt**
2 cloves	**2–3 cloves**	**garlic, unpeeled (optional)**
1 tablespoon	**2 tablespoons**	**fat (either butter or bacon, goose, duck, or chicken fat)**

1. Combine the kasha and egg in a bowl and stir to moisten all the grains thoroughly. Heat a heavy saucepan (preferably one with a nonstick surface) and scrape in the mixture. Stir over moderate heat until all the grains are separated and dried.
2. Add the boiling liquid, salt, and garlic cloves and bring to a boil. Turn the heat to its lowest point, cover the pot, and cook 15 minutes. Remove from the heat and let stand 15 minutes longer.
3. Remove the garlic cloves. Add the fat. Fluff the kasha into a buttered or greased shallow baking/serving dish and season with salt and pepper. Let cool, then cover with foil and store in the refrigerator up to 1 1/2 days.
4. *To serve:* Set the foil-covered dish in a cold oven. Turn the heat to 375° and bake for about 30 minutes, fluffing once during heating to redistribute the grains.

CRACKED WHEAT (BULGUR, WHEAT PILAF)

Not surprisingly, when the whole-wheat kernel is cracked, it is called cracked wheat. Most often, however, cracked wheat refers to a partly cooked, then dried cracked wheat, also called bulgur, burgul, and sometimes wheat pilaf. It is sold in many supermarkets and health-food stores. Check the ingredients on the box or bag to be sure you're paying for wheat only; no seasonings are needed. For cooked dishes, such as the following recipe, you'll want the coarse or medium granulation, not the fine.

4 servings	*6 servings*	
1 1/2 tablespoons	**2 1/2 tablespoons**	**butter or chicken fat**
1 tiny	**1 small**	**onion, finely minced**
1 1/4 cups	**2 cups**	**medium- or coarse-grained cracked wheat**
1/2 teaspoon	**3/4 teaspoon**	**salt (if broth is not salted)**
2 cups	**3 1/4 cups**	**chicken broth or water**

1. Melt the butter in a heavy saucepan and stir in the onion. When softened slightly, stir in the cracked wheat and stir for a few minutes over moderate heat to brown the grain slightly.
2. Add the salt and liquid and bring to a boil. Turn the heat to its lowest point, cover the pot, and cook for 15 minutes. Remove from the heat and let stand 15 minutes longer.
3. Scrape into a buttered, shallow baking/serving dish and let cool. Cover with foil and store in the refrigerator up to 1 1/2 days.
4. *To serve:* Set the foil-covered dish in a cold oven. Turn the heat to 375° and bake for about 35 minutes, stirring once to redistribute the grains.

Winter

17
A Picnic Lunch for Winter Holidays

A large, informal meal, a picnic in spirit, is the easiest type to manage during the holidays. The buffet service allows for an expandable guest list, which can be most useful at this time of year when long-lost friends suddenly appear, and when kids of all ages are home from school. The lunchtime hour encourages the inclusion of small children, who can make a vacation-time festivity particularly lively.

The suggested meal works well for Christmas, New Year's Day, or any wintry morning or afternoon party. The dishes will generously feed about a dozen people, with the exception of the ham, which could take care of more. Familiarity with your guests should help determine just how much you'll really need for this open-ended kind of meal.

A PICNIC LUNCH FOR WINTER HOLIDAYS, FOR TWELVE

Sliced Fresh Pineapple and Oranges
*Country Ham
*Deviled Eggs
*Creamy Watercress and Pea Purée
*Christmas Rye Bread, Swedish Style/Sweet Butter
Hard Cider/Selection of Beers
(the above arranged on the main serving table)
*Hot Apple Cider/*Mocha Punch
*Filbert-Glacéed Fruit Biscuits
*Spicy Cut-Out Cookies
A Bowl of Nuts in the Shell
(the above set out on a side serving table)

COUNTRY HAM

For this special holiday occasion, enjoy a richly flavored, old-fashioned country ham from one of the many smokehouses in this country. The various brands of country hams have little in common except for the fact that they are slow-cured and smoked. Broadly considered, there are two distinct kinds of ham-curing procedures, which produce different tastes and textures. The dry-cured (salt-rubbed or salt-packed) aged hams, mostly from the South, are tangy-savory, have an abundance of translucent fat, and are very firm-fleshed and extremely salty. They can be stored indefinitely without refrigeration, as their moisture content is too low for the survival of microorganisms. The brine-cured smoked hams, which often hail from the Northeast, although they are produced in other areas, are usually sweeter and more tender, and require refrigeration for storage. They do not need soaking, as do the dry-cured hams. They take particularly well to glazes of all kinds, and are delicious either hot or cold.

Hams are available by mail, in sizes ranging from 10 to 16 pounds. Allow 2 weeks for delivery. Most smokehouses also offer completely cooked, ready-to-eat hams, if you prefer to have your *fête* even more *accomplie* beforehand. If you do not have a source for hams, there are suggestions in the mail-order listing, page 353.

TO PREPARE A DRY-CURED COUNTRY HAM:

1. Whatever the size of your ham, leave plenty of time for soaking it, and make sure that you have a vessel large enough to soak it in. Country hams are hefty creatures, and their shank bones are often left in, which makes them even more unwieldy. Cut off the shank and save it for soup if it won't be coaxed into your largest clam/lobster pot or preserving kettle. At any rate, unless you like terribly salty ham, soak it in cold water to cover for 2–3 days (3 days for the Smithfield and Virginia cures), changing the water 3–4 times during the soaking period. Scrub off any spice coating or the harmless mold that remains, using a stiff brush.

2. Put the ham in the pot with water to cover and bring to a bare simmer. Maintain at this level and cook for about 20 minutes per pound. Pierce the meat to check its tenderness, but do not expect it to become as soft as the tenderized or supermarket varieties.

3. When the ham has cooked sufficiently, set it on a cutting surface and cool it enough to be able to handle it. Carefully cut off the rind. Slice off as much fat as you care to but leave a minimum of 1/4–1/2 inch intact. Reserve, skim, and freeze as much of the stock as will fit into your freezer for use in soups and stews.
4. If you wish to glaze the ham, place it fat side up in a roasting pan on a rack. Rub with a mixture of 1 1/2 tablespoons brown sugar, 1 teaspoon dry mustard, and 1 teaspoon cider vinegar. Place the ham in a preheated 400° oven and bake until well browned, about 15–20 minutes.
5. *To store and serve:* When the ham has cooled completely, you can cover it loosely and leave at room temperature for up to 24 hours. Or you can refrigerate it, covered, for weeks. Let the meat return to room temperature before serving. At serving time, carve the ham into extremely thin slices and arrange on a platter. Sliced, the ham can remain at room temperature for 3–4 hours.

TO PREPARE A BRINE-CURED COUNTRY HAM:
1. Most hams in this category simply require baking. They should be cooked, fat side up, at 325° for about 20 minutes per pound. If the rind has not been removed, slice it off carefully about 20 minutes before you estimate that the ham should be finished. Rub with a mixture of 1 1/2 tablespoons brown sugar, 1 teaspoon dry mustard, and 1 teaspoon cider vinegar to form a light coating. Turn heat to 400° and bake about 20 minutes longer. If the rind has already been removed, simply cook the estimated time.
2. *To store and serve:* Serve the ham hot, warm, or at room temperature. You can let it cool completely, then cover it loosely and let stand at room temperature for up to 4 hours. Sliced, the ham can remain at room temperature up to 2 hours. Or you can refrigerate it, covered, for about 1 week.

DEVILED EGGS

Although this may appear to be a large amount of nibbles for a dozen guests, the eggs move quickly. Children enjoy them, as a rule. They're delicious the next day, even if you overestimate.

Makes 32 halves

16 eggs
2 tablespoons mustard
6 tablespoons (3/4 stick) butter
About 1 tablespoon very finely minced fresh dill (or use 1/2 teaspoon dried dillweed)
2 teaspoons very finely minced scallion (white part only)
1/4 teaspoon white pepper
About 2 teaspoons lemon juice
GARNISH: **Tiny dill sprigs**

1. Hard-cook the eggs in your favorite way, or as follows: Place the eggs in a large, *heavy* pot with water to cover by an inch or more. Bring to a boil, cover, and remove from the heat. Let stand, covered, for 18 minutes. Drain the eggs and place them in a large bowl of ice water. Tap each egg gently to crack the shell all over. Return to the ice water and let cool through. Eggs can be refrigerated for several hours, until you need them.
2. Drain and peel the eggs carefully. Halve them lengthwise. Shave a very thin sliver off the bottom of each white half, so it won't tip over on the serving dish.
3. Press the yolks through the fine disc of a food mill or a sieve. Combine the mustard, butter, dill, scallion, pepper, lemon juice, and salt to taste with the yolks and beat well to blend. Season to taste.
4. Fit a pastry tube with a large star tip and pipe the yolk mixture into the hollows of the whites. Arrange the eggs in a deep serving dish. Tuck a tiny sprig of dill in each. Cover the dish with plastic wrap and store in the refrigerator up to 24 hours.
5. *To serve:* Let stand at room temperature, uncovered, for about 1/2 hour before serving.

CREAMY WATERCRESS AND PEA PURÉE

This creamy purée, meant to be used almost as a sauce, complements the saltiness and compact texture of the aged ham. Prepare the day that you'll serve the ham.

Makes about 12 servings

2 cups water
6 packages (10 ounces each) frozen green peas
3/4 cup thinly sliced scallions
6 tablespoons (3/4 stick) butter
6 bunches watercress, rinsed, heavy stems removed
About 1 1/2 cups sour cream

1. In a large pot combine the water and peas and cook over highest heat until the peas are broken apart and the water boils. Reduce the heat, cover the pot, and simmer for 5 minutes, or until the peas are tender.

2. Stir the scallions in 3 tablespoons of the butter in a very large skillet over moderate heat until softened. Add the watercress, then turn the heat to high and cook, covered, for 4 to 5 minutes, or until the cress is soft and most of the liquid has evaporated, stirring several times.

3. Drain the peas. Combine them with the scallion-cress mixture and 1 cup sour cream. In batches, whirl to a very fine purée in a blender or food processor. Force through the fine disc of a food mill. Add 1/2 cup sour cream or to taste. Season with salt and pepper and let cool completely. Cover with plastic. Let remain at room temperature until ready to heat.

4. *To serve:* Melt the remaining 3 tablespoons butter in a very large skillet. Stir in the purée and cook over low heat until it is hot through. Scrape into a heated serving dish.

CHRISTMAS RYE BREAD, SWEDISH STYLE

The following recipe is an adaptation of the bread served in Sweden for the Christmas feast. Traditionally, after the Christmas ham has been cooked, the water in which it was poached is maintained at just under a simmer while each member of the family dunks in a slice of the good brown loaf. The fairly heavy bread, flavored with dark beer, is surprisingly fine textured. The combination of orange, fennel seeds, and rye is typically Scandinavian, and it perfumes the kitchen with the pleasantest of baking aromas.

The full, complex flavor blooms if you allow this bread to mellow for a day or two before serving. Refresh in a 275° oven for about 15 minutes shortly before serving. Or, if you prefer, you can freeze the bread for several months. To serve, let the bread reach room temperature, wrapped, then heat briefly, minus wrapping, in a very low oven.

Makes 2 loaves (each about 1 pound 10 ounces)

3 tablespoons butter
20 ounces dark beer (2 1/2 cups)
1 tablespoon salt
1/4 cup molasses
2 packets dry yeast
1/4 cup warm water
1 teaspoon sugar
1 1/2 tablespoons grated orange rind
1/2 teaspoon anise seeds
1 teaspoon caraway seeds
1 teaspoon fennel seeds
1 1/2 cups pumpernickel flour (also called rye meal; see list of mail-order sources, page 353)
1 1/2 cups rye flour (see list of mail-order sources, page 353)
About 4 1/4 cups bread flour (available in specialty stores and many supermarkets)
Cornmeal for sprinkling the pan
3 tablespoons hot water
About 1/2 tablespoon honey

1. In a saucepan heat the butter, dark beer, salt, and molasses until the butter begins to melt. Pour into a large bowl and let cool to lukewarm.

2. Combine the yeast, warm water, and sugar in a cup and stir; let stand until the mixture is fluffy, about 5 minutes. If the yeast does not puff up, begin again with fresh ingredients. Add the yeast to the cooled beer mixture. Add the orange rind. Lightly crush the anise, caraway, and fennel seeds in a mortar, then add them to the liquid. Stir in the pumpernickel and rye flours. Gradually mix in 3 cups bread flour.

3. Spread the remaining bread flour on a kneading surface. Drop the dough into the center and knead in as much flour as you can to make a firm dough. Knead as long as necessary to make a dough that is bouncy and no longer sticks to your hands, about 5–8 minutes. Remember that whole-grain doughs never become as smooth as white ones; they remain a bit tacky.

4. Form the dough into a ball and place it in a large buttered bowl. Turn to coat all sides. Cover the bowl with plastic and let the dough rise (preferably at about 75–80°) until it has doubled in bulk, approximately 1½ hours.

5. Punch down the dough and divide it into 2 equal parts. Form each piece into a ball, pinching together the dough on the bottom until you have a neat, tight shape. Place each ball, pinched side down, in a 9-inch round cake pan sprinkled with cornmeal. Cover the dough with a towel and let the loaves rise until *not quite* doubled (three-quarters proof), about 1 hour.

6. Preheat the oven to 425°. With a single-edged razor or sharp knife slash a cross about ¼-inch deep in the center of each loaf, holding the blade almost parallel to the surface.

7. Set the pans in the center of the oven and bake 10 minutes. Lower the heat to 350° and bake 25 minutes longer. Mix the honey and hot water and brush evenly over each loaf to cover completely. Switch the pan positions. Bake 25 minutes longer. Remove from the pans and set on the oven rack. Bake until nicely browned and hollow sounding when you thump the undersides, about 5–10 minutes. Cool on a rack.

8. *To serve:* Cut the loaf in half, then slice each half crosswise.

HOT APPLE CIDER

The amount of cider you'll need will depend upon the number of children and teetotalers you invite. For variety, mix the apple with cranberry juice and add a few peppercorns—but not for children, who are often sensitive to spices with "heat."

Makes about 6 cups

6 cups unfiltered apple cider
1/4 cup maple syrup
1 cinnamon stick, broken up
1/2 teaspoon whole allspice
1/4 teaspoon whole cloves

Simmer all the ingredients, covered, for 5 minutes. Strain into a hot serving bowl or pitcher and serve hot, in cups. Or assemble the drink, then reheat when needed.

MOCHA PUNCH

Strong and brisk, unspiced and only slightly sweetened, this brew serves as a foil for the fragrant Filbert-Glacéed Fruit Biscuits and Spicy Cut-Out Cookies (for which recipes follow). If you serve the punch without the cookies alongside, grind a few cardamom seeds and a bit of cinnamon stick with the coffee beans, or add a small amount of powdered spices to ground coffee when you brew it.

Makes about 6 1/2 cups

1/4 cup sugar
3 cups freshly brewed dark-roast coffee or espresso
1 1/2 cups milk
1 cup light cream or half-and-half
2/3 cup Cognac, Armagnac, or brandy
1/3 cup rum

Stir the sugar into the coffee and let cool. Add the remaining ingredients and chill for several hours or more before serving. Taste and adjust flavors when the punch has chilled several hours.

FILBERT-GLACÉED FRUIT BISCUITS

These crunchy biscuits (the word *biscuit* is French; it means twice-cooked or baked) are prettily flecked with candied fruit bits.

Makes about 32

$^3/_4$ cup hazelnuts (filberts)
$^2/_3$ cup mixed glacéed fruits (one 4-ounce container)
$2^1/_4$ cups sifted flour
$2^1/_2$ teaspoons baking powder
$^1/_2$ teaspoon salt
1 stick (8 tablespoons) unsalted butter, softened
$^2/_3$ cup plus 1 tablespoon sugar
$^1/_2$ teaspoon almond extract
1 teaspoon orange extract
2 eggs

1. Preheat the oven to 325°. Spread the nuts in a pan and bake about 15 minutes, until the husks are cracked open. Place the nuts in a coarse sieve and rub around, protecting your hands with a pot holder, until most of the husks are removed. Let the nuts cool completely, then pick them out of the sieve and chop coarsely.
2. Turn the oven to 375°. Empty the glacéed fruits into a sieve and rinse briefly with boiling water. Spread the fruits on a paper towel to dry. Sift the flour, baking powder, and salt into a bowl. Remove 2 tablespoons and toss them with the fruits; chop finely.
3. In the small or medium bowl of an electric mixer beat the butter until pale. Gradually beat in the $^2/_3$ cup sugar, scraping down the sides as needed. Add the almond and orange extracts. Beat in the eggs, one at a time. On lowest speed incorporate about two thirds of the flour. Remove the bowl from the stand and stir in the remaining flour; add the nuts and fruit and mix well with a rubber spatula.
4. Smooth aluminum foil over a large baking sheet to cover it completely. Spoon lumps of the batter across the sheet to form 2 strips that run from one long side to the other and are equidistant from both short ends and from each other. Shape the batter with your hands or a spatula into even rectangles, each about 9 inches long and 3 inches wide. Smooth with a wet spatula, spreading the batter to cover nuts that protrude through the surface. Sprinkle the loaves with the 1 tablespoon sugar.
5. Bake in the upper third of the oven until almost firm and colored a pale golden brown, about 15–20 minutes. The loaves should *not* be baked until browned.

(Continued)

6. Gently pull the foil and loaves off the sheet onto the counter and let stand 10 minutes. Remove the loaves very gently from the foil, place them on a rack, and cool about 20 minutes. Lower the oven temperature to 300°.
7. Set the loaves on a cutting board. Using a sharp serrated bread knife, and cutting with a slow, sawing motion, cut each loaf across on the bias into about 16 slices. Place the slices flat on the baking sheet, very close together (be careful, they're fragile), and bake for about 10–15 minutes on each side, until the slices are very lightly golden and dried out.
8. Place the biscuits gently on a rack and cool completely. Pack airtight for at least 1 day before serving.

SPICY CUT-OUT COOKIES

This recipe combines Christmas-y elements from cookies of several nations but doesn't represent any single country: It has the dark complex spiciness of German cookies, the butteriness of Scandinavian cookies, and the charm of *any* cookies that can be cut into appealing shapes and iced. Crisp, slightly flaky, brown sugary, they keep very well. I prefer to ice them the day I serve them, or a day before that, as the more complicated decorations dry and crack off if kept longer.

Makes about 5 dozen 2½-inch cookies

DOUGH:
3 cups all-purpose flour
½ teaspoon baking powder
¼ teaspoon baking soda
2 teaspoons ground cinnamon
1 teaspoon ground ginger
2 teaspoons ground coriander
¼ teaspoon black pepper
½ teaspoon salt
½ teaspoon ground mace
1¾ sticks (14 tablespoons) unsalted butter, softened
½ cup dark brown sugar
¼ cup molasses
½ cup white sugar
1 egg

GLAZE AND ICING:
Milk
1 egg white
About 1½ cups confectioners' sugar
Pinch of salt
⅛ teaspoon anise or lemon extract

1. Sift together the flour, baking powder, baking soda, cinnamon, ginger, coriander, pepper, salt, and mace into a bowl.
2. In the smaller bowl of an electric mixer beat the butter until it is light. Gradually beat in the brown sugar, first squeezing it through your fingers to remove any lumps. Beat in the molasses and white sugar. Add the egg and beat well. Gradually add half the flour mixture on lowest speed. Stir in the remainder with a wooden spoon.
3. Form the dough into a block, wrap it in plastic, and refrigerate for 1–2 days.
4. Preheat the oven to 375°. Cut off one third of the dough and refrigerate the remainder. Place on a large sheet of well-floured waxed paper. Sprinkle the dough with flour and place another sheet of waxed paper on it, then roll it out to form a thin sheet about 12 × 9 inches. Cut the dough into circles using a 2½-inch round cutter or into fancy shapes (but not too elaborate—the dough is soft). Reroll the scraps, cut more cookies, and place all the cookies on a nonstick or parchment-covered or greased baking sheet. Brush each cookie with milk, using a soft brush.
5. Bake the cookies in the center of the oven for about 10 minutes, or until the rims are lightly browned. Cool completely on a rack.
6. Repeat the entire process twice with the remaining dough, using about half for each sheet. When all the cookies are thoroughly cooled, pack them airtight.
7. When you are ready to decorate the cookies, make the icing by combining the egg white, confectioners' sugar, salt, and anise or lemon extract in the smallest bowl of an electric mixer. Beat on high speed for several minutes, or until the icing is thick and forms softish peaks. If necessary, add confectioners' sugar or drops of water to achieve a proper piping consistency.
8. Scrape half the icing into a small pastry tube. Cover the icing in the bowl with a wet paper towel to prevent drying out. Pipe half the cookies. Refill the tube (at this point you can lightly color the remaining icing, if you like two-color cookies) and decorate the remaining cookies. Let the cookies dry completely before arranging on serving platters, or leave them overnight.

18
As Noble to Give as to Receive

Holiday Foods to Have on Hand

Tuck away long-lived holiday delicacies to serve to unexpected guests or to take to your hosts when you go visiting during this most social season. Although cookies and candies are the traditional gifts, a wider selection of sweet and savory nibbles is more useful. These recipes for cocktail comestibles, teatime tidbits, luncheon munchables, or even a breakfast bite will provide you with prepared-ahead food to trot out at just about any time of the day (or night, as my friends and I prefer when we're on holiday time). Ribboned, wrapped, or enclosed in handsome crocks or jars, any of these festive foods makes a most present-able offering to tote along from your refrigerator or freezer.

SPECIALTIES OF THE HOUSE, FOR GUESTS OR GIVING

*Rillettes d'Oie (Goose Spread)
*Sharp Cheddar and Walnut Spread
*Pickled Fish and Scallops
*Potted Ham
*Coiled Christmas Bread
*Black Cake with Almond Paste Topping
*Pound Cake with Pistachios, Apricots, and Glacéed Pineapple
*Sugared Almonds

RILLETTES D'OIE (GOOSE SPREAD)

This practical recipe makes use of every bit of the fat and meat of the goose—that full-flavored, rich-textured bird which is, sadly, unfamiliar to many American cooks. Since one goose yields around six good-sized jars of this pâté-spread, what might at first appear to be an expensive affair is really quite sensibly priced.

In this adaptation of one of the simplest of French peasant dishes, the meat is given an untraditional spicing prior to cooking, and only goose, rather than the usual pork/goose combination, is used. The spread is neither ravishing nor delicate, but, rather, heavy, creamy-shreddy in texture—and utterly delicious. If, though, you cannot bear a detour into the realm of unctuosity, do not venture here. Likewise if you shudder at the thought of running your fingers through goose grease. *But* if you have ever loved rillettes, or rich country pâtés, chances are you and your gift-ed friends will be more than seasonably merry consuming every morsel of such a worthwhile bird.

For those who are fortunate enough to be starting with the absolute basics, there is a recipe—"To pot Geese the French way"—that directs you to "confine what number of geese you choose to pot; feed them on corn and water, clean out their place every day, and give them clean straw to lie on; they must be fed very fat, or they are not worth doing. . . ." Incidentally, for cooks who think that adding nitrates to meat is a fairly modern invention, the goose is then to be "rubbed very well with saltpetre [now called potassium nitrate]" (*Cookery and Pastry, as Taught and Practised by Mrs. Maciver, Teacher of Those Arts in Edinburgh*, 1800).

Makes about 12 cups, but yield varies considerably

1 goose (about 10 pounds), defrosted if frozen, giblets reserved for another use
4–5 teaspoons black peppercorns
3 tablespoons coarse (kosher) salt
2 teaspoons dried thyme
2 bay leaves, crumbled or snipped small
8 whole cloves
1 1/2 pounds fresh hard pork fat (fatback), cut into 1-inch cubes
2 cups water
5–6 medium-size garlic cloves, sliced

1. Have the butcher cut the goose into 8–10 pieces (they needn't be neat), or—armed with a hefty hacking knife—cut up the goose yourself. Pull off and reserve the goose fat that can be removed easily. Wrap and refrigerate the fat. Place the goose pieces in a large, nonmetal bowl or dish.

2. Combine 2 teaspoons peppercorns, the salt, thyme, bay leaves, and cloves in an electric spice mill or mortar and grind or pound to a medium-fine texture. Rub the mixture into the goose pieces on all sides, cover with plastic, and refrigerate for about 24 hours.

3. When you're ready to cook the goose, combine the goose fat, pork fat, and water in a very large (at least 6-quart) pot and simmer for 15–20 minutes. Add the garlic and goose pieces, pressing them down well into the fat, and simmer for about 15 minutes longer. Press the pieces down again so they are almost submerged.

4. Cover the pot tightly and place it in the oven. Turn the heat to 250° and cook the goose for 5–6 hours, barely bubbling in the fat. Open the pot now and then to stir and submerge the poultry. The goose should become meltingly tender, but should never be allowed to brown.

5. Pour the goose and fat into a large colander set over a bowl and let the fat drip through. Reserve the fat. When the meat is cool enough to handle, take a handful at a time and remove and discard all bones (be sure to remove any tiny sharp ones) and the skin. Shred the meat with your fingers into fine fibers and return to the rinsed-out pot. There will probably be about 8 cups of meat.

6. Skim off about 2 cups of the drained fat and set aside. Combine the remainder with the shredded meat in the pot. Bring to a simmer, stirring. Cover and cook at a bare simmer, stirring often and vigorously, for 30 minutes.

7. Coarsely crack 2–3 teaspoons of the remaining pepper, depending upon your preference, and add to the mixture. Season to taste, then let cool a bit.

8. Turn the meat mixture into a bowl (you'll probably need to do this in two batches) and set in a larger bowl of ice water. Beat with a wooden spoon every 10 minutes or so, then every 5 minutes as the fat hardens slightly, until the mixture is completely cooled and somewhat fluffy. This can take 30–45 minutes.

9. Meanwhile, wash about six 2-cup canning jars or glazed crocks in hot soapy water. Rinse and dry them well. Pack the meat mixture tightly into the jars. Pour the reserved fat over the rillettes to fill the jars or crocks.

10. *To store:* Cover containers and refrigerate for a minimum of several days, a maximum of several months.

11. *To serve:* Spread the cool, but not cold rillettes on thin, crunchy rounds of French bread that have been toasted and cooled.

SHARP CHEDDAR AND WALNUT SPREAD

Potted cheeses were originally produced by frugal housewives as an economical means of keeping surplus cheese, or of finishing up drying bits and pieces. They have since become a great commercial favorite, and as such have unfortunately gotten out of hand—as is quickly verifiable by a glance over the technicolor, nut-studded creations in the dairy cases of supermarkets and delicatessens. Why not control what goes into your cheese spread by making it yourself with fresh, flavorful cheese of your own choosing? With a food processor, the task is accomplished in a matter of moments.

Makes about 3 cups

1 pound sharp Cheddar cheese, cut into 1-inch cubes, at room temperature
1/2 stick (4 tablespoons) unsalted butter, softened
1/4 cup sour cream
1/8 teaspoon cayenne pepper
1/4 teaspoon ground mace
2 tablespoons Madeira or Port
1 cup chopped walnuts

1. Combine the cheese, butter, sour cream, cayenne, mace and Madeira in the container of a processor and whirl until the mixture is smooth and creamy (see note below).

2. Scrape into a bowl and stir in the nuts. Taste and correct the seasoning.

3. *To store:* Pack the spread into two 1 1/2- to 2-cup glazed crocks (onion soup bowls are nice for this). Cover closely and refrigerate for 2 days or more before serving; the spread will keep at least 2 weeks.

4. *To serve:* Let the mixture soften slightly before serving with dry biscuits and Madeira, Sherry, or Port.

NOTE: If you're not using the processor, grate the cheese, then press it through a fine sieve into a bowl. Beat in the remaining ingredients with a wooden spoon.

PICKLED FISH AND SCALLOPS

As with most of the recipes in this holiday group, the one for pickled fish is adapted from several "receipts" that were originally devised to preserve highly perishable foods for quite some length of time. Such foods may now be purchased as needed and refrigerated. In this case, the fish no longer needs heavy salting, as it did in pre-refrigerator times.

Makes about 2 quarts

$1\frac{1}{2}$ pounds fairly rich "steak" fish (such as salmon or swordfish), $1\frac{1}{2}$ inches thick
1 pound sea scallops
2 tablespoons coarse (kosher) salt
2 teaspoons coriander seeds
2 bay leaves, crumbled
2 tablespoons sugar
$\frac{1}{2}$ cinnamon stick, broken in two
$\frac{1}{2}$ teaspoon whole allspice
$\frac{1}{4}$ teaspoon dried thyme
$\frac{1}{2}$ teaspoon black peppercorns
$1\frac{1}{2}$ cups white wine vinegar or rice vinegar
$1\frac{1}{4}$ cups water
$\frac{1}{3}$ cup olive oil
5 scallions, thinly sliced
1 medium carrot, thinly sliced
Bibb lettuce
Minced fresh parsley

1. Carefully remove any skin and bones from the fish and cut the flesh into $1\frac{1}{2}$-inch cubes. Cut the scallops in half lengthwise and crosswise, to make quarters. Spread the seafood on a large plate and sprinkle the pieces on all sides with the salt. Let stand for about an hour. Drain, rinse lightly, and drain again.
2. Combine the coriander, bay leaves, sugar, cinnamon, allspice, thyme, peppercorns, vinegar, and water in a stainless-steel, enameled, or glass saucepan. Bring to a boil, then simmer, covered, for 10 minutes.
3. Add the olive oil, then add the fish and scallop pieces and turn the heat to its highest point. When the liquid comes to a simmer, remove the pan from the heat. Do not allow to cook further.
4. Ladle the seafood pieces into two 1-quart canning jars (preferably straight-sided), arranging them more or less in layers separated by sliced scallions and carrot. Pour in the pickling liquid, dividing the spices between the two jars. Let cool.

5. *To store:* Cover and refrigerate the pickled fish and scallops for at least 3 days, or up to about 8, gently stirring now and then with a chopstick.
6. *To serve:* Drain the fish and scallops. Arrange them on a plate with a little lettuce, then sprinkle with parsley. Accompany with toasted French bread.

POTTED HAM

Leftover ham was given almost the same treatment as cheese by early English and American cooks: It was pounded with butter and spices—usually mace or allspice—and mellowed to use as a spread. Although beef, hare, venison, woodcock, pigeon, and swan were once standard pot-ables, ham and tongue are the meats most commonly encountered in this form today.

Susannah Carter supplied several recipes for potting meat and fish in her cookbook *The Frugal Housewife* (1772). This one is typical of many of the time:

> When you have boiled or baked, and cut your meat small, let it be well beaten in a marble mortar, with some butter melted for that purpose, and two or three anchovies, till you find it mellow, and agreeable to your palate. Then put it close down in pots, and pour over them a sufficient quantity of clarified butter. You may season your ingredients with what spice you please.

To this recipe I've added an unorthodox—and all-American—"secret ingredient," cranberries. They lend tartness, moisture, and a fruitiness, rather than the sourness you might expect from such an acid fruit. As hams vary considerably in saltiness, smokiness, fattiness, and water content, it is best to add the softened butter gradually, and to adjust the seasonings to match the ham at hand. Because good ham is not inexpensive, you may want to make the potted ham from the leftovers of a holiday ham (see the chapter preceding, "A Picnic Lunch for Winter Holidays"), which is why the recipe has been developed for a small amount. If you plan to use a great deal of ham especially purchased for the dish, double or triple the quantities of cranberries, ham, shallots, and butter, but increase the spices slowly, tasting as you go. The best flavor and texture result when a combination of firm ham fat and butter is used to smoothen the pâté-spread; but the fat on some hams is insufficient to provide the amount called for, in which case more butter must be substituted.

Makes about 1½–2 cups

½ cup fresh cranberries, rinsed (see note below)
2½ cups cubed ham (about ¾ pound)
1 medium shallot, minced
¼ teaspoon white pepper
½ teaspoon dry mustard (mustard powder)
¼ teaspoon ground allspice
¼ teaspoon grated nutmeg
Big pinch of cayenne pepper
¼ cup diced firm ham fat (or substitute unsalted butter)
½ stick (4 tablespoons) unsalted butter

1. Bake the cranberries in a covered baking dish in a preheated 400° oven (or toaster oven) until they split and soften, about ½ hour. Let them cool, uncovered.
2. Coarsely chop half the ham in a food processor (or chop it by hand) and scrape into a bowl.
3. Combine the remaining ham, cranberries, shallots, pepper, mustard, allspice, nutmeg, cayenne, ham fat (or the butter substitute) and 2 tablespoons of the butter in a processor or blender container and whirl to a very fine purée. Scrape into the bowl with the coarsely chopped ham and combine the two thoroughly. Add the remaining butter, then taste and season.
4. Pack the spread into 2 small crocks or dishes of about 1-cup capacity. Cover the crocks closely and refrigerate for 2 days to 2 weeks.
5. *To serve:* Accompany the spread with thin-sliced dark bread or rye crackers.

NOTE: Freeze the unused portion of the bag of berries for just about as long as you like. I've used frozen berries (do not defrost before cooking) after upwards of a year in storage.

COILED CHRISTMAS BREAD

This simple, fat, sleek egg bread is light textured, not too sweet, gently spiced, and slightly fruited. Although the bread's cardamom flavoring suggests that its next of kin might be *Julekake* (Danish Christmas bread), it could otherwise belong to any country that celebrates Christmas or Easter, as so many breads for both those occasions resemble one another.

Makes 2 large round loaves

1 1/2 cups mixed glacéed fruits, or a combination of glacéed orange and lemon peel (about 7 ounces)
2 packets dry yeast
1/2 cup warm (not hot) water
1 1/4 sticks (10 tablespoons) unsalted butter, chilled
1/2 cup brown sugar (dark or light), packed
1 1/2 teaspoons salt
2 teaspoons ground cardamom
Rind of 1 lemon, grated
3/4 cup milk, heated to a simmer
About 5 1/2 cups all-purpose flour
3 eggs plus 1 yolk, beaten together
GLAZE: 1 egg yolk beaten with 1 tablespoon cold water

1. Rinse the glacéed fruit and/or peel in a strainer under warm water for a moment. Spread on a towel to dry.
2. Stir together the yeast and warm water with a pinch of sugar. Allow to puff up for about 10 minutes, until doubled. If the mixture doesn't fluff, start again with fresh ingredients. In a large bowl of an electric mixer stir together the butter, brown sugar, salt, cardamom, lemon rind, and hot milk until the butter more or less melts.
3. Set the large bowl on the mixer stand and stir in 1 cup flour. Scrape in the yeast mixture, and beaten eggs and yolk. On low speed beat in 1 cup more flour. Beat the mixture on high speed for 3 minutes.
4. Gradually add about 3 cups more flour to make a soft dough—stirring either by hand, or with a dough hook. Use as much flour as necessary to keep the dough from sticking, but keep it as soft as possible. Knead by hand or machine until the dough is very bouncy and smooth. Form into a ball.
5. Place the dough in a buttered bowl and turn to coat the top. Cover the bowl with plastic and let the dough rise until doubled, about an hour.

(Continued)

6. Meanwhile, dust the fruits with a few tablespoons of flour and chop them fine.
7. Turn the dough onto a floured surface and knead in the fruits, a bit at a time. Cover and let relax about 10 minutes. Divide the dough in half.
8. Form a rope about 36 inches long with one piece of dough. Coil the dough in a buttered round cake pan, 9 inches in diameter. Start the coil about an inch from the side of the pan and spiral inward. Make a second loaf with the other half of the dough. Cover the pans and let the dough rise until doubled in volume, about 45 minutes. Meanwhile preheat the oven to 350°.
9. Brush each loaf thoroughly with the glaze, taking care to prevent it from dripping into the pans. Bake the loaves in the lower third of the oven for about 45 minutes, switching places and turning the pans halfway through baking. The breads should be a rich, even brown and produce a hollow sound when thumped on the bottom. Cool thoroughly on a rack.
10. *To store:* If serving within a day, leave uncovered at room temperature. Wrap tightly and store up to a week in the refrigerator, or for months in the freezer.
11. *To serve:* Unwrap (and thaw, if frozen), then warm the bread through in a low oven, or slice and toast it lightly. Serve with unsalted butter and honey at breakfast or teatime.

BLACK CAKE WITH ALMOND PASTE TOPPING

Recipes for black cake and black fruit cake abound in nineteenth-century American cookbooks. These old cakes are clearly related to the English fruitcake and Scottish black bun, both carried by settlers to their New World home. Black cake seems to have been a favorite in the South, where whortleberries or huckleberries were occasionally added to the basic fruit mixture. Brandy, rosewater, sweet wine, mace, and nutmeg (several recipes called for two whole nutmegs for each small cake) were stirred in with a lavish hand. Some of the cakes were covered with almond paste, and all were sealed with a thick coat of sugar icing for long storage. By 1837 the trend to store-bought was already apparent, as one can read in this description of how to ice the cake:

> Spread [the icing] evenly over the cake with a bread knife or a feather; if you find it too thin, beat in a little more powdered sugar. Cover with it thickly the top and sides of the cake, taking care not to have it rough and streaky. When dry, put on a second coat; and when that is nearly dry, lay on the ornaments. You may flower it with coloured sugar-sand or nonparels; but a newer and more elegant mode is to decorate it with the devices and borders in white sugar; they can be procured at the confectioners, and look extremely well on icing that has been tinted with pink by the addition of a little cochineal (*Directions for Cookery, in Its Various Branches* by Miss Leslie, first published in 1837).

The following recipe does not include a sugar icing, but simply a top covering of almond paste. The cake is slightly sweet, close-grained, spicy, and rather alcoholic. If you fancy a cake with a less defined liquor presence, substitute apple cider for part of the brandy.

Makes two 8-inch round cakes

BATTER:

1 1/4 cups raisins
1 1/4 cups currants
2/3 cup brandy or Calvados
2/3 cup Madeira or Port
1 cup unblanched whole almonds
1/3 cup glacéed lemon peel (2 ounces)
2/3 cup glacéed orange peel (4 ounces)
2 cups all-purpose flour
1 teaspoon grated nutmeg
1 teaspoon ground mace
1 tablespoon ground cinnamon
1/2 teaspoon salt
1 teaspoon baking powder
2 sticks (1/2 pound) unsalted butter, at room temperature
1/4 cup dark brown sugar, packed
1/4 cup light (unsulphured) molasses
5 eggs, at room temperature

ALMOND PASTE TOPPING:

2 cups blanched whole almonds
2 cups confectioners' sugar
2 egg yolks
1/4 cup brandy
1/2 teaspoon almond extract

GLAZE:

2 egg whites beaten with 2 tablespoons brandy or Calvados

1. Combine the raisins, currants, brandy, and Madeira in a large jar. Cover and let stand at least 24 hours, or longer. When ready to bake, drain the fruit and spread on a paper towel, reserving the liquor. Preheat the oven to 300°.
2. Spread the almonds in a pan and bake for 15 minutes, stirring occasionally. Let them cool.
3. Grease two 8-inch round cake pans with vegetable shortening. Cover the bottoms with rounds of waxed paper cut to size, then grease the paper. Sprinkle each pan with flour; turn to coat evenly, then knock out the excess.
4. Rinse the glacéed lemon and orange peels under warm running water, then drain and dry on a paper towel. Chop very fine and place in a large bowl. Chop the reserved almonds to a medium-coarse texture and add to the fruit peels.
5. Sift together into a bowl the flour, nutmeg, mace, cinnamon, and salt. Remove 1/2 cup of this mixture and sift it together with the baking powder into a bowl. Preheat the oven to 425°, having first set a large pan of hot water on the bottom of the oven.
6. Cream the butter in a large bowl of an electric mixer until it is light. Gradually beat in the brown sugar, removing lumps with your fingers as you add it. Add the molasses. Beat in 1/2 cup of the flour mixture without the baking powder. On high speed beat in the eggs, incorporating them one at a time. On low speed beat in the remaining portion of the flour mixture without baking powder. Slowly beat in the reserved liquor.
7. Sprinkle the reserved flour–baking powder mixture over the peels and almonds. Add the currants and raisins and toss to coat. Add to the batter slowly, folding with a rubber spatula to incorporate evenly.
8. Divide the batter between the prepared pans. Smooth evenly. Set the pans in the center of the oven. Turn the heat to 325° and bake the cakes for 45–50 minutes, or until the center can no longer be easily dented by the pressure of a finger.
9. Cool 15 minutes on a rack. Unmold the cakes onto the rack and turn them right side up. Cover lightly with a towel and let cool completely. When cooled, either wrap tightly in plastic and refrigerate for up to a week before frosting, or wrap them airtight and freeze indefinitely.

10. *To make the almond paste topping:* Grind half the blanched almonds to a powder in a food processor. Add half the confectioners' sugar and whirl to blend. Beat together 1 of the egg yolks, 2 tablespoons of the brandy, and 1/4 teaspoon of the almond extract. Add gradually to the almond mixture through the feed tube with the motor running. Process only until the mixture forms a single mass on top of the blade. Repeat with the remaining ingredients to make the topping for the second cake. Wrap and chill each batch until needed.

11. *To assemble the cakes:* Roll the paste for each cake between sheets of waxed paper dusted with confectioners' sugar. Make rounds that will fit each cake top exactly, trimming the paste and saving the scraps. Using the tip of a chopstick, press an indentation every inch or so around the perimeter of each circle to make a scalloped edge. Remove one of the chilled cakes from the refrigerator (if frozen, thaw in the refrigerator), set it on a baking sheet, and brush all over with the egg white glaze. Set a scalloped round of almond paste on top and press down to adhere. Form half the scraps into berries and leaves, brush the glaze over the almond coating, and press on the decorations. With the rounded end of the chopstick, pierce a shallow indentation into each of the scallops. Brush the decorations with the glaze. Repeat the entire procedure with the second cake.

(Continued)

12. Set the baking sheet with the cakes on it quite close to the broiling element, turn on the heat, and broil for 2–4 minutes, or until the surfaces of the cakes are light golden beige, not browned. Check frequently to be sure the cakes do not burn.
13. *To store:* Wrap the cakes airtight and store for several weeks in the refrigerator, up to a year in the freezer.
14. *To serve:* Allow to come to room temperature before serving in thin slivers with afternoon tea or coffee, or with a glass of Sherry, Port, or Madeira.

POUND CAKE WITH PISTACHIOS, APRICOTS, AND GLACÉED PINEAPPLE

For those who prefer a light, buttery cake at holiday time, this delicately flavored, prettily fruit/nut-flecked loaf may be the answer. Although rich in butter and eggs, it is in no way heavy, but subtle and fresh tasting, suitable for a dessert, teatime, or breakfast confection any time of the year.

Makes 3 cakes (each about 1 pound)

6 ounces dried California apricots
5–6 ounces glacéed pineapple
1/3 cup Calvados, Armagnac, or brandy
3/4 cup coarsely chopped, shelled, unsalted pistachios (see note below)
3 cups all-purpose flour
2 1/4 teaspoons baking powder
1/4 teaspoon ground mace
1/4 teaspoon salt
2 1/2 sticks (10 ounces) unsalted butter, at room temperature
1/3 cup dark rum
6 extra-large eggs, at room temperature
1 1/2 cups sugar
1/4 teaspoon almond extract
Confectioners' sugar

1. Cut the apricots into very thin slivers and place them in a small bowl. Set the pineapple in a sieve and rinse with boiling water. Cut into tiny slivers and add to the apricots. Add the Calvados, cover the bowl, and let stand 1/2 hour or more, stirring occasionally. Preheat the oven to 325°.
2. Spread the nuts in a pan and toast them in the oven for 10 minutes, tossing a few times. Cool and reserve; turn the oven heat to 350°.

3. Grease and flour three 4- to 5-cup loaf pans (or use small bundt or kugelhopf molds). Sift together the flour, 2 teaspoons of the baking powder, the mace, and salt onto a sheet of waxed paper. Reserve 2 tablespoons of the mixture and stir the remaining 1/4 teaspoon baking powder into this.

4. In the large bowl of an electric mixer cream the butter until light and creamy-pale. Gradually beat in the flour mixture to form a smooth paste. Beat in the rum. Remove the bowl from the stand and wash the beaters thoroughly.

5. In another large beater bowl combine the eggs and sugar. Beat on high speed until the mixture is very thick, pale, and quite firm. This will take at least 10 minutes; do not underbeat. Add the almond extract. Remove the bowl from the stand and replace it with the one containing the butter-flour mixture. Add the nuts to the bowl of fruits and sprinkle with the reserved flour and baking powder mixture. Toss well.

6. On lowest mixer speed add one third of the egg mixture to the flour-butter and blend thoroughly. Add half the remaining eggs and mix in partially, at the same speed. Remove the bowl from the stand. Using a rubber spatula, gently fold in the remaining egg mixture, folding to blend only partially. Add the fruit and nut mixture, about one quarter at a time, folding gently until well incorporated.

7. Delicately divide the batter among the pans. Smooth the tops and set the pans in the oven center. Bake 1 hour or more, or until the interiors, which will be visible, as the cakes will crack, no longer appear foamy and the sides separate from the pans.

8. Let the cakes cool on a rack for about 15 minutes. Run a knife carefully around each mold and invert the cakes onto the rack. Set loaf cakes on their sides, bundt or kugelhopf on their wide, undecorated end. Let cool completely.

9. *To store and serve:* Wrap the cakes tightly and let them mellow for at least a day at room temperature, or several days in the refrigerator. Or you can freeze them for months, properly wrapped. To serve, sieve a little confectioners' sugar over the top of each cake.

NOTE: If shelled pistachios are not available in your neighborhood, or if you don't have the patience to shell nuts, you can order shelled, unroasted, unsalted pistachios. See page 353 for list of mail-order sources.

SUGARED ALMONDS

These tawny bonbons have a sugary-sandy (not glassy or smooth) coating, demonstrating yet another guise of that remarkably transformable substance—sugar. To think that lollipops, spun sugar, fondant, liquid caramel, taffy, and this sugar coating are all made from the same simple sugar-water syrup (plus flavorings) merely subjected to different temperatures and handling methods!

Warning: Working with hot sugar is tricky, so be careful and follow directions exactly. To be sure that your candy thermometer is registering properly, test it first. Lower into a pot of boiling water. If it doesn't measure 212° F, add or subtract as needed to adjust to this.

Makes about 5 cups

3 cups unblanched whole almonds
2 cups sugar
1/2 cup plus 2 tablespoons water
1 1/2 teaspoons ground cinnamon
1 1/2 teaspoons vanilla extract
3/4 teaspoon salt

1. Preheat the oven to 325°. Spread the nuts in a large baking pan and bake for 20 minutes, stirring occasionally. Cool completely.
2. Combine the sugar and 1/2 cup water in a 2 1/2-quart heavy saucepan and bring to a full boil, stirring. Let the syrup boil gently—do not stir—until it registers 250° on a candy thermometer.
3. Without removing the pan from the heat, quickly stir in the cinnamon, vanilla, and salt. Add the almonds and stir briskly with a wooden spoon to coat well. Without stopping the stirring, remove the pan from the heat. Continue mixing vigorously until the nuts are separated and dry, about 2–3 minutes. Do not stop stirring until the nuts are separated. At this point the nuts will be unevenly coated with sugar and the pan will contain a good deal as well.
4. With a strainer or slotted spoon lift out the nuts and set them aside on a baking sheet, letting any loose sugar fall back into the pot. Separate any nuts that might stick together and add the loose sugar to the pot.
5. Add the 2 tablespoons water to the pot and stir and scrape to loosen as much sugar as possible. Over low heat bring the sugar and water to a simmer, stirring constantly and scraping the sugar from

the pot. Turn to medium heat and let the syrup come to a thick, rolling boil. Add the nuts and stir quickly over the heat to coat them well.

6. Remove the saucepan from the heat and again stir vigorously until the syrup turns granular and the nuts are evenly coated and all are separated. Keep stirring until all separate. Spread on the baking sheet to cool.

7. *To store:* Pack into jars, seal tightly, and store in the freezer indefinitely.

19
Twelfth Night Supper—to See Out the Holiday Season

Twelfth Night, also called "Epiphany," "Twelfth Day," or "Three Kings' Day," falls on January 6. Celebrations ranging from polite tea parties to full-scale carnivals have long taken place in France—and its New World "colony," Louisiana—and in England, Germany, Scotland, Spain, Mexico, Puerto Rico, and other Latin countries. These, and other nations, observe in their own ways the close of the holiday period called "the twelve days of Christmas" by marking the day of the Three Kings' arrival in Bethlehem to view the infant Jesus. In most cultures the coming of the gift-bearing Magi is remembered by an exchange of presents. In Spanish-speaking countries children fill small boxes with grass or hay to feed the horses and camels of the kings of the Orient. Morning finds the boxes filled with presents.

Today winter holidays are shorter than they used to be. Often the celebration of Chanukah or Christmas is more frantic than felicitous. Why not try to lengthen the season a bit and dawdle back into reality, rather than crash full force the day after the New Year begins? A Twelfth Night Supper is a peaceful way to avoid the post-festivity blues. If January 6 is not the ideal night for a small-scale feast, simply use Twelfth Night as an excuse, and let the party fit into your life when possible.

A few final words on the subject: Twelfth Night, in this case, has nothing whatsoever to do with Mr. Shakespeare's comedy of errors. In fact, the whole recipe scheme has been devised to avoid anything of the kind!

TWELFTH NIGHT SUPPER FOR EIGHT

*Canapés of Smoked Turkey and Hazelnut Butter
Wine: Gewürztraminer *or* a Full-Bodied Champagne
or Monterey Pinot Blanc
*Celery Consommé
*Cold Spiced Beef
*Potato Salad with Horseradish Cream Dressing
*Watercress, Beet, and Orange Salad
Dark Breads *or* *Christmas Rye Bread, Swedish Style (page 188)
Dark Ale *or* Beer *or* Sparkling Cider
Coffee/Port
*Kings' Cake
Candied Fruit Peels/Chocolates

CANAPÉS OF SMOKED TURKEY AND HAZELNUT BUTTER

Smoked turkey or chicken of good quality is an economical and delicious food to have on hand for the holiday season. If you don't know a shop that carries smoked poultry, you can substitute smoked ham, or see the list of mail-order sources, page 353.

Makes 30–36 canapés

1/2 cup hazelnuts (filberts)
3/4 stick (6 tablespoons) unsalted butter, cold
About 10 slices thin, firm, dark, whole-grain bread
About 6 ounces thin-sliced smoked turkey, chicken, or ham
GARNISH: Parsley sprigs and black olives

1. Preheat the oven to 350°. Toast the nuts in a pan in the oven for 15 minutes. Transfer the nuts to a coarse sieve and rub them around, protecting your hand with a pot holder, until all the skins have been loosened or removed. Scrape any stubborn nuts against the mesh to take off most of the skin. Cool completely.

(Continued)

2. Pick the nuts out of the sieve, discarding the skins. Place them in the container of a food processor with the butter. Process, stopping the motor often to scrape the mixture off the sides, until the nuts and butter are well blended but the nuts retain a coarse texture. (If you have no processor, cream the butter in a bowl until fluffy-soft; chop the nuts medium coarse and mix them in.) Chill the butter for several hours or more.
3. Spread the slices of bread lavishly with the butter. Top with the meat, closely and neatly arranged. Trim the edges straight with a very sharp knife. Cut each slice into about 3 "fingers." Arrange on a serving dish and chill until dinner, covered.
4. *To serve:* Garnish with the parsley and olives.

CELERY CONSOMMÉ

Warm up guests with this brisk, full-flavored, clear amber soup. The pungent, herbal aroma is enhanced if the soup is piping hot. Offer it in small bowls or mugs, preferably glass, or at least light colored, to show off the sparkling clarity.

Makes 8 servings

8 cups homemade beef stock or beef and veal stock (or use a nonsalty brand of canned beef broth)
About 4 large celery stalks with their leaves, very finely chopped (to make at least 2½ cups)
4 egg whites (reserved, if convenient, from the Kings' Cake, page 217)
1 medium-small leek, meticulously washed and thinly sliced (1¼ cups)
1 large carrot, scrubbed and finely chopped (about 1 cup)
¼ pound ground beef, as lean as possible
½ teaspoon dried thyme
¼ teaspoon black peppercorns
¼ teaspoon dried tarragon
GARNISH: Finely chopped fresh chives, tarragon, or parsley

1. Heat 7 cups of the stock and the celery to simmering. Turn the heat to low.
2. In a large bowl whisk the egg whites until frothy. Add the remaining 1 cup stock, the leek, carrot, ground beef, thyme, peppercorns, and dried tarragon. Beat 2 cups of the hot broth into this, using a whisk. Pour the contents of the bowl into the stockpot.

3. Over moderate heat, stir the mixture until it just begins to boil. Immediately turn the heat to low, allowing the mixture to barely simmer for 20 minutes, undisturbed. Do not stir or the consommé will not be limpid. Remove from the heat and let stand undisturbed for 15–20 minutes.
4. Line a sieve set over a bowl with 2 layers of dampened fine-mesh cotton cheesecloth (or 4–5 layers of the loose-weave variety). Gently ladle the broth through this. When all has dripped through, press down lightly on the solids to extract as much liquid as possible without making the broth cloudy. Taste for salt. Cool the consommé, then chill as long as several days, or as convenient.
5. *To serve:* Discard any specks of chilled fat. Heat the consommé until very hot, then sprinkle lightly with fresh herbs.

COLD SPICED BEEF

Recipes for spiced beef have existed in some form or another for just about as long as people have been cooking meat. Before refrigeration, salting the beef to cure it for long keeping was obviously a necessity; spicing it for flavor was a refinement that has kept the dish alive. Traditional recipes call for a good deal of saltpeter (potassium nitrate), which helps to keep the meat from spoiling and gives it the bright pink color characteristic of pickled meats. Indeed, the hue of meat that has been cured in saltpeter gave the dish one of its older names—"scarlet beef" (boeuf à l'écarlate). As refrigeration preserves the meat's freshness without the saltpeter, which has acquired a rather dubious reputation as a possible carcinogen, it has not been included here. This results in meat that is a deep, leathery brown color, rather than rosy.

Cold spiced beef has been the Christmas specialty for hundreds of years in England and Ireland. The British carried it to the New World, where it underwent many minor transformations, but its uses and ingredients remained basically unchanged. "Christmas beef," or spiced round, is still very much a part of holiday time in Canada and in the southeastern United States, where it is served with beaten biscuits. Both the Southern and Canadian version are sweeter and spicier than the Old English originals.

The following recipe, about halfway between the ancient British and "colonized" styles, yields firm-textured, slightly sweet-spiced meat that can be carved into the thinnest slices imaginable to be served in much the way one might a salt-cured country ham. In fact, although the meat certainly tastes like beef, those who appreciate the rather dry, dense texture and intense flavor of old-fashioned dry-cured pork will probably be taken with this treatment for beef.

NOTE: You will need to plan on 2–3 weeks of curing time for the beef before it is cooked.

Makes 8 or more servings

1/2 cup coarse (kosher) salt
1/2 cup dark brown sugar
3 tablespoons juniper berries
2 tablespoons whole allspice
1 teaspoon ground cinnamon
2 tablespoons black peppercorns
1/2 teaspoon grated nutmeg
4 pounds bottom round of beef (or use rump roast)
3/4 cup water
GARNISH: Watercress

1. Mix the salt and sugar in a large jar. Combine the juniper berries, allspice, cinnamon, peppercorns, and nutmeg in a small electric spice mill and grind medium fine. (If you do not have a mill you can use a mortar and pestle—and plenty of elbow grease.) Add the spices to the jar, cap, and shake well to blend.
2. Cut a slit along the length of the beef about 3/4 of the way through. Open the meat like a book, and prick holes in the meat on all sides, using a skewer or large trussing needle. Rub a generous handful of the spices into the opened meat, then close it up and coat with about one quarter of the mixture. Enclose the meat in a tightly fitting heavy plastic bag; set in a dish and refrigerate overnight.
3. The next day, open the bag, open up the meat, and rub it on all sides with about one third of the remaining mixture. Close up the meat, seal the bag, and refrigerate for another day.
4. Repeat for 2 more days, to use up the mixture. After that, you can leave the meat for 2–3 weeks in the refrigerator before cooking. Each day turn the bag to distribute the liquid that will accumulate, and squeeze to work in the spices.
5. *To cook the meat:* Take the beef out of the bag and give it a very quick rinse to remove a little of the spice mixture. Discard the plastic

bag and the juices that have accumulated. Tie the meat into a neat shape and set in a Dutch oven as close to the size of the meat as possible. Pour in the 3/4 cup water. Cover the pot with heavy-duty foil, then cover with the lid. Place the pot in the lower third of your oven and set the heat at 275°. Roast for 4 hours, until the meat is very tender when pierced gently with the tip of a knife. The timing can vary at least an hour in either direction, so test the meat. Remove the foil and pot lid and let the meat cool.

6. When cooled, wrap the meat in foil and set in a dish. Place a weight of about 3 pounds on top of it. Refrigerate for about a day before serving, or longer, if you prefer.

7. *To serve:* Remove the strings and cut the beef into very thin slices. Arrange in a neat, overlapping pattern on a platter and surround with watercress.

POTATO SALAD WITH HORSERADISH CREAM DRESSING

Potato salad, assertively seasoned, creamily dressed, provides just the right foil for the chewy, firm beef. You can make the salad a day ahead and serve it cold. Or, for an even better, softer, lighter texture, cook and dress the potatoes, without chilling them, several hours before serving. Two words of caution: Don't oversalt. The salad is made to be a complement to the salty beef, almost a sauce.

Makes about 8 servings

3 pounds even-size all-purpose potatoes, peeled
2 tablespoons finely minced shallots
2 tablespoons sharp mustard
1/4 cup (one 4-ounce bottle) prepared horseradish, not drained
1/2 cup Celery Consommé (page 212), or beef broth
1 cup sour cream
2 tablespoons white or red wine vinegar
1 cup finely minced celery
1 large Cortland or Red Delicious apple

1. Drop the potatoes into a large pot of boiling water. Boil for 20 minutes, or until the potatoes are just barely tender; they must not fall apart. Drain and let stand 5–10 minutes to firm up.

(Continued)

2. Mix the shallots, mustard, horseradish, and consommé in a large bowl and set aside.
3. When the potatoes have cooled a few minutes, slice them in half lengthwise, then into 1/2-inch slices crosswise. Gently mix the potatoes into the dressing, using a rubber spatula. Let stand until cool, mixing gently a few times.
4. Mix together the sour cream and vinegar and pour over the potatoes. Add the celery. Mix gently with a rubber spatula. Taste for salt. Leave as long as 5 hours at room temperature, or refrigerate.
5. *To serve:* Core and thinly slice the apple (without peeling). Arrange the slices over the top of the salad.

WATERCRESS, BEET, AND ORANGE SALAD

Oranges have long been a traditional Christmas pleasure, and the colorful addition of beets and watercress makes a salad that is festive to behold. The alliance of earthy and citrusy sweetness, along with the bite of cress, creates a bright background for the saline beef.

Makes about 8 servings

8 medium-size beets
3 bunches watercress
1/3 cup fresh lemon juice
1/3 cup French walnut oil (see list of mail-order sources, page 353; or use peanut oil)
1 teaspoon coarse (kosher) salt
1/4 teaspoon black pepper
4 scallions, very thinly sliced
3–4 medium-size navel oranges

1. Cut off and discard all but 2 inches of the beet tops. Drop the beets into boiling water and cook as long as needed to produce tender beets. Timing varies considerably with beets, so begin testing after about 1/2 hour.
2. Meanwhile, wash and dry the watercress thoroughly. Cut off and discard thick stems. Place in a serving bowl and refrigerate.
3. Drain the beets, pull off their skins, and trim them. Cool until easy to handle, then cut into thin julienne strips. Reserve.
4. In a jar combine the lemon juice, walnut oil, salt, pepper, and scallions. Cap the jar, shake, and taste for seasoning on a sprig of cress.

5. Remove all the skin and pith from the orange. Cut in half lengthwise, then cut each half across into 1/4-inch-thick semicircular slices. Reserve.
6. *To serve:* Arrange the beets over the cress at serving time, not before. Arrange the oranges over this. Shake the dressing and pour it over all. Toss gently and serve.

KINGS' CAKE

A rich cake-bread, in which a bean or china figurine is hidden, is the traditional focus of Twelfth Night. The person who finds the charm chooses a mate, and the two reign over a willing populace for a specified period.

Until the Reformation, Twelfth Night was observed in England with spectacular feasting. When Christmas groaning boards were emptied of their boars' heads, the Twelfth cakes, stocked by all confectioners for the occasion, made their appearance, signaling the start of a new round of revels. In Scotland, a rich plum cake, black bun, marked Kings' Day. When Christmas and Twelfth Night festivities were banned during the Reformation, the cake was served on New Year's Day (Hogmanay) instead, a custom that has continued until today in Scotland.

In Mexico, rosca de Reyes, a ring-shaped egg bread, slightly sweetened, hides a tiny china Jesus. The finder of the infant is promised good luck throughout the year. But a bit of good will and cold cash must be attached to the luck, for the finder is obliged to give a party on February 2, Candlemas Day.

The New Orleans Mardi Gras carnival had its origin in the celebration of Kings' Day. The traditional Spanish celebration was adopted by the French Creoles, who called the day Petit Noël. Grand balls took place on the night of January 6, at which a king and queen were chosen to lead subsequent nights of festivity, until the dawn of Ash Wednesday. While the Mardi Gras season saw a new king and queen selected weekly by various means, the original pair was chosen by the finding of a bean (or, in finer fashion, a jewel) in the gâteau de Roi.

In France the gâteau des Rois shows up in many forms: it can be a simple, flattish round of pastry sprinkled with sugar; puff pastry enclosing egg-enriched almond paste; or a tart. Most commonly, however, one finds the egg-butter-yeast dough shaped into a ring, similar to the recipe that follows. This soft-textured cake is sugar sparkled, cherry bedecked, and sweet smelling. If any remains after dinner, serve it in the morning with fresh fruit and café au lait for a royal breakfast.

NOTE: The dough should be made a day before you bake the cake, so remember to leave time for this.

Makes 1 large, ring-shaped cake

1 packet dry yeast
1/4 cup warm water
1 egg, at room temperature
2 1/4 cups all-purpose flour
4 egg yolks (use the whites to clarify the Celery Consommé, page 212)
1 stick (8 tablespoons) unsalted butter, softened
1/2 teaspoon salt
1/3 cup dark brown sugar, firmly packed
Grated rind of 1 lemon
Grated rind of 1 orange
1/3 cup dried currants
4 ounces glacéed cherries (2/3 cup)
Milk for glazing
2–3 teaspoons large sugar crystals (decorating sugar—see list of mail-order sources, page 353) or granulated sugar

1. Mix the yeast, water, and a big pinch of sugar in a small mixing bowl. Allow to become foamy and fluffy, which takes about 10 minutes. If the mixture doesn't puff up, begin again with fresh ingredients. Beat in the egg and 3/4 cup flour until the mixture is smooth. Cover the bowl with plastic, set in a warm place, and let the mixture (the sponge) stand until it rises, then falls. This usually takes about 2 hours. You can tell that the sponge has fallen by checking the "high water mark" on the side of the bowl.

2. In a large mixing bowl combine the yolks, butter, salt, brown sugar (remove any lumps with your fingers), and lemon and orange rinds. Blend well. Beat in 3/4 cup flour, then the sponge. Use a dough hook, if your machine has one, or a strong wooden spoon. Vigorously beat in the remaining flour. Cover the bowl and refrigerate overnight, which will develop the flavor and texture.

3. On a well-floured board, pat out the cold dough, which will be very soft, to form a rectangle about 12 × 8 inches. Spread the currants over this and lightly pat into the dough with the heel of your hand. Spread all but 8 cherries evenly on the dough and press them into the dough lightly. Without letting the dough warm up, make a neat cylinder by rolling, not stretching or pulling, from one long side to the other. Brush off excess flour as you roll. Pinch the seam closed. Gently roll, with the palms of your hands, to form a cylinder of even circumference about 2 feet long.
4. Set the roll on a nonstick or parchment-covered baking sheet. Being careful to keep the fruits on the inside, carefully pinch the ends together to form a ring. Stretch the center opening to be sure it is at least 5 inches in diameter. Grease a small oven-glass dish or custard cup and set it in the middle of the ring to prevent closing up. Grease an 11- to 12-inch flan ring, plain or fluted, and set it around the dough to help the ring keep its shape and rise evenly. (Or you can shape a triple thickness of aluminum foil into a ring about 12 inches in diameter.)
5. Cover the dough with a clean cloth and let rise until almost doubled, about 2 hours.
6. Set a rack in the center of the oven, then preheat the oven to 350°. Brush the ring with a little milk, then sprinkle with the sugar crystals. Gently press in the reserved cherries to decorate the top. Bake for 15 minutes. Turn the sheet around in the oven and bake 15–20 minutes longer, or until the cake is evenly light brown. Carefully transfer to a rack to cool until you can remove the center dish and flan ring. Cool completely on the rack.
7. *To serve or store:* You should, ideally, serve the cake fresh, the day it is baked. Or you can wrap it tightly and keep for several days in the refrigerator, or a month in the freezer. Warm the cake briefly in a low oven (thaw first in the fridge, if it was frozen), being careful not to brown anymore. The softness and richness of the cake are not apparent if you serve it cold.

20
Coldly Calculating
Frozen Vegetable Casseroles to Fill Out a Meal

Although one can dine spontaneously on a quick salad on a sultry day, wintry evenings call for real hot food. So when an impromptu company meal seems a pleasant notion, but there isn't enough cold roast on hand to graciously include guests, a substantial vegetable casserole, handily kept in cold storage until you need it, fills out a meal nicely. Or, if you know you'll be having company but can't get home in time to prepare dinner, defrost the vegetables a day ahead and simply pop them into the oven when you get home; then grill or sauté a meat or fish accompaniment.

The combination vegetable dishes that follow are good enough to double up on, and so have twofold practicality: When time permits, make one of the recipes (all are devised for twelve), serve or refrigerate half, and freeze the remainder. When you next need a rather complex side dish to fill out a skimpy or too-plain meal, you'll be able to withdraw your "frozen assets" and enjoy the company. The major part of two nights' meals will be produced from one kitchen stint.

If you don't have enough space, or pots, or company, all the recipes can be halved. Or, on the other hand, if you are inclined to entertain more ambitiously, and you own baking and serving dishes of a generous size, fit all of one recipe for twelve into one casserole, then bake or freeze according to your needs.

If you have the time and foresight, you can attain a more perfectly uniform texture by defrosting the vegetables before reheating. Leave them for at least 24 hours in the refrigerator, or 8 hours at room temperature. But if you prefer to whisk the package right from the freezer, you will still produce predictably fine results, as the vegetables suggested here all successfully withstand the freezing-defrosting process.

Please read Reminders about Freezing, page 352.

SUGGESTED MENU FOR SIX

Roast Pork or Turkey
*Sweet Potatoes Baked with Rum, Cider, and Raisins
Broccoli *or* Kale
Light Beer
Baked Apples with Cream

SWEET POTATOES BAKED WITH RUM, CIDER, AND RAISINS

This rather sweet dish, so easy to assemble, complements fresh or cured pork, or roasted duck, chicken, or turkey.

Makes 2 casseroles (each about 6 servings as a side dish)

6 pounds sweet potatoes (about 12 medium-size potatoes)
1 stick (8 tablespoons) butter
2 1/2 cups apple cider
2/3 cup dark rum
1/2 cup brown sugar, lightly packed
2 teaspoons salt
1 teaspoon ground allspice
1/2 teaspoon ground mace
2 teaspoons ground ginger
2/3 cup raisins

1. Preheat the oven to 375°. Peel the potatoes and cut them into 3/4- to 1-inch cubes. There should be about 16–18 cups. Foil-line a 2-quart casserole and butter another.
2. Combine the butter, cider, rum, brown sugar, salt, allspice, mace, and ginger in a small pan and heat, stirring, until the butter and sugar have melted.
3. Divide half the potatoes between the prepared casseroles. Stir the cider mixture and pour about 1 cup over each dish. Sprinkle 1/3 cup raisins over each. Divide the remaining potatoes between the dishes, which should be almost overflowing, as the potatoes will shrink considerably. Stir the liquid again and pour it evenly over the two dishes. It should reach one half to three quarters of the way up the sides of the casseroles.

(Continued)

4. Cover the dishes tightly and bake for about 1 hour, or until the potatoes are almost tender, mixing gently and checking for doneness a few times. If you are going to freeze one casserole, remove it from the oven at this point.
5. *To finish baking for immediate serving:* Turn the oven to 425°, uncover the casserole, and bake about 1/2 hour, or until the juices are thickened and bubbling. Baste several times.

To freeze: Cool the mixture in the foil-lined dish, cover with foil, and freeze. When frozen solid, you can remove the foil package from the dish, seal, label, and date it, and return it to the freezer for up to 3 months.

To reheat: Unwrap the package and place in the casserole in which it was frozen. Cover, place in the oven, turn the heat to 350°, and bake until the vegetables are defrosted, about 1 1/2 hours. Remove the foil (or cover), turn the heat to 425°, and bake for 15–30 minutes, or until the juices are bubbling and thickened and the top is browned.

If the casserole was thawed prior to heating, you can cut the initial covered-baking time to about 45 minutes, then bake uncovered.

SUGGESTED MENU FOR SIX

Roast Lamb, Pork (cold or hot), *or* Ham
*Gratin of Turnips
Wine: Grignolino *or* California Pinot Noir
Chicory Salad
*Apricot Kissel (Purée) with Cream (page 233)
or Baked Pears in Wine

GRATIN OF TURNIPS

A lovely, creamy, herb-flavored side dish that could be served with any plain-cooked meat, whether roasted, grilled, broiled, baked, or sautéed. Or, if you're a vegetable lover, serve as a main course, as we do, with a side dish of brown rice or kasha.

Makes 2 casseroles (each about 6 servings as a side dish, 4 as a main dish)

2 1/2 cups milk
1 large garlic clove, peeled, with several cuts in it
3/4 cup heavy cream
1/2 stick (4 tablespoons) butter
3 tablespoons all-purpose flour
1/4 teaspoon grated nutmeg
1/2 teaspoon dried thyme
1/4 teaspoon black pepper
1/4 teaspoon dried rosemary
1 teaspoon salt
4 pounds small white turnips, peeled, halved lengthwise, then cut across into slices 1/4 inch thick (13–14 cups)
1/2 cup fine dry bread crumbs
2/3 cup grated or shredded Parmesan or Swiss cheese (2–3 ounces)

1. Combine the milk, garlic, and heavy cream in a heavy saucepan and bring just to a simmer. Preheat the oven to 375°.
2. Melt the butter in a skillet; stir in the flour and cook for 1 minute. Add the hot milk and stir with a whisk over moderate heat until the mixture is thick and boiling. Lower the heat and simmer for 5 minutes, stirring often. Remove the garlic clove; add the nutmeg, thyme, pepper, rosemary, and salt. Stir and remove from the heat.
3. While the sauce is cooking, bring a large pot of lightly salted water to a boil. Drop in the sliced turnips and return to a boil over highest heat. Drain well.
4. Butter a 1 1/2- to 2-quart baking dish and foil-line another. Arrange half the turnips in each dish. Pour half the sauce over each dish of turnips, then cover with foil.
5. Bake for 30 minutes. Remove the foil covers and sprinkle each casserole with half the crumbs, then half the cheese.
6. *To finish baking for immediate serving:* Turn the oven to 425°. Bake the casserole, uncovered, for 15–30 minutes, or until the sauce is lightly browned and bubbling.

To freeze: Cool the turnips in the foil-lined dish, then cover with foil and freeze. When frozen solid, you can remove the foil package, seal, label, and date it, and return to the freezer for storage (up to about 3 months).

To reheat: Unwrap the vegetables and place in the casserole in which they were frozen. Cover, place in the oven, and turn the heat to 350°. Bake for 1–1 1/2 hours, or until the turnips are entirely defrosted. Uncover, turn the heat to 400°, and bake for about 30 minutes longer, until the top is browned slightly and the sauce is bubbling. If the vegetables have been defrosted, cut the initial heating time to about 45 minutes, then go on to the uncovered baking.

SUGGESTED MENU FOR SIX

Roasted Duck, Turkey, *or* Chicken
*Winter Squash and Apple Purée with Walnuts
Wine: California Chenin Blanc *or* Sauvignon Blanc
*Orange, Onion, and Chicory Salad (page 124)
Coffee/Gingerbread

WINTER SQUASH AND APPLE PURÉE WITH WALNUTS

A surprisingly simple and subtle preparation that has more flavor than you might imagine. Try to find squash of equal weight so you don't need to hang around to remove them from the oven at different times.

Makes 2 casseroles (each about 6 servings as a side dish)

6 pounds winter squash (preferably a combination of butternut, acorn, and Hubbard—be sure to include the butternut), washed
6 large baking apples (use Rome Beauties or York Imperials), washed
3/4 stick (6 tablespoons) butter
1 teaspoon ground coriander
1/4 teaspoon black pepper
1 cup walnuts
1 cup fine dry bread crumbs
2 tablespoons frozen butter

1. Set the squash on a large baking pan or sheet, preferably one with sides. Place in the oven, turn to 350°, and bake until the squash is soft. Timing will vary considerably, but you might figure that a 3-pound squash will take about 1 3/4 hours, and a 2-pound squash about 1 1/4 hours.
2. About 45 minutes before you expect the squash to be cooked through, poke a few holes in the apples, using a skewer or knife tip. Set them in the pan with the squash.

3. When both squash and apples are tender (about 45 minutes), remove them from the oven and cut in half to cool a bit. Scrape out seeds and pull off stems and peels. Remove the apple cores as well.
4. Press the apples and squash together through the medium disc of a food mill into a bowl. Beat in the butter, coriander, pepper, and salt to taste.
5. Combine the walnuts and crumbs in a blender or processor and chop to a medium-coarse texture.
6. Spread the purée in two fairly shallow baking/serving dishes, about 10 × 6 × 2 inches; one buttered, the other foil-lined. Sprinkle the nut-crumb mixture evenly over each. Shave a tablespoon of the frozen butter over each.
7. *To finish cooking for immediate serving:* Bake the buttered casserole in the top third of a preheated 425° oven for 30 minutes, or until the topping is browned and the squash is bubbling.

To freeze: Cool the purée in the foil-lined dish, cover with foil, and freeze. When frozen solid, you can remove the foil package, seal, label, and date it, and return to the freezer for storage up to 3 months.

To reheat: Remove the foil and set the purée in the same dish in which it was frozen. Cover, turn the oven to 350°, set the dish in the oven, and bake for about 45 minutes, or until heated through and softened. Uncover and bake at 400° for about 30 minutes longer, or until the top is slightly browned. If the dish was defrosted prior to reheating, bake only 20–25 minutes for the covered period, then go on to the uncovered baking.

SUGGESTED MENU FOR SIX

Cucumber Salad with Dill
Sautéed Liver, *or* Roast Duck *or* Chicken
*Barley, Mushroom, and Onion Casserole
Wine: Egri Bíkaver (from Hungary) *or* a Red Wine from Yugoslavia
Fresh Persimmons *or* *Apricot Kissel (Purée) with Cream (page 233)

BARLEY, MUSHROOM, AND ONION CASSEROLE

Barley, a mainstay in homes in Scotland, Scandinavia, and Eastern Europe, deserves considerably more attention from American cooks. It is hearty, flavorful, and nutritious and has a firm texture that holds up well when frozen. Tasty alongside lamb, beef, liver, or chicken, it adds a robust character to meals. When you are serving it with chicken or livers, brown the barley in a combination of chicken fat and butter, and use chicken stock for the cooking liquid. Similarly, use duck stock when you serve roast duck, beef stock when the grain accompanies beef, and lamb broth to follow suit.

Makes 2 casseroles (each about 6 servings)

3 cups barley
1 stick (8 tablespoons butter) (or 1/4 cup chicken, goose, or duck fat plus 1/2 stick butter)
4 medium onions chopped (about 3 cups)
1 medium-large garlic clove, minced (about 1 teaspoon)
2 teaspoons dried savory
1 bay leaf, crumbled or snipped small
1 pound mushrooms, thinly sliced (about 6 cups)
9 cups stock or broth
About 1 teaspoon salt (more if stock is not salted)

1. Preheat the oven to 350°. In a very large, heavy casserole brown the barley lightly in the butter. Add the onions and garlic and stir over moderate heat for 5 minutes. Add the savory, bay leaf, and mushrooms and stir for a few minutes. Add the stock and salt and bring to a simmer.
2. Cover tightly and bake for about 1 hour, or until the liquid is absorbed and the barley is tender, adding liquid if necessary.
3. Spoon half the mixture into a heated serving dish, or cool and refrigerate to reheat the next day.
4. *To freeze:* Spoon the remaining half of the barley mixture into a foil-lined baking dish. Cool, cover with foil, and freeze. When the barley is frozen solid, remove the wrapped mixture, seal, label, and date it, and return it to the freezer for storage up to 3 months.

To reheat: Unwrap the barley mixture and return it to the casserole in which it was frozen. Cover tightly, place in the oven, and turn the heat to 350°. Bake about 1 1/2–2 hours, or until heated through.

If you have defrosted the casserole beforehand, it will heat through in about an hour.

SUGGESTED MENU FOR SIX

*Crisp Savory Almonds (page 289)
Sautéed Fish Filets *or* Roast Cornish Hens
*Lima Bean Purée with Creamed Spinach
Wine: Mâcon-Villages *or* Muscadet
Green Salad
*Poached Apples with Rum and Lemon (page 237)

LIMA BEAN PURÉE WITH CREAMED SPINACH

Although, as a rule, convenience foods leave a good deal to be desired, both frozen limas and frozen spinach are worthwhile time-savers—if they have been properly handled by retailers. If your vegetables appear dried out and withered, or are covered with ice crystals, they have been defrosted—and should be returned.

Serve this rich, creamy dish as an accompaniment to simply prepared fish or such meats as roast lamb, poultry, veal, sautéed liver, or ham.

Makes 2 casseroles, each to serve 6 people

1 stick (8 tablespoons) butter
1 medium-large onion, minced (about 1 cup)
6 cups blanched, chopped spinach (about 6 pounds) or 4 packages (10 ounces each) frozen chopped spinach, thawed
1/4 cup all-purpose flour
1 1/2 teaspoons dried tarragon
2 cups milk
1 1/2 teaspoons salt
5 cups fresh lima beans (about 5 pounds in the pod) or 3 packages (10 ounces each) frozen lima beans
3/4 cup heavy cream
1/4 teaspoon grated nutmeg
White pepper
1 cup grated cheese (Gruyère, Swiss, or Jarlsberg)

1. Melt the butter in a very large skillet (or divide between 2 skillets). Add the onion and cook for about 5 minutes, until softened. Squeeze the moisture from the spinach and add it. Cook over high heat until the juices are almost completely evaporated. Add the flour and stir a few minutes. Add the tarragon and milk and 3/4 teaspoon of the salt. Stir over low heat for 5 minutes. Season to taste. Reserve.

(Continued)

2. Drop the limas into boiling water. Boil until tender, which can take as little as 5 minutes for small frozen beans and as long as 25 minutes for large, fresh beans. Drain the beans, then press them through the medium disc of a food mill into a large bowl. Beat in the cream. Add the nutmeg, the remaining salt, and white pepper to taste.
3. Butter one baking dish and foil-line another (each about 10 × 6 × 2 inches). Spread half the lima purée in each. Top each with half of the creamed spinach. Sprinkle half the cheese evenly over each.
4. *To finish cooking for immediate serving:* Set the buttered dish in the upper third of a preheated 425° oven and bake for about 30 minutes, or until the top is lightly browned and bubbling. If you prefer, you can cool the vegetables, cover, and refrigerate for up to 24 hours before heating.

To freeze: Cool the vegetables in the foil-lined dish, cover with foil, and freeze. When frozen solid, you can remove the foil package from the dish, seal, label, date, and return it to the freezer for storage up to 3 months.

To reheat: Place the vegetables, unwrapped, in the casserole in which they were frozen. Cover, place in the oven, turn heat to 350°, and bake until the vegetables are defrosted, about 1 1/2 hours. Remove the foil, turn the heat to 425°, and bake the casserole in the upper third of the oven until the topping is lightly browned and bubbling, about 15–30 minutes.

If you have defrosted the dish beforehand, you'll need only about 45 minutes covered heating time, then the higher-heat browning.

21
White Nights Suppers
Two Informal Meals for Chilly Times

On some busy winter evenings I can just about muster the energy to reheat food for dinner. The cold weather does not stimulate my senses, as it does for some, but makes me feel sleepy. Because a desire to cuddle up in a mohair blanket does not mix well with the exigencies of entertaining, completely prepared-ahead food is an absolute necessity during the nippiest months.

The two dinners that follow—one of Russian parentage, the other of German—are ones that need attention beforehand but require virtually none the night you serve them. You might set the table with trivets, serving utensils, and flowers as well as the place settings; arrange the hors d'oeuvres and refrigerate them; and lay out the tea or coffee accoutrements on a side table early in the day. That way you need only heat the food when you slump in the door.

DINNER À LA RUSSE FOR SIX

Iced Russian and Polish Vodkas
Sliced Dry Sausages/Pickles/Radishes
*Borsch
*Mushroom-Egg Pirozhki
*Apricot Kissel (Purée) with Cream
Russian Tea with Lemon

BORSCH

Aside from the fact that borsch (or borsch*t*) is of Slavic origin and contains beets, the many versions have little in common. Among the numerous guises are a delicate, clear, sweet-sour one; a creamy, smooth version; a borsch made with potatoes and beets only; a hefty one with pork, beef, and sausages; another hearty kind with duck. Some borsch stocks are based on meat, others on the beer-y homemade brew kvas.

As any recipe for a main-course soup with a large ingredient list is merely a guide, you can experiment with different root vegetables and stocks, but keep more or less the proportion of liquid and vegetables indicated in the recipe. When you make the soup in the summer, be sure to use some of the tender green tops of the beets, which add a pleasantly bitter edge. Whatever you do end up with, let the soup mellow for at least a day before serving, then taste and season to achieve a lightly sweet-sour balance.

By the way, if a processor ever came in handy, it's in making borsch.

Makes about 6 servings

2 smoked ham hocks (about 2 pounds)

3 quarts water

2 tablespoons lard (or use goose or bacon fat)

1 large onion, chopped (about 1 cup)

1 large garlic clove, minced

1 medium celery root (also called celeriac; about 8 ounces, without leaves), peeled and cut into very fine julienne, or coarsely grated or shredded

8 or 9 medium-size beets, peeled and cut into very fine julienne, or coarsely grated or shredded (about 6 cups)

1 tiny red cabbage (about 1 pound), or 1/2 small one, cored and finely shredded (about 5 cups)

1 large bay leaf, crumbled or snipped into tiny bits

1 can (1 pound) tomatoes

1/4 teaspoon black pepper

1/2 cup red wine vinegar or cider vinegar

Big pinch of ground cloves

1 tablespoon brown sugar

1. Combine the ham hocks and water and simmer, covered, until the meat is tender, about 1 hour. Remove and cool the meat. Reserve the broth.
2. In a very large pot melt the fat over moderate heat and stir in the onion. Cook until softened. Add the garlic, celery root, beets, cabbage, and bay leaf and cover the pot while you press the tomatoes through the medium disc of a food mill. (Or purée the tomatoes in a blender or processor, then press through a sieve.) Add to the vegetables with the pepper, vinegar, cloves, and brown sugar. Cover and cook over moderately low heat for 15 minutes, stirring occasionally.
3. Remove the rind and fat from the ham and discard it. Sliver the meat and set aside. Add the meat stock to the vegetables and simmer the soup, partly covered, for about 1 hour, or until the vegetables are tender. About 15 minutes before the soup is cooked through, add the ham pieces.
4. Cool the soup, then chill it for at least 1 day—longer if you like.
5. *To serve:* Heat the soup through and season to taste with salt and additional vinegar, sugar, and pepper.

MUSHROOM-EGG PIROZHKI

There are a number of filled dumplings, turnovers, loaves, and tartlets in the Slavic pastry repertoire: vatrushki—cheese-filled tartlets; pirogi—literally "pies"; pirozhki—"little pies"; pelmeni—boiled meat dumplings similar to Chinese wonton; vareniki—Ukrainian boiled dumplings that are either savory or sweet.

Since some cooks can't seem to leave well enough alone, I'm not making any of the above in traditional form, but rather a sort of Russian-flavored composite turnover of eggy yeast dough filled with hard-cooked eggs, mushrooms, onions, and dill. These are particularly cute little turnovers—plump and golden. Serve them warm, or at room temperature. Although the recipe yield is quite large, the leftover pirozhki are no hardship to have on hand for the next day or two. Just refresh briefly in a low oven. Do not freeze.

Makes 24 turnovers

PASTRY:

3/4 cup milk
3 tablespoons butter
1 1/2 teaspoons salt
1 packet dry yeast
1/4 cup warm (not hot) water
1 teaspoon sugar
2 eggs, beaten
About 4 cups all-purpose flour

FILLING:

1/2 stick (4 tablespoons) butter
1 medium onion, finely chopped
1 pound mushrooms, very finely chopped
1 1/2 teaspoons salt
1/2 teaspoon black pepper
1/8 teaspoon grated nutmeg
5 hard-cooked eggs, very finely chopped
1/4 cup snipped dill
2 cups cooked, cooled rice
1/4 cup sour cream

GLAZE:

1 egg
1 tablespoon water
1 teaspoon sugar
1 tablespoon poppy seeds

1. *To make the pastry:* Scald the milk in a small pan. Pour it into a large mixing bowl, add the butter and salt, and let cool to lukewarm. Meanwhile, combine the yeast, water, and sugar in a small bowl and let stand until doubled in volume, about 5–10 minutes. If the mixture doesn't puff up, begin again with fresh ingredients.
2. Add the yeast mixture to the milk and stir. Add the eggs and 2 cups flour and mix well. Add another cup of flour and mix well. Spread the remaining flour on a working surface and drop the dough onto it. Knead well, adding flour if needed, but keeping the dough quite soft. Knead until the dough is very smooth and shiny.
3. Place in a greased bowl and turn to coat all sides. Let rise at room temperature (about 75°) until doubled in bulk, 1 1/2–2 hours.
4. *To make the filling:* While the dough is rising, melt the 1/2 stick butter in a large pan and cook the onion until wilted. Add the mushrooms and cook over high heat, stirring constantly, until almost no juices remain. The vegetables should almost form a paste. Add the salt, pepper, and nutmeg and spread on a plate to cool. When cooled, mix lightly in a bowl with the eggs, dill, rice, and sour cream. Season assertively (add more dill if desired) and cool. Cover and store in the refrigerator up to 2 days, or until you form the pirozhki.

5. Divide the dough into four parts. Cut each part into six equal pieces and cover them with a sheet of plastic. Remove one piece at a time and roll it out on a floured surface to make a circle about 4 inches in diameter.
6. Spread a heaping tablespoon of the filling toward one side of each circle. Moisten the rim with water and fold the dough over the filling to make a neat half-moon. The package will be tightly filled. Press down the edge very firmly to seal it, then press again with the tines of a fork to seal very thoroughly. Place the filled pirozhok on a nonstick, or parchment-covered, or lightly greased baking sheet. Preheat the oven to 350°.
7. When twelve pirozhki have been filled, mix together the egg, water, and sugar for the glaze. Brush a thin, even layer on each turnover. Sprinkle the pirozhki with half the poppy seeds. Bake for about 30 minutes in the center of the oven, until well browned. Cool on a rack.
8. While the first batch is baking, make up the rest of the turnovers and complete as above. When all are completely cooled, wrap and store in the refrigerator for 1–2 days.
9. *To serve:* Unwrap the pirozhki, place on a baking sheet, and bake in a preheated 300° oven for about 15 minutes, until crisped. Serve warm, or cooled to room temperature.

APRICOT KISSEL (PURÉE) WITH CREAM

This Russian-style fruit purée is usually made from very tart berries. Although it is sometimes thickened sufficiently to be shaped in a mold, I prefer it softly spoonable, as it is in the following recipe. Add the honey gradually when you sweeten the purée, as some tartness lends a refreshing contrast to the very smooth fruit consistency and the rich cream. American, rather than Middle Eastern dried apricots, are recommended because they are not as sugary.

Makes 6 servings

2 cups dried California apricot halves
4 cups water
4–8 tablespoons honey (not the strong, dark kinds)
1½ tablespoons potato starch stirred into 3 tablespoons water
3–4 tablespoons Calvados or brandy
1 cup heavy cream
Extrafine sugar

1. Combine the apricots and water and bring to a boil. Simmer, partly covered, for 20–30 minutes, or until the fruit is very tender.
2. Purée the fruit and liquid to a very smooth consistency in the blender or processor. Rub through a fine sieve. Sweeten to taste with honey. Return to the pot.
3. Stir the starch mixture and add it to the apricots. Add the Calvados gradually, tasting. Bring to a simmer, stirring vigorously. Simmer, stirring, for 2 minutes. Spoon into 6 glasses or glass dishes; cool and refrigerate.
4. *To serve:* Whip the cream to barely form peaks, adding extrafine sugar to taste. Serve in a bowl along with the kissel.

DINNER GERMAN-ESQUE FOR SIX

*Smoked Fish Canapés with Horseradish Butter
*Sauerbraten en Casserole
*Diced Potatoes with Crumb Topping or *Kasha (page 179)
German or Czech Beer
Cucumber Salad
*Poached Apples with Rum and Lemon
Coffee/Ginger Cookies

SMOKED FISH CANAPÉS WITH HORSERADISH BUTTER

The German-style meal begins with smoked fish canapés. If you've never made them, a few suggestions might be useful. Chub, sturgeon, whitefish, salmon, sable, trout, or eel are all delicious openers for a sturdy meal. Buy whatever your neighborhood has to offer. Cream some sweet butter and beat in freshly grated (or drained bottled) horseradish and a little bit of scallion or chives. Or else mix the butter with a German mustard, if you're not a horseradish fan. Spread the mixture on very thin, small pieces of black bread and refrigerate until serving time. To serve, top with the fish pieces, cut to size.

SAUERBRATEN EN CASSEROLE

Perhaps sauerbraten is the dish most often thought of when German food is mentioned. Unfortunately, it is more often than not too sharply vinegared or overly sweetened. The following recipe produces meat that is tender, with a rich, brown, slightly thickened, gently sweet sauce. The flavor is not too acid because the meat is marinated in twice as much red wine and water as vinegar. The slicing and saucing of the meat before storage and subsequent reheating keep it moist and ensure a minimum of last-minute preparation. If you have a larding needle, you might want to insert strips of pork fat into the beef, running with the grain, for an even more succulent dish.

Makes about 6 servings

About 3 1/2 pounds beef roast (either rump or top or bottom round, in a neat piece without muscle separation)
1 tablespoon coarse (kosher) salt
1 cup red wine vinegar
2 cups red wine
2 cups water
4 tablespoons sugar
2 carrots, thinly sliced
2 onions, thinly sliced
2 bay leaves, crumbled or snipped small
1/2 teaspoon black peppercorns
6 whole cloves
1/2 teaspoon whole allspice
1/2 teaspoon coriander seeds (optional)
2 tablespoons all-purpose flour
2 tablespoons lard or vegetable oil
1 tablespoon water

1. Trim excess fat from the meat and rub the roast with the salt. Place in a bowl that is deep enough to allow for a covering of the marinade.
2. Combine the vinegar, red wine, water, 2 tablespoons of the sugar, the carrots, onions, bay leaves, peppercorns, cloves, allspice, and coriander seeds in a nonaluminum saucepan. Simmer for 5 minutes.
3. Pour the marinade over the meat and let cool. Cover with plastic wrap and refrigerate for 2–5 days, depending upon how much flavoring you like. Turn the meat daily in the marinade.
4. Preheat the oven to 350°. Drain the meat and reserve the marinade. Dry the beef and coat it with the flour. If the meat is not a firm, even shape, tie it with string to make a neat package. In a heavy pot

(Continued)

or Dutch oven just large enough to hold the meat comfortably, melt the lard or oil. Deeply brown the meat on all sides over moderate heat. Transfer the meat to a plate and pour out all but a thin slick of fat.

5. With a slotted spoon remove the carrots and onions from the marinade and cook them in a Dutch oven, stirring, over high heat until they are lightly browned. Add 2½ cups of the marinade and bring to a boil, stirring.

6. Add the meat, cover, and bake for about 2½ hours, or until very tender. Timing can vary considerably, so check often. Remove the meat to a cutting board.

7. Strain the sauce into a bowl, pressing down hard to extract all the juices and forcing through some of the soft vegetables. Skim off whatever fat you can.

8. Boil the remaining 2 tablespoons sugar and the 1 tablespoon water in a small, heavy pan, swirling often until the sugar caramelizes to a medium brown. Remove from the heat, and with your face averted to avoid splatters, add ½ cup of the sauce. Boil to dissolve the caramel. Pour the mixture into a larger pan and add the remaining sauce. Simmer for a few minutes. If you like a thicker sauce, boil a little longer. Taste and season, then cool.

9. Carve the meat into ¼-inch-thick slices and arrange them, overlapping, in a baking/serving dish. Spoon the sauce over all, cover the dish with foil, and store in the refrigerator up to 2 days.

10. *To serve:* Set the meat in the oven, turn to 400°, and bake with the foil cover in place for about 40 minutes, or until the meat is hot through and the sauce is bubbling.

DICED POTATOES WITH CRUMB TOPPING

This is not a creamy-buttery dish, although both cream and butter are included. They keep the potato pieces from drying out when reheated, without contributing any visible sauce. The potatoes emerge from the oven tender, in separate cubes, under their browned crumbs.

Makes 6 servings

$2\frac{1}{2}$–3 pounds all-purpose potatoes, peeled and cut into ½-inch dice (7–8 cups)
⅔ cup heavy cream
½ teaspoon salt
3 tablespoons butter
$1\frac{1}{4}$ cups fine dry bread crumbs

1. Cook the potatoes in a very large pot of boiling salted water for 3 minutes, or until they are just barely cooked through. Drain. Spread in 2–3 layers in a buttered wide, shallow baking/serving dish.
2. Boil the cream in a small pan to reduce it to ½ cup. Stir in the salt and sprinkle the cream over the potatoes.
3. Melt the butter in a pan and stir in the crumbs. Stir over low heat until the crumbs are crisp and golden, about 3–4 minutes. Sprinkle the crumbs very evenly over the top of the potatoes. Press down to make an even layer. Cover with foil and refrigerate.
4. *To serve:* Set the potatoes, still covered with the foil, in a cold oven. Turn the heat to 400° and bake for 20 minutes. Remove the foil and continue baking for about 20–25 minutes longer, or until the potatoes are hot through and the crumbs are crisp and browned.

POACHED APPLES WITH RUM AND LEMON

This dessert is about as simple as can be, but to be worthwhile it must not be mushy. Choose only very firm, fresh apples and keep a close watch on their cooking progress.

Makes about 6 servings

2 cups water
⅔ cup sugar
Grated rind of 1 lemon
8–9 medium-large apples (preferably Golden Delicious, Rome Beauties, or York Imperials)
About 2 tablespoons rum
Crème fraîche or sour cream (optional)

1. In a large, deep skillet or wide saucepan combine the water, sugar, and lemon rind and bring to a boil, stirring. Simmer for 5 minutes. Set aside.

2. Peel, quarter, and core the apples. There should be about 7–8 cups apples. Add to the syrup and bring to a bare simmer. Barely simmer the apples, covered, until they are not quite tender, stirring them around in the syrup gently, and often. Poaching time can take from 5 to 15 minutes, depending on the apple variety. Take care not to let the fruit get too soft, as it will continue to cook in the syrup after having been removed from the heat. Add rum to taste.

3. Spoon the apples into a serving dish and pour the syrup over. Cool completely, then cover and refrigerate.

4. *To serve:* You can stir a little of the syrup into a small bowl of crème fraîche or sour cream and serve on the side. Or enjoy the apples plain, which is lovely when the fruit is at its flowery, fragrant peak.

22
Valentine Weekend for Two

An Amorous Antidote to Winter Doldrums

Romantic, for me, means no need to get dressed, no watching the clock, and plenty of fine food and wine, consumed in leisurely fashion. Hence, this two-day affair for homebodies, with main dishes that double for both days. Comestibles and potables for this continuous pleasure have been chosen for their amorous connotations as well as their deliciousness.

MENUS FOR AN AT-HOME WEEKEND

SATURDAY

MORNING, MORE OR LESS

*Love Feast Buns
*Coeurs à la Crème
Sliced and Sugared Strawberries
Tea

AFTERNOON

Roasted Nuts/Tangerines
Sherry *or* Port

(Continued)

EVENING

*Nu et Cru *or* Oysters on the Half Shell
Wine: Muscadet with Nu et Cru, Champagne *or*
Dry White Sparkling Wine with the Oysters
*Roast Marinated Tenderloin of Beef
Wine: Elegant Red Burgundy such as Chambolle-Musigny,
Les Amoureuses, *or* a Saint-Amour from Beaujolais
*Love Apples (Tomatoes) with Herbs
*Wild Rice with Mushrooms
Espresso/*Lemon Sighs (or Kisses)

NIGHTCAP

*Hot Chocolate

SUNDAY

MORNING-ISH

Café au Lait
*Bread Custard with Strawberry Sauce

AFTERNOON

Amuse-Bouche ("amuse-the-mouth"): Canapés of white bread
topped with avocado, sprinkled with salmon eggs and lime
juice/Cherry Tomatoes or Sweet Red Pepper Strips
Iced Vodka, briefly infused with cracked grains of paradise
(a rare spice) or cracked peppercorns and lemon peel

EVENING

*Mushroom Broth with Dill
*Cold Tenderloin of Beef
Wine: Paradiso or Inferno (depending on how the weekend is going)
or another wine from the Valtellina area such as
Sassella, Grumello, *or* Valgella
*Wild Rice Salad with Walnuts and Fennel
Cheese, such as *Fol Amour *or* Caprice des Dieux/Ripe Pears

NIGHTCAP

*Angel's Dream

SATURDAY MORNING

LOVE FEAST BUNS

Although the name of these sweet, soft buns seems to have a carnal connotation, it is, in fact, religious in origin. Moravian settlers in Pennsylvania and North Carolina served the rolls and other sugary baked goods at church services celebrating the spiritual brother/sisterhood of man/womankind. The love feast was originally served to commemorate the Last Supper—not the first breakfast, as here.

Makes 12 buns

1 large all-purpose potato, peeled and quartered
1 packet dry yeast
3/4 cup sugar
1/2 teaspoon salt
2 eggs
1 stick (8 tablespoons) unsalted butter, softened
About 4 1/2 cups all-purpose flour
GLAZE: 2 tablespoons milk mixed with 1 tablespoon sugar

1. Boil the potato in water to cover until tender. Drain off the water and reserve it; let cool to lukewarm. Press the potato through a food mill or a strainer into a large bowl and let it cool. There should be roughly 3/4 cup.
2. While the potato is cooling, mix the yeast, a large pinch of sugar, and 1/2 cup of the lukewarm potato water in a cup. Let stand until very fluffy, about 10 minutes. If the mixture doesn't puff up, begin again with fresh ingredients. Add to the potato with the 3/4 cup sugar, the salt, eggs, and butter. Beat to blend well.
3. Gradually mix in 3 1/2 cups flour. Spread the remaining flour on a work surface and plop the soft dough into the center. Knead well, adding as little additional flour as possible, to make a soft, shiny dough that is elastic and no longer sticky.
4. Place the dough in a buttered bowl and turn to coat, then cover the bowl with plastic wrap. Let the dough stand at room temperature until doubled in bulk—about 2 hours, as rich doughs require a longer rise.

(Continued)

5. Punch down the dough, divide it into 4 pieces, and cover 3 of the pieces with plastic wrap. Divide the uncovered piece into 3 portions. Form each piece into a neat ball by pinching the underneath side to make a smooth shape. Place the balls well apart on a parchment-covered, nonstick, or lightly greased large baking sheet. Repeat the operation with the rest of the dough. Cover the buns with a cloth and let rise until almost doubled in bulk, about 1½ hours. Meanwhile, preheat the oven to 350°.
6. Bake the buns in the center of the oven for 15 minutes. Brush with the glaze and bake 10–15 minutes longer, or until the buns sound hollow when you thump the bottoms. Cool on racks.
7. *To store and serve:* Set aside enough buns for breakfast, plus two for the Bread Custard with Strawberry Sauce (page 250). You can leave these unwrapped, at room temperature, for as long as 2 days. Tightly wrap and freeze the remainder for as long as 3 months. Refresh the buns, either frozen and thawed or freshly baked ones, in a 200° oven shortly before serving. If the buns were frozen, thaw them overnight in the refrigerator before heating.

COEURS À LA CRÈME

Makes 2 small cream hearts

½ small package (3 ounces) cream cheese, at room temperature
2 tablespoons sour cream
1 tablespoon confectioners' sugar
⅛ teaspoon salt
¼ cup heavy cream (or use homemade crème fraîche)

1. Blend the cream cheese, sour cream, confectioners' sugar, and salt in a small bowl with an electric beater or whisk.
2. Beat the heavy cream or crème fraîche in a small chilled bowl until soft peaks form. Fold thoroughly into the cheese mixture, blending with a rubber spatula.
3. Line 2 small porcelain coeur à la crème molds (see list of mail-order sources, page 353) with 1 layer of fine-mesh or 2 layers of loose-mesh dampened cheesecloth. Divide the cream mixture between them, fold over the cloth, place the molds on a plate, and let them drain several hours at room temperature. (If you are going to sleep, leave them overnight.) Refrigerate at least 8 hours before unmolding to serve as a spread on the Love Feast Buns (page 241).

SLICED AND SUGARED STRAWBERRIES

Strawberries are, at their best, rosy, tender little fruits with valentine qualities. Mention of them provides the happy opportunity to quote one of the most delightful observers of human nature and food—the Reverend Sydney Smith (1771–1845), who once commented on his clerical status as it related to the luscious berries: "What is real piety? What is true attachment to the Church? How are these fine feelings best evinced? The answer is plain: by sending strawberries to a clergyman. Many thanks."

You'll need about a pint of berries. Rinse them briefly before hulling, in case they came from sandy beds, then slice and sugar to taste.

SATURDAY AFTERNOON

SHERRY

For a languorous late-afternoon nip, a full-flavored sweet Sherry is a nice change of pace. Oloroso (Spanish for fragrant) is the term that characterizes a group of Sherries that might suit the occasion, although unfortunately the word does not always appear on the bottle. Despite labeling inconsistencies, the common characteristics of Olorosos do exist: They are all a deep amber color; they range from semisweet to sweet; they have an intense, rich perfume.

Perhaps the Sherry best named for this romantic weekend is the delicate Oloroso called "Amoroso." Julian Jeffs in his book *Sherry* (2nd ed.; London: Ebenezer Baylis & Son, Ltd., 1970) defines the term "amoroso" as one

> used chiefly in England for a type of light and not very dry *oloroso* sherry. *Amorosos* are smooth, sweet *olorosos* that justify their name, which in Spanish means loving. But the name of the wine has nothing to do with *amor;* it was that of a famous vineyard which was noted for such wines. The name is still sometimes used owing to its beauty, though sherries of this style are more often called cream.

SATURDAY EVENING

NU ET CRU

Nu et cru (translated straight: naked and raw) is a simple Provençal treatment for raw fish described by Mireille Johnston in her book *The Cuisine of the Sun* (Random House, 1976). The name of the dish seemed irresistible for this chapter, but in fact any easy-to-assemble seafood hors d'oeuvre would do well here—including simple canapés of smoked salmon or trout, if you don't fancy raw fishies. Instead of making Ms. Johnston's strips of whiting, I prefer to cut very small cubes of salmon, tuna, or scallops, and then toss them with her recommended seasonings—lemon juice, oil, parsley, chives, pepper, and a sprinkle of capers. Be very light-handed when flavoring raw fish, as it is easily overpowered. Chill the dish for a few hours to blend the tastes, then serve. If the oil has congealed, let the fish stand briefly at room temperature before serving.

OYSTERS ON THE HALF SHELL WITH LEMON

These bivalves have such a long and lascivious history that it is almost unnecessary to dwell on their aphrodisiac past—but one description for the occasion can't hurt:

> Oisters do justly deserve a full treatice, being so common and withall so wholesome a meat; they differ in colour, substance, and bigness, but the best are thick, little and round-sheld, not slippery nor flaggy through abundance of a gellied humour, but short, firm and thick of flesh, riseing up round like a woman's breast, being in manner all belly and no fins (*Health's Improvement* by Thomas Muffet, 1655).

CHAMPAGNE

Speaking of bosoms, the origin of the wide, shallow-stemmed glass that is often used for Champagne is Marie Antoinette's perfect breast, molded in Sèvres porcelain. Beautiful as it may have been, most agree that Champagne is better served in either a tulip-shaped glass or a tall, slender glass (a "flute") to maintain a slow fizzle of the precious bubbles, rather than the barrage produced by pouring Champagne into the more usual saucer shape.

ROAST MARINATED TENDERLOIN OF BEEF

This is one of the few made-ahead meals in this book in which actual cooking, rather than reheating, takes place at dinner time. But the idea is the same: There is no last-minute adjusting to be done. The dish is assembled beforehand; it just needs to be put in the oven and a timer set. Note that you'll need a day to marinate the meat before roasting.

Makes 2 servings (with half reserved for Sunday's dinner)

1½ pounds beef tenderloin, without added barding (wrapping) fat
¼ cup red wine
1 tablespoon brandy
3 tablespoons olive oil
1 garlic clove, thinly sliced
2 teaspoons green peppercorns (see list of mail-order sources, page 353), drained (if liquid packed) and crushed
½ teaspoon salt
1 large bay leaf, crumbled or snipped into tiny pieces

1. Tie the beef in a neat cylinder, if the butcher has not done this already. Place it in a heavy plastic bag.
2. Combine the wine, brandy, oil, garlic, peppercorns, salt, and bay leaf in a dish and mix well. Pour over the beef, close the bag tightly, and place on a dish in the refrigerator. Marinate for 1 day or more, turning the bag over whenever you think of it.
3. Preheat the oven to 425°. Remove the beef from the bag and scrape off clinging garlic bits. Roast the meat in a pan in the center of the oven for about ½ hour, or until a meat or instant-reading thermometer registers 120° (for rare meat).
4. Set the meat on a carving board and let it rest for 15 minutes. Meanwhile, turn the oven down to 375° and bake the tomatoes (see following recipe). Cut off, wrap, and refrigerate half the beef for Sunday's meal. Carve the rest for dinner.

LOVE APPLES (TOMATOES) WITH HERBS

Love apples are tomatoes, and cherry tomatoes are among the oldest forms of love apples. The etymological exercise required to explain how the old name came about is far too strenuous for such a lazy weekend.

Makes 2 servings

1 tablespoon olive oil
1 box (1 dry pint) cherry tomatoes, washed and hulled
1–2 tablespoons mixed finely minced fresh herbs (such as a combination of parsley, chives, and tarragon or dill or thyme)

1. Select a baking/serving dish that will hold the tomatoes close together in one layer. Pour the oil in the dish and roll the tomatoes around to coat them well.
2. Sprinkle the tomatoes with the herbs, a sprinkle of sugar, and salt and pepper to taste. Cover with foil and leave at room temperature until you're ready to make dinner—which can be hours later.
3. *To bake:* When you've roasted the Marinated Tenderloin of Beef (see preceding recipe), set the dish of tomatoes in the 375° oven for 5 minutes. Remove the foil and bake about 10 minutes longer, or until the tomatoes are softened and just beginning to split. Do not overcook or they'll burst. Serve hot.

WILD RICE WITH MUSHROOMS

This is a lavish amount of rice for two, so cut down if you're less wild about wild rice than some of us!

Makes 2 generous servings (plus plenty for the Wild Rice Salad with Walnuts and Fennel—see following recipe)

1/2 pound wild rice (about 1 1/2 cups; see list of mail-order sources, page 353)
1 1/2 teaspoons salt
About 3 cups water
2 tablespoons butter
6 ounces small mushrooms, rinsed and sliced
1 tablespoon finely minced shallots
Grated nutmeg

1. Rinse the rice and remove any bits of soil or pebbles. Combine in a saucepan with the salt and 3 cups water and bring to a boil over high heat.
2. Reduce the heat to its lowest point and cover the pot. Cook 1/2–1 hour, until rice is tender but still chewy, not soft. Timing varies considerably, so begin tasting after 30 minutes. Add water, if needed, then drain if necessary when the rice is done.
3. Remove half the rice from the pot and spread in a strainer to dry. This is for Sunday's salad, which may be made at this point (see following recipe).
4. Melt the butter in a pan. Add the mushrooms and shallots and cook over high heat, stirring, until lightly browned. Add to the rice in the pot and season with nutmeg, salt, and pepper. Scrape into a buttered baking/serving dish. Cool, cover with foil, and store in the refrigerator.
5. *To serve:* Place the foil-covered dish in the oven with the beef for the last 15 minutes or so of roasting time. Uncover and stir lightly with a fork. Lower the heat to 375° and bake about 10 minutes longer, or until the rice is heated through and the tomatoes (page 246) cooked.

WILD RICE SALAD WITH WALNUTS AND FENNEL

The recipe for wild rice salad is provided here instead of on Sunday's schedule because it makes more sense to prepare it at this point. Warm rice absorbs dressing and flavors more willingly than cold.

The distinctive, nutty flavor of this grain, the seed of a wild grass, is particularly apparent in cold preparations. Although the interesting combination of textures is immediately discernible, the subtle flavors of this salad develop slowly on the palate. Yet you might call this dish downright blatant when compared to the recipe created by Li Liweng, a seventeenth-century Chinese gastronomer-philosopher. He explained that "when the rice is just cooked, pour a little . . . dew on it. . . . The dew on wild roses, cassis, and citron flowers is best, as these fragrances are not easily distinguished from that of rice. The dew collected from garden roses is too easily identified" (*Chinese Gastronomy* by Hsiang Ju Lin and Tsuifeng Lin, 1972).

Makes 2 servings

1/4 cup walnut halves or pieces
About 2 1/2 cups cooked wild rice (see preceding recipe)
3 tablespoons walnut oil (see list of mail-order sources, page 353) or use peanut oil
1 tablespoon white wine vinegar
1/8 teaspoon salt
1/8 teaspoon black pepper
1 scallion green, thinly sliced
1/2 small fennel bulb

1. Preheat the oven to 325°. Toast the walnuts in a pan in the oven for 15 minutes. Cool them and set aside until serving time.
2. Transfer the reserved wild rice (step 3, page 247) from the strainer to a serving dish. Combine the oil, vinegar, salt, pepper, and scallion green in a cup; mix. Pour over the rice and mix gently with a rubber spatula. Cover and refrigerate until serving time, which can be the next day.
3. *To serve:* Pull off any heavy "strings" from the fennel. Slice the stalks across into small, very thin pieces; mince the leaves (tops). Add the sliced stalks to the rice salad with the toasted nuts, then toss gently. Sprinkle with the minced fennel leaves and serve.

LEMON SIGHS (OR KISSES)

Of the several pastries given a "sigh" appellation, the majority are meringue-based. Curiously, the same cookie poufs called sighs (soupirs, suspiros) in Romance languages are known as kisses in English. Even more curious is the etymological route followed by the popular French souffléed fritter called soupir de nonne (nun's sigh), commonly called pet de nonne (nun's fart), but originally called soupir de putain (whore's sigh)!

All meringues are sweet by nature, but they can be chewy or powder-dry, which dramatically changes the impact of the sweetness. The following recipe is for the dry variety, aromatic with lemon, crunchy with almonds. Since sighs or kisses last very well, you may want to double the small recipe.

Makes 12 cookies

1/4 cup blanched almonds
2 egg whites ("extra-large")
1/8 teaspoon cream of tartar
1/4 teaspoon vanilla
1/8 teaspoon almond extract
2/3 cup confectioners' sugar
2 teaspoons grated lemon rind

1. Preheat the oven to 325°. Spread the almonds on a pan and bake for about 15 minutes, tossing occasionally, until lightly golden. Turn the oven to 250° and remove the nuts. Let them cool completely, then sliver or chop coarsely.
2. Beat the egg whites in a small bowl with an electric mixer until foamy. Add the cream of tartar and beat 30 seconds. Add the vanilla and almond extract and beat 30 seconds longer on high speed.
3. Beat in the confectioners' sugar, about 1 1/2 tablespoons at a time, beating on high speed for 30 seconds after each addition. Blend often with a rubber spatula. Gently fold in the lemon rind and almonds.
4. Using a rubber spatula to dislodge the mixture, drop tablespoons of the meringue onto a nonstick or parchment-covered baking sheet to form about 12 equally spaced mounds.
5. Bake at 250° for 1 1/2 hours. Turn off the oven and leave the kisses for several hours, or overnight. Remove from the oven and store airtight, for weeks.

HOT CHOCOLATE

Chocolate's reputation as an aphrodisiac is as ancient as its written history. In what is probably one of the earliest references to this New World food (1519), Bernal Díaz, chronicler of the conquistador Cortés, wrote that Montezuma was served "in cups of pure gold a drink made from the cocoa-plant, which they said he took before visiting his wives. We did not take much notice of this at the time, though I saw them bring in a good fifty large jugs of this chocolate" (*The Conquest of New Spain*, tr. by J. M. Cohen, Penguin Books, 1963).

If Mexican chocolate is available to you, it makes a splendid nightcap. The chocolate, which has been mixed with ground almonds, sugar, and considerable quantities of cinnamon, can be melted in water and/or milk. Froth up the mixture with an eggbeater or a molinillo, the Mexican hand swizzle, or beater, created specifically for this job. If you can't get the Mexican chocolate, melt semisweet chocolate in the milk, and flavor with cinnamon and a tiny drop of almond extract.

SUNDAY MORNING

BREAD CUSTARD WITH STRAWBERRY SAUCE

Makes 2 generous servings

2 reserved Love Feast Buns (page 241)
2 eggs
1 1/2 cups milk
1/4 cup heavy cream
1/8 teaspoon grated nutmeg
1/8 teaspoon ground cinnamon
1/8 teaspoon salt
2 tablespoons sugar
1 pint strawberries, rinsed and hulled

1. Trim the crust off the buns and discard it. Cut each bun in half, then cut each half into slices 1/2 inch thick. Butter a circular or oval dish at least 2 inches deep that will hold the bread in 2 layers; arrange the bread in the dish.
2. Beat together the eggs, milk, cream, nutmeg, cinnamon, salt, and sugar. Strain over the bread, cover with foil, and refrigerate overnight. Or, if you prefer to assemble the custard in the morning, let it stand 1/2 hour or more before baking.
3. *To bake and serve:* Preheat the oven to 350°. Place the pudding, covered, in a larger pan or dish and pour boiling water around it to come about halfway up the custard. Bake for 35 minutes. Uncover and bake about 10 minutes longer, or until the surface is lightly golden.
4. While the custard is baking, purée the strawberries in a blender or processor with sugar to taste. Strain into a small pitcher and serve with the hot bread custard.

SUNDAY EVENING

MUSHROOM BROTH WITH DILL

Makes 2 servings

6 ounces small mushrooms, cleaned
1 medium shallot, chopped
$2^1/_2$ cups beef stock, skimmed of all fat
Few tablespoons of the dinner wine
Few tablespoons finely snipped dill

1. Combine about two thirds of the mushrooms, the shallot, and half the broth in the container of a blender or processor and chop fine. Transfer to a saucepan, add the remaining stock, and simmer gently for about 15 minutes.
2. Strain through a sieve lined with fine-mesh cotton cheesecloth, then season. Either go on to the next step, if you're serving the soup at once, or cool and refrigerate for the next day.
3. *To serve:* Thinly slice the remaining mushrooms and add them. Simmer for a minute to just barely cook the mushrooms. Add the red wine and dill to taste. Serve hot.

FOL AMOUR OR CAPRICE DES DIEUX

These whimsical names belong to two soft, double-cream cheeses made from cow's milk. Translated "mad love" and "whim of the gods," either might serve ideally as a grand finale to this fling. If you can't locate them, use another ripe, rich dessert cheese.

NIGHTCAP

ANGEL'S DREAM

This drink is nothing more than crème de cacao, with heavy cream floated gently on top, which is heavenly, if you're fond of crème de cacao. Anyway, the thought suits for a nightcap.

If you imagine that the name is a bit fanciful, there are quite a few liqueurs from times gone by that could easily compete: Melancholy Water, The Longer the Better, Rose without Thorns, Bitter Suffering, and Venus Oil—to name a few.

23
Made and Waiting

Frozen Entrées for Economical, Easy Entertaining

Herewith a helpful handful of inexpensive main-dish casseroles to be frozen, then reheated in the months to come for casual, inexpensive dining.

Please read Reminders about Freezing, page 352.

SUGGESTED MENU FOR FOUR

*Spicy Lamb and Chickpea Stew
Cucumber and Yogurt Salad (to serve on the same plate as the stew, like a relish or condiment)
Cherry Tomatoes
Wine: Chilean Cabernet Sauvignon *or* California Petite Sirah
Turkish Coffee/Tangerines/*Sugared Almonds (page 208)

SPICY LAMB AND CHICKPEA STEW

Rack of lamb is not exactly an economy cut these days, but it was when Lydia Maria Child (the very same remarkable woman who worked as abolitionist, women's rights reformer, poet, magazine editor, newspaperwoman, and novelist) wrote in her book of household tips, *The American Frugal Housewife* (1832): "That part of mutton called the rack . . . is cheap food. It is not more than four or five cents a pound." But flavorful, chewy lamb shank is, comparatively, a "bargain cut," which takes well to slow cooking and freezing.

Makes 2 casseroles (each about 4 servings)

About 1½ pounds (4 cups) dried chickpeas
6 cups water
6 small lamb shanks, trimmed
3 tablespoons vegetable oil
4 medium-size leeks, trimmed of roots and dark green tops, well washed and thinly sliced
3 medium garlic cloves, sliced
2 tablespoons ground coriander
4 teaspoons ground cumin
1 teaspoon ground cinnamon
1 tablespoon salt
Finely minced fresh parsley or cilantro (fresh coriander or Chinese parsley)
Thin lemon slices

1. Soak the chickpeas overnight in a large pot of water to cover by at least 4 inches. Drain. Add the 6 cups water, then simmer the chickpeas, covered, until they are not quite tender. Timing can vary considerably; start checking at about 1 hour.
2. Broil the lamb shanks, turning often, until they are browned lightly on all sides, about 20 minutes. Preheat the oven to 325°.
3. Heat the oil in a very large pot (which later will hold everything). Stir in the leeks and cook until softened. Stir in the garlic, coriander, cumin, cinnamon, and salt. Add the chickpeas and their liquid, then the browned meat.
4. Bake, covered, for about 40 minutes, or until the lamb is tender. Remove the meat with tongs and let cool. Meanwhile, set the pot in a sink containing cold water. When the meat has cooled somewhat, cut it into bite-size pieces and discard the bones. Stir the meat into the pot of chickpeas. Divide the mixture between two foil-lined containers, cover with foil, and freeze. When solidly frozen, remove the foil packages, seal, label, and date and return to the freezer for storage (up to 3 months).
5. *To serve:* Defrost the stew entirely in the appropriate pot. Heat, covered, in a 350° oven until it is bubbling throughout, about 1 hour. Stir gently several times while the dish is heating. Sprinkle with cilantro or parsley. Arrange lemon slices over this and serve.

SUGGESTED MENU FOR FOUR

*Pork and Sweet Potato Stew
Pumpernickel Bread *or* *Christmas Rye Bread, Swedish Style (page 188)
California Fumé Blanc Wine *or* Beer
Salad of Cooked Broccoli Florets and Red Pepper *or* *Gingered Red Cabbage Slaw (page 311)
Coffee/Caramel Custard

PORK AND SWEET POTATO STEW

A thick, pungent, sweetish stew to warm the evening.

Makes 2 casseroles (each about 4 servings)

3 pounds boneless pork shoulder (preferred) or loin, cut into 1-inch cubes
1/3 cup all-purpose flour
About 2 tablespoons vegetable oil
About 2 tablespoons butter
2 large garlic cloves, sliced
3 pounds sweet potatoes, peeled and cut into 1-inch cubes
1/2 cup dry Sherry
2 cups orange juice
1/2 cup lemon juice
5–6 strips dried orange peel
2 teaspoons salt
1 teaspoon dried marjoram
1/3 cup honey
1/2 teaspoon black pepper

1. Preheat the oven to 325°. Toss the pork with the flour to coat it lightly. Shake off the excess. Brown the pieces over moderate heat in a large skillet in batches, using as much of the oil and butter as needed. Transfer the pieces to a large flameproof casserole as they are browned. Sauté the garlic for a moment in the remaining fat and add to the pork. Set aside.
2. Drop the potatoes into a large pot of boiling water; boil for 2 minutes—no more. Drain and add to the pork.
3. Pour the Sherry, orange juice, and lemon juice into the skillet; add the orange peel, salt, marjoram, honey, and pepper and bring to a boil, stirring. Pour the mixture over the meat and potatoes and bring to a simmer.

4. Place the casserole in the oven and bake for about 45 minutes, or until the pork and potatoes are almost but not quite tender. Set the pot to cool in a sink containing cold water. Stir the stew occasionally and gently, to avoid mushing the potatoes. When cooled, divide between two foil-lined dishes, cover with foil, and freeze. When frozen solid, remove the foil packages, seal, label, and date, and return to the freezer for storage (up to 3 months).
5. *To serve:* Defrost the stew entirely in the appropriate dish. Cover with foil and bake in a preheated 350° oven for about 45 minutes, until hot through. Uncover, stir gently, being careful not to break the potatoes, and bake about 15 minutes longer, until bubbling.

SUGGESTED MENU FOR FOUR

*Oxtail Soup-Stew
*Crusty Whole-Wheat Loaves (page 100)
or *Cracked-Oat Bread (page 347)
Wine: California Zinfandel
or Light Spanish Red from the Rioja Region
Sharp Cheddar Cheese/Apples
Coffee

OXTAIL SOUP-STEW

Oxtail, one of the lesser-known parts of beef, is a rich, gelatinous meat that often goes unnoticed in market meat cases in this country—where boneless, fatless, quick-cooking meat cuts rule the kitchen. (The often useful *Meat Board Meat Book* does not even acknowledge the existence of this appendage!)

Although cooked oxtail freezes exceptionally well, it is bulky with bones, so freeze only half the recipe. Refrigerate and serve the rest within a few days. Or pull the meat off the bones before freezing, if you're feeling energetic. If you've left in the bones, supply knives and forks with the soup spoons when you serve the stew, so guests can pull off the meat without wading about in the plates up to their elbows.

Makes 8 servings or 2 casseroles (each about 4 servings)

5 pounds oxtail, fresh or defrosted, cut up and well trimmed of fat
4 quarts water
1 1/2 teaspoons dried thyme
1 tablespoon salt
2 tablespoons vegetable oil or lard
3 medium-size green bell peppers, thinly sliced (about 3 cups)
3 medium-size carrots, thinly sliced (about 1 cup)
4 medium-size onions, thinly sliced (about 4 cups)
2 tablespoons sweet Hungarian paprika
1 teaspoon black pepper
2 large garlic cloves, thinly sliced
1/3 cup all-purpose flour
1 1/2 pounds cabbage, coarsely chopped (7–8 cups)
1/4 cup wine vinegar

1. Combine the oxtails and water in a very large stockpot and bring to a boil. Simmer, skimming, for 3–4 minutes. Add the thyme and salt and simmer the meat, partly covered, for 2 hours, or until it is tender but not falling off the bones.

2. Meanwhile, heat the oil in a large saucepan. Add the peppers, carrots, and onions and stir over moderate heat for a few minutes to soften. Add the paprika, pepper, garlic, and flour and stir for a few minutes. Stir in the cabbage and cook over moderate heat, covered, for a few minutes, until the cabbage begins to wilt. Stir vigorously.

3. Pour about 1 quart of the oxtail broth into the vegetable mixture and bring to a simmer, stirring up any bits from the bottom of the pan. Pour into the stockpot; add the vinegar. Simmer for 15–20 minutes, or until the meat is very tender.

4. Set the pot in a sink containing cold water and cool, stirring. Divide the meat and broth and vegetables evenly between two storage containers. Freeze one, and save the other for dinner within a few days.

5. *To serve:* Defrost the soup, if frozen, and reheat until it is bubbling hot, about 15 minutes. If you prefer, the frozen stew can be warmed over low heat without thawing first.

SUGGESTED MENU FOR FOUR

Dried Sausage *or* Salami, Olives, and Radishes
*Pinto Beans with Tomatoes and Paprika
Italian White Bread *or* *Processor "French" Bread (page 139)
Wine: Robust Red Wine from Spain or Chile *or* Mexican Beer
Green Salad
Coffee/Baked Pears *or* *Apple Slices in Anise Syrup (page 162)

PINTO BEANS WITH TOMATOES AND PAPRIKA

If you would like to turn this into a meatier main course, substitute 1 1/2 pounds garlic sausage for the slab bacon and make these changes: Slice the sausage into 1/2- to 3/4-inch-thick rounds and cook them in a large skillet over moderate heat, covered, for 3–4 minutes. Uncover the pan and brown the meat on both sides. Transfer the pieces to a 6-quart casserole and reserve the fat in the pan to use in place of the salt pork fat.

Makes 2 casseroles (each about 4 servings)

2 pounds dried pinto (or kidney) beans
3 quarts water
1/2 pound lean slab bacon, rind removed and cut into 1/4- to 1/2-inch dice
3 medium-size onions, coarsely chopped (about 3 cups)
3 large garlic cloves, finely minced (about 1 tablespoon)
1 1/2 tablespoons sweet Hungarian paprika
2 bay leaves, crumbled or snipped into small bits
1 teaspoon dried thyme
1 teaspoon dried marjoram
2 tiny dried hot chile peppers, seeded and crumbled (or use 1/4 teaspoon crushed red pepper)
3 tablespoons tomato paste
1/2 teaspoon black pepper
2 cups strong meat broth (from fresh or cured pork, turkey, duck, chicken, or beef)
1 can (35 ounces) tomatoes
Yogurt or sour cream for topping (optional)

1. Combine the beans and water in a large bowl and let stand about 8–12 hours. (Or, if you prefer, boil the beans and water for 2 minutes, cover, and let stand 1 hour.) Simmer gently, partly covered, for 45 minutes, or until the beans are not quite tender. The time needed to cook the beans will vary considerably depending upon their state of dehydration, so begin testing for doneness at about 1/2 hour—although cooking may take as long as 1 1/2 hours. Drain the beans and preheat the oven to 350°.
2. In a large casserole or Dutch oven brown the bacon on all sides. Drain off a little of the fat if you think there is too much. Add the onions and cook over moderate heat, covered, for 5 minutes, stirring a few times. Uncover and add the garlic, paprika, bay leaves, thyme, marjoram, and hot pepper and stir for 1 minute. Add the tomato paste, black pepper, and broth. Using kitchen shears, snip the tomatoes in the can into small pieces. Add, along with the juices, and bring to a simmer, stirring.
3. Add the beans and bring to a simmer. Bake, covered, for about 45 minutes, or until the beans are tender. Timing will vary, so taste. Add salt, if necessary. Divide the beans between two foil-lined containers. Cool, wrap, and freeze. When frozen solid, remove the foil packages, seal, label, and date, and return to freezer for storage (up to 3 months).
4. *To serve:* Defrost the stew in the appropriate dish. Set in a preheated 350° oven for 1 hour, until hot throughout, stirring a few times. Spoon into large bowls and top with the yogurt, if desired.

SUGGESTED MENU FOR FOUR

*Layered Brown Rice, Spinach, and Cheese
Baked Crumb-Topped Tomatoes
Wine: Chianti *or* Bardolino Chiaretto
Italian or French Bread
Fresh Pineapple/*Petite Macaroons (page 43) *or* Bakery Nut Cookies

LAYERED BROWN RICE, SPINACH, AND CHEESE

Firm-textured brown rice is topped with a soft, savory combination of herbed spinach and cheese for a filling, meatless entrée.

Makes 2 casseroles (each about 4 servings)

2½ cups long-grain brown rice
4¼ cups chicken stock or broth
4–5 pounds fresh spinach or 3 packages (10 ounces each) frozen spinach, thawed
2 medium onions, finely chopped
¾ stick (6 tablespoons) butter
¼ cup all-purpose flour
1½ teaspoons salt
½ teaspoon dried thyme
About ¼ teaspoon black pepper
2½ cups milk
1 teaspoon dried basil
¼ teaspoon grated nutmeg
1¾ cups (15-ounce container) ricotta cheese, preferably part-skim
About 5 ounces firm cheese (such as Jarlsberg, Swiss, or Parmesan), grated

1. Combine the rice and broth in a large, heavy saucepan and bring to a rolling boil, stirring occasionally. Turn the heat to its lowest point, cover, and cook 35 minutes. Remove from the heat and let stand, covered, for at least 30 minutes.
2. Meanwhile rinse fresh spinach thoroughly, so that no sand or soil remains. Remove the stems and discard them. Cook the spinach leaves in a large, nonaluminum pot, stirring often, over highest heat until it is wilted. Drain and chop coarsely and press out the liquid. (Do the same to the thawed spinach, if you're using it.)
3. In a large skillet cook the onions in the butter until soft. Add the spinach and toss over moderate heat for a few minutes. Add the flour and stir for a minute or two. Add the salt, thyme, pepper, and milk. Simmer gently, stirring often, for about 4–5 minutes. Set aside.
4. Stir the basil and nutmeg thoroughly into the ricotta. Add half the grated cheese to this and mix to blend.
5. Foil-line two baking dishes, each measuring about 10 × 6 inches or 8 × 8 inches and about 2 inches deep. Divide the rice between the dishes and flatten firmly with a spatula. Divide the cheese mixture over this, dropping it first in dollops to distribute evenly, then spreading to make a smooth layer. Divide the spinach mixture between the dishes and sprinkle the remaining grated cheese over the tops. Cool, cover with foil, and freeze. When solidly frozen, remove the foil packages from the freezer, seal, label, and date, then return to the freezer for storage (up to 3 months).
6. *To serve:* Defrost the mixture in the appropriate dish. Set on the upper shelf of a preheated 350° oven and bake, covered, for about 25 minutes. Remove the foil, raise the heat to 425°, and bake 15 minutes longer, until the surface is bubbling and lightly browned.

24
A Warming Rabbit Dinner, When March Winds Blow

What better focus for a March meal than March Hare (or March rabbit, to be precise)? Although the renowned character from *Alice's Adventures in Wonderland* made his mark on literary history at a Mad Tea-Party, our rabbit is the center of attention at a most peaceful affair—a substantial dinner for six, made before the guests arrive.

While a celebrated hare is the point of departure for this menu, hares at present seem to be more departed than celebrated in the United States, when considered in culinary terms. "Bunny rabbits" have been so romanticized in children's books, cartoons, and stuffed toys that eating them may appear to be a form of sacrilege to some. This has not always been so, nor is it true today all over Europe and Latin America, where rabbits often wind up as main dishes. Whether hare or rabbit, the lack of interest in the animal is very recent. Nineteenth- and early twentieth-century American cookbooks overflowed with rabbit recipes. One early nineteenth-century book in my library supplies several recipes for each of these forms of the animal: scollops, filets, mince (hash), blanquette, fried, giblotte (a stew), pie, en caisses (parchment-wrapped), quenelles, soufflé, croquettes, boudins (minced and formed into sausage shapes), boned legs and saddles, skewered cubes, soup, rissoles (fried turnovers), and fricassee. For centuries our English forebears cooked conies (rabbits over a year old), sucking rabbits (the youngest ones), and hare, although during the Elizabethan period diners stayed clear of hare, which was considered nutritionally deficient and a cause of melancholia.

For dining purposes, the contemporary distinction between hares and rabbits is as follows: Rabbits are commercially raised, white-fleshed members of the leporid family; hares are the wild, dark-fleshed members of the same clan—represented by cottontails and jackrabbits in the United States. As rabbits require only a few feet of space in which to live and breed (which they do as prolifically as legend suggests), need little upkeep, and feed on not very large amounts of hay, barley, wheat, and alfalfa, why are they so expensive (the cost of beef round) at present? Probably because the demand for them is small. Since rabbit is nourishing, meaty, versatile, lean, easy to prepare, and composed entirely of white meat, one would think that it would be clamored for in this land of chicken-breast fanciers. It should be.

RABBIT DINNER FOR SIX

Iced Dry Sherry
*Clear Mushroom Soup with Ginger
*Salted Rusks *or* Breadsticks
*Rabbit in Orange-Walnut Sauce
Wine: Serradayres *or* Periquita (from Portugal)
*Kasha and Red Peppers *or* *Saffron Rice (page 175)
*Salad of Celery Root, Carrots, and Watercress
Coffee
*Pumpkin or Squash Flan

CLEAR MUSHROOM SOUP WITH GINGER

This simple-to-make soup has a gingery sprightliness that makes it just right to begin a rich meal.

Makes 6 servings

1 pound mushrooms, quickly rinsed, then trimmed
2 large shallots, sliced
1 piece ginger, about 1 inch in diameter and 2 inches long, peeled and thinly sliced
6 cups chicken or veal stock (or both), completely grease-free
Soy sauce
Fresh lime juice
GARNISH: Thin lime slices and a few sprigs of cilantro

1. Reserve about one third of the mushrooms, preferably small ones. Combine the remaining mushrooms in the container of a processor or blender with the shallots, ginger, and 2 cups stock. Process until finely chopped but not puréed. Transfer to a pot and add the remaining stock.
2. Simmer, partly covered, for 20 minutes. Strain through a sieve (you can save the chopped vegetables for a sauce). Line the sieve with cheesecloth and strain again. Slice the reserved mushrooms very thin and add them to the broth. Bring to a bare simmer. Add soy sauce, salt if needed, and lime juice to taste. Cool, then refrigerate, covered.
3. *To serve:* Reheat slowly and taste for seasoning. Serve in small Japanese-style bowls, from which you can sip; or use cups. Garnish each bowl with a slice of lime and a sprig of cilantro.

SALTED RUSKS

This is simply a useful and delicious way to use up homemade or firm bakery bread. Begin by cutting the loaf into very thin, uniform slices, trimming for neatness. Brush one side of each slice with a tiny bit of olive oil, then sprinkle sparingly with coarse salt. Set the slices directly on an oven rack, turn to 200–225° and bake until the bread is dried through but not browned, about 1 hour. (If you have a convection oven, it is ideal for this.) Cool and pack airtight. You can vary the flavor if you like, by rubbing the slices before baking with a cut garlic clove, or sprinkling them with a little powdered fennel or whatever spice or herb suits your meal.

RABBIT IN ORANGE-WALNUT SAUCE

Most rabbits are sold frozen—and remain miraculously unaffected by the process. In fact, the frozen small rabbits I've sampled were better than fresh. Rabbits weighing up to 6 pounds (the large females for breeding) are available, but the tender 2- to 3-pound leverets are the ones most commonly obtainable. These "fryers" and the large

(5-pound) "mature" or "roasting-stewing" rabbits are sold skinned, cut into portions of equal weight, pinkly smooth and pristinely packaged in cardboard boxes. Although it may be slightly less economical to buy the small fryers, which have a larger proportion of bone, I heartily recommend them. The "mature" rabbits do not compare in tenderness or succulence. If, however, you can get only mature rabbit, increase the cooking time by at least 30 minutes.

Because the flesh of rabbits is bland and tends to dryness, there is a rich, highly flavored sauce—and plenty of it. Unless your company has often partaken of rabbit, they will probably have no idea what lies beneath the fragrant, brown sauce. Once tasted, the meat is reminiscent of veal and turkey, not game. At my table, no one blinked when my daughter (who by this time had shared enough tests to never want another nibble of rabbit) asked for "another wing, please."

Makes about 6 servings

2 small rabbits (about 2 1/4 pounds each), cut up into small serving pieces (reserve the heart, kidneys, and liver)
3 medium-size garlic cloves
1/2 teaspoon dried thyme
1 large bay leaf, crumbled or snipped small
1 teaspoon ground cinnamon
2 tablespoons brown sugar
1/4 cup brandy or rum
1/2 cup Sherry
2 teaspoons salt
3 tablespoons olive oil, plus the amount needed for browning
1 1/4 cups fresh orange juice
3/4 cup mild red wine vinegar or sherry vinegar
1/2 teaspoon black pepper
1/2 cup all-purpose flour
2 medium onions, chopped
1 or 2 small navel oranges
1 cup walnuts
1 1/2 cups brown stock or strong broth

1. Remove and discard any loose fat from the rabbits. Slice one of the garlic cloves and combine in a bowl with the thyme, bay leaf, cinnamon, brown sugar, brandy, Sherry, 1 teaspoon of the salt, 3 tablespoons olive oil, the orange juice, vinegar, and pepper; stir. Add the rabbit, cover, and refrigerate for about 24 hours, or until convenient to cook—up to 2 days. Turn occasionally.

2. When ready to cook, lift out the rabbit pieces and lay them on several layers of paper toweling; pat dry. Reserve the marinade.

(Continued)

3. Mix the remaining 1 teaspoon salt with the flour in a plate. Dredge the rabbit pieces in the mixture and tap off the excess. Brown well in a little oil in a skillet, preferably a nonstick one. Transfer the pieces to a heavy flameproof casserole as you finish browning them. Chop the reserved innards; lightly brown them in oil and add to the casserole.
4. Cook the onion in the same skillet until deeply browned, stirring often and adding oil if necessary. Mince the remaining garlic cloves, add to the skillet, and stir for a minute.
5. Preheat the oven to 300°. With a zester or swivel peeler remove one third of one orange's peel. (If using a zester, you can remove the peel in a decorative pattern of strips running from stem to blossom spaced about 1/2 inch apart, and then reserve the orange for garnish.) Place the peel in a small saucepan, add water to cover, and bring to a boil. Drain and reserve the peel.
6. Add the reserved marinade to the onions and garlic in the skillet. Grind 1/2 cup of the walnuts to a very fine texture and add them. Add the stock and orange peel and bring to a boil, stirring.
7. Pour this sauce over the rabbit pieces, place the casserole over moderate heat, and bring to a simmer. Bake, covered, for about 1–1 1/4 hours, or until the thickest pieces of meat are very tender. Transfer the pieces to a deep, wide baking/serving dish (preferably earthenware) to form one overlapping layer.
8. Press the sauce through the medium disc of a food mill into a bowl. Return the sauce to the pot and boil for about 10 minutes, or until it is reduced to about 3 1/2 cups. It should be thick enough to coat the pieces. Press the sauce through a fine sieve onto the rabbit. Cool, then refrigerate, covered with foil.
9. *To serve:* Set the foil-covered rabbit (the kasha, too, if you're serving it—see following recipe) in the oven. Turn to 375°. After 15 minutes remove the foil from the rabbit. Baste each piece with the sauce. Bake about 15–20 minutes longer, basting once or twice, until the sauce is bubbling and the rabbit glazed. Slice the remaining orange (or reserved decorated orange) lengthwise, then crosswise into half rounds and arrange with the remaining walnuts over the rabbit.

KASHA AND RED PEPPERS

The toasted, earthy flavor of kasha, also called roasted buckwheat groats, is well loved in my family. But if you're not a fan, or if a lot of brown on the plate doesn't delight your eye, add the red peppers to Saffron Rice (page 175) instead.

Makes 6 servings

3–4 medium-size red bell peppers (or use a combination of red and green)
1 medium-large onion, cut into 1/2-inch dice
2 tablespoons olive oil
1 egg
1 1/2 cups whole-grain kasha (roasted buckwheat groats; see list of mail-order sources, page 353)
1 1/2 teaspoons salt
1 teaspoon dried summer savory
2 1/4 cups boiling water

1. Drop the peppers into a large pot of boiling water. Let them boil for 5 minutes, turning to cook all sides. Run under cold water to cool. Gently and carefully pull off the skins. Remove stems, ribs, and seeds. Cut into 1/2-inch dice.
2. Cook the onion in a heavy saucepan in the oil until slightly softened. Add the peppers and cook a minute over high heat. Scrape into a dish and set aside. Don't rinse out the pan; you'll need it again.
3. In a small bowl beat the egg. Add the kasha and stir until all grains are coated. Scrape the mixture into the pan in which the vegetables were cooked and stir over moderate heat for a few minutes, until all the grains are dried and separated. Add the salt, savory, boiling water, pepper to taste, and the cooked vegetables. Bring to a boil.
4. Turn the heat to its lowest point, cover the pan, and cook 15 minutes. Remove from the heat and let stand 15 minutes or so. Turn into a fairly wide ovenproof serving dish (earthenware is nice), fluffing the grains. Let rest at room temperature until you serve dinner or cool, cover, and refrigerate overnight.
5. *To serve:* Set the foil-covered dish in a 375° oven with the rabbit (see preceding recipe) and heat along with it until hot through—about 1/2 hour if chilled, slightly less if room temperature.

SALAD OF CELERY ROOT, CARROTS, AND WATERCRESS

This salad is vervy and clean, with a fresh herbal flavor. It keeps well and looks lovely.

Makes 6 servings

1 teaspoon coarse (kosher) salt
1 1/2 tablespoons Dijon-style mustard
2 tablespoons lemon juice
1/4 cup olive oil
1/4 cup sour cream
About 1 1/4 pounds firm celery root (also called celeriac), weighed without leaves and roots
About 1 pound carrots (6 or 7 medium-size ones)
2 tablespoons finely minced fresh dill
2 scallion greens, thinly sliced
1 bunch watercress, trimmed, washed, and dried

1. In a bowl mix the salt, mustard, and lemon juice; gradually stir in the olive oil, a tablespoon at a time. Stir in the sour cream, a bit at a time.
2. Peel and quarter the celery root. Cut out the core, if it is spongy. Using a fine julienne blade or the coarse shredder on a food processor or a vegetable cutter, cut up all the root. Mix it in a bowl with two thirds of the dressing. Using your hands, toss and separate the strands until they are all lightly coated. Cover with plastic wrap and refrigerate.
3. Peel and shred the carrots as above. Using your hands, mix thoroughly with the remaining dressing, dill, and scallion greens. Refrigerate in a bowl, covered.
4. *To serve:* Arrange the cress around the edge of a serving platter. Spread the celery root within the circle of cress, then mound the carrots in the center.

PUMPKIN OR SQUASH FLAN

This custard is rather soft and creamy—not firm and sliceable, as flans sometimes are. The pumpkin or squash, almost unidentifiable, adds a golden coloring and distinctive depth of flavor, which is further enhanced by the caramelized sugar.

Makes 6 servings

Grated rind of 1 lemon
1½ cups milk
½ cup heavy cream
2 tablespoons water
½ cup plus 2 tablespoons sugar
¾ cup canned, fresh, or frozen pumpkin or butternut squash purée, pressed through a fine sieve (see note below)
Scant ⅓ cup honey (not a very strong, dark variety)
¼ cup dark rum
¼ teaspoon salt
3 eggs plus 2 egg yolks

1. In a heavy saucepan combine the lemon rind, milk, and cream; bring to just under a simmer over moderate heat, stirring occasionally. Remove from the heat and cover.

2. Turn the oven to 325°. Set a 4½- to 5½-cup metal mold in the oven. (It can be a loaf pan, or a charlotte or brioche mold.)

3. Combine the water and ½ cup sugar in a small, very heavy saucepan or skillet. Stir over moderate heat until the sugar syrup boils up and becomes clear. Turn down the heat, cover the pot, and let boil gently for about 2 minutes to dissolve sugar crystals on the side of the pot. Remove the cover and boil the syrup over moderately high heat, swirling the pot occasionally to prevent burning, until the syrup turns an amber brown.

4. Immediately pour the syrup into the hot mold. Holding the mold with pot holders, tip and tilt it to coat the interior as evenly as possible (which will not be too evenly). Continue tipping until the syrup has ceased to run easily as you turn the mold, has begun to solidify; then turn the mold upside down on a piece of waxed paper or foil.

(Continued)

5. If using frozen or canned purée, press it through a fine sieve set over a bowl. Beat in the honey, the 2 tablespoons sugar, the rum, and salt. Blend the eggs and yolks in a separate bowl. Strain into the pumpkin through a sieve. Strain in the milk mixture, stirring constantly.

6. Pour the custard mixture into the prepared mold and cover closely with foil. Set in a dish of hot water to come at least halfway up the sides. Check that the foil does not extend into the water. Bake for 1 hour. Remove the foil gently. Continue baking for about 30 minutes, or until a knife inserted halfway down into the center of the custard comes out clean. Cool the custard in the water, then remove it, cover with plastic, and refrigerate for at least 3 hours.

7. *To unmold and serve:* Run a knife carefully around the edges of the mold. With one hand flat on the custard, *gently* ease it away from the edge of the mold until the sides are released all around. Place a serving dish over the mold and invert. Serve at once, as the soft flan will crack if left unmolded.

NOTE: If you are making a fresh purée to flavor the custard, butternut squash has more flavor and a finer texture than most pumpkins. To make the purée, place a 1½-pound squash in a dish or pan and set it in the oven. Turn the oven to 350° and bake for about 1 hour, or until the squash is very tender. Halve the squash and scoop out and discard all seeds and fibers. Press the pulp through the medium disc of a food mill, then through a fine sieve. Cool, then refrigerate. If you'd like extra, choose larger squash, increase the cooking time, and pack into 1-cup containers, leaving ½-inch headspace. Freeze for several months.

Spring

25
No Fool Like an Old Fool

An April Fool's Day Dinner for Eight

*Asparagus with Avocado Dressing
*Chickens Stuffed with Almonds and Orange Peel in Vermouth Sauce
*Saffron Rice (page 175) *or* *Millet (page 178)
Wine: Saint-Véran, Quincy, *or* Mâcon Blanc
*Salad of Chicory and Jerusalem Artichokes
*Rhubarb Fool

An old fool—rhubarb, to be precise—gives this chapter its frivolous title and is the nominal excuse for a spring dinner party. For those not familiar with them, fools are the most popular surviving members of a venerable English family of desserts. Although the family members are distantly related by ingredients, what they do have conspicuously in common are their endearing names, to wit: fools, flummeries, trifles, and syllabubs. Generally speaking, fools are fruit purées, fresh or cooked, which are chilled, then combined with rich cream or custard.

The origin of the word "fool" is obscure, although it has provided food writers with plenty of food for thought. Some suggest that the word comes from the French verb *fouler*, to crush. But the editors of the *Oxford English Dictionary* will not trifle with such flummery, stating flatly that "the derivation from the F[rench] *fouler* . . . is not only baseless, but inconsistent with the early use of the word." The same authority offers the possibility that the word is most likely a "use of the obsolete adjective 'fool' (meaning silly, or foolish) suggested by the synonym trifle." This is supported by a late sixteenth-century quotation in which there is mentioned "a kind of clouted creame called a foole or a trifle in English."

Whatever the provenance of this simple, rich fruit-cream, the recipe has held its own in cookbooks dating from the seventeenth century. Although the name of the dessert often switches from fool to cream, the recipe has remained pretty much the same. It is to be found in many old texts, tucked between such fine companions as Tender Curd and Fairy Butter.

But enough fooling around. On to dinner.

ASPARAGUS WITH AVOCADO DRESSING

Slim, tender-crunchy asparagus stalks are the *only* possible commencement for a celebration of springtime. You'll note that instead of cooling the cooked asparagus in ice water, which is the French method, you fan them. Elizabeth Andoh, who teaches traditional Japanese cooking, has demonstrated to me the superiority of this technique. The asparagus lose none of their flavor or vitamins when treated this way. If you're fresh out of fans, a large light pot top or baking sheet does the trick quickly and admirably.

Makes 8 servings

3½ pounds very, very thin asparagus
1 egg
1 ripe medium-size avocado, peeled and chunked
1 teaspoon coarse (kosher) salt
1 teaspoon extrafine sugar
¼ cup fresh lime juice
2 teaspoons finely minced chives
¼ teaspoon Tabasco
Chopped fresh basil (optional)
3–6 tablespoons buttermilk

1. Rinse the asparagus gently. Holding the ends, swish the tips around in a bowl of water to rid them of sand. Snap off the butts where they bend easily.

2. Set the asparagus on a steamer rack over boiling water, cooking half at a time if the entire amount doesn't fit. (Or tie the asparagus in bunches and stand on end in the bottom part of a double boiler in 2–3 inches of boiling water, then cover with the other boiler pot, inverted.) Steam, covered, until the asparagus just barely bend, about 5–8 minutes.

3. Spread in a single layer on a towel and fan until cooled. Set the stalks in a dish, cover, and store in the refrigerator up to 12 hours.
4. Combine the egg, avocado, salt, sugar, lime juice, chives, Tabasco, and optional basil to taste in a processor or blender. Whirl to a purée. Add buttermilk gradually, until the thickness of the sauce is to your liking. Taste for seasoning. Scoop into a serving dish. Cover tightly and refrigerate. You can keep the sauce at least 12 hours, as the acid and egg prevent discoloration.
5. *To serve:* Arrange the asparagus on individual plates. Spoon a little dressing over each and pass the remainder separately.

NOTE: If you can get only large asparagus, it is important to peel the stalks before cooking, and to increase the steaming time. Buy 4 pounds.

CHICKENS STUFFED WITH ALMONDS AND ORANGE PEEL IN VERMOUTH SAUCE

For this recipe the chickens are split down the backs, then spread flat, stuffed under the skin, and roasted. The presentation is not only plumply, brownly beautiful, it is ideal for a made-ahead meal because the stuffing keeps the flesh moist when reheated. The birds, treated this way, are simple to carve at the table. You cut down on the opened-out chickens as you would a cake, to make even quarters that follow the contours.

Makes about 8 servings

2 chickens (3 pounds each), with no holes pierced in the skin (reserve gizzard and neck for another use; use heart and liver for stuffing)
2 large juice oranges
2 large shallots, finely minced
1 cup unblanched almonds
2 teaspoons dried rosemary
2 teaspoons coarse (kosher) salt
3/4 stick (6 tablespoons) butter, softened
2 slices bread, cut into cubes
1 cup water
1 1/3 cups sweet vermouth
4 teaspoons cornstarch
1 cup fresh orange juice
1/2 cup fresh lemon juice
1 teaspoon green peppercorns, drained and crushed lightly (optional; see list of mail-order sources, page 353)
1 bunch watercress

1. Set one chicken on its breast. Using poultry shears, cut along the length of the spine from tail to neck. Cut out the backbone. Open out the bird, skin side down, and using the palm of your hand press firmly on the breast with enough force to break the breastbone and ribs. Turn the bird over.
2. Starting at the neck, slip your hand between skin and breast and loosen all the skin that covers the breast, which is very easy to do. Continue working under the skin of the leg and second joint until you have loosened all but the attaching points at the tip of the drumsticks and the wings. Refrigerate the chicken.
3. Repeat steps 1 and 2 with the second chicken.
4. With a swivel peeler remove the rind from the oranges, avoiding the bitter white pith. Drop the rind into a small pot of boiling water. Boil 2 minutes. Then drain, cool, and dry. Mince very fine. Mince the shallots. Chop the almonds to a medium-fine texture.
5. Combine the rosemary and salt in a spice mill or mortar and crush fine. Mix in a processor or blender with the orange peel, almonds, shallots, and reserved chicken hearts and livers. Blend in the butter and work to a fairly smooth texture. Add the bread and whirl to just blend. Scrape the mixture into two small bowls, dividing it evenly. Preheat the oven to 375°.
6. Gently work the stuffing from one bowl under the skin of one chicken to cover the flesh as evenly as possible. Use one hand to stuff, the other to distribute the stuffing from the outside. If there are any tears, sew them up with white cotton thread. Repeat the stuffing operation with the second bird and remaining stuffing.
7. Set the birds, skin side up, in a buttered roasting pan to fit closely. Pull the neck flaps over the openings and tuck the skin under the breast to seal in the stuffing. If there is not enough skin to cover, extend the stuffing only partway to the edge. Fold the wing tips under the bird. Smooth the skin and press the stuffing firmly against all contours. Turn under any skin that overhangs.
8. Roast the birds for 20 minutes. Sprinkle with salt and pepper. Turn the heat to 325° and roast 25 minutes longer, tipping the pan and using a bulb baster to moisten the birds several times. Roast until the skin is nicely brown but the birds are not quite done, about 160° on an instant-reading thermometer pushed into the thickest

part of the thigh. Transfer carefully to a baking/serving dish to fit the size fairly closely. Cool, then cover and refrigerate. You can store the chicken for a day, if you like. Do not wash the roasting pan.

9. Add the water and vermouth to the roasting pan and bring to a boil over direct heat, scraping up the solids. Pour into a large measuring cup and skim off as much fat as possible. Stir the orange and lemon juice gradually into the cornstarch. Add the optional peppercorns. Add to the vermouth-stock mixture. Bring to a boil, stirring constantly. Boil 1 minute, stirring. Add salt to taste. Cool, uncovered. Then cover and refrigerate until time to reheat the chicken.

10. *To serve:* Place the chicken in the baking dish in a cold oven. Turn the heat to 375°. (Heat the rice or millet—see the menu, page 271—at the same time.) Warm the sauce in a small pan. After the chicken has heated for 20 minutes, pour 1 cup of sauce evenly over it. Continue cooking and basting for about 20 minutes, or until the sauce is hot and bubbling. Tuck the watercress around the bird and bring to the table. Using shears or a knife, cut each bird down the center, then halve each piece, dividing at the natural separations of breast and thigh. Reheat the remaining sauce and serve at the table.

SALAD OF CHICORY AND JERUSALEM ARTICHOKES

It was a pleasant surprise to discover that Jerusalem artichokes (also called sunchokes) can be julienned and marinated well in advance, with no loss of crispness or flavor. Springy, bitter chicory provides just the right balance for the sweet, crunchy artichoke shards.

Makes 8 servings

1/4 cup lemon juice
1 teaspoon salt
1/4 teaspoon black pepper
2 scallion greens, finely minced
1/2 cup olive oil
1 pound Jerusalem artichokes, the larger the better
About 2 tablespoons finely minced fresh or 3/4 teaspoon dried dill
1 1/2 pounds curly chicory (a medium-large head), washed and well dried

1. In a jar combine the lemon juice, salt, pepper, scallion greens, and olive oil. Cap and shake to blend.
2. Peel the Jerusalem artichokes (see note below) and cut them into the finest matchsticks possible. Pour half the dressing over the julienne, add the dill, and toss to coat well. Cover and store in the refrigerator for at least an hour, up to 24 hours. Reserve and refrigerate the remaining dressing.
3. *To serve:* Cut the chicory into small pieces and combine in a serving bowl with the artichokes. Pour the remaining dressing over and toss gently.

NOTE: Although Jerusalem artichokes look neater when peeled, they can be scrubbed aggressively instead. The peel will simply contribute an uneven beige coloring instead of a uniform paleness.

RHUBARB FOOL

Gooseberries and rhubarb are the fruits most commonly used in fools. This is probably because their extremely acid properties offer a welcome contrast to the rich English clotted cream or sweet eggy custard with which they are blended. Since clotted cream is difficult to obtain in the United States, heavy cream, boiled to a thick consistency, is substituted.

Rhubarb stalks range from palest shell-pink to vibrant flamingo-red and are adorned with curly chartreuse leaves. These leaves are high in poisonous oxalic acid and should not be eaten. When cooked, the bright color briefly leaves the rhubarb, but the fruit regains some of its brilliance as the purée cools. Even those who don't love rhubarb seem to enjoy it this way. If you are firm in your loathing, however, Pineapple Snow (page 330) makes a lovely alternative.

Makes 8 servings

3 pounds rhubarb stalks, rinsed and cut into 1-inch pieces, to make about 10 cups (frozen will do, if you can't find fresh)
3/4 cup sugar
Pinch of salt
1 1/2 cups heavy cream (not ultrapasteurized)

1. Preheat the oven to 350°. Place the rhubarb in a close-fitting nonmetallic dish and cover tightly, being sure there are no openings, or the rhubarb will scorch. Bake for 35–60 minutes, or until the rhubarb juices boil up and the vegetable is so tender it becomes a purée when stirred.

2. Remove from the oven and stir to form a coarse purée. Stir in the sugar and salt. Taste and add more sugar as needed. Cool, cover, and refrigerate until chilled. Or store for several days in the refrigerator, if you like.

3. Pour the cream into a small, heavy pot and boil gently, stirring constantly, until reduced to about 1 1/8 cups, which will take 5–10 minutes. Pour the cream into a small mixing bowl and set the bowl in a larger one containing ice water. Let the cream cool entirely, stirring often to prevent a skin from forming. Cover and store in the refrigerator—for days, if you like.

4. *To serve:* At serving time, or several hours before, whip the cream until it forms soft ribbons that do not dissolve into the larger mass when you lift the beaters above the surface of the cream. Mix the cream and the cold purée together in a serving dish. Stir only enough to distribute the two evenly, but not to blend. Both tastes and colors should remain distinct. You can serve at once, or cover and refrigerate for several hours.

26
Small Simple Breakfasts

I love the simplicity of breakfast food, the casual tone of a small morning meal—although I always wish that the morning would arrive less early. But breakfast is a quirky, individual affair. While one person's preference may be for café au lait, cold toast, butter, and orange marmalade at 1:00 P.M., having just arisen, another might wake up perky at 5:00 A.M., ravenous for griddle cakes and sausages. When you eat your breakfast, and what you eat, appear to be most personal decisions.

Although the meals proposed here for breakfast are certainly intended for consumption at a reasonable hour of the morning, thinking varies about the necessity of early rising. "Sir John Sinclair, who has written a large work on the Causes of Longevity, states, as one result of his extensive investigations, that he has never yet heard or read of a single case of great longevity where the individual was not an early riser" (*The American Woman's Home* by Catherine E. Beecher and Harriet Beecher Stowe, 1869). These good ladies add that early rising is

> indispensable to a systematic and well-regulated family. . . . A late breakfast puts back the work through the whole day, for every member of a family; and if the parents thus occasion the loss of an hour or two to each individual who, but for their delay in the morning, would be usefully employed, they alone are responsible for all this waste of time.

The breakfast hour has changed radically over the course of history. In Europe during the Middle Ages it was dinner that was served at 9:00 or 10:00 A.M. (at what time breakfast must have been dished out I cannot bear to imagine). By the fifteenth century meals were served forth a bit later, and by the eighteenth, the meal timetable had begun to approach our modern arrangement. A journal of 1451 (cited in *Good Cheer* by Frederick W. Hackwood, 1911) details the fifteenth-century hours for feeding in one English home: "*Six o'clock* (a.m.) Breakfasted. The buttock of beef rather too much boiled and the ale a little the stalest. . . . *Ten o'clock* (a.m.) Went to dinner. . . . *Seven o'clock* (p.m.) Supper at the table. . . . The goose pie too much baked, and the loin of pork almost roasted to rags."

As to the question of *what* we eat for breakfast, there are practically as many answers as there are people. Clodius Albinus, a Roman politician of ancient times, "could swallow of a morning five hundred figs, a hundred peaches, ten melons, twenty pounds of grapes, a hundred figpeckers [tiny birds popular in the Mediterranean, eaten bones and all] and four hundred oysters" (*Consuming Passions* by Phillipa Pullar, 1970)—all admirably delicate morning comestibles, if taken in moderation.

In the Orient, traditional morning meals are composed of highly salted foods, usually pickled eggs, or dried and pickled fish and vegetables, to be served with fluffy or soup rice. A "Continental" breakfast is usually tiny, consisting of little more than bread in some form and coffee or hot chocolate, while the morning meals served in the United States, England, and Scotland have been known to fell even the most robust trencherman. Meg Dods described a Scottish déjeuner in *The Cook and Housewife's Manual* (1826):

> Besides the ordinary articles of eggs, broiled fish, pickled herrings, Sardinias, Finnans, beef, mutton, and goat hams, reindeer's and beef tongues, sausages, potted meats, cold pies of game, etc., a few stimulating hot dishes are . . . set apart for the . . . gourmand and sportsman. Of this number are broiled kidneys, calf's and lamb's liver with fine herbs, and mutton cutlets à la Vénitienne.

In turn-of-the-century America, breakfasts were frequently gala affairs, with menus as lengthy as the Scottish one. But such extravaganzas were part of a fast-disappearing life style; breakfast was becoming the quick, "necessary" meal it so often is today. By the early part of the twentieth century, breakfast had already been limited to most of the foods with which we're familiar, although meat and fish made more frequent appearances.

Although reindeer's tongue is not recommended in any of the menus that follow, neither are the breakfasts strictly traditional. They are breakfasts—not brunches or lunches—and deserve to be called that for reasons of brevity, content, and structure. They are smallish meals, not meant to be lingered over or stretched out, but to be served when you have a full day planned. Perhaps you're taking off with friends for a day in the country and want a pleasant snack before hopping in the car? Maybe you're expecting to visit museums and have the thought of a big lunch in mind? Or could you be coming home at 4:00 A.M., having danced yourself cockeyed? Let's hope you'll find one breakfast in this group to suit *your* morning mode.

SMALL, SIMPLE BREAKFASTS

Fresh Fruits
*Whole-Wheat Citrus Bread
*Honeyed Cheese Mold
Russian or English Breakfast Tea

Sliced Bananas with Yogurt
*Warm Pear Cake
Canadian Bacon *or* Bacon
Café au Lait

*Smoked Chicken with Oranges and Almonds
California Johannisberg Riesling *or* Lapsang Souchong Tea

Tomato Juice
*Cheese, Ham, Chile, and Bread Pudding
Grapefruit and Orange Slices
Coffee

*Baked Sweet Potatoes and Breakfast Sausages
Fresh Pineapple
Coffee with Cream

WHOLE-WHEAT CITRUS BREAD

This is a full-flavored bread—pungent with lemon and orange, densely whole-wheat textured, not too sweet. The curious treatment of the peels—which are simmered in syrup before being added to the batter—is borrowed from a recipe that appeared in *Maida Heatter's Book of Great Desserts* (New York: Alfred A. Knopf, 1975). It produces a unique, chewy texture and remarkably fresh flavor. When the bread is toasted, the surface develops an almost crackly hard finish that is delicious.

Makes 2 loaves (one to freeze, one to serve)

3 medium oranges
2 lemons
1/3 cup water
1/2 cup white sugar
1 cup brown sugar, packed
3/4 stick (6 tablespoons) butter
4 eggs, lightly beaten
2 1/2 cups all-purpose flour
1 1/2 cups whole-wheat flour
1 tablespoon baking powder
1 teaspoon baking soda
3/4 teaspoon salt
1 cup walnuts, coarsely chopped

1. Butter two 5- to 6-cup loaf pans. Press a piece of buttered waxed paper into each to cover the bottom; dust the interiors with flour. Preheat the oven to 350° (or 325°, if glass pans are used).
2. With a swivel peeler remove the colored peel from the oranges and lemons. Squeeze and reserve the juice from both fruits; there should be 1 1/2 cups. If not, add juice to make that amount. Stack about 6 pieces of peel at a time on a cutting board and with a very sharp knife cut into the thinnest strips possible.
3. Combine the peel with the water and white sugar in a heavy, medium-size saucepan and bring to a boil, swirling the liquid. When the syrup has come to a full boil, turn down the heat and simmer for 7–8 minutes. Remove from the heat and stir in the brown sugar and butter; stir to melt. Add the juices and mix well. Mix in the eggs.
4. Sift into a large bowl the flour, whole-wheat flour, baking powder, soda, and salt. Pour the liquid into the dry ingredients, add the nuts, and mix, using a spoon, until the batter is well blended. Do not overbeat.

(Continued)

5. Turn the batter into the prepared pans, tap against a counter to level the mixture, and place in the center of the oven. Bake for 45 minutes, or until a tester inserted in the center comes out clean. Cool for 5 minutes, then invert the breads on a rack, peel off the paper, and set on their sides to cool completely. Serve, or wrap and refrigerate for a few days. Or freeze up to a few months.
6. *To serve:* Warm or toast the bread and serve with Honeyed Cheese Mold (see following recipe).

HONEYED CHEESE MOLD

This is a lightly sweetened, fairly rich spread halfway between the French fromage blanc and the cheese mixture molded to make coeur à la crème. It takes minutes to assemble, but needs to drain overnight to achieve the right consistency. The recipe makes a generous amount to accompany one loaf of Whole-Wheat–Citrus Bread (see preceding recipe).

Makes about 12 ounces (1¼ cups)

1 package (7½ ounces) farmer cheese
½ cup sour cream
2–3 tablespoons honey
½ cup heavy cream, chilled

1. Press the farmer cheese through a fine sieve 3 times to make it smooth. Add the sour cream and honey to taste, and blend well.
2. In a small bowl whip the cream to form soft peaks. Fold gently into the cheese mixture, using a rubber spatula.
3. Line a sieve just large enough to hold the cream mixture with dampened cheesecloth (either 3 or 4 layers of wide-mesh or 2 layers of fine-mesh) and set it over a bowl. Scoop in the cheese, fold the cheesecloth over it, and refrigerate the whole assembly for at least 12 hours.
4. *To serve:* Peel back the cheesecloth and very gently invert the cheese onto the center of a serving plate. Remove the cheesecloth.

WARM PEAR CAKE

An easy, quick coffee cake that takes less than 30 minutes to put together. Pop it into the oven shortly before your friends arrive, then serve fresh baked or kept warm on a heating tray.

Makes 4–5 servings

1 cup plus 1 tablespoon all-purpose flour
6 1/2 tablespoons sugar
1/4 teaspoon salt
1 teaspoon baking powder
3/4 teaspoon ground cinnamon
2 1/2 tablespoons cold butter, cut into small bits
1/3 cup milk
2 eggs
1 1/2 teaspoons vanilla
1/2 cup sour cream
2 hard-ripe medium-size pears
Confectioners' sugar

1. Preheat the oven to 375°, having first placed one rack in the upper third. Generously butter a 9-inch pie plate.
2. Whisk together thoroughly in a bowl the 1 cup flour, 4 tablespoons of the sugar, the salt, baking powder, and cinnamon. Work in the butter, using a pastry blender or your fingers to form tiny particles.
3. In a small bowl blend the milk, 1 egg, and the vanilla. Pour into the dry ingredients and stir to just blend. Spread the batter evenly in the pie plate with a spatula.
4. Whisk together in a bowl the 1 tablespoon flour, 2 tablespoons of the sugar, the remaining egg, and the sour cream. Pour this over the batter.
5. Quarter, core, and peel the pears. Cut them into very thin lengthwise slices. Make a ring of overlapping slices, laid petal fashion on the batter close to the edge. Arrange the remaining slices in the center. Cover with foil.
6. Bake in the upper third of the oven for 20 minutes. Remove the foil, sprinkle with the remaining 1/2 tablespoon sugar, and bake 20 minutes longer, until the cake is firm and the pears are tender and lightly browned.
7. *To serve:* Set the cake on a heating tray. Sieve over a bit of confectioners' sugar just before serving.

SMOKED CHICKEN WITH ORANGES AND ALMONDS

At first glance, you might consider this combination an odd breakfast choice, but the no-cook, easily assembled meal can be a welcome change from the more traditional breakfast foods. Although some might hesitate to serve the suggested wine for a morning meal, it was customary to serve *only* liquor for breakfast in England through the seventeenth century. Breakfast was not considered a meal of much importance, but the morning ale, served with bread or meat, was the usual eye-opener. Children drank beer from infancy onward, for although chocolate, tea, and coffee were known by that time, they were far too expensive to be served in most families.

Makes 4 servings

2/3 cup heavy cream
3 tablespoons grated fresh ginger
2/3 cup whole, blanched almonds
1 smoked chicken (2 1/2 pounds) (see list of mail-order sources, page 353)
3 navel oranges, peeled, halved, and thinly sliced (see note below)
2 heads Belgian endive, sliced across into narrow crescents
1 bunch watercress, washed and trimmed
2 tablespoons lime juice
1 teaspoon sugar
1/2 teaspoon salt
1 tablespoon walnut, almond, or peanut oil

1. Combine the cream and ginger in a small bowl and refrigerate for at least 1/2 hour. Preheat the oven to 325°.
2. Spread the almonds in a pan and toast them for about 20 minutes, until lightly golden. Let cool.
3. Bone, skin, and thinly slice the chicken. Arrange it with the oranges on a platter over the endive and watercress.
4. Strain the cream into a small bowl, pressing out as much juice as possible from the ginger. Discard the ginger. Using a whisk, beat in the lime juice, sugar, and salt, then the oil.
5. *To serve:* Chop the almonds coarsely and scoop into a serving bowl. Pass the dressing and nuts along with the platter of salad.

NOTE: Honeydew or cantaloupe can replace the oranges when nature provides tastier specimens of the former.

CHEESE, HAM, CHILE, AND BREAD PUDDING

In an essay on Elizabethan England, M. F. K. Fisher, doyenne of culinary philosophers, discussed the lighter eating habits, copied from the Italians, that the English began to affect during the late sixteenth century. But the "Queen, God be thanked, paid no attention to the new style finicking, and make her first meal of the day light but sustaining: butter, bread (brown, to stay in the stomach longer and more wholesomely than white), a stew of mutton, a joint of beef, one of veal, some rabbits in a pie, chickens, and fruits, with beer and wine to wash all down in really hygienic fashion" (*The Art of Eating*, 1976). Fortunately, the main meal of the day was served at about 11:00 A.M., so the queen was not likely to suffer stomach rumblings from hunger after such a petite repast.

For those who find the breakfast menus thus far to be too delicate, here is a hearty breakfast meal-in-one-dish that may leave you happily filled. Use a compact, smoky country ham to flavor the egg-cheese-chile custard, as a soft, water-cured one will be lost. If you can't get country ham, perhaps you can find Westphalian, or Black Forest, or Canadian bacon, or another richly flavored variety. Or you might use a smoked tongue. Unless you're a very early riser, you'll want to assemble this dish for baking the night before.

Makes 4 generous servings

About 10 thin slices firm bread (whole-wheat, rye, or white), crusts trimmed off and the slices halved
1 large Spanish onion, coarsely diced
1½ tablespoons bacon fat or butter
1½ cups coarsely chopped cooked ham or tongue (about 6 ounces)
3–4 tablespoons diced, roasted green chiles (fresh, frozen, or canned)
½ teaspoon dried oregano
6 ounces sharp Cheddar cheese, grated (about 2 cups)
2½ cups milk
4 eggs

1. Spread one third of the bread slices, edges almost touching, in a shallow baking dish of about 6-cup capacity, preferably about 10 × 6 inches.
2. Sauté the onion briefly in the fat until it softens. Sprinkle half over the bread. Top this with half the ham, half the chiles, half the oregano, and a third of the grated cheese.

(Continued)

3. Spread another layer of bread over this, using about half the remaining slices, or enough to barely cover the filling. Over this sprinkle the remaining onion, ham, chiles, oregano, and half the remaining cheese. Arrange the remaining bread slices on top, edges touching.
4. Beat together the milk and eggs to blend. Slowly pour over the bread. Sprinkle the remaining cheese evenly over this. Cover and refrigerate overnight (or for at least 2 hours).
5. Preheat the oven to 325°. Bake the pudding, uncovered, for 45 minutes, until the center is puffed and golden. Serve hot.

BAKED SWEET POTATOES AND SAUSAGES

Plain, fresh-baked sweet potatoes in the skins are a surprisingly satisfying breakfast food and probably need no explanation in the way of a recipe—nor do breakfast sausages. What follows, then, is simply some general information about amounts and times that might be helpful.

For 6 people you'll need 6 to 9 medium-size sweet potatoes, depending on appetites, and about 1½ pounds small breakfast sausages, preferably the ones without preservatives. Preheat the oven to 400°. Place the washed, dried potatoes in a pan, set in the oven, and bake until the potatoes are tender when pressed—about 30 minutes or more. Ten minutes after the potatoes have been put in the oven, spread the sausages in a single layer in a baking pan and set them in the oven with the potatoes. Bake until they are well browned on all sides, turning often. This should take about 25 minutes, by which time the potatoes will be done as well. Both can be kept hot for a while in a low oven. *To serve:* Tuck the sweets into a napkin in a basket to keep warm. Drain the sausages and arrange them in a hot dish. If you've never tried sweet potatoes without butter, you might. Their creamy smoothness and the salty-rich sausage should suffice without added fat.

Having discussed briefly some of the whens, whats, and wherefores of breakfasting, herewith a small coda to deal with a few of the important aspects of serving. The breakfast tablecloth, for example, "should above all, be gay. If we need gayety at any one time more than another, it is in the morning when . . . spirits are likely to be a little low" (*Table Setting and Service for Mistress and Maid* by Della Thompson Lutes, 1934). In a proper household, Mrs. Lutes explains, breakfast begins with fresh fruit and is followed by cereal. To serve this, she writes: "The deft maid brings a dish of cereal to the table in her right hand, goes to the left of the guest, and with her left hand removes the fruit plate and places the cereal on the service plate with her right." Next comes the main course, in this instance waffles, sausages, and creamed potatoes. To serve the waffles they are cut apart, then "put one on the plate before you (the hostess). The maid, who has an extra plate in her hand, will set that before you, take the one with the waffle to whomever is serving the sausage and potatoes, and then carry this plate to one of the guests where, *always from the left*, she will exchange it for the plate before him." Take heed, slovenly servers.

27
Paschal Pork

A Meal for Many

Although ham is the meat most commonly served for Easter, it is seldom served in its "natural" state, that is, uncured. A hefty part of the pig, fresh ham (the plump hind leg) merits a casual crowd—perhaps a large group of relatives. Easter, or any other spring celebration, is a fine excuse for such a family get-together. Despite the beautiful brown, shiny finish that a fresh roasted leg presents, it is more difficult to carve than a cured ham, because the meat is not as compact. But the rich, burnished fat and the marbling of the green stuffing make this a pretty, if somewhat challenging presentation. If pristine slices are important to you, let the meat cool and it will carve more tidily.

Since you'll need to be in the house to oversee the lengthy roasting of the pork, you may as well confine most of the cooking to the day of the party. Everything, as usual, can be completed before the company comes.

AN EASTER FAMILY MEAL FOR FIFTEEN

*Crisp Savory Almonds
*Cracklings (see recipe for Fresh Ham)/
Dish of Celery and Radishes
Wine: Sparkling White Wine *or* Bardolino Chiaretto
*Fresh Ham (Pork Leg) with Lemon-Herb Stuffing
*Rice, Fennel, and Apple Salad
*Processor "French" Bread (page 139)
*Pineapple-Strawberry Ice
*Orange Sugar Wafers (page 65; double or triple the recipe)

NOTE: If you like to serve a first course, in addition to the predinner nibbles, the chilled Spring Green Soup (quadruple recipe, page 307) or a light spinach or asparagus soup is nice.

CRISP SAVORY ALMONDS

Serve these lightly flavored, golden almonds with wine or drinks.

Makes about 5 cups

2 egg whites
1 1/2 tablespoons sharp mustard
Big pinch of cayenne
4 cups unblanched whole almonds (about 1 1/4 pounds)
2/3 cup freshly grated Parmesan cheese (about 2–3 ounces)
1/2 teaspoon salt

1. Preheat the oven to 300°. Whisk the egg whites in a mixing bowl until frothy. Whisk in the mustard and cayenne to taste. Add the almonds and toss to coat evenly. Set in a sieve and toss to remove excess coating.
2. Spread the cheese and salt on a sheet of waxed paper. Toss the almonds in the mixture until none of it is left on the paper. Spread the coated almonds in a single layer on a nonstick or parchment-covered baking sheet.
3. Bake the nuts for 25 minutes, until nicely browned, tossing several times. Turn off the oven and leave the nuts for 30 minutes longer. Cool. Store in an airtight container in refrigerator or freezer.

FRESH HAM (PORK LEG) WITH LEMON-HERB STUFFING

Fresh ham is available all year round, with supplies varying from one region to another according to local demand. It is generally sold at about 13–15 pounds, but can be found both smaller and larger. Choose a leg that shows very firm, creamy fat under the rind, and, if possible, order a leg that has had none of the rind removed, so you can have plenty of "cracklings." These crispy, hard strips of roasted skin and fat sound inelegantly like seashells, when crunched, but they're great favorites.

Makes about 15 servings

Small pork leg (about 14 pounds)
1 tablespoon dried summer savory
1 tablespoon dried rosemary
1 tablespoon dried sage
5 teaspoons coarse (kosher) salt
1 teaspoon black peppercorns
2 large garlic cloves, finely minced or pushed through a press
Finely grated rind of 2 lemons
2 slices fresh white homemade or bakery bread, finely crumbled (or enough to make 1–1¼ cups)
¼ cup dry vermouth
6 ounces Westphalian ham (or use another firm, highly smoked variety), cut into 3 thick slices
2 bunches fresh parsley, very finely minced
6 garlic cloves, unpeeled
2 bunches watercress
GARNISH: Lemon slices

1. Remove the aitch bone (hip bone): Set the leg on a working surface so that the side that is completely covered with rind is downward (see diagram). With a boning knife cut a slit running from one exposed bone tip to the other. Keeping the blade parallel to the aitch bone's surface, keep scraping the flesh free from the bone, folding back the meat from the bone as you proceed. Continue cutting all around the bone to loosen it until you get to the ball joint that connects the aitch bone to the leg bone. Grasp the aitch bone and wiggle and twist it to expose the ball joint and attaching cartilage. Cut through the cartilage to free the aitch bone, which can be reserved for stock or discarded.

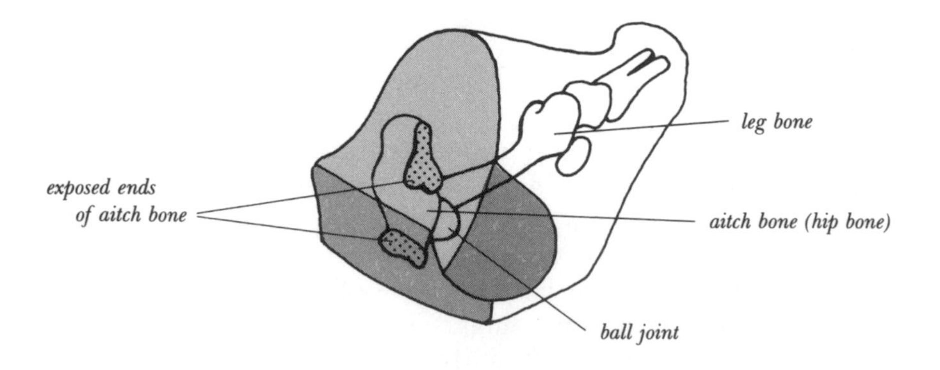

2. Slit the pork skin lengthwise along the leg, cutting off some of the fat with the skin, but leaving a covering of at least 1/4 inch. To do this, hold the knife blade tilted slightly upward toward the skin and cut almost parallel to the meat's surface, pulling off the skin as you progress. Wrap and refrigerate the skin. Trim off the ragged parts of meat and fat to make 1 cup or so of pieces, at least half fat. Cut off and discard any bits of tough tendon or ligament that are exposed. Chill the leg.

3. In a spice mill or mortar combine the savory, rosemary, sage, coarse salt, and peppercorns. Grind to a fine texture. Remove 2 tablespoons of this mixture and combine in a tiny bowl with half the minced garlic.

4. Combine the remaining spice mixture in a bowl with the remaining minced garlic, lemon rind, bread crumbs, and vermouth. Beat to blend well. Using a meat grinder or food processor, chop the reserved cup of pork scraps to form a coarse purée. Cut the smoked ham into tiny dice and add, along with the parsley. Blend well with your hands.

5. Cut a deep slit into the cut face or along the meatier side of the leg, running more or less parallel to the leg bone, reaching in as far as possible. Widen the opening by inserting the handle of a wooden spoon. With your fingers, stuff the tunnel tightly. Continue making and filling tunnels almost parallel to the leg bone, spacing them evenly around the ham, until the stuffing is used up.

6. Rub the reserved spices into the pork. Tie the leg around in several places with white cotton string to make a neat shape and to prevent the stuffing from squeezing out. Enclose the ham in a large plastic bag, close tightly, and store in the refrigerator for about 24 hours to flavor, turning and rubbing whenever you think of it.

7. About 8 hours before you plan to serve the meat, set it fatty side up on a strong rack in a large pan and set in the oven. Turn the heat to 325°.

(Continued)

8. *Make the cracklings:* Cut the reserved skin with attached fat into 4–5 large pieces and drop into a large pot of salted water. Boil gently, partly covered, for 10 minutes, stirring now and then. Drain and cool, then cut into strips about 2 inches long and 1/2 inch wide. Spread in a large roasting pan.

9. When the roasting leg has produced some melted fat, in about 1 1/2 hours, spoon a few tablespoons over the strips. Set the pan in the oven on the upper rack and roast until slightly colored, about an hour, pouring off the fat several times and tossing the strips carefully (they spatter). Split the unpeeled garlic cloves and add to the pan, tossing gently. Roast until the cracklings are well browned, tossing often. Remove from the oven and toss generously with coarse salt and pepper. Drain, remove the garlic, and reserve for cocktail time, when the pieces can be reheated briefly, if you like.

10. Baste the roast every 45 minutes or so with the fat that accumulates in the pan. Turn the pan occasionally, so that the pork roasts evenly. By the time the leg has cooked sufficiently, it should be a deep, rich mahogany brown. To determine when the meat is finished roasting, use an instant-reading thermometer, or insert a meat thermometer into the thickest part of the meat (avoiding the bone) after the leg has cooked for several hours. It should register from 170° to 180°. To plan your time, you can figure about 30 minutes per pound roasting time. A time of 6 1/2 hours for a 14-pound leg is usual.

11. Set the leg on a carving board and let stand 30 minutes–3 hours before carving.

12. *To serve:* Slice the meat carefully, as it is tender, and arrange on a platter with the watercress. Garnish with the lemon slices and serve.

NOTE: When you are working with raw pork, it is extremely important that the working utensils and surfaces be scrupulously clean, both while you're stuffing the pork and after you have cleaned up. Be sure, as well, that the ingredients are chilled.

RICE, FENNEL, AND APPLE SALAD

This is a crispy, clean, fresh-tasting salad that kindly provides both starch and vegetable accompaniment for the pork. If you have trouble finding fennel, you might substitute tender celery hearts, sliced paper thin.

Makes 15 servings

3 3/4 cups long-grain white rice
5 cups water
3 1/2 teaspoons salt
1/2 cup plus 2 tablespoons fresh lime juice
1/2 cup cider vinegar
1/2 cup olive oil
1/3 cup peanut oil
1/2 teaspoon Tabasco
6–8 scallions, thinly sliced
3 medium-large fennel bulbs
2 Red Delicious apples
1 Granny Smith apple

1. In a large, heavy pot combine the rice and water (the 5 cups is correct; do not use more) and 1 1/2 teaspoons of the salt. Bring to a rolling boil over highest heat. Turn the heat to its lowest point, cover the pot, and cook 20 minutes. Remove from the heat and let stand 20 minutes longer.
2. Meanwhile, mix the remaining 2 teaspoons salt, the lime juice, cider vinegar, olive oil, peanut oil, and Tabasco in a large jar. Cover and shake well to blend.
3. Turn the rice into a large bowl with two thirds of the dressing and mix gently with a rubber spatula. Add the scallions and let cool to lukewarm, folding occasionally.
4. Meanwhile peel off and discard the "strings" and feathery tops from the stalks and outer part of the fennel bulbs, using a knife or swivel peeler. Slice all into very thin, small pieces. There should be 7–8 cups. If there is not enough, prepare more fennel or celery to make this amount.
5. Without peeling, core the apples and cut into very thin, small slivers or tiny dice. Combine the apples and fennel in a bowl and toss with the remaining dressing, coating each piece well. Add to the rice mixture, toss, and season.
6. Refrigerate for at least 3 hours before serving.

PINEAPPLE-STRAWBERRY ICE

Cooling, sweet-tart, snowy water ice is refreshing, easy-to-make, and a delightful candy pink. Before you begin, check to see that you have plenty of space cleared in the coldest part of your freezer, which should be operating at about 0° or less. This is a generous amount of ice, but you can keep the dessert, tightly packed and covered, for at least a week without loss of texture or flavor.

Makes about 3½ quarts

1 medium-size ripe pineapple, peeled, cored, and coarsely cut up
2 pints ripe strawberries, hulled and sliced
1¾ cups sugar
2½ cups freshly squeezed orange juice
2½ cups water
Lime juice

1. Combine the pineapple, berries, sugar, and orange juice in a large bowl and let stand at least ½ hour, stirring occasionally.
2. Stir in the water. In a blender or processor purée the fruit mixture in batches. Strain each batch through a fine sieve into a bowl, pressing down to force through the fruit pulp, but not the seeds and fibers. Stir and taste. The mixture should be rather tart. Add lime juice to taste, or sugar if you like a particularly sweet ice.
3. Pour the purée into 4 metal ice-cube trays minus dividers for fastest freezing. Or you can use any wide metal pan. Set in the coldest part of your freezer. Freeze until almost firm in the center, not solid. Timing can vary considerably. Begin checking at about an hour.
4. Scrape 2 trays of the ice at a time into the large bowl of an electric mixer. Beat to a uniform slush. Do not liquefy. Return to the trays and to the freezer. Repeat with the other ice trays.
5. Freeze again until almost solid, which will take a little less time.
6. Again, working 2 trays at a time, beat the ice to a fluffy, even texture, scraping down the sides of the bowl with a rubber spatula. Scrape into a freezer container, packing tightly. Repeat with the other 2 trays.
7. Cover closely, replace in the freezer, and allow to "ripen" for a day before serving. There is no need to soften the ice to serve.

NOTE: If at any point the ice becomes too frozen to beat up easily, simply set the ice trays in the refrigerator to soften a little.

28
A Budget Freeze for Tax Time

Inexpensive Entrées for Cold Storage

Inexpensive meals are often a necessity in early spring, when the government "take" dampens the pleasure of entertaining. "Perhaps there never was a time when the depressing effects of stagnation in business were so universally felt . . . as they are now . . . by all grades of society." These words were written in 1832 by Lydia Maria Child—abolitionist, women's rights reformer, novelist, poet, journalist and author of *The American Frugal Housewife.* They come from a section of that book entitled "Hard Times," which is logically followed by "How to Endure Poverty." Mrs. Child warned particularly against those "men who rush into enterprise and speculation [and] keep up their credit by splendour," a way of life that is as common in this era of "plastic money" as it was in Roman times, when sumptuary laws were drawn up by some of the most celebrated big spenders in history. These laws were designed to regulate the amount of money that private citizens could spend on their food and/or dress, but more often than not they served to distinguish the upper crust from the crumbs.

Alexis Soyer, celebrated chef, writer, and reformer of the nineteenth century, supposed that the early sumptuary laws in Greece and Rome evolved for ethical reasons, that they came about for the purpose of maintaining friendship and solidarity, rather than as a result of abuses. But, he goes on (in the *Pantropheon,* 1853), "man abuses everything. The Romans, tired of eating merely to support life, and disdaining, little by little that austere sobriety which rendered them the masters of the world, gave themselves up at last to unbridled luxury." As a result, numerous laws were passed and ignored, remade and revoked. A law was passed limiting the number of guests allowed to visit on a single evening. Julius Caesar stationed officers in the markets to seize provisions forbidden by law and sent soldiers to banquets to remove any illegal edibles. Augustus permitted dinners for 12, in honor of the 12 great gods, and stipulated the amounts of money that could be spent on all food, from ordinary repasts to weddings. "Caligula, Claudius, and Nero—doubtless better judges of liberty than their predecessors—allowed every one the right to ruin himself as joyously as he pleased," continued the wry M. Soyer.

The "wild pagans" were not the only group guilty of considerable overeating. During the fourteenth century, a proclamation was issued in England against the "outrageous and excessive multitude of meats and dishes which the great men of the kingdom use in their castles" as well as against those men who "imitated the nobles beyond what their stations required and their circumstances could afford." Mid-century, a law was passed that limited the servants of gentlemen to one meal of fish or flesh daily, permitting only milk, butter, and cheese the rest of the day. In 1443 the English heads of state found a new way of keeping their fingers in as many pies as possible—quite literally. A law was passed that forbade the pleasures of pies and baked meats to those under the rank of baron.

Sumptuary laws are not limited to the West, nor to ancient history. In China, in the 1920s, the Communist-led Peasants Association set down a number of highly specific rules about banquets, a long-popular form of entertainment in that country. They stipulated that

> sumptuous feasts are generally forbidden. In Shaoshan . . . it has been decided that guests are to be served with only three kinds of animal food. . . . It is also forbidden to serve bamboo shoots, kelp, and lentil noodles. . . . Only five dishes are allowed in the East Three District in Li-ling country and only meat and three vegetable dishes in the North Second . . . while in the West Third District New Year Feasts are forbidden entirely (*Food in Chinese Culture*, edited by K. C. Chang, 1977).

While the government does not directly limit our intake in the United States at present, merry mid-April usually finds us in straitened circumstances. Mrs. Child has a few further words on the subject, when she reminds us that "those who have had wealth, have recently had many and bitter lessons to prove how suddenly riches may take to themselves wings" (*The American Frugal Housewife*).

Following are four inexpensive, main-dish casseroles to freeze before your spirit sags, then defrost and reheat in the months to come for really casual, easy, moderate-priced entertaining.

Please read Reminders about Freezing (page 352).

SUGGESTED MENU FOR FOUR OR EIGHT

*Deep-Dish Chicken Pie
Wine: California Chenin Blanc *or* Muscadet
Light, Leafy Green Salad
Strawberries and Pineapple
*Sugared Almonds (page 208)

DEEP-DISH CHICKEN PIE

Speaking of cockeyed sumptuary laws:

> The cock, always honoured as a warlike bird, did not at first enjoy a high culinary reputation. And when . . . the Consul thought that hens, owing to the enormous consumption of them, would soon become extinct, he ordered that for the future Romans should dispense with fattening and eating this delicious table bird. But the law said nothing about cocks, a silence which saved Roman gastronomy, for the capon was invented (*Good Cheer* by Frederick Hackwood, 1911).

To freeze chicken pie most successfully, bake and freeze the rich pastry tops separately. This prevents them from getting soggy, and is easier and tastier, as well.

Makes 2 pies (each 4 servings)

PASTRY:

2 1/2 cups all-purpose flour
3/4 teaspoon salt
1 stick (8 tablespoons) unsalted butter, chilled and cut small
1/3 cup lard, chilled and cut small
About 1/2 cup ice water

FILLING:

2 chickens (3 1/2 pounds each), cut up
4 celery stalks with leaves, cut in large pieces
6 cups water
1 1/2 teaspoons dried thyme
2 teaspoons salt
Butter, if needed
1/2 cup all-purpose flour
6 scallions, thinly sliced
1/4 teaspoon grated nutmeg
1/2 teaspoon dried tarragon
2 cups canned corn kernels, drained or frozen
1/2 cups pimientos (one 4-ounce container), rinsed and drained
1/2 teaspoon Tabasco

GLAZE:

1 egg beaten with 2 tablespoons milk

1. Mix the flour and salt for the pastry in a bowl. Cut in the butter and lard, using a pastry blender or your fingers, continuing until the mixture is crumbly. Toss with a fork as you gradually add enough water to hold the pastry together firmly when pressed into a ball. Flatten into a block, wrap, and chill for at least 2 hours, preferably more.
2. Place the chickens, celery, and water in a large pot. Bring to a boil, then skim. Add the thyme and salt and simmer gently, partly covered, for 25 minutes. With tongs, remove the chicken pieces to cool.
3. Boil the chicken stock until it is reduced to 3 1/2 cups. Discard the celery. Pour the stock into a large, transparent measuring cup and reserve it. Rinse out the pot.
4. Remove the skin, bones, and gristly bits from the chickens and discard them. Cut the meat into good-size chunks.
5. Measure the layer of fat on top of the broth. If there is less than 1/2 cup, add butter to make that amount; if more, discard excess. Heat the fat (and butter, if needed) in the rinsed-out pot.

6. Stir in the flour and scallions and stir for 2 minutes over moderate heat. Add the reduced stock, stirring vigorously with a whisk. Add the nutmeg and tarragon and simmer for a few minutes, stirring; the sauce will be very thick. Add the corn, pimientos, Tabasco, and chicken pieces and mix well.

7. Divide the chicken mixture between two foil-lined round baking/ serving dishes of 4- to 5-cup capacity each, preferably 7–9 inches in diameter. Spread the mixture evenly, then cool. Cover tightly and freeze. When frozen solid you can remove the packages from the dishes, and seal, label, and date them. Freeze up to 3 months.

8. *To make the pastry topping:* Preheat the oven to 425°. Divide the pastry in half. Roll out a piece of dough to form a rough circle an inch or two larger than the baking dish. Trim to make a circle with a diameter that is 1/2-inch larger than the top of the dish. Place the pastry on a baking sheet. Repeat the process with the other half of the dough, using a second sheet if necessary. Brush the crusts very lightly with the egg glaze, being careful not to drip any on the sheet. Prick designs with a fork or skewer all over each circle and cut a small hole in each. If you like, decorate the tops with shapes cut from the pastry scraps, affixing them with a little of the glaze.

9. Bake for 12–15 minutes, or until the pastry is nicely browned. Carefully slide the tops onto a rack and cool them completely. Wrap each top airtight, label "fragile," and freeze up to 3 months.

10. *To assemble and reheat:* Unwrap and defrost the chicken filling in the appropriate dish. Bake in a preheated 375° oven for about 40 minutes, or until the filling is bubbling hot. Set the frozen pie crust on top (do not defrost beforehand), turn the heat to 425°, and bake for 15 minutes. The heat will seal the pastry to the edge of the dish.

11. *To serve:* With a sharp knife cut the crust into portion-wedges and lift them onto a plate. Ladle the filling into serving bowls and place pieces of crust on top.

SUGGESTED MENU FOR FOUR OR EIGHT

Olives/Breadsticks
*Macaroni Layered with Spinach and Meat Sauce
Wine: Inferno *or* Sassella from Valtellina Region
Green Salad
Baked Pears in Wine
Espresso

MACARONI LAYERED WITH SPINACH AND MEAT SAUCE

When it comes to macaroni, some feel more lyrical than others: "Italian sunshine and blue skies, concentrated in flour paste, wrought into tubes and ribbons and squares and lozenges, come to gladden the sinking heart and cheer the drooping spirits" (*Food Products From Afar* by E. H. S. Bailey and H. S. Bailey, 1922).

Makes 2 casseroles (4 servings each)

SPINACH MIXTURE:

1/2 cup finely chopped onion
1/2 stick (4 tablespoons) butter
2 packages (10 ounces each) chopped frozen spinach, thawed (or use 3 pounds fresh spinach, trimmed, blanched, squeezed dry, and chopped)
1/4 cup all-purpose flour
2 cups milk
1/2 teaspoon salt
1 cup grated cheese (Swiss, Jarlsberg, or Parmesan)

TOMATO-MEAT SAUCE:

1/2 cup chopped onion
2 tablespoons butter
1 1/4 pounds ground beef, preferably round
2 medium-size garlic cloves, minced
2 teaspoons dried basil
1 teaspoon salt
1/2 teaspoon black pepper
3 tablespoons tomato paste
1 can (2 pounds 3 ounces) Italian plum tomatoes (or 4 cups peeled, seeded, and diced fresh plum tomatoes)

MACARONI:

1 pound imported Italian macaroni or a "high protein" brand
2 tablespoons butter
1 cup grated cheese (Swiss, Jarlsberg, or Parmesan)

1. *Prepare the spinach:* In a large skillet sauté the onion in butter until softened; add the spinach and cook over high heat for 2 minutes. Add the flour and cook, stirring, a few minutes more. Add the milk and salt and stir over moderately low heat for 5 minutes. Remove from the heat and stir in the cheese.
2. *Prepare the meat sauce:* In a large skillet sauté the onion in butter until softened. Add the meat and garlic and stir over moderate heat until the meat just loses its pinkness, breaking it up as you cook. Add the basil, salt, pepper, and tomato paste. With kitchen scissors, snip the tomatoes into small pieces in the can. Pour into the skillet. Simmer, partly covered, for 15 minutes.
3. Meanwhile, *prepare the macaroni:* Boil the pasta in a large pot of salted water until it is not quite tender; it should be undercooked. Drain, then toss with the butter and half the cheese.
4. Butter or foil-line two 2-quart baking dishes, preferably the circular, straight-sided glass soufflé dishes. In each dish make layers as follows: first spread one quarter of the tomato sauce in each dish; on this spread one sixth of the macaroni; over that one quarter of the spinach; then another sixth of the macaroni; another quarter of the tomato sauce; one sixth macaroni; one quarter spinach. When you have filled the casseroles, sprinkle the top of each with half the remaining grated cheese. Cool, then cover tightly and freeze. When frozen solid, remove the foil packages from the dishes, then seal, label, and date. Return to the freezer for further storage (up to 3 months).
5. *To serve:* Unwrap and defrost the mixture in the appropriate dish (or simply thaw, if you've frozen the casseroles directly in the dishes). Bake, foil covered, in a preheated 375° oven for 45 minutes, until hot through. Uncover and bake about 15 minutes longer, until the top is bubbling.

SUGGESTED MENU FOR FOUR OR EIGHT

*Radishes with Anchovy Butter (page 5)
*Creole Veal Stew
*Brown Rice (page 176) *or* *Millet (page 178) *or*
*Saffron Rice (page 175)
Wine: Côtes du Rhône *or* California Pinot Noir
Watercress and Orange Salad
Coffee/Almond Toast *or* Anise Toast

CREOLE VEAL STEW

Moist, tender breast of veal is a wonderful, but often overlooked, stewing cut. If you want the benefit of its natural succulence, you must cook it with the bone and cartilage attached. This is a bit messy, and the bones take up too much freezer space, but the taste and price are right *because* the bones are there. Breast of veal creates such a thick, savory, rich sauce that even freezing cannot affect the texture.

Makes 2 casseroles (4 servings each)

4½–5 pounds meaty, trimmed veal breast, with bones in
⅓ cup all-purpose flour
2 teaspoons salt
1 pound boneless shoulder of veal, cut into 2-inch pieces
About 2 tablespoons butter
About 2 tablespoons vegetable oil
1 cup finely minced carrot
2 cups finely minced onion
1 cup finely chopped green pepper
1 cup finely minced celery, with leaves
1 large garlic clove, minced
2 teaspoons dried thyme
2 bay leaves, finely crumbled or snipped small
¾ teaspoon ground cloves
¼ teaspoon cayenne pepper
1 can (2 pounds 3 ounces) Italian plum tomatoes, plus their liquid, pressed through the medium disc of a food mill
1 cup water
1 cup dry vermouth or white wine

1. Have the butcher cut the veal breast (including bones) into 2-inch pieces. Combine the flour with ½ teaspoon of the salt and toss the breast and shoulder to coat well.

2. Heat 1 tablespoon each butter and oil in a very large Dutch oven. Brown the meat lightly on all sides, transferring each batch to a bowl as it browns. Add butter and oil as needed.
3. Preheat oven to 325°. Add the carrot and onion to the pot and stir over moderate heat for about 5 minutes, or until lightly colored. Add the green pepper, celery, and garlic and stir for a few minutes longer. Add the thyme, bay leaves, cloves, cayenne, and remaining 1 1/2 teaspoons salt and stir for a moment. Pour in the tomatoes, water, and wine and bring to a boil, stirring. Add the meat and bring to a simmer.
4. Cover and bake for 2 hours, or until the meat is just tender, stirring a few times during the cooking. Skim off some of the fat and set the pot in a sink containing cold water. Stir often until cooled.
5. Divide the stew between 2 foil-lined containers, cover tightly, and freeze. When frozen solid, you can remove the packages from the containers, seal, label, and date them. Return them to the freezer for storage (up to about 3 months).
6. *To serve:* Unwrap and thoroughly defrost the stew in a heavy pot. Bake, covered, in a preheated 350° oven for about 1 hour, until hot, stirring occasionally.

SUGGESTED MENU FOR FIVE OR TEN

*Smoked Oysters and Horseradish Cream in Cucumber Cups
(page 50; halve the recipe to serve 5)
*Chickpea, Tomato, and Eggplant Casserole
Whole-Wheat Pita
Wine: Chianti *or* Grumello
Bowl of Fruit/Cheese

CHICKPEA, TOMATO, AND EGGPLANT CASSEROLE

This time-honored Mediterranean/Middle Eastern blend of flavors, gently spiced, freezes remarkably well. Serve either hot or at room temperature.

Makes 2 casseroles (each about 5 servings)

1 pound dried chickpeas
1 tablespoon salt
4 pounds eggplant, washed (unpeeled), cut into 1-inch cubes (about 5 quarts)
1 cup olive oil
3 medium onions, chopped (2 cups)
2 large garlic cloves, finely minced
4 teaspoons ground coriander
2 teaspoons ground cumin
2 cans (2 pounds 3 ounces each) tomatoes
2 tablespoons sugar
GARNISH: Lemon slices

1. Soak the chickpeas overnight in water to cover them by at least 3 inches. Drain, then pour into a pot and add water to cover by about 3 inches. Simmer, partly covered, until the peas are almost tender, adding 2 teaspoons of the salt toward the end. Check the peas after 1 hour. Timing can vary, taking as long as 3 hours. Add water, if needed, to keep the chickpeas covered during cooking. Drain.
2. Preheat the oven to 375°. Heat 1/3 cup oil in a very large skillet and toss half the eggplant over high heat until it is lightly browned but not cooked through. Transfer to a large, flameproof casserole. Add another 1/3 cup oil to the skillet and sauté the remaining eggplant cubes. Add them to the casserole.
3. Pour the remaining 1/3 cup oil into the skillet and cook the onions over moderately low heat for 5 minutes. Stir in the garlic and cook another minute. Stir in the coriander and cumin. Using kitchen scissors, snip the tomatoes in the cans into small pieces. Pour into the skillet with the sugar and remaining 1 teaspoon salt. Bring to a simmer, stirring, then add to the casserole with the chickpeas.
4. Bring the mixture to a simmer, stirring. Cover and bake for 30 minutes. Uncover, raise the heat to 400°, and bake 30 minutes longer, stirring a few times.
5. Spoon into two foil-lined dishes of about 3-quart capacity. Let cool, cover with foil, and freeze. When frozen solid, you can remove the packages from the dishes, seal, label, and date them. Return to the freezer for storage (up to 3 months).
6. *To serve:* Unwrap and defrost the mixture in the dish in which it was frozen. Cover with foil and set in a cold oven. Turn to 350° and bake about 45 minutes, stirring gently a few times. Uncover, raise heat to 400°, and bake 30 minutes longer, or until the juices are bubbling. Season; garnish with lemon slices.
NOTE: If you want to serve the dish cool, it need only be defrosted and stirred, then left briefly at room temperature.

29
Positively Ducky

A Small Spring Dinner for Four

Wild (and domestic) ducks once figured as daily fare in America, from the simple suppers of the earliest settlers to the gala dinners of Gay Nineties socialites. For centuries forests, fens, lakes, and ponds teemed with widgeon, teal, canvasbacks, mallards, gadwells, black ducks, garganey, poachards, wood ducks, pintails, lake ducks, sheldrakes, spirit ducks, red-headed ducks, and more—all edible. After Charles Dickens visited the United States in the mid-nineteenth century he wrote, in *American Notes* (1842): "En route from Philadelphia to Washington, we crossed by wooden bridges, each a mile in length, two creeks, called respectively Great and Little Gunpowder. The water in both was blackened with flights of canvasback ducks, which are most delicious eating, and abound hereabouts at this season of the year." It will come as a surprise to no one that the wildlife population of this country has been decimated since Mr. Dickens's sojourn.

Feathered game, once the most readily available of viands, has now become a "gourmet item," with per capita consumption at only 1/2 pound annually (as compared, for example, with 51 pounds of chicken). Nature's "natural" bounty no longer fills the needs of a nation as large as ours. We must produce our food using foolproof methods, taking advantage of strains that are predictable, high-yielding, untroublesome. Enter the white Pekin duck (about a hundred years ago, shipped from China), which suits our requirements admirably. A fat, handsome, fast-growing creature, it produces year round, can be raised indoors, and has pure white feathers. This last is no small virtue, because it means that after plucking no ugly 5 o'clock shadow is visible, as with most other birds, which have colored plumage. The quick weight gain of white Pekins allows for "collecting," a euphemism I've seen used in reference to wild game, at a mere 49 days to yield a dressed weight of about 5 pounds. Once raised almost exclusively on Long Island, the Pekin now flourishes as well in Wisconsin, Virginia, and Indiana. While the breed is neither the meatiest nor the most flavorsome, it is remarkably tender for a duck; it is quite bland, not gamy—an unpopular quality for most Americans—adapts easily to a wide variety of cooking techniques, produces a crisp skin when roasted or broiled, and is virtually impervious to the freezing process. All in all, a most reasonable candidate for commercial production.

If you fancy a more intense flavor and extremely firm flesh, you can try to get your hands on a Muscovy duck (nothing to do with Moscow—they originated in South America) or the even leaner, firmer mallard, from which all domestic ducks have descended. Both are marketed at a limited level; both are best-suited to braising, as they tend to dry out and toughen. You might, however, hesitate to have anything to do with domesticated mallards when confronted with this inside information from the lady who had a little something to say about everything, Mrs. Isabella Beeton. She wrote in 1861, in her *Book of Household Management:* "It is to be regretted that domestication has seriously deteriorated the moral character of the duck. In a wild state, he is a faithful husband . . . but no sooner is he domesticated, than he becomes polygamous, and makes nothing of owning ten or a dozen wives at a time."

Because production of ducks other than the Pekin is so difficult, the major breeders feel that the market will always be limited to a "gourmet" audience, willing to pay for such specialties. Thus far, the most promising hybrid is the one that results from the cross of a Muscovy, also called a Barbary, and a white Pekin or Rouen duck, which, except for the dark mallardlike plumage, closely resembles the Pekin. The crossbreed, called a mulard, is leaner and more flavorful than a white Pekin, but it cannot reproduce.

At present, ducks are a more popular food in restaurants than at home, particularly as prepared by Chinese, whose cuisine has found favor all over the United States. The national favorites, beef and shellfish, have become so expensive that diners are seeking alternatives to these standbys, and duck is considered special enough to be ordered as "going-out" food. If you would rather enjoy your company "in," the following ducky dinner for homebodies might fill the bill, rather than present you with a stunning one, as a restaurant dinner might.

A DUCK DINNER FOR FOUR

*Crisp Savory Almonds (page 289; halve the recipe)
Wine: Alsatian Sylvaner *or* Dry Johannisberg Riesling from California
*Chilled Spring Green Soup
*Aromatic Duck
Wine: California Zinfandel *or* Gewürztraminer
*Gingered Red Cabbage Slaw
*Fresh Grapefruit Gelatin with Cream

CHILLED SPRING GREEN SOUP

This soup started out life as a simple, unthickened asparagus purée, but the color and texture needed improvement. When thickened with potatoes, the asparagus was overpowered; with flour, the purée was too slippery. The peas, which function as thickener, sweetener, "smoother," and color enhancer, proved to be just the right thing.

Makes 4 servings

1 pound asparagus
3 cups water
3 tablespoons long-grain white rice
1 medium-size onion, coarsely chopped
1 celery stalk with leaves, coarsely chopped
2 tablespoons safflower, corn, or other light vegetable oil
1 pound fresh peas in the pod, shelled (makes about 1 cup)
1 1/2 teaspoons salt
1/4 teaspoon sugar
White pepper
Grated nutmeg
About 1/2 cup milk
About 1/4 cup heavy cream
Lemon juice
Minced fresh basil and chives (optional)

1. Break any heavy, woody bottom parts off the asparagus stalks and discard them. Cut the asparagus into slices, reserving the 8 prettiest tips. Bring the 3 cups water to a boil and drop in the tips. Boil for a few minutes, until barely tender. Scoop out the tips (reserve the water in the pot); cool them in ice water. Dry and refrigerate, wrapped, until serving time.
2. Add the rice to the pot of water; cover and simmer until very soft while you prepare the rest of the soup.
3. In a larger pot cook the onion and celery in the oil until they are well softened, about 10 minutes, stirring often. Add the asparagus and peas and stir over high heat for about 2 minutes. Add the salt, sugar, rice, and the water in which it cooked. Cover and simmer until all the vegetables are soft, about 15 minutes.
4. Press the mixture in batches through the medium disc of a food mill to remove the fibers. Purée the soup in a blender or processor until it is very smooth, again working in batches. Stir enough milk into the purée to make a somewhat too thick soup. Season with salt, white pepper, and nutmeg to taste. Chill, covered.
5. *To serve:* Stir enough cream into the soup to give it the desired consistency and flavor. Season the soup with lemon juice, salt, and white pepper. Divide among 4 chilled bowls. Into each bowl sprinkle a small amount of the optional basil and chives. Float 2 asparagus tips on each and serve.

AROMATIC DUCK

This manner of flavoring and roasting duck produces meat that is so succulent and rich tasting that it is possible to feed four with an amount that is usually suggested for two or three. The precooking seasoning—which takes two days, so plan accordingly—and slow, fat-melting roasting make for a successful presentation at room temperature, which is unusual for such a fat bird—except as prepared in China. At this temperature the flesh is more compact and juicy, the flavor more complex than when hot. And with no worry about coordinating the serving of hot roasted duck with the arrival of guests, the cook can relax.

It is important to serve the duck in little pieces, each with a neat covering of deeply browned, shiny skin; the petite portions are not only more appealing to behold, but tend to satisfy diners more quickly than large chunks of hot, plain-roasted meat. As no small bonus, the cleavering or shearing of the duck can take place in the privacy of the kitchen, before guests arrive, avoiding carving antics such as these:

> We then have learned to walk around
> The dining room and pluck
> From off the window sills and walls
> Our share of father's duck.
> While father growls and blows and jaws
> And swears the knife was full of flaws,
> And mother laughs at him because
> He couldn't carve a duck.

(From "When Father Carves the Duck" by E. V. Wright)

Makes 4 servings

1 duckling (about 5 pounds), fresh or frozen (thawed)
2 teaspoons black peppercorns
1 teaspoon dried thyme
2 bay leaves, crumbled or snipped small
6 whole cloves
1 tablespoon coarse (kosher) salt
1 tablespoon brown sugar
1 tablespoon gin, vodka, or brandy
1 garlic clove, peeled
5–6 large, neat red cabbage leaves (reserve them from the slaw recipe that follows)

1. Cut off the duck's wing tips and wrap up with the giblets to freeze for future stock making. Pull out and discard any loose interior fat. Rinse the duckling inside and out and pat dry.
2. Mix together in a spice mill or mortar the pepper, thyme, bay leaves, cloves, and salt. Grind to a fine texture. Combine in a small dish with the brown sugar and gin. Place the duck in a snug-fitting heavy plastic bag. Rub half the spice mixture inside the duck, the remainder over the outside. Place the garlic in the duck's cavity. Close the bag tightly and refrigerate for about 24 hours, rubbing the surface and squeezing in the spices when you happen to think of it.

(Continued)

3. Remove the duck from the bag and lightly pat it dry. Set on a cake rack set over a plate and return, uncovered, to the refrigerator for about 24 hours, turning once.
4. Pat the duck if any moist spots remain. Let it reach room temperature, which takes about 2 hours. Preheat the oven to 300°. Using a large needle and white cotton thread, sew closed the duck's neck and tail openings. Set the duck on its side on a rack set in a roasting pan.
5. Roast 45 minutes. With the needle prick the fatty parts on the upper side; do not prick deeply enough to pierce the flesh. Using wadded-up paper towels to protect your hands, hold the duck's legs and turn it onto the other side.
6. Increase the heat to 350° and roast 30 minutes. Prick the fatty parts on the upturned side and turn the duck onto its breast.
7. Roast 25 minutes longer. Prick the upturned side. Turn the duck breast upward.
8. Increase the heat to 400° and roast about 30 minutes longer, or until the duck is deeply browned and most of the fat has melted off. Remove from the oven and let cool 1–2 hours before carving and serving.
9. *To serve:* Using a heavy cleaver or poultry shears, cut through the flesh and bone of the duck to make about 12–14 serving pieces. Cut carefully, keeping the skin neatly intact on each piece. Spread the cabbage leaves on a platter or shallow basket or wooden bowl and arrange the duck on them.

NOTE: If you prefer duck that is sizzling hot, you can easily heat the pieces. Arrange the cut pieces in a pan in a single layer, cut side down, and roast in a preheated 350° oven for 15 minutes, or until hot.

GINGERED RED CABBAGE SLAW

What coleslaw *isn't* is *cold* slaw, although most salads made from cabbage are served cold. Old American cookbooks, in an effort to anglicize *koolsla,* one form of the Dutch word for cabbage salad, went so far as to suggest that if a cabbage salad were not served ice cold, it could not properly be termed "cold slaw." Recipes for cold and warm slaws appeared to reinforce the confusion. "Cole" is one of the oldest terms for cabbage, while the word "cabbage" comes from the French word *caboche,* meaning "head."

Makes 4 servings

1 small red cabbage (about 2 pounds)
2 medium-size red bell peppers
3 scallions, thinly sliced
1 teaspoon coarse (kosher) salt
1/4 cup cider vinegar
1 tablespoon grated fresh ginger
1 teaspoon honey
3 tablespoons light vegetable oil (such as safflower or corn)

1. Carefully remove 5 or 6 outer leaves of the cabbage, keeping them whole. Reserve these for the Aromatic Duck (see preceding recipe). Quarter the cabbage, then cut out the core and discard it. Shred the leaves very fine.
2. Drop the shredded cabbage into a large pot of boiling salted water. When the water has returned to a boil, cook the cabbage for about 2 minutes, or just until it has begun to soften but not lost its crispness. Drain, cool in ice water, then drain again. Dry in a salad spinner (or use towels), then spread on paper towels. (Cabbage will be restored to fuchsia when dressed; don't worry.)
3. Remove the stems, ribs, and seeds from the peppers. Cut them into 2-inch pieces, then stack the pieces and cut them into thin slivers. Combine in a bowl with the scallions and cabbage.
4. Combine the salt, vinegar, ginger, and honey in a small jar; mix. Add the oil and shake to blend. Pour the dressing over the vegetables and toss. Cover with plastic and refrigerate at least 4 hours or as long as overnight, tossing occasionally. Taste and season before serving.

FRESH GRAPEFRUIT GELATIN WITH CREAM

Delicate, refreshing, old-fashioned "jelly" will probably surprise you, if you've forgotten just how delicious real fruit gelatin can be. Happily, grapefruit seems to retain its pleasant astringency and distinct aroma in this form. If you prefer a firmer gelatin to be shaped in a mold, use 1 1/4 cups water and omit the lemon juice. Personally, I find the melting soft texture and bright citrus flavor of the spoonable form more attractive.

Makes 4 servings

1/2 cup sugar
1 1/2 cups water
2 envelopes unflavored gelatin
2 or 3 large grapefruits
1/4 cup fresh lemon juice
Few drops red and yellow food coloring (optional)
1/2 cup heavy cream, whipped to very soft peaks

1. Combine the sugar, water, and gelatin in a pot. Rinse the grapefruits. Using a swivel peeler remove all the colored part, avoiding the bitter white pith, and add to the pot.
2. Halve and squeeze the juice from 2 grapefruits. There should be about 1 1/2 cups juice. If there is less, squeeze the third grapefruit to make that amount; if a little more, use it all. Add to the pot, along with the lemon juice.
3. Stir the mixture over low heat until it just simmers and becomes clear, about 5 minutes. Strain the liquid through a fine sieve into a bowl; discard the solids. If desired, add coloring to the gelatin to restore a pale grapefruit color. Strain the gelatin mixture through the sieve again into a clear glass serving dish. Chill for at least 3 hours.
4. *To serve:* Mound the gelatin into glass serving dishes and spoon a bit of soft-whipped cream on each. (For a somewhat fancier presentation, whip the cream to a slightly firmer peak, scoop into a pastry bag, and decorate the gelatin in the serving bowl.)

30
A-Fin-Ities

Made-Ahead Fish Menus

Preparing seafood in advance of company presents many problems, to which there are only a few solutions. Plain-broiled, fried, or sautéed fish—the most common cooking techniques—are obviously not useful answers.

One way to prevent the delicate flesh from drying out is to layer the raw seafood along with the seasonings and vegetables in a baking/serving dish and to refrigerate until needed. When guests arrive, set the assembly in the oven and turn on the timer. This method is used in the recipes given here for Baked Shad with Fruits and Ginger (page 314), Bluefish with Fennel and Tomato Sauce (page 316), Striped Bass Filets with Pink Peppercorns and Pistachios (page 318), and Spiced Fish Filets with Tahini (page 319). An embellished version of this approach is used for the Turban of Flounder with Leek Mousse and Tomato Cream (page 320), where a raw fish mousse set into filets lining a ring mold replaces the simple fish filets and baking dish.

Another way to retain moisture is to cook minced fish patties and reheat them in a sauce, as in Steamed Shrimp-Fish Cakes in Lemon Sauce (page 323). Or you can handle the made-ahead problem by making a heady broth with vegetables and marinating an assortment of fish pieces for later inclusion. When you are ready to serve dinner, remove the soup from the refrigerator and stir in the fish while the soup heats, as in American Bouillabaisse (page 325).

SUGGESTED MENU FOR SIX

*Baked Shad with Fruits and Ginger
*Saffron Rice (page 175) *or* *Brown Rice (page 176)
Wine: Alsatian Riesling, Sylvaner, *or* California Fumé Blanc
String Beans Vinaigrette
*Pineapple Snow (page 330) *or* Sherbet

BAKED SHAD WITH FRUITS AND GINGER

On the East Coast, this is the fish that signifies spring. American shad (*Alosa sapidissima*) is a tender, buttery-rich fish whose only shortcoming is that its "flesh is cursed with a superfluity of small bones" (*Canadian Fisheries Manual* for 1942)—about 700 minute ones, as a matter of fact—which are generally removed before the fish goes to market. Early recipes suggested cooking the fish 5 hours or more to soften the bones, which I've not tried.

Like two of our greatest fish, salmon and striped bass, shad are anadromous, spending most of their lives in the sea but returning to their natal streams to spawn. Found in great profusion by the early American colonists, they were at first scorned—although the native Americans had wisely cooked and smoked them. But as the shad population dwindled, their popularity increased, an unfortunate but not infrequent phenomenon: Oysters, when available in masses, were considered fit for the poorest and least discriminating members of society. As their numbers declined, they became the precious province of the elite.

Shad is extraordinarily receptive to a wide range of cooking techniques and seasonings. It might be compared to pork in the way its distinctive, sweet flavor can be subjected both to delicate herbs and creams, or to spicy, sharp sauces without losing its identity. The recipe that follows, which could not be simpler, is a bit acid, a bit sweet, and preserves the fish's delectable texture.

Makes about 6 servings

5 tablespoons olive oil
$2^1/_2$ pounds shad filets, with skin
Fresh ginger, a piece about 2 inches long and 1 inch wide, peeled
2 scant tablespoons drained tiny capers (or use chopped larger ones)
$^1/_4$ cup golden (yellow) raisins, loosely measured
2 small grapefruits, peeled and sectioned
2 medium navel oranges, peeled and sectioned

1. Spread 2 tablespoons of the oil in a large, shallow baking/serving dish that will hold the fish in one layer. Cut the fish across into 6–9 pieces, and fit them neatly into the dish, skin side down. Salt and pepper the fish very sparingly.
2. Using a swivel peeler, shave the ginger into transparent-thin slices and spread these over the fish. They should almost cover the surface. Sprinkle the capers and raisins evenly over the ginger.
3. Arrange the grapefruit and orange sections, alternating, to neatly cover the fish slices in an attractive design. Evenly drizzle the remaining oil over all.
4. Cover and refrigerate until time to cook. Fish can be stored up to 12 hours, but a shorter time is preferable.
5. *To bake and serve:* Remove the fish from the refrigerator at least $^1/_2$ hour before cooking. Preheat the oven to 450°. Spoon the oil and accumulated juices over the fish, then set in the upper third of the oven, uncovered. Bake for about 20 minutes, until the fish is opaque in the center and registers about 140° on an instant-reading thermometer.

NOTE: If you are serving the suggested rice with the fish, you can heat this through before baking the fish. It will remain hot while the fish bakes.

SUGGESTED MENU FOR FOUR

*Marinated Mushrooms (page 3)/
*Processor "French" Bread (page 139)
*Bluefish with Fennel and Tomato Sauce
Wine: Beaujolais
*Millet (page 178)
Crisp Green Salad
*Blackberry (or Blueberry) Pie (page 94) *or* Apple Tart

BLUEFISH WITH FENNEL AND TOMATO SAUCE

This simple, aromatic recipe comes from cooking teacher and friend Michèle Urvater, whose *Fine Fresh Food—Fast* has recently been published by Irena Chalmers Cookbooks, Inc.

Bluefish are fierce fighters and voracious eaters. As with other frenzied feeders, bluefish have in their systems extremely powerful enzymes to help them digest their enormous intake of food. Unfortunately, these same enzymes also cause the fish to spoil extremely rapidly if it is left ungutted or un-iced. In addition, the high oil content of bluefish prevents it from being successfully transported over long distances. All told, you had better sniff and prod your fish before buying. It should be bright-eyed, silvery, firm, and clean smelling. If fresh bluefish is not available, you can substitute mackerel or mullet. But do try for blues; when they are truly fresh, they are sweet, flavorful, and delicate.

Makes about 4 servings

1 fresh fennel bulb (about 1 pound)
1/2 stick (4 tablespoons) butter
1 tablespoon olive oil
2 medium-size garlic cloves, minced
1-inch piece orange rind
1/2 teaspoon fennel seeds
1/4 cup anise-flavored liquor (Pernod or Ricard)
3/4 teaspoon salt
1/4 teaspoon black pepper
1 cup peeled, seeded, chopped tomatoes (canned or fresh—see note below)
1 1/2 pounds bluefish filets, with or without skin

1. Cut off and discard the feathery tops of the fennel and cut the bulb into 1-inch pieces. Melt 2 tablespoons of the butter with the olive oil in a 9-inch skillet. Stir in the garlic, then the fresh fennel, orange rind, fennel seeds, liquor, salt, and pepper. Cover and simmer for 10 minutes.
2. After 10 minutes add the tomatoes, re-cover and simmer 10 minutes longer. Remove the cover and check the liquid in the pan. If there is a good deal remaining, evaporate it over high heat until the mixture looks syrupy. Remove the orange rind. Turn off the heat and stir in the remaining 2 tablespoons butter. Taste and adjust seasoning. Cool.
3. Season the filets lightly with salt and pepper and place them, skin side down, in a generously buttered baking/serving dish large enough to hold them in one layer.
4. Spoon the cooled vegetable mixture over the fish and cover the dish with foil. Store in the refrigerator up to 12 hours or so.
5. *To bake and serve:* Remove the fish from the refrigerator about 1/2 hour before you plan to bake it. Preheat the oven to 375°. Bake for about 20–25 minutes, covered with the foil, until the center of the fish no longer looks translucent but opaque (about 140° on an instant-reading thermometer).

NOTE: If you're using fresh tomatoes, 3 medium ones, or 3/4 pound, will do. Drop them into boiling water and let the water return to a full boil. Remove and peel the tomatoes, then halve them across and squeeze out their seeds. Chop coarsely.

SUGGESTED MENU FOR FOUR

*Leek and Potato Soup with Cucumbers (page 344; halve the recipe)
*Striped Bass Filets with Pink Peppercorns and Pistachios
*Perfect White Rice (page 174) *or* *Saffron Rice (page 175)
Wine: Pouilly Fumé *or* California Chardonnay
Salad of Boston Lettuce and Mushrooms
with Lemon-Oil Dressing
*Watermelon Ice (page 37) *or*
Strawberries and *Orange Sugar Wafers (page 65)

STRIPED BASS FILETS WITH PINK PEPPERCORNS AND PISTACHIOS

While striped bass (also called "rockfish" in parts of this country) is not on the list of endangered species, neither is it to be found in the abundance described by Captain John Smith in 1623: "There are such multitudes that I have seene stopped close in the river adjoining to my house . . . so many as will loade a ship of 100 tonnes. I myselfe, at the turning of the tyde have seen such multitudes pass out of a pounde that it seemed to me that one might go over their backs drishod" (quoted in *The Encyclopedia of Fish* by A. J. McClane, 1977).

Like salmon and shad, striped bass is anadromous—an ocean inhabitant dependent upon fresh rivers for its reproduction. It is deservedly popular, both for its delicacy of flavor and versatility. Wrote William Wood in 1634: "The basse is one of the best fishes in the Countrey, and though men are soone wearied with other fish, yet are they never with Basse. It is a delicate fine fat, fast fish" (*New England Prospect*).

The recipe that follows is extraordinarily simple to put together, yet elegant, beautiful, and delicious.

Makes about 4 servings

1½–2 pounds striped bass filets, with skin
3 tablespoons butter
1½ teaspoons pink peppercorns, drained—if vinegar packed, or freeze-dried (see list of mail-order sources, page 353)
2 scallion greens, very thinly sliced
¼ teaspoon salt
2 tablespoons dry vermouth
2 tablespoons coarsely chopped unsalted pistachios (see list of mail-order sources, page 353) or use blanched, chopped almonds

1. Arrange the fish filets, skin side down, in a single layer in a well-buttered baking/serving dish.
2. Melt the butter in a small skillet. Stir in the pink peppercorns, scallion greens, salt, and vermouth. Crush the peppercorns slightly with the back of a spoon to release their flavor. Remove from the heat and let cool.
3. Spoon the sauce over the fish. Scatter the nuts on top. Cover and store in the refrigerator up to 12 hours or so.
4. *To bake and serve:* Uncover the dish and let it stand at least 1/2 hour at room temperature. Preheat the oven to 425°. Set the dish on the upper rack of the oven and bake, basting 3–4 times, until the thickest part of the fish is opaque and registers 140° on an instant-reading thermometer, about 20 minutes for 3/4-inch-thick filets.

NOTE: If you can't get striped bass in peak condition, you might substitute red snapper or sea bass.

SUGGESTED MENU FOR FOUR

*Radishes with Anchovy Butter (page 5)/*Salted Rusks (page 262)
*Spiced Fish Filets with Tahini
*Millet (page 178) *or* *Saffron Rice (page 175)
Wine: Spanish Red Wine from the Rioja Region
Salad of Cucumbers, Mint, Vinegar, and Sugar
Honeydew and Cantaloupe Balls
with Fresh Ginger, Lime Juice, Honey

SPICED FISH FILETS WITH TAHINI

Tahini (sesame cream) is the oily, rich, nutty-flavored product of hulled, ground sesame seeds. It works very efficiently to keep the fish moist. You can find it in almost all health-food and Middle Eastern stores (or see list of mail-order sources, page 353).

Makes about 4 servings

1 medium garlic clove, minced or pushed through a press
1 1/2 teaspoons ground cumin
1 teaspoon paprika
1 teaspoon coarse (kosher) salt
1 1/2–2 pounds full-flavored fish filets (such as mackerel, sea bass, bluefish), with skin
Scant 1/2 cup tahini
2 tablespoons lemon juice
1 small red bell pepper, very finely minced

1. In a small dish combine the garlic, cumin, paprika, and salt and blend well. Rub into the fish on both sides.
2. Spread 2 tablespoons of the tahini in a baking/serving dish large enough to hold the fish in a single layer. Arrange the fish over this, skin side down. Drizzle the remaining tahini evenly over the fish, then spread to coat each piece evenly. Sprinkle with the lemon juice. Spread the minced red pepper over this. Cover with foil and store in the refrigerator for about 12 hours, or less.
3. *To bake and serve:* Remove the fish from the refrigerator while you preheat the oven to 400°. Set, covered with the foil, in the center of the oven and bake for 15 minutes. Uncover, baste, and bake for about 15 minutes longer, or until the thickest part of the fish is no longer translucent and an instant-reading thermometer registers 140° when inserted there. Serve immediately.

SUGGESTED MENU FOR SIX

*Crisp Savory Almonds (page 289; halve the recipe)
*Turban of Flounder with Leek Mousse and Tomato Cream
*Perfect White Rice (page 174)
Wine: Chablis *or* Meursault
Salad of Endive and Mushrooms
Dish of Whole Strawberries/*Lemon Sighs (page 248)

TURBAN OF FLOUNDER WITH LEEK MOUSSE AND TOMATO CREAM

The many varieties of sole and flounder are all members of the flatfish family, and all can be cooked in the same ways. Although many market fish are dubbed sole of one kind or another, strictly speaking, virtually none is available commercially. Therefore, the fish called for in this recipe is flounder, which is what most of those so-called soles are.

You'll need about 8 thin, medium-size filets to fit, just barely overlapping, in a 6-cup ring mold. To save time and expense, bring the mold with you to the market to measure the number you'll need.

When you're buying skinned, white fish filets—whatever they may be called—keep these qualities in mind: Filets should be translucent, not opaque; the pieces should be firm, evenly tapered, and uniformly cut, with no ragged edges; and fish that has begun to divide along the center seam or appears watery or limp is not desirable.

If you buy filets that fit this description, you should produce a beautiful ring of pure white fish, enclosing a soft green mousse, lightly flavored with leek and sorrel and studded with bits of pink shrimp. The cream-based, coral-orange sauce that cloaks the whole is flavored with shrimp shells and tomato. This is an elegant presentation for those who like a formal look.

Makes about 6 servings

FISH AND MOUSSE:

3/4 pound shrimp in the shell
1 teaspoon salt
1 medium leek
1/4 pound fresh sorrel (sour grass) leaves
About 8 thin, even-size flounder or sole filets (1 3/4 pounds)
1 1/2 tablespoons all-purpose flour
3 tablespoons cold butter, cut into 6 pieces
2 extra-large eggs, chilled
1/4 teaspoon grated nutmeg
1/4 teaspoon white pepper
1/2 cup heavy cream, chilled

SAUCE:

2 medium shallots
Reserved fish trimmings and shrimp shells
1 tablespoon butter
3/4 cup dry white wine
1 cup water
1/4 teaspoon salt
1/2 teaspoon dried tarragon
1/2 cup heavy cream
1 large ripe tomato, coarsely sliced
1/4 teaspoon sugar

1. Peel the shrimp and reserve the shells. Chop half the shrimp into small dice, toss with 1/4 teaspoon of the salt, and set over a bowl in a strainer to drain. Chill the remaining shrimp.
2. Quarter the leek lengthwise and wash thoroughly. Cut in half crosswise and set on a steaming rack in a pot of boiling water. Cover and cook for about 10 minutes or longer, or until thoroughly tender. Lift out the rack and drain and cool the leek. Wrap in paper towels and refrigerate.

(Continued)

3. Strip the leaves off the sorrel stems and rinse them. Place in a small, heavy pot, cover, and cook over low heat for a minute. Uncover and stir for a minute, until the leaves are all softened and "melted." Set in a sieve over a bowl to drain and cool, then refrigerate.

4. Halve the filets lengthwise by cutting out their central "zipper" of tiny bones. Reserve these for the sauce, refrigerated. Spread the filets on waxed paper, with room between them, and cover with another sheet of paper. Gently pound or roll them with a meat pounder or rolling pin to flatten them somewhat. Reserve 2 ounces of the least neat filets for the mousse.

5. Heavily butter a 6-cup ring mold. Lay the filets, very slightly overlapping, in the mold, their ex-skin sides (the darker sides) facing up toward you, their broad ends dangling a little over the outside edge, their pointed tips dangling slightly over the center hole. Pat into the mold and refrigerate.

6. Combine the whole shrimp, reserved bit of flounder, leek, sorrel, and flour in the container of a processor. Whirl to a fine purée. Add the butter, eggs, nutmeg, remaining 3/4 teaspoon salt, and the pepper. Whirl until the bits of butter are no longer visible. Scrape into a bowl. Pat dry the diced shrimp and add to the purée.

7. Whip the cream in a small bowl to form soft peaks, then fold very delicately into the purée. Taste for seasoning.

8. Sprinkle the fish filets with salt and pepper. Distribute dollops of the mousse evenly around the mold, then spread with a spatula. Tap the mold against a counter to settle the mousse. Fold the fish over the purée; do not press them into it. Cover with foil and store in the refrigerator up to 12 hours or so.

9. *To make the sauce:* In an enameled or stainless-steel skillet, sauté the shallots, fish trimmings, and shrimp shells for a minute in the butter. Add the wine, water, salt, and tarragon and gently simmer, partly covered, for 15 minutes. Strain through a sieve and discard the solids. Rinse out the skillet.

10. Combine the fish stock with the cream in the skillet and boil gently, stirring, to reduce the liquid to a scant 2/3 cup. It should be shiny and thickish. Set aside.

11. Purée the tomato in the blender. Press through a sieve into a skillet. Add the sugar. Boil gently, stirring, until the tomato is reduced almost to a paste, about 1/4 cup. Stir the tomato gradually into the

cream mixture. Taste and season. Cool, cover, and store in the refrigerator until serving time.
12. *To bake and serve:* Set a large roasting pan in the oven and place a cake rack in it. Fill the pan halfway with hot water. Preheat the oven to 325°. Cut a piece of waxed paper to fit the top of the mold (cut out the center hole) and butter it. Remove the foil from the mold and set the paper on top.
13. Place the mold on the rack in the pan in the oven and bake for about 40 minutes, or until the mousse mixture is quite firm when prodded with a finger. It should measure 140° on an instant-reading thermometer.
14. Remove the mold from the oven and set on a rack for 10 minutes. Over the sink, invert the mold with cake rack held against it to drain off any accumulated juices. Turn back over, then hold a large, heated serving dish over the mold and invert again.
15. Stir the reserved sauce over low heat to warm it. Drizzle a tablespoon or two over the fish. Serve the rest at the table on each serving of the turban; a little goes a long way.

SUGGESTED MENU FOR FOUR

*Feta-Walnut Pastries (page 16)
*Steamed Shrimp-Fish Cakes in Lemon Sauce
*Saffron Rice (page 175)
Wine: Warmed Sake *or* Iced Dry Sherry
Salad of Slivered Fennel and Cucumbers *or* Cucumbers and Endive
*Peaches with Cream and Almonds (page 105)

STEAMED SHRIMP-FISH CAKES IN LEMON SAUCE

These delicate cakes are light, gingery, with a fresh crunch from the water chestnuts. They are substantial enough to serve without a first course for lunch, but for dinner they need an introduction of some richness, such as the Feta-Walnut Pastries. Their sharp-sweet-sour sauce would overpower most wines, but the sake works well.

Makes about 4 servings

FISH CAKES:

1/2 pound shrimp in the shell
3/4 pound flounder or sole filets, skinned
1 1/2 tablespoons minced fresh ginger
3 scallions, sliced
3/4 teaspoon salt
3 tablespoons Sherry
1 tablespoon cornstarch
1 egg
1 teaspoon grated lemon rind
1 cup water chestnuts (about 8 ounces), drained (if canned)

SAUCE:

1/3 cup fresh lemon juice
3 tablespoons sugar
1/4 cup rice vinegar or mild white wine vinegar
1/4 cup Sherry
1/2 teaspoon salt
1 tablespoon cornstarch
1/2 cup water
2 teaspoons butter
1/2 teaspoon tomato paste
1 teaspoon or more grated fresh ginger

GARNISH: 1 scallion green, thinly sliced

1. Shell and clean the shrimp. Cut the fish into 1-inch pieces.
2. Combine the ginger, scallions, salt, Sherry, cornstarch, egg, and lemon rind in the container of a processor. Whirl to a fine purée, then pour into a small pitcher.
3. Combine half the shrimp and half the fish in the processor and chop very coarsely; just turn the machine on and off a few times. With the motor running, pour in the egg mixture. Process to just barely blend; do not purée. Scrape into a bowl.
4. Chop the remaining shrimp by hand to a medium-fine texture. Blend into the fish mixture. Mince the water chestnuts in the processor to a medium-fine texture and add them. Chill the mixture, covered, for an hour or more.
5. Heat water in the bottom part of a large steamer. Remove the steamer rack and set a large piece of oiled foil on it. Turn up the edges to form a dish.
6. Taking 1/4 cup of the fish mixture at a time, form the paste into ovals about 3/4 inch thick, wetting your hands with cold water to keep the mixture from sticking. Set as many cakes as will fit close together on the oiled foil.
7. Set the rack over the boiling water and cover the steamer. Steam for about 5 minutes over moderate heat, or until the cakes are no

longer mushy in the center. Remove the rack and with a spatula transfer the cakes to a large flameproof serving pan or dish.

8. Repeat step 7 as needed to steam all the cakes.

9. Cool the cakes in their juices, then cover and store in the refrigerator up to 24 hours.

10. *To make the sauce:* Stir together in a nonmetal saucepan the lemon juice, sugar, vinegar, Sherry, salt, cornstarch, water, butter, tomato paste, and ginger. Cook over moderate heat, stirring, until the mixture boils up and thickens. Stir a minute longer over low heat. Set aside for as long as a few hours, or cool, then cover and chill.

11. *To serve:* Heat the sauce to bubbling and pour over the fish cakes. Heat the pan over low heat for a few minutes, or until the cakes are hot through, turning them once with a spatula. Sprinkle with the scallion green and serve.

SUGGESTED MENU FOR SIX OR SEVEN

*American Bouillabaisse
*Processor "French" Bread (page 139)
or *Cracked-Oat Bread (page 347)
Wine: Muscadet *or* Rosé d'Anjou
*Salad of Chicory and Jerusalem Artichokes (page 275)
or Green Salad
Ripe Pears/Creamy Dessert Cheese

AMERICAN BOUILLABAISSE

This recipe is based on one devised by Susan Holland, a stylish New York caterer. She developed it to be ready before the arrival of guests, no small feat for a fish soup, which can be overcooked so easily.

Based ever-so-slightly on the Mediterranean fish soup, bouillabaisse, this version uses American fish, lighter seasonings, and different cooking techniques from its distant cousin in the south of France. A generous amount of fish and a modicum of rich, flavorful, garlic-scented stock produce a dish that is both elegantly balanced and a substantial meal. It is, as well, pretty to serve—with its large seafood chunks in a coral-colored broth, garnished with pale lemon slices.

Makes 6–7 servings

TO MARINATE:

3/4 pound medium-size shrimp in the shell
1 1/2 pounds scrod (or some member of the cod family), fileted, skinned, and cut into pieces about 2 1/2 inches square (see note)
1 pound striped bass filets (or use sea bass or red snapper), with skin, cut into pieces about 2 inches square (see note)
1 1/2 teaspoons coarse (kosher) salt
1–2 teaspoons fennel seeds
1/4 teaspoon dried thyme
1 garlic clove, minced

FOR THE STOCK:

1 onion, sliced (no need to peel)
1 carrot, sliced (no need to peel)
1 celery stalk with leaves, sliced
1 garlic clove, unpeeled
1 bay leaf
1/2 teaspoon black peppercorns
1/2 cup parsley stems
Bones from fish, plus heads and bones to make about 3 pounds of lean fish, chopped into manageable pieces (see note below)
2 1/2 cups dry white wine
1/2 teaspoon dried thyme

SOUP ASSEMBLY:

5 cups water
1/4 cup olive oil
1 medium onion, finely minced
2 medium carrots, finely minced
1 can (1 pound) peeled tomatoes
1/2 teaspoon dried basil
About 2 teaspoons salt
1/4 teaspoon saffron threads
1/2 teaspoon black pepper
2 1/2 dozen mussels (about 2 pounds)
1/2 lemon, very thinly sliced

NOTE: Save any bones and heads from filets. Remove and discard gills, if there are any, in any of the fish skeletons you use.

1. Rinse and shell the shrimp, placing the shells in one bowl, the shrimp in another. Add the fish pieces to the shrimp meat.
2. Crush together in a mortar the coarse salt, fennel seeds to taste, and the thyme. Add the garlic and blend. Sprinkle the mixture over

the fish and shrimp and distribute evenly. Cover the dish and store in the refrigerator up to 24 hours (or marinate for at least 6 hours, if you're making the soup in one day).

3. In a stainless-steel or enameled pot combine the reserved shrimp shells, and all ingredients for the stock. Bring to a simmer, then skim for a few minutes. Simmer, partly covered, for 30 minutes.

4. Meanwhile, heat the oil in a large pot, preferably the one in which you'll be serving the soup. Stir in the minced onion and carrots and stir occasionally over medium-low heat until the vegetables are well softened but not browned, about 10–15 minutes.

5. With kitchen scissors, snip the tomatoes in the can into small pieces. Pour the contents of the can into the pot. Add the basil, salt to taste, saffron, and black pepper. Stir over moderate heat for a few minutes, then set aside.

6. Strain the fish stock through a colander to remove the solids. From this, pick out and refrigerate any good chunks of fish meat to use later in the soup. Strain the stock into a bowl through a sieve lined with dampened cheesecloth, using one layer of cloth if you have a very fine weave, 2 or 3 if it is loose. There should be 7–7½ cups; if there is less, add water to make this amount.

7. Add the broth to the vegetable mixture and bring to a simmer. Remove from the heat. Place in a sink containing cold water and stir until cooled. Cover and store in the refrigerator until serving time, or up to 24 hours.

8. Some time before serving, scrub the mussels under running water and pull off their "beards." Soak for 15–20 minutes in a large pot of salted water into which you've stirred a handful of flour. Lift out the mussels carefully to leave any sand in the bottom. Place them in a large pot with a few tablespoons of water and steam, covered, over high heat for a few minutes; discard any that do not open. Strain, reserve, and freeze the broth for another use; it is too strong for this soup. Remove the mussel shells and cover and refrigerate the meat until serving time.

9. *To serve:* Bring the soup to a simmer. Add the reserved fish and shrimp combination and stir gently over moderate heat for 2 minutes, until the outside of the fish is white but the interior still uncooked. Add the mussels and reserved cooked fish bits. Spread the lemon slices over the soup. Cover the pot and barely simmer for 1–2 minutes, until the fish is just cooked. Serve at once.

31
A Memorable Memorial Day Weekend
Three Made-Ahead Menus with One-Dish Meals

Since the forces of nature are particularly unpredictable during this transitional season, here are three meals to cover the various whims of the weather. The first, of Creole parentage, might be served during just about any customary climatic caprice that might take place in the spring; the second, which has Russian/Polish ancestors, would suit a misty, coolish day; the third, a more or less Mediterranean mélange, begs for sunshine.

MEMORIAL DAY DINNER 1 (FOR SIX)

*Shrimp-Ham Jambalaya with Rice and Okra
Wine: Medium-Bodied Spanish Red from the Rioja Region
or California Pinot Noir
*Pineapple Snow/*Jumbles

SHRIMP-HAM JAMBALAYA WITH RICE AND OKRA

Jambalaya, a Creole-Acadian stew that can include just about anything with rice, has been variously called jimbalaya, jombalaya, and jumbalaya. Evoking images of nineteenth-century Louisiana, the name alone carries with it the confusion characteristic of many Creole dishes, which have both Spanish and French antecedents. Some historians contend that the name derives from the Spanish word *jamon* (ham), while others think it comes from the Provençal word *jambalaia*, meaning a dish of fowl and rice. There are many other theories about the origin of the word, but most seem far-fetched.

Although jambalaya is usually made with rice and shrimp (but often with chicken, sausages, and oysters, too) combined in one pot, the textures hold up better if the rice and stew are prepared separately. If the procedure is unorthodox, the tastes are representative of the cuisine, though in the case of a few ingredients, compromises have been made here. It is not feasible, for example, to stipulate, as one recipe did, that the dish be made with "100 fine small lake shrimp."

Makes about 6 servings

TO MAKE THE SHRIMP-HAM JAMBALAYA:

1½ pounds medium-small shrimp in the shell
Few celery leaves
1 carrot, sliced
Few peppercorns
3 cups water
3 tablespoons butter
1 large onion, minced (1 cup)
1 tablespoon all-purpose flour
3 large garlic cloves, minced (1½ teaspoons)
½ cup chopped green bell pepper
½ cup minced celery
About ⅛ teaspoon cayenne pepper
2 bay leaves, crushed or snipped small
¼ teaspoon ground cloves
1 teaspoon dried thyme
1 can (1 pound) peeled tomatoes
¾ pound firm, well-flavored ham, cut into ¾-inch dice

1. Rinse the shrimp and peel them, reserving the shells in a pot. Devein the shrimp, if needed, then refrigerate, covered.
2. Add the celery leaves, carrot, peppercorns, and water to the reserved shrimp shells. Cover, and simmer 20–25 minutes. Strain the stock and discard the shells. There should be 2 cups stock.
3. Melt the butter in a heavy saucepan; add the onions and cook until softened and lightly browned. Add the flour and stir until well browned, not just pale beige. Add the garlic, green pepper, and celery, and stir for a few minutes. Add ⅛ teaspoon cayenne (or to taste), bay leaves, cloves, thyme, and reserved shrimp stock. Snip the tomatoes in the can with kitchen scissors and pour into the saucepan. Simmer gently, covered, for 30 minutes, stirring occasionally.

(Continued)

4. Uncover, add the ham, and simmer 10 minutes, uncovered, stirring often. Taste for seasoning. Add the shrimp and remove the pan from the heat (do not cook the shrimp). Set the pot in a sink containing cold water and stir the mixture gently until lukewarm. Store in the refrigerator up to 24 hours.

TO MAKE THE RICE AND OKRA:

3–4 ounces lean slab bacon, cut into 1/4-inch dice
1/2 cup sliced scallions
1 1/4 cups long-grain white rice
2 1/2 cups chicken stock or broth
1 package (10 ounces) frozen okra, partly defrosted, cut into 1-inch-wide slices

1. In a heavy pot cook the bacon over medium heat, covered, for a few minutes. When it has rendered some fat, cook uncovered, stirring often, until lightly browned.
2. Add the scallions and rice and stir until the rice is opaque. Add the chicken stock and bring to a boil, stirring occasionally. Turn the heat to its lowest point and cook the rice, covered, for 20 minutes.
3. Remove the pot from the heat and let stand, covered, 20 minutes longer. Stir in the okra. Scrape into a wide, fairly shallow baking/serving dish and let cool. Cover tightly with foil and store in the refrigerator for up to 24 hours.
4. *To serve:* Set the rice in the center of a cold oven. Turn the heat to 350° and bake, covered, for 35–40 minutes, or until the rice mixture is hot. When almost ready, stir the jambalaya over moderately low heat for a few minutes, until hot throughout; do not overcook. Spoon the shrimp-ham mixture over the rice, or serve separately.

PINEAPPLE SNOW

The light, fluffy, appealing family of simple desserts known as "snows" or "snow creams" was popular summer fare around the turn of the century, and has remained a favorite in many parts of the United States. Sometimes the "creams" were composed only of puréed fresh fruit mixed with meringue, but more often whipped cream was included. Later versions incorporated gelatin to make a stable dessert that could be unmolded. The following recipe, an uncomplicated blend of sweet-smooth cream and tart, textur-y pineapple, follows the earlier versions.

Makes 6 servings

1 small ripe pineapple, peeled, cored, and cut into chunks
2 tablespoons rum
6 tablespoons extrafine sugar
2 egg whites (use those reserved from the Jumbles recipe that follows)
1 cup heavy cream, chilled
GARNISH: Small, ripe strawberries, halved

1. In a processor or by hand, coarsely grate or shred the pineapple; there should be about 2 cups. Stir in the rum and 2 tablespoons of the sugar. Cover and refrigerate until serving time.
2. Beat the egg whites until fluffy on medium speed in the small bowl of an electric mixer. Running the machine on high speed, add the remaining sugar, 1 tablespoon at a time, beating 1 minute between additions.
3. Whip the cream until it forms soft peaks. Gently fold it into the whites, using a rubber spatula. Spoon the mixture into a sieve lined with a layer of dampened, fine-mesh cotton cheesecloth (or two layers of the loose-mesh kind) that has been set over a bowl. Store in the refrigerator, covered, up to about 5 hours.
4. *To serve:* Gently loosen the cream from the cheesecloth into a large, chilled serving dish. Gradually fold the pineapple into the cream with a rubber spatula. Garnish with the berries and serve at once, in chilled dishes.

JUMBLES

These plain, sugared butter cookies have been making their way around cookery books since the seventeenth century. Their ancestor was probably the "gimbal," which was a ring-shaped cookie, or one "wreathed into knots." Mary Randolph, in *The Virginia Housewife* (1860), refers to the cookies as "jumbals," while the Louisiana version (in *The Picayune's Creole Cookbook*, 1901) is dubbed "Melee-Creole." The quaint nomenclature is suited to this tidbit from the past century, a time when fashionable women were constantly on the verge of collapsing: "She feels a little faint with walking, and intends eating a tart or jumble, or drinking a glass of lemonade."

Rose water, the flavoring commonly used in old recipes, has been included, but if it is not to your taste, substitute 2 tablespoons lemon or orange juice and 1 teaspoon grated lemon or orange rind.

Makes 20 cookies

1 stick (8 tablespoons) unsalted butter, at room temperature
1/2 cup sugar
2 egg yolks (reserve the whites for the Pineapple Snow, page 330)
1–2 tablespoons rose water
1 1/4 cups all-purpose flour
1/8 teaspoon salt
1/8 teaspoon grated nutmeg
1/4 teaspoon baking powder
Confectioners' sugar (preferably vanilla-flavored)

1. Cream the butter and sugar in a bowl until light. Add the yolks and rose water to taste and beat until pale and fluffy.
2. Sift together the flour, salt, nutmeg, and baking powder. Sift, a little at a time, into the butter mixture and blend. Scrape the dough into a ball, form into a brick, and wrap in floured plastic. Refrigerate for several hours, or overnight.
3. Preheat the oven to 375°. Cut the dough into 20 equal pieces. Dust your hands with confectioners' sugar, if necessary to prevent sticking, and roll each piece to form a rope about 5 inches long. Moisten the ends, then seal to form a ring. Place on a nonstick or parchment-covered baking sheet. Repeat until all the dough is used.
4. Bake the cookies in the center of the oven for about 12 minutes or until they are *pale* beige: Do not overbake.
5. Transfer to a rack and sieve confectioners' sugar over the tops. Cool, then store in an airtight container. When serving, sieve additional confectioners' sugar over the cookies.

MEMORIAL DAY DINNER 2 (FOR SIX)

*Bitki (Veal Patties) with Noodles and Peas
Wine: Alsatian Pinot Blanc *or* California Fumé Blanc
*Salad of Crisp-Cooked Carrots with Herbs
*Fruit-Filled Honeydew

BITKI (VEAL PATTIES) WITH NOODLES AND PEAS

These traditional Russian/Polish meat patties can be made with beef, pork, or veal. For a warm-weather meal, veal is leaner and lighter. The bitki (plural of bitok, which simply means a patty) always contain onions and are finished in sour cream, but beyond that, there is little agreement among recipes.

Be sure to arrange the meat around the sides of the baking dish, touching the edge, with the noodles in the center—otherwise the meat will heat through too slowly and the noodles will get mushy. In any case, the noodles will be pleasantly soft and sauced, not *al dente*; if you prefer more bite to your pasta, substitute ditali or shell macaroni.

Makes 6–8 servings

1 large onion, minced (1 cup)
About 3 tablespoons butter
3 slices soft white bread, crusts removed, torn into coarse crumbs
2/3 cup milk
1 1/2 teaspoons salt
2 teaspoons caraway seeds
2 eggs
1/4 teaspoon black pepper
2 pounds well-trimmed veal, ground
1/2 cup all-purpose flour
About 1 tablespoon vegetable oil
1 package (12 ounces) egg noodles
1 1/2 cups veal or chicken broth
1 1/2 cups sour cream
2 pounds fresh peas, shelled, or 1 package (10 ounces) frozen peas, partially thawed
Few tablespoons minced fresh parsley
Few tablespoons snipped fresh chives

1. Cook the onion in 2 tablespoons of the butter in a small skillet until softened. Scrape into a mixing bowl. Cool slightly.
2. Combine the bread and milk in a small bowl, pressing down on the crumbs to cover them with milk. Mash with a fork until soft, then add to the onion with the salt, 1 1/2 teaspoons of the caraway seeds, the eggs, and pepper and beat well with a fork or whisk. Add the veal and beat until fluffy and well blended.
3. Form 18 patties with the mixture. Dredge half of them heavily in the flour so that all sides are covered; do not remove the excess.

(Continued)

4. Brown the patties on each side in the remaining 1 tablespoon of the butter and the oil in a very large skillet. Transfer carefully to a plate.
5. Dredge the remaining patties in flour and brown them, adding butter and oil if needed. Return the other patties to the pan and cook them over low heat, covered, for 5 minutes.
6. Add the stock and remaining 1/2 teaspoon caraway seeds. Bring to a simmer and cook, stirring gently and turning a few times, for 5 minutes. Transfer the patties to the plate.
7. Add the sour cream to the stock and bring to a bare simmer, stirring with a whisk. Season to taste. Set the sauce aside.
8. Simmer the fresh peas, covered, with a small amount of water until half cooked. Drain, cool in water, and drain again. (If you are using frozen peas, there is no need to cook them.)
9. Boil the noodles in a large pot of salted water for about 3 minutes, or until half cooked. Drain. Pour half the reserved sauce into a very large, fairly shallow baking/serving dish large enough to hold the noodles, peas, and veal (a lasagne-style dish does well). Add the noodles and peas and toss to coat well.
10. Mound the noodles and peas in the center of the dish, leaving a margin around the sides. Surround the noodles with the veal, overlapping the patties to fit all around. Pour the remaining sauce over the meat. Let cool, then cover with foil and refrigerate up to 1 day.
11. *To serve:* Place the dish in the oven and turn the heat to 350°. Bake, covered, until hot through, about 45 minutes. Remove the foil and sprinkle with the parsley and chives.

SALAD OF CRISP-COOKED CARROTS WITH HERBS

Makes 6 servings

2 pounds small-medium carrots, peeled and trimmed
1/4 cup fresh lime juice
3 tablespoons light vegetable oil (such as corn)
1/2 teaspoon salt
1/4 teaspoon black pepper
About 1–2 tablespoons minced fresh basil, dill, mint, or oregano

1. Drop the carrots into a large pot of boiling salted water and cook on highest heat for about 3–5 minutes, or until they have just barely lost their raw, crunchy texture. Do not overcook. Cool in a bowl of ice water.
2. Slice the carrots into very thin rounds. A processor or mandoline works well for this.
3. Combine the lime juice, oil, salt, and pepper and blend. Pour over the carrots. Add the chosen herb and toss to mix.
4. Cover the salad and chill for several hours or more.

FRUIT-FILLED HONEYDEW

This cooling dessert, not unusual for a Russian or Polish meal, adapts to all manner of spring-summer fruits. General procedural indications should take care of the variables that a specific recipe could not cover, in this instance:

Select a very large, ripe honeydew melon and cut out a lid about 4 inches in diameter with a zigzag edge around the stem end of the melon. Remove and reserve this cap, first scraping off and discarding the seeds. Spoon out and discard all the seeds from the melon cavity. With a melon ball cutter scoop out the flesh, being careful not to pierce the skin. Place the balls in a bowl.

Add a generous selection of sliced soft fruits—strawberries, peaches, plums, halved and seeded grapes, nectarines, blueberries, apricots, and raspberries all respond well to this treatment. Add enough to make a quantity that will almost fill the melon cavity. Add vanilla sugar (or sugar and some scrapings from a vanilla bean) to taste. Add kirsch or another fruit-flavored eau-de-vie or brandy. Taste; the fruit should be slightly oversweetened and overflavored to compensate for the chilling. Pour the fruit mixture into the melon, cover with the cap, and chill several hours.

Serve the fruits directly from the melon—which looks pretty surrounded by leaves and flowers, if you're lucky enough to have them for the picking.

MEMORIAL DAY DINNER 3 (FOR SIX)

*Jellied Chicken Provençal
Wine: Italian Tocai *or* Montepulciano d'Abruzzo Cerasuolo
*Salad of White Beans in Tomato Shells
Cherries/*Orange Sugar Wafers (page 65)

JELLIED CHICKEN PROVENÇAL

A full-flavored, easy-to-serve dish of chicken chunks, chilled in their natural aspic, which has been tinted a lovely orangy-pink by the tomatoes and red peppers. Garnished with orange, watercress, and black olives, the dish becomes a meal. It can be made a day or two ahead, to suit your schedule.

Makes 6 servings

1½ pounds ripe tomatoes, preferably Italian plum tomatoes
Enough small onions, peeled and sliced, to make 2 cups
1 medium-small carrot, very thinly sliced
2 large garlic cloves, minced (2 teaspoons)
2 cups thinly sliced red bell peppers
2 tablespoons olive oil
1 cup dry vermouth
¼ cup white wine vinegar
¼ cup lemon juice
2 teaspoons salt
1 teaspoon sugar
1 teaspoon fennel seeds
½ teaspoon black peppercorns
1½ teaspoons dried thyme
2 bay leaves, crushed or snipped small
1 roasting chicken (5½ pounds), cut up
2 navel oranges, peeled, halved through the stem end, then cut into crosswise slices
Black olives, preferably the small Niçoise variety
Watercress or arugula sprigs

1. Drop the tomatoes into a large pot of boiling water and let the water return to a boil. Drain, peel, and reserve the tomatoes.
2. In a large skillet cook the onions, carrots, garlic, and peppers in the olive oil until they are only very slightly softened—a few minutes will do.

3. Press the tomatoes through a fine disc of a food mill into the skillet. Add the dry vermouth, vinegar, lemon juice, salt, and sugar. Preheat the oven to 350°.
4. Tie into a small doubled piece of fine-mesh cotton cheesecloth the fennel seeds, peppercorns, thyme, and bay leaves and add to the vegetables. Simmer for 5 minutes, pressing on the herb bag now and then.
5. Layer the chicken pieces and vegetables (with their liquid) in a heavy pot. Bring to a simmer, then cover and place in the oven. Bake for 50–60 minutes.
6. Remove the chicken pieces to a platter to cool. Strain the stock into a bowl and reserve the vegetables. When the chicken is cool enough to handle, remove and discard the skin and bones and cut the meat into good-sized cubes, as neatly as possible. Skim all the fat off the stock.
7. Spread the chicken in a wide serving dish that is deep enough to hold all the vegetables and stock (as well as the garnish, later). Spread the vegetables over the chicken, pour the skimmed stock over all, and chill overnight or longer.
8. *To serve:* Arrange the oranges, olives, and watercress or arugula around the platter and over the chicken and vegetables.

SALAD OF WHITE BEANS IN TOMATO SHELLS

Makes 6 servings

6 medium-large tomatoes
2 medium garlic cloves, finely minced
1/2 cup olive oil
2 1/2 cups cooked white beans
1/3 cup minced fresh basil
2 teaspoons vinegar
Very finely minced fresh parsley
GARNISH: Tiny basil sprigs

1. Slice the stem ends from the tomatoes. Squeeze out the seeds gently. Scoop out most of the pulp, chop it, and toss in a sieve with a sprinkle of salt and pepper. Let drain 15 minutes or longer. Reserve the tomato shells.

(Continued)

2. Sauté the garlic in the oil for a minute or two. Add the beans and toss gently for a few minutes to absorb the oil. Off the heat stir in the basil, tomato pulp, vinegar, and salt and pepper to taste.
3. Broil the tomato shells close to the heat for about 5 minutes, or until they have softened very slightly. Invert on a rack and let drain briefly. Sprinkle the interiors of the shells with enough minced parsley to coat lightly.
4. Spoon the bean mixture into the tomato shells and refrigerate, or let stand at room temperature until serving time.
5. *To serve:* Let the tomatoes reach room temperature. Poke a sprig of basil in each for garnish.

32
House Guests for the Weekend, Late Spring

This group of recipes is designed to fit the mealtime needs of those fortunate enough to be in the country with weekend guests—but you needn't be a country squire to enjoy the rolling feast.

So that the weekend won't be one long KP shift, several parts of each meal can be put together during the week and a few recipes are for double-duty dishes: Saturday's hot soup, for example, becomes a chilled cream soup on Sunday, while the roasted pork forms the basis for the next day's main-course salad. If you have time during the week, you might prepare the chickpea dip, bake the bread and cookies, and marinate the pork before you leave for the weekend. We'll assume that you'll arrive at your country house Friday, and that guests will show up on Saturday for brunch. The scenario is for six—adults and children, or just adults.

A WEEKEND WITH HOUSE GUESTS

SATURDAY

BRUNCH FOR SIX

Berries with Sour Cream or Crème Fraîche and Sugar
*Rolled Soufflé with Tomato Filling
Coffee/*Cinnamon-Sugar Strips (page 42) *or* Bakery Cookies

COCKTAILS

Drinks
*Chickpea Dip with Vegetable Strips
*Crisp Savory Almonds (page 289) *or*
*Tiny Tomatoes Stuffed with Taramosalata (page 49)

DINNER FOR SIX

*Leek and Potato Soup with Cucumbers
*Roasted Marinated Pork Loin
Salad of Watercress and Thinly Slivered Apples, Lightly Dressed with Lemon and Oil
Wine: Bourgueil *or* Beaujolais, slightly chilled
*Cracked-Oat Bread *or* *Crusty Whole-Wheat Loaf (page 100)
Espresso/Basket of Peaches or Pears

SUNDAY

LATE BREAKFAST FOR SIX

Honeydew Melon *and/or* Figs with Prosciutto or Westphalian Ham
*Cracked-Oat Bread
Selection of Mild Goat Cheeses
Coffee

LATE AFTERNOON PICNIC OR BUFFET FOR SIX

*Chilled Cream of Leek and Potato Soup with Dill
*Pork, Rice, and Carrot Salad with Capers
Wine: Iced Soave *or* Vernaccia di San Gimignano
Grapes/Plums
Iced Tea/*Cinnamon-Sugar Strips (page 42)

SUGGESTED PREPARATION SCHEDULE

During the week
Prepare Savory Almonds or Taramosalata
Prepare Cracked-Oat Bread
Prepare Chickpea Dip
Marinate Pork Loin

Friday afternoon or evening
Shop for remaining ingredients
Prepare Leek and Potato Soup with Cucumbers
Bake Cinnamon-Sugar Strips

Saturday morning
Clean berries
Prepare Rolled Soufflé with Tomato Filling
Prepare and refrigerate raw vegetable strips for cocktails

Saturday afternoon
Roast pork
Prepare salad
Shred cucumbers into soup

Saturday night or Sunday morning
Prepare Pork, Rice, and Carrot Salad with Capers

NOTE: Recipes for meals follow in the order in which they appear in the menu plan.

ROLLED SOUFFLÉ WITH TOMATO FILLING

Although it is obviously more bothersome to make this filled soufflé for breakfast than it would be to scramble eggs, the lovely spiral slices are certainly more appealing, and the dish is easier to serve, as it can wait for hours. You can prepare the filling the day before, then put together the soufflé the next morning—or make the two parts at once. Once filled, the roll can wait until everyone is ready to eat. Or, if you prefer, make the entire recipe the night before and let it reach room temperature the next morning. Although this doesn't look quite as perky-fresh, the flavors are remarkably vivid.

Makes 6 servings

FILLING:

3 pounds ripe tomatoes
2 tablespoons butter
1/2 teaspoon dried tarragon (or use 1 teaspoon minced fresh)
1/2 teaspoon sugar
1/2 teaspoon salt
Black pepper to taste

SOUFFLÉ:

1/2 stick (4 tablespoons) butter
1/3 cup all-purpose flour
1 3/4 cups milk, heated to almost simmering
1/4 teaspoon white pepper
1/2 teaspoon salt
5 eggs (large or extra-large) at room temperature, separated
1/2 cup grated Parmesan cheese, lightly packed
2 tablespoons finely cut fresh chives
1/4 cup finely minced fresh parsley

GARNISH: Mustard cress or cucumber slices

1. *To make the filling:* Drop the tomatoes into a pot of boiling water; return to a boil. Drain, peel, then core the tomatoes. Halve crosswise and squeeze out and discard the seeds. Cut the flesh into small dice.
2. Melt the 2 tablespoons butter in a skillet; add the tomatoes, tarragon, sugar, and salt and cook, covered, over moderate heat for about 2 minutes. Uncover and stir over high heat until the tomatoes are soft and most of the liquid has evaporated, which takes about 5 minutes. Season with pepper and let stand overnight at room temperature. (If you are making the filling in the morning, spread it on a plate to cool more rapidly.)
3. *To make the soufflé:* Melt the 1/2 stick butter in a heavy 3-quart saucepan and stir in the flour. Stir over moderately low heat for 2 minutes, or until the mixture is light golden. Stir in the hot milk all at once and whisk vigorously until smooth. Simmer, stirring constantly, for 2 minutes. Add the pepper and salt.
4. Preheat the oven to 400°. Line a greased jelly-roll pan (15 × 10 inches) with buttered waxed paper. Sprinkle the paper with flour and knock off any excess.
5. Add the yolks to the white sauce, one at a time, beating well after each addition.
6. Beat the egg whites in a large bowl until they form firm but not too stiff peaks. Stir a few large dollops thoroughly into the sauce. Fold in the remaining whites gently, adding 1/4 cup of the grated Parmesan when they are nearly incorporated.
7. Carefully pour the mixture into the pan, taking care not to deflate it. Smooth with a spatula to even it out. Sprinkle with the remaining 1/4 cup cheese.
8. Bake in the center of the oven for 15–20 minutes, or until the soufflé is well puffed and browned but not dried out.
9. Remove the soufflé from the oven. Sprinkle it evenly with 1 tablespoon of the chives and the parsley. Place on top of this 2 sheets of waxed paper several inches longer than the pan and cover with a baking sheet. Invert all onto a table. Remove the hot pan and very carefully peel off the paper. Trim any dry edges off the rectangle of soufflé. Sprinkle with the remaining chives.
10. Spread the tomato filling on the roll and gently, tightly, roll up the soufflé from a short end, lifting the paper to help roll. Let the soufflé cool until you are ready to serve.

11. *To serve:* Gently cut the roll into 12 equal slices with a sharp serrated knife and arrange them on a platter, surrounded by the mustard cress or cucumber slices.

CHICKPEA DIP WITH VEGETABLE STRIPS

Make this two days to a week before serving. Film the purée with olive oil and refrigerate until ready to eat. Prepare and refrigerate the vegetable strips the day that you'll serve the dip.

Makes about 3 cups

1 cup dried chickpeas (or use 3 cups cooked chickpeas)
1/2 cup olive oil
1/4 cup lemon juice
2 tablespoons grated fresh ginger
2 teaspoons Oriental sesame oil (see list of mail-order sources, page 353)
1 1/4 teaspoons salt
1 medium-small garlic clove, finely minced or pushed through a press
About 1/3 cup water
Finely minced cilantro (also called fresh coriander or Chinese parsley) or fresh parsley
Vegetable strips (fennel, fresh red and green bell peppers, carrots, cucumbers, celery, endive—and whatever else is available)
Thinly sliced, toasted bread or pita

1. Soak the chickpeas in cold water (to cover by several inches) overnight in a large enameled or stainless-steel saucepan. Add water as needed to cover again by several inches. Simmer, partly covered, for several hours, or until the chickpeas are tender, adding water as needed to keep them covered. Timing can vary considerably—from 1 to 3 hours, so keep tasting. Drain the peas.
2. Combine the drained peas in a food processor container with the olive oil, lemon juice, ginger, sesame oil, salt, and garlic and process briefly to mix. Continue processing, adding 1/3 cup water, or the amount needed to achieve a desirable consistency. Stop the machine often to check the texture, which should be somewhat chunky, not smooth. Season to taste.

(Continued)

3. Spoon the purée into small earthenware crocks or bowls. Smooth the tops and cover the purée with oil. Cover the dishes with close-fitting lids or plastic wrap and store in the refrigerator until needed.
4. *To serve:* Stir the surface oil into the purée and sprinkle with the cilantro or parsley. Serve with the vegetable strips and crisp toast.

NOTE: If you wish to use a blender instead of a processor, make the purée in 2 batches, adding about 3 tablespoons of water to each batch along with half the seasonings. You will need to stop the blender often to scrape down the mixture from the sides of the container.

LEEK AND POTATO SOUP WITH CUCUMBERS

The flavor of this soup improves if you refrigerate it for a day or two before serving, so prepare it up to step 4—the addition of the cucumbers—and finish the soup sometime Saturday afternoon or evening.

Makes 6 servings (when half is reserved for the next evening)

3/4 stick (6 tablespoons) butter
4 medium leeks, light green and white parts only, meticulously washed, then thinly sliced (to equal about 3 1/2 cups)
3 medium onions, thinly sliced (about 3 cups)
1 tablespoon salt
About 3 pounds baking potatoes, peeled and thinly sliced (about 8 cups)
8 cups water
4 medium cucumbers
About 1/2 cup heavy cream
About 1/2 cup milk
White pepper
Fresh chives

1. Melt the butter in a large pot, then stir in the leeks and onions and cook over moderately low heat, stirring often, until softened, about 10 minutes.
2. Add the salt, potatoes, and water and bring the soup to a simmer. Cover and maintain the soup at a simmer until the potatoes are soft, about 25 minutes. Cool the soup to lukewarm, uncovered.

3. Process the soup in batches to a very fine purée in a blender or food processor. Strain it through a sieve and return to the pot. Season. Reserve and refrigerate for a day or two.
4. *To finish and serve:* Peel, seed, and coarsely shred the cucumbers, using the shredding blade on a processor or vegetable slicer or the largest opening on a hand grater. There should be about 1½–2 cups. Remove half the soup from the refrigerator. Add the cucumber to this and simmer for about 5 minutes, or until the cucumber is tender, stirring occasionally. Stir in the cream and milk, adjusting to the desired thickness. Season with white pepper and salt and sprinkle with chives. Serve hot.

ROASTED MARINATED PORK LOIN

Marinate the pork for 2 to 3 days before roasting. Both texture and flavor of pork loin are improved by being served at room temperature, a condition that also allows for greater flexibility at dinnertime, when the pressure of delivering a just-cooked roast to the table can be distracting. Remember to save about 1½ pounds for Sunday's salad.

Makes 6 servings (when 1½ pounds of the cooked roast are reserved for Sunday)

About 5½ pounds boneless pork loin (not tied up)
4 teaspoons coarse (kosher) salt
½ cinnamon stick
1 teaspoon black peppercorns
2 bay leaves
1¼ teaspoons dried thyme
1 teaspoon juniper berries
1 large garlic clove, crushed or minced
1 tablespoon brown sugar
2 tablespoons gin
2 tablespoons olive oil
2 tablespoons peanut oil
About ⅓ cup dry vermouth or white wine
About 2 teaspoons sharp mustard
About 1–2 tablespoons sour cream
1 good-size bunch small radishes with leaves

1. Stab the meat through all over with the point of a thin skewer or small knife. Trim away excess interior fat, but leave a good amount on the outside of the meat.

(Continued)

2. Combine in a spice mill or mortar the salt, cinnamon, pepper, bay leaves, thyme, and juniper berries and grind to a fine consistency. Pour into a small bowl and stir in the garlic and brown sugar to distribute evenly. Add the gin and olive oil and mix.

3. Set the loin on a large sheet of waxed paper or parchment. Rub the marinade evenly over the meat. Tie strings around the meat to form a neat, even cylinder. Wrap in the paper, then a layer of foil. Enclose the whole in a plastic bag and fasten tightly. Refrigerate for 2–3 days.

4. Several hours before you expect to cook the meat, remove from the refrigerator and unwrap. Find a large casserole or roasting pan that will fit the meat as closely as possible. Heat the peanut oil in this. Blot the meat dry and brown it well on all sides. Pour out all fat from the pan. Cover tightly with heavy foil or a lid. Set in an oven turned to 325°.

5. Depending upon the conformation and tenderness of the pork, roasting times vary considerably, from about 1½ hours to about 3 hours for a loin like this. If the meat is very tender, long, and narrow, it will take less time to roast than a thick, dense piece. In any case, roast the meat until it registers 170–175° on a meat thermometer or instant-reading thermometer. Begin checking after about 1 hour and 15 minutes. When the meat is done, remove the foil and let the meat stand from ½ hour to 2½ hours before carving, as convenient.

6. While the meat is resting, pour the juices from the pan into a cup and skim off the fat. Combine the meat juices in a small pan with enough vermouth or wine to make about 1⅓ cups. Boil down by half. Stir in the mustard with a whisk and boil for a minute. Remove from the heat and cool. Whisk in sour cream to taste. Leave at room temperature.

7. *To serve:* Slice about two thirds of the meat and arrange it, overlapping, on a large platter. Surround with the rinsed radishes, their leaves intact. Spoon a tiny bit of the concentrated juices over each slice of meat. Wrap and refrigerate the remaining pork for Sunday's salad.

CRACKED-OAT BREAD

The gently sweet flavor of oats is delicate, and easily masked by spices and sugar, which often accompany them. Here, the taste is underscored by a double dose of grain—in cracked or cut form, to improve moisture retention and create an interesting texture, and as ground-oat "flour," for additional substance. The second rising further develops the subtle grain taste, as does the undertone of pungent pepper. The loaves have a crackly crisp crust and moist, close-textured interior.

Makes 2 large loaves (each about 1 pound 6 ounces)

1¼ cups water
1 tablespoon salt
1 cup steel-cut oats (also called cracked oats; see list of mail-order sources, page 353)
2 tablespoons butter
2 tablespoons brown sugar
1 packet dry yeast
1¾ cups warm water
2½ cups quick-cooking oatmeal
½ teaspoon ground black pepper
About 4 cups bread flour (available in specialty stores and many supermarkets)

1. In a small heavy saucepan bring the 1¼ cups water to a boil with ½ teaspoon salt. Stir in the steel-cut oats. Bring to a boil and remove from the heat. Cover and let stand 20 minutes. Add the butter and brown sugar and stir. Set aside, uncovered.
2. Stir together the yeast, ¼ cup of the warm water, and a pinch of brown sugar. Let the mixture stand until very fluffy, about 5 minutes. If it doesn't puff up, begin again with fresh ingredients. Meanwhile, mix the remaining 2½ teaspoons salt and 1½ cups warm water in a large mixing bowl. Add the cracked-oat mixture and yeast and stir.
3. Grind 2 cups of the quick-cooking oatmeal to a very fine texture in a processor or blender. Add to the oat-yeast mixture with the pepper and 1½ cups of the bread flour. Stir for a minute or two, vigorously, to develop the gluten.

(Continued)

4. Spread 2 cups bread flour on a kneading surface. Pour the wet dough into the center of this and mix into the flour roughly, using a dough scraper, putty knife, heavy pancake turner, or spatula. Knead with your hands when the dough is sufficiently stiff. Continue kneading constantly until the dough is no longer very sticky. (Whole-grain doughs never become as sleek as white ones; they always remain a bit tacky.) Add flour as needed to keep the dough from sticking—but add slowly, to be sure it is necessary. About 10 minutes of forceful kneading should do the trick.
5. Form the dough into a ball and turn it around in a large buttered bowl to coat all sides. Cover the bowl with plastic wrap and let the dough rise at room temperature (ideally about 70–75°) until doubled in bulk, about 1¼ hours. Punch down the dough, turn it over, and re-cover the bowl. Let rise again until doubled, about 1 hour.
6. Turn the dough onto a floured surface and flatten it. Divide in two equal pieces. Form each piece into a ball, using as little pulling and pinching as possible. Cover the balls with a towel and let the dough relax for about 10 minutes. Meanwhile, grind the remaining ½ cup quick-cooking oatmeal in the processor or blender and sprinkle half evenly over a large baking sheet.
7. Flatten one piece of dough with your hands or with a rolling pin to form an oval about 12 inches long. With the side of your hand press a narrow trough in the center running the length of the oval. Roll the dough tightly, but stretching as little as possible, from one long edge to the center line. Pinch the edge to seal to the center. Roll the other long edge to meet this and pinch the two together firmly. Turn under the ends and pinch to seal. Turn over the loaf and shape as needed to form a neat oblong about 10 inches long. Set on the sheet. Repeat the forming process with the other ball.
8. Cover the loaves with a towel and let rise until not quite double, about 45 minutes. Preheat the oven to 400°.
9. When loaves have risen, sprinkle each with the remaining ground oatmeal. Using a single-edged razor or a very sharp knife, hold the blade edge almost parallel to the surface of the loaves and cut 3–4 diagonal slashes about ¼ inch deep in each.

10. Using a plant mister, spray the oven fiercely for 30 seconds, then immediately set the loaves in the center. (If there is a light bulb in your oven, turn it off so it won't shatter.) Bake for 25 minutes. Turn the pan around, lower the heat to 350°, and bake 20 minutes longer, until browned. Set the loaves directly on the oven rack and bake about 10–15 minutes longer, until well browned. Cool completely on a rack.

11. *To store and serve:* If you'll be using the bread within a day or two, leave the loaves unwrapped, on a rack. Recrisp in a 275° oven for 15 minutes shortly before serving. For longer storage (up to 3 months), wrap the bread tightly in freezer paper, seal, label and freeze. To serve, unwrap the bread and rewrap it in a clean towel. Let defrost completely at room temperature. Crisp for 15 minutes in a 275° oven shortly before serving.

CHILLED CREAM OF LEEK AND POTATO SOUP WITH DILL

Although there are very few changes to be made in the Leek and Potato Soup to transform it into a cold purée, the result is distinctively different—creamy and herbal.

Makes 6 servings

1/2 cup heavy cream
1/2 cup sour cream
About 6 cups reserved Leek and Potato Soup (from Saturday's dinner)
Lemon juice
White pepper
About 1/4 cup finely snipped fresh dill

1. Whisk together the heavy cream and sour cream. Whisk into the reserved cold soup. Season with lemon juice, pepper, and salt to taste. If the soup is quite thick, thin it with cold water.

2. Sprinkle the soup with the dill. Serve, or chill until needed.

PORK, RICE, AND CARROT SALAD WITH CAPERS

Assemble this salad either Saturday night or during the day on Sunday, whichever is more convenient.

Makes 6–7 servings

About 1 1/2 pounds pork reserved from Saturday's dinner
2/3 cup cider vinegar
1 tablespoon brown sugar
1 teaspoon Dijon mustard
1/4 teaspoon black pepper
1/4–1/2 teaspoon Tabasco
1/2 cup corn oil
2 1/2 teaspoons coarse (kosher) salt
1 1/2 cups long-grain white rice
2 1/2 cups water
3 large garlic cloves, peeled
6–7 medium-large carrots (about 1 1/4 pounds, weighed without leaves)
1 bunch (6 large) scallions, trimmed and thinly sliced
1/4 cup drained capers (if the tiny nonpareil variety, leave whole; if large, chop them coarsely)
1/4 cup finely minced fresh parsley
1 bunch watercress, trimmed, rinsed, and dried

1. Trim the fat off the pork. Cut the meat into fine julienne strips about 1 1/2 inches long. A cleaver does this job best.
2. In a jar combine the vinegar, brown sugar, mustard, pepper, Tabasco, corn oil, and 1 1/2 teaspoons of the salt and shake to blend. Pour one third to one half of the mixture over the pork and toss to coat. Leave at room temperature. The marinating will soften and flavor the meat while you cook the rice.
3. In a heavy 1 1/2- to 2-quart saucepan combine the remaining 1 teaspoon salt, the rice, water, and whole garlic cloves. Bring to a boil over highest heat, stirring. Turn the heat to its lowest point, then cover the pot and cook 20 minutes. Remove from the heat and let stand 20 minutes longer. Do not uncover.
4. Meanwhile, peel the carrots and cut them into fine julienne strips about 1 1/2 inches long. Drop them into a large pot of boiling salted water and let return to a boil over highest heat. Drain immediately and spread in a single layer on a towel to cool.

5. When the rice has rested the allotted time, remove the garlic cloves. Scoop the rice into a large mixing bowl. Pour the remaining dressing over it. Add the scallions and toss gently with a rubber spatula until the rice is barely lukewarm, not hot. Add the carrots, pork, capers, and parsley and toss to blend thoroughly. Cover with plastic and chill for at least 3 hours.
6. *To serve:* Arrange the watercress around the edge of a large platter and mound the rice salad in the center. Let stand at room temperature for about 1/2 hour before serving.

Reminders about Freezing

• Freezing alters the texture and flavor of foods in unpredictable ways. Be wary of substituting different spices, thickeners, or vegetables in foods to be frozen.
• Frozen foods often require extra spicing up and thickening. Don't be alarmed at the quantity of herbs and spices in the dishes; they fade.
• All foods soften somewhat when frozen, defrosted, and reheated. Beware of overcooking.
• To prevent pots and dishes from being consumed by a voracious freezer, line each container with aluminum foil, smoothing it in without wrinkles. Spoon in the food to be frozen, then cover closely with foil. Set in the freezer until frozen solid, then remove the foil-wrapped package of food from the dish. If the package doesn't drop out easily, run hot water on the bottom of the dish. Seal all seams with tape, then label and date the package and return to the freezer for storage.
• As cooked combination dishes tend to fade quickly, freezer storage time of no more than 3 months at 0° or below is recommended.
• All combination dishes retain their texture and taste better if defrosted slowly in the refrigerator before reheating. Thawing takes longer than some might think. For a solidly frozen casserole to soften uniformly through, remove the foil, set the food in the dish in which it was frozen, cover with foil and let thaw in the refrigerator for about 36 hours, or at room temperature for about 12 hours.

Mail-Order Sources

Mail-order sources for hard-to-find products are listed below. See the particular ingredient for the specific sources that are able to supply it. Sources are numbered; numbers refer to the names and addresses listed below.

1. The Birkett Mills
   P.O. Box 440
   Penn Yan, NY 14527
   315/536-3311

2. Casados Farms
   P.O. Box 852
   San Juan Pueblo, NM 87566
   505/852-2433

3. The Complete Cook
   405 Lake Cook Plaza
   Deerfield, IL 60015
   312/272-3833

4. La Cuisine
   323 Cameron Street
   Alexandria, VA 22314
   703/836-4435

5. Dean & DeLuca
   121 Prince Street
   New York, NY 10012
   212/254-7774

6. Erewhon, Inc.
   3 East Street
   Cambridge, MA 02141
   617/354-2001

7. Great Valley Mills, Inc.
   P.O. Box 260
   Quakertown, PA 18951
   215/536-3990

8. Harrington's in Vermont, Inc.
   Main Street
   Richmond, VT 05477
   802/434-3411

9. John Ritzenthaler Co.
   40 Portland Road
   West Conshohocken, PA 19428
   215/825-9321

10. Lawrence's Smokehouse Inc.
    Route 30
    Newfane, VT 05345
    802/365-7751

11. Maison E. H. Glass Inc.
    52 East 58th Street
    New York, NY 10022
    212/755-3316

12. Moneo & Son, Inc. (Casa Moneo)
    210 West 14th Street
    New York, NY 10011
    212/929-1644

13. Moose Lake Wild Rice
 P.O. Box 325
 Deer River, MN 56636
 208/246-8143

14. New Braunfels Smokehouse
 P.O. Box 1159
 New Braunfels, TX 78130
 512/625-7316

15. Pacific Trader
 19 Central Square
 Chatham, NY 12037
 518/392-2125

16. H. Roth & Son
 1577 First Avenue
 New York, NY 10028
 212/734-1111

17. The Vermont Country Store Inc.
 Weston, VT 05161
 802/824-3184

18. Walnut Acres
 Penns Creek, PA 17862
 717/837-0473

19. Williams-Sonoma
 Mail Order Dept.
 P.O. Box 3792
 San Francisco, CA 94119
 toll free 800/862-4999

INGREDIENTS

Angelica, candied, 3, 4, 16
Balsamic vinegar, 3, 4, 5, 11, 17, 19
Buckwheat noodles, Japanese (soba), 6, 15
Bulgur (cracked wheat), 5, 6, 7, 15, 16, 17, 18
Chestnuts, dried, 3, 12, 15, 16
Chestnuts, roasted, peeled, vacuum- or moisture-packed, 3, 4, 5, 11, 16, 19
Chicken, smoked, whole, 11, 14
Chiles, whole dried (California, Mexican, or New Mexican), 2, 5, 12
Chiles, ground, mild (powder), 2, 12
Coriander seeds, ground, 3, 4, 5, 11, 12, 16, 17
Coriander seeds, whole, 3, 5, 11, 12, 15, 16, 17
Cracked wheat, 5, 6, 7, 15, 16, 17, 18
Cumin, ground, 3, 5, 11, 12, 15, 16, 17
Cumin seeds, whole, 3, 5, 11, 12, 15, 16, 18
Decorating sugar (large crystals), 3, 4, 11, 16
Fennel seeds, 3, 5, 11, 12, 15, 16, 17, 18
Ginger, preserved in sugar syrup, 4, 11, 12, 15, 16

Green peppercorns, packed in water or brine, 3, 4, 5, 11, 12, 15, 16
Ham, smoked, New England or Southern-style, 7, 8, 10, 11, 14
Hazelnut oil, 3, 4, 5, 11, 16, 19
Juniper berries, 3, 4, 11, 15, 16, 17
Kasha, medium, 1, 16, 18
Kasha, whole, 1, 5, 6, 7, 15, 16, 18
Mint leaves, candied, 3, 4, 11, 16
Mushrooms, dried Oriental varieties, 3, 4, 5, 11, 15, 16
Oats, steel-cut (cracked), 5, 6, 11, 16, 18
Olives, Calamata, 4, 5, 11, 15, 19
Olives, Niçoise, 4, 5, 11, 19
Orange flower water, 3, 4, 5, 11, 12, 15, 16, 19
Paprika, sweet Hungarian, 3, 4, 5, 11, 15, 16, 17, 19
Pink peppercorns, 3, 4, 5, 11, 12, 16, 17
Pistachios, shelled, unsalted, 16
Pumpernickel flour (rye meal), 7, 16, 18
Rose petals, candied, 3, 4, 11, 16
Rose water, 3, 4, 5, 11, 15, 16, 19
Rye flour, 1, 7, 16, 17, 18
Saffron (threads), 3, 4, 5, 11, 12, 15, 16
Sesame oil, 3, 4, 5, 6, 11, 15, 16, 18
Szechuan peppercorns, 3, 4, 5, 11, 15, 16
Tahini (sesame cream), 5, 6, 11, 15, 16, 18
Turkey, smoked, whole, 3, 7, 8, 11, 14
Vinegar, balsamic, 3, 4, 5, 11, 17, 19
Violets, candied, 3, 4, 11, 16
Walnut oil, 3, 4, 5, 11, 16, 19
Wheat pilaf, 5, 6, 7, 15, 16, 17, 18
Wild rice, 3, 4, 5, 6, 8, 11, 13, 15, 16, 17

EQUIPMENT

Cheesecloth, fine, all cotton, 3, 4, 9, 16, 17
Coeur à la crème molds, 3, 4, 5, 10, 16, 19
Meat thermometer, Taylor instant-reading, 3, 4, 16, 17, 19

Bibliography

For those who enjoy reading about food in the past, many of the following books are facsimile editions.

Banfield, Walter T. *Manna*. London: Maclaren & Sons, 1937(?).

Beecher, Catherine E., and Stowe, Harriet Beecher. *The American Woman's Home*. Reprint of the 1869 edition. Hartford, Conn.: Stowe-Day Foundation, 1975.

Beeton, Isabella. *Beeton's Book of Household Management*. Reprint of the 1861 edition, published in London. New York: Farrar, Straus, and Giroux, 1969.

Benson, Evelyn Abraham, ed. *Penn Family Recipes*. York, Pa.: George Shumway, 1966.

Blot, Pierre. *Hand-Book of Practical Cookery for Ladies and Professional Cooks*. Reprint of the 1876 edition, published in New York. New York: Arno Press, 1973.

Carter, Susannah. *The Frugal Colonial Housewife*. Reprint of the 1772 edition, published in London and Boston. Garden City, N.Y.: Dolphin Books, 1976.

Child, Lydia Maria. *The American Frugal Housewife*. Reprint of the 1832 edition, published in Boston. Worthington, Ohio: Worthington Historical Society, 1965.

Dallas, E. S. *Kettner's Book of the Table*. Reprint of the 1877 edition. London: Centaur Press, Ltd., 1968.

David, Elizabeth. *French Provincial Cooking*. 2nd rev. ed. Harmondsworth, Middlesex, England: Penguin Books, Ltd., 1969.

———. *Elizabeth David Classics: Mediterranean Food; French Country Cooking; Summer Cooking*. New York: Alfred A. Knopf, 1980.

———. "The Harvest of the Cold Months," *Petit Propos Culinaires 3*. London: Prospect Books, 1979.

Davidson, Alan. *North Atlantic Seafood.* New York: The Viking Press, 1979.

Farmer, Fannie Merritt. *The Original Boston Cooking-School Cook Book.* Reprint of the first edition, 1896. New York: Weathervane Books, n.d.

Filippini, Alessandro. *The Table.* New York: Charles L. Webster & Company, 1891.

Fisher, M. F. K. *The Art of Eating.* New York: Vintage Books, 1976.

Francatelli, Charles Elmé. *The Modern Cook.* Reprint of the 1880 edition, published in Philadelphia, based on the 9th edition, published in London in 1853. New York: Dover Publications, 1973.

Glasse, Hannah. *The Art of Cookery Made Plain and Easy.* Reprint of the 1796 edition, published in London. Hamden, Conn.: Archon Books, 1971.

The Good Housekeeping Hostess. Springfield, Mass.: The Phelps Publishing Co., 1904.

Hackwood, Frederick W. *Good Cheer.* London: T. Fisher Unwin, 1911.

Hess, Karen, ed. *Martha Washington's Booke of Cookery.* New York: Columbia University Press, 1981.

Leslie, Eliza. *Directions for Cookery in Its Various Branches.* Reprint of the 1848 edition, published in Philadelphia. New York: Arno Press, 1973.

Lin, Hsiang Ju, and Tsuifeng Lin. *Chinese Gastronomy.* New York: Pyramid Publications, 1972.

Lutes, Della Thompson. *Table Setting and Service for Mistress and Maid.* Boston: M. Barrows & Company, 1934.

McClane, A. J. *The Encyclopedia of Fish Cookery.* New York: Holt, Rinehart and Winston, 1977.

McNeill, F. Marian. *The Scots Kitchen: Its Traditions and Lore with Old-Time Recipes.* First published in Great Britain by Blackie & Son, 1929. Published in 1974 by Mayflower Books Ltd., Frogmore, St. Albans, Herts.

Marshall, Agnes B. *Ices Plain and Fancy.* Reprint of the 1885 edition, published in London under the title *The Book of Ices.* New York: The Metropolitan Museum of Art, with a new introduction and annotations by B. K. Wheaton.

The Picayune's Creole Cook Book. Reprint of the 2nd edition, 1901. New York: Dover Publications, 1971.

Pullar, Philippa. *Consuming Passions.* Boston: Little, Brown and Company, 1970.

Randolph, Mrs. Mary. *The Virginia Housewife.* Reprint of the 1860 edition, published in Philadelphia. New York: Avenel Books/A division of Crown Publishers, Inc., by arrangement with the Valentine Museum of Richmond, Virginia, n.d.

Simmons, Amelia. *American Cookery.* Reprint of the 1796 edition, with an introduction by Martin Rywell. Harriman, Tenn.: Pioneer Press, 1966.

Soyer, Alexis. *The Pantropheon.* Reprint of the 1853 edition, published in London. New York and London: Paddington Press, 1977.

Index